DUMBARTON OAKS COLLOQUIUM
ON THE HISTORY
OF LANDSCAPE ARCHITECTURE
X

Edited by

ELISABETH BLAIR MACDOUGALL

ANCIENT ROMAN VILLA GARDENS

Dumbarton Oaks Research Library and Collection

Trustees for Harvard University

Washington, D.C.

© 1987 DUMBARTON OAKS
TRUSTEES FOR HARVARD UNIVERSITY
WASHINGTON, D.C.

Library of Congress Cataloging-in-Publication Data

Dumbarton Oaks Colloquium on the History of Landscape
　　Architecture (10th : 1984)
　　Ancient Roman villa gardens.

　1. Gardens, Roman—History—Congresses. 2. Garden
archaeology—Italy—Congresses. 3. Rome—Antiquities—
Congresses. I. MacDougall, Elisabeth B. II. Dumbarton
Oaks. III. Title.
SB458.55.D86　1984　　712'.6'0937　　86-24255
ISBN 0-88402-162-9

Contents

Introduction   1
WILHELMINA F. JASHEMSKI

Ancient Literary Evidence for the Pleasure Gardens of Roman Country Villas   7
A.R. LITTLEWOOD

Recently Excavated Gardens and Cultivated Land of the Villas at Boscoreale and Oplontis   31
WILHELMINA F. JASHEMSKI

The Sculptures of the Villa of Poppaea at Oplontis: A Preliminary Report   77
STEFANO DE CARO

The Importance of Water in Roman Garden Triclinia   135
EUGENIA SALZA PRINA RICOTTI

Town in Country and Country in Town   185
NICHOLAS PURCELL

Montmaurin: A Garden Villa   205
JEAN-MARIE PAILLER

Land Use at the Via Gabina Villas   223
WALTER M. WIDRIG

Introduction

WILHELMINA F. JASHEMSKI

The second Dumbarton Oaks Symposium on Ancient Roman Gardens was held in May 1984. The year 1979 marked a first in the history of Dumbarton Oaks, for it was in that year that the first Dumbarton Oaks Symposium on Ancient Roman Gardens took place. Many in the audience for the second symposium had been present on that occasion. It was an exciting event, for it was the first time, as far as we could discover, that a group of people had ever gathered together to discuss the gardens of the ancient Romans and their role in ancient Roman life, in both Italy and the provinces. There have been countless symposia and conferences on almost every aspect of antiquity—on Roman law, government, religion, architecture, wall painting, mosaics, pottery, the provinces, the *limes,* shipping, numismatics, to name only some of them—but on gardens, no. It seems strange indeed, to anyone who has worked on Roman gardens, that this subject should have been so long neglected. For the garden was intimately related to most aspects of Roman life: art, religion, architecture, economics, public and private life.

When I began to invite the participants for that first symposium, the response was from the beginning overwhelmingly enthusiastic, even though several said that they knew little about the gardens in the sites that they had excavated. When we finally assembled it was with a sense of excitement that we were embarking on something new. Animated and fruitful exchanges took place in the discussion periods after each paper, during the coffee breaks, and at mealtime. And I know that since the symposium, discussion has continued in correspondence and in visits.

It was even said that a new area of formal study in antiquity, the study of Roman gardens, was born at the 1979 symposium. It is only recently that some archaeologists have for the first time become aware of the importance of salvaging every possible bit of information relating to gardens. Until very recently most archaeologists have either ignored or destroyed the precious evidence for gardens in their sites, not realizing that such evidence was there. The architectural setting of the garden was all that was noticed. The findspots of garden furnishings were not even noted. Any evidence of plant material, wood, seeds, fruit, pollen, bones, the role of water, soil contours, planting beds, etc., which could be salvaged only at the time of excavation, was lost forever.

Garden archaeology is a very complex discipline requiring the close cooperation of many specialists: soil experts, palynologists, botanists, charcoal experts, microbiologists, bacteriologists, ornithologists, ichthyologists, geologists. All of these experts, and many more, have cooperated closely with me in my work. A number of these scientists were at our first symposium and were immensely helpful; they were present again for the second symposium and generously shared their specialized knowledge.

Five years ago I noted that in the first Dumbarton Oaks Garden Symposium, which had as its subject the Italian Renaissance garden, Professor Elisabeth MacDougall in her paper pointed out the Renaissance desire "to imitate models from antiquity." But she noted that the Renaissance patron or humanist wishing to emulate antiquity was faced with a dilemma for "he had little concrete evidence to draw upon. Actual remains of ancient gardens were scarce and frequently misinterpreted."[1] It is only within recent years that our knowledge of Roman gardens has increased markedly. The discoveries since our first Roman Garden Symposium have been significant, and many are the subject of papers in this book.

In the first Roman Garden Symposium we first looked back to the Greek heritage of Roman gardens and then examined the evidence for the Campanian peristyle garden. Quite appropriately our symposium was held in 1979, the year of the 1900th anniversary of the eruption of Vesuvius, for it was this tragedy that by overwhelming Pompeii, Herculaneum, and many villas in the surrounding area preserved our most complete evidence about early Roman gardens. The emphasis in our first symposium was on the peristyle garden, and most of the gardens discussed were city gardens.

In thinking of a profitable focus for our second symposium it occurred to me that it would be interesting to give our attention this time to the country villas, noting not only the character of their gardens, but also the extent to which they differed from and were similar to the gardens in the city. Attention is also given to the cultivated land connected with the villas, a subject that is today of increasing interest and significance. The topic of villa gardens is a timely one. Much exciting work has been done on villa gardens and the cultivated land connected with villas since our first symposium, and many important new discoveries have been made. Fortunately we were able to assemble the people involved to report on their findings.

Five years ago all the symposium papers were archaeological in character. In planning this symposium it seemed good to begin with a discussion by a classicist who would glean any information available from Latin literature regarding the gardens of the country villas and speak of the attitude of the Romans toward their villas. Who better to do this than Professor A.R. Littlewood, who was our first speaker.

When we next turn to the archaeological evidence for country villa gardens and cultivated land connected with villas, it is not surprising that important and perfectly preserved evidence comes from the area covered by Vesuvius. One of the most exciting sites in recent years has been the luxurious villa at Oplontis (modern Torre Annunziata), believed to be the villa of Poppaea, the wife of Emperor Nero. The excavation of the villa is not yet completed, but thus far I have excavated thirteen individual gardens in this villa. A remarkable collection of sculpture was found in the villa at Oplontis, most of it garden sculpture. Dr. Stefano De Caro, Director of the Excavations at Pompeii, who has made a careful study of this sculpture, reported on his research at this symposium. In the second essay I describe recent garden discoveries there and the *villa rustica* discovered in the locality of "Villa Regina," at Boscoreale, which afforded the first opportunity to excavate and examine the use of farmland in the Vesuvian area.

After this discussion of recent discoveries in Campania, we next examined new

---

[1] Elisabeth MacDougall, "Ars Hortulorum: Sixteenth-Century Garden Iconography and Literary Theory in Italy," in *The Italian Garden*, ed. David R. Coffin, Dumbarton Oaks Colloquium on the History of Landscape Architecture, I, Washington, D.C., 1972, 40.

INTRODUCTION

finds elsewhere in Italy. Dr. Eugenia Salza Prina Ricotti reported on her research at the villa of Tiberius at Sperlonga and at the Villa Adriana. In closing she announced the spectacular results of her recent excavations—the discovery of Pliny the Younger's Laurentine villa. Dr. Nicholas Purcell spoke of new discoveries relating to the great imperial villas that ring the city of Rome and reinterpreted their meaning and significance. There was also a rethinking of an important old site, the villa of Montmaurin, by Professor Jean-Marie Pailler, for the gardens of this villa have heretofore been given only scant attention. The symposium was appropriately closed by a survey of land use at the Via Gabina villas by Professor Walter M. Widrig.

The symposium was rich in dialogue between those who dig and those who spend their time with the literary texts. The breadth of backgrounds represented by the participants, both the speakers and those in the audience, resulted in much animated exchange of ideas and fertile discussion, both in the formal sessions and in small groups during the ample time provided by coffee breaks and at mealtime. A generous spirit of cooperation and sharing of information led to the solution of more than one problem. As the symposium came to an end plans were already being made for the next one.

During the closing remarks at the end of the last session, the various speakers enthusiastically summarized the new insights and new directions of research that had resulted from the symposium. Warm appreciation was expressed to Dumbarton Oaks for its encouragement and nurture of the newly developing field of Roman garden history.

Scholars are beginning to realize as never before that a study of the gardens of any culture results in new insights into the values of that civilization. Roman history has long been a topic of intensive research. But it may well be that this complex civilization cannot be fully understood until we inquire more deeply into the character and significance of the garden in Roman life. It was our pleasant assignment to continue this inquiry in the sessions of the second Dumbarton Oaks Symposium on Ancient Roman Gardens.

Ancient Literary Evidence for the Pleasure Gardens of Roman Country Villas

A.R. LITTLEWOOD

Any history of the pleasure gardens of Roman country villas based solely upon written records describing them is necessarily fragmentary since the evidence of Roman paintings and the discoveries of modern excavation are as, or in many aspects more, informative; extrapolation too may profitably be made from our knowledge of not only the gardens attached to urban Roman residences but also the older gardens of more easterly Mediterranean countries. However, because of the Roman fascination with quotidian matters abhorrent to a writer of classical Greece and the at times serendipitous choices of the goddess Fortuna, whose portfolio includes the transmission of texts from antiquity, a rigorously literary survey of the subject may be of some utility.[1] Less rigorous, however, must be the definition of "pleasure garden," since from at least the first half of the first century B.C. house, garden, agricultural land (the *villa*), and even sea and surrounding countryside were regarded not as discrete units but as an aesthetically integral entity. Indeed, divisions between all parts were blurred, since, for instance, open-air colonnades adorned with shrubs frequently served as a transition from house to terraced garden, which itself contained shrines, grottoes, and arbors.

Utilitarian cultivation of a kitchen garden is assuredly of considerable antiquity in Rome,[2] but there is no conclusive evidence of pleasure gardens earlier than those of the

---

[1] Archaeological evidence proves that in general the type of information provided by literature, at least up to the mid-second century A.D., is reliable, exaggeration being restrained and fantasy eschewed. Thereafter the situation is somewhat less clear: statements in the *Historia Augusta* must always be subjected to suspicion and in many cases to outright disbelief; ostensibly factual descriptions of real gardens, like those of their fictional counterparts, are increasingly affected by the dictates of the literary topos of the garden, but not sufficiently, I believe, to vitiate seriously the general picture that they create of the later Roman garden. The standard history of Roman gardens is still P. Grimal, *Les jardins romains*, 2nd ed., Paris, 1969; the monograph of K. Woksch, *Der römische Lustgarten*, Leitmeritz, 1881, is only twenty pages in length and of scant importance. Geographically restricted but more recent than Grimal and of great importance for both text and illustrations is W.F. Jashemski, *The Gardens of Pompeii, Herculaneum and the Villas Destroyed by Vesuvius*, I, New Rochelle, N.Y., 1979. Of considerable complementary value are J.H. d'Arms, *Romans on the Bay of Naples: A Social and Cultural Study of the Villas and Their Owners from 150 B.C. to A.D. 400*, Cambridge, Mass., 1970; and, for the necessary economic background, T. Frank, ed., *An Economic Survey of Ancient Rome*, 6 vols., Baltimore, 1933–40; M.I. Rostovtsev, *The Social and Economic History of the Roman Empire*, 2nd ed., ed. and rev. P.M. Fraser, 2 vols., Oxford, 1957; A.H.M. Jones, *The Later Roman Empire, 284–602: A Social, Economic and Administrative Survey*, 3 vols., Oxford, 1964; R. Duncan-Jones, *The Economy of the Roman Empire: Quantitative Studies*, 2nd ed., Cambridge, 1982. These and other modern authorities are cited with extreme parsimony in the present survey which aims merely to present ancient literary evidence. All abbreviations for ancient authors and their works are those found in N.G.L. Hammond and H.H. Scullard, eds., *The Oxford Classical Dictionary*, 2nd ed., Oxford, 1970, ix–xxii. All translations are my own.

[2] The tale, even superficially improbable, according to which Tarquinius Superbus, the last king of Rome (traditional dates 534–510 B.C.), decapitated the tallest poppies "in his garden" as a cryptic answer to his son's emissary from Gabii (Livy 1.54.6; Pliny *HN* 19.53.169 etc.) is no evidence for an early Roman garden, since not only did *hortus* originally signify "farm" rather than "garden" according to Pliny (ibid. 19.19.50), but the whole incident, with the substitution of poppies for corn, is taken from Herodotus' narrative of Thrasybulus and Periander (5.92.6).

Younger Scipio (185/84–129 B.C.).³ The creation of a garden as an aesthetic adjunct of a country estate can probably be similarly placed soon after the middle of the second century B.C. The retirement of the Elder Scipio to his estate at Liternum (near Lago di Patria) on the Campanian coast in 184 B.C. to avoid standing trial for bribery⁴ appears to have set a fashion that led to the conversion of the *villa rustica* into what Vitruvius later terms the *villa pseudourbana*.⁵ This rural incubus was castigated as early as 164 B.C., as may be inferred from a fragment of Cato's speech as censor in that year, in which he boasts that his own villas were "unadorned, rough and not even plastered."⁶ About twelve years later, in his speech against the holding of a second consulship, he specifies the citronwood, ivory, and marble with which others' villas were then embellished.⁷ Yet it is to this same Cato that we owe our earliest expressed faint hint of delight in a country estate, lurking amid that disorderly compilation of agricultural wisdom that constitutes our oldest piece of continuous Latin prose, the *De Agri Cultura;* for there Cato counsels that the living quarters of a farm be built well and in a good situation, so that visits will be "more pleasurable and more frequent."⁸ Of the nine parts of an estate he grants second place (the vineyard alone ranks higher) to a watered garden,⁹ in which should be grown, if near a town, vegetables and chaplet flowers.¹⁰ To judge from Cato's practical and mercenary character, his insistence upon the propinquity of a town,¹¹ and the whole tenor of the treatise, these are to be grown merely for profitable sale, and we may safely reject as anachronistic the romantic fantasy of the Elder Pliny who presents our austere agronomist captivated by "the ineffable delicacy of the flowers" painted by a sportive Nature joyously reveling in her variegated creativity.¹²

Early in the following century, certainly before 88 B.C., we hear of C. Marius building an expensive villa at Misenum on the Bay of Naples which caused his archrival Sulla to declare that "compared with Marius other men were blind." It presumably included gardens, but any quickened sense of aesthetic anticipation is swiftly stilled by the statement that its owner and designer made use of his expertise in laying out an army

---

³ Cic. *Amic.* 7.25; *Rep.* 1.9.14; Grimal, *Jardins*, 121–122. According to Cicero, the Younger Scipio possessed also a coastal estate where he entertained friends (*Fat.* frag. 4 apud Macrob. *Sat.* 3.16.3–4) and himself visited Laelius who had a villa at Formiae (*Rep.* 1.39.61).

⁴ Livy 38.52.1, 53.8 etc. The estate is briefly described by the Younger Seneca who visited it (*Ep.* 86).

⁵ *De Arch.* 6.5.3. For further literary evidence of Roman rural extravagance in the 2nd century B.C. see d'Arms, *Romans*, 1–17.

⁶ Frag. 174 Malcovati apud Gell. 13.24.1.

⁷ Frag. 185 Malcovati apud Fest. p. 282.4.

⁸ Cato *Agr.* 4.1.

⁹ Ibid. 1.7. Varro later challenged the priority of the vineyard by putting meadowland first (*Rust.* 1.7.9–10).

¹⁰ Cato *Agr.* 8.2.

¹¹ He adds that the farm near a town should be planted "as productively as possible" (loc. cit.). Varro makes the point even more clearly (*Rust.* 1.16.3).

¹² *HN* 21.1.1. Pliny proceeds to discourse on the variety of chaplets and their history in Greece and Rome (ibid. 21.1.2–9.13: cf. 16.4.9–5.14). Cicero, writing about 106 years after the dramatic date of his dialogue, represents Cato in his eighty-fourth year enthusiastically praising to his younger auditors not only monetary profit but also the pleasurable toil of farming, by which occupation he is "delighted to an incredible degree" (*Sen.* 15.51–16.58).

camp.¹³ In 82–81 B.C. gardens, we learn from Plutarch, were among the possessions that could gain for their owners the dreaded publicity of proscription under the rapacious dictator Sulla.¹⁴

Tantalizing fragments of information about the country seats of the multimillionaire L. Licinius Lucullus (consul in 74 B.C.) suggest an extravagance in design of house and garden¹⁵ that few of his contemporaries, if any, could emulate.¹⁶ Plutarch describes his seaside establishment, again on the Bay of Naples, where "he suspended hills over huge tunnels, surrounded his buildings with circuits of the sea and channels for breeding fish, and constructed residences in the sea,"¹⁷ a veritable "Xerxes in a toga."¹⁸ In addition, his country seat near Tusculum had "observatories, open-air banqueting chambers and colonnades." When Pompey on a visit criticized him for designing his villa "in the best possible way for summer, but uninhabitable in winter, Lucullus responded with a laugh, 'Do you think me more stupid than cranes and storks that I do not change my residences with the seasons?'"¹⁹ His attempt to combine house and garden is illustrated also in Varro's description of Lucullus' enclosure for birds under the same roof as a dining room, so that he could see some birds cooked upon his plate and others fluttering around in captivity. Varro, however, adds the caustic remark that the scheme was not a success, for Roman noses were offended more than eyes delighted by this avian display.²⁰

Cicero possessed eight residences outside Rome. These were his ancestral demesne at Arpinum (Arpino), his preferred estate at Tusculum (Poggio Tulliano?), about a dozen miles from Rome, and six villas on the coast,²¹ especially around the Bay of Naples which was rapidly becoming the millionaires' playground. At Arpinum he made a profit through leasing out farms, but his other residences were what he would have called "properties of pleasure."²² They served two main purposes: first, to afford respite from both the aestival heat of Rome and, a thing especially valued in time of political

---

¹³ Pliny *HN* 18.7.32: cf. Sen. *Ep*. 51.11. Plutarch, however, condemns it for its "extravagant and effeminate appurtenances" that did not become so experienced a soldier (*Mar*. 34.3). It later came into the hands of Lucullus (ibid. 4). See further d'Arms, *Romans*, 23.

¹⁴ *Sull*. 31.10. Plutarch adds (ibid. 11–12) that when the inoffensive Q. Aurelius saw his own name he declared, "Alas, my Alban estate is prosecuting me."

¹⁵ His most famous gardens were, however, in Rome itself. According to Pliny (*HN* 15.30.102) and Athenaeus (2.50f–51a), it was Lucullus who introduced the cherry to Italy from Pontus.

¹⁶ For an exhaustive inventory with bibliographical details of villas on the Bay of Naples owned by prominent Romans between ca. 75 B.C. and A.D. 400 see d'Arms, *Romans*, 171–232.

¹⁷ Plut. *Luc*. 39.3: cf. Varro *Rust*. 3.17.8–9. Such a description was a standard topos.

¹⁸ Plut. loc. cit.; Vell. Pat. 2.33.4; Pliny *HN* 9.80.170. Lucullus embellished one estate also with a preserve for wild animals (Pliny *HN* 8.78.211).

¹⁹ Plut. *Luc*. 39.4–5.

²⁰ *Rust*. 3.4.3. Lucullus received another public rebuke for lack of taste from a censor who remarked on one of his estates that "there was less [ground] to plough than [floor] to sweep" (Pliny *HN* 18.7.32).

²¹ From north to south these were at Antium (Anzio; house in town rather than villa), Astura, Formiae, Cumae, Puteoli (cf. Philostr. *VA* 7.11), and Pompeii. In addition, Cicero possessed several rest houses or lodges (*deversoria*) so that he could stay overnight on his own property when traveling between villas. Tusculum was becoming an exceedingly popular area of magnificent estates (Strabo 5.3.12 [C 239]).

²² *Voluptariae possessiones* (*Att*. 12.25.1).

uncertainty, from the quotidian cares or dangers of public life in the capital, although he does complain, perhaps with some pride, that callers made his villa at Formiae (Formia) seem like a public building[23] and that at Cumae (near Naples) "a Rome in miniature";[24] and second, to enhance his social standing, as is shown by his purchase of residences once owned by the multimillionaire Crassus[25] and the dictator Sulla[26] and most revealingly by his own comment that he had proved to the public the legitimacy of buying property with loans from friends "to reach a certain position" in society.[27]

At his villas Cicero devoted himself in the main to reading, "devouring books" as he once says,[28] and writing.[29] His comments on gardens and, far more frequent, on the more distant scenery, are for the most part, though genuine, brief and repetitious,[30] while his great encomium of rural life in the *De Senectute* not only is placed in the mouth of Cato but also is largely tralatitious.[31] For our purposes his most informative passage is a progress report on work being done at five of his brother's properties. This work includes a bath, promenade, colonnade, aviary, and fishpond with fountains.[32] Cicero has particular praise for the landscape gardener who "has so clothed everything with ivy, both the foundation wall of the villa and the spaces between the columns of the promenade, that to be sure those Greek statues seem to be landscape gardeners themselves offering their ivy for sale."[33] The sole instance Cicero gives us of landscaping on one of his own properties may be found in a request to his friend Atticus for plans of the latter's shrine to Amalthea (a Cretan nymph who nursed the infant Zeus) on his estate at Buthrotum (Butrinto), so that Cicero could have a replica constructed at Arpinum.[34] It probably involved a grotto, approached by a path between plane trees, and running water.[35] Cicero planned also a shrine to his daughter Tullia, who died in mid-

---

[23] Ibid. 2.14.2.

[24] Ibid. 5.2.2.

[25] *Fam.* 5.6.2.

[26] Pliny *HN* 22.6.12.

[27] *Att.* 1.13.6. Similarly indicative of his competitive social vanity, doubtless exacerbated by the fact that he was a *novus homo* or "new man," is the proximity to each other of his villas at Antium and Astura and of those at Cumae and Puteoli.

[28] Ibid. 4.11.2. He claims that books are a possession superior to hamlets and meadows (ibid. 1.4.3) and that he can read even when there are workmen in the house (*QFr.* 2.9.3). Just once he admits to dividing his time between reading and "counting the waves" (*Att.* 2.6.1).

[29] Villas, both his own and those of others, serve also as the dramatic setting of many of his oratorical and philosophical dialogues and treatises: *De Oratore* (1.7.28–29, in stated imitation of Plato's *Phaedrus*; 2.5.20–22; 3.5.18), *De Republica* (1.9.14; 1.12.18), *De Legibus* (1.4.14), *Brutus* (2.10), *Academica* (1.1.1; 2.3.9), *De Finibus* (1.5.14; 3.2.7), *Tusculanae Disputationes* (1.4.7), *De Natura Deorum* (1.6.15), *De Divinatione* (1.5.8), *De Fato* (1.2), *De Senectute* (1.3), *De Amicitia* (1.2).

[30] Typical is his comment in 45 B.C. that "nothing could be more charming than the villa, the shore, the view of the sea" at Astura (*Att.* 12.9), although most probably of the same place he writes the following year that the "artificial prettiness" tends to cloy (ibid. 15.16a).

[31] See above, n. 12.

[32] *QFr.* 3.1.1–6: cf. ibid. 3.7.7.

[33] Ibid. 3.1.5. See further Grimal, *Jardins*, 88–95. Pliny points out that ivy is destructive to walls (*HN* 16.62.144).

[34] *Att.* 1.16.18.

[35] Cf. *Leg.* 2.3.7. The mythical archetype is lengthily described by Diodorus Siculus (3.68.5–69.4). See further Grimal, *Jardins*, 302–304.

February 45 B.C., to ensure her apotheosis. Many letters to Atticus attest his search for a suitable garden. He rejected his own estates because either the shrine would not be held sacred by a subsequent owner of the land or by being too remote would not adequately protect her fame.[36] Very soon he combined projected shrine and garden with retirement home for himself, but before midsummer of the following year the whole scheme had collapsed.[37] Elsewhere we find Cicero anxious to purchase through Atticus objets d'art and especially statues for his villa and garden at Tusculum. Quantity appears to be the prime requisite.[38] Finally, a curious passage sheds obscure light on the appreciation of a garden from within. Cicero's architect, Vettius Cyrus, answered an objection that his windows were too narrow with the following argument: "Views of greenery through wide openings are not so pleasant; for let vision be A, the object seen BC, the rays, etc." (Shackleton Bailey wonders if Cicero knew how to continue.) "You understand the rest. If our vision were dependent upon the impact of images, the images would have great trouble in the narrow spaces, but in reality the emission of rays works very nicely."[39]

In 36 B.C. the great polymath M. Terentius Varro, then in his eightieth year and aware that "if, as the saying is, man is a bubble, an old man is all the more one," wrote a manual on agriculture for the use of his prospective widow who had recently purchased a farm.[40] In it we find the expected criticism of a member of the landed gentry against city dwellers who created country seats for display and luxury to the detriment of the state[41] and dined amid piles of rural produce bought and transported from the markets of Rome,[42] a mockery of old-fashioned rusticity exotically complemented by Grecian appellations for the chambers of these edifices.[43] Nevertheless, despite his detailed practical advice, Varro, as befits the owner of not only the ancestral demesne at Reate (Rieti) but also a luxurious farm at Casinum (Cassino) and villas at Tusculum and Cumae, states profit and pleasure as husbandry's twin goals;[44] and the greatest importance of

---

[36] According to a late and surely misguided source, "Aelius Spartianus," Cicero's estate at Puteoli was, however, chosen for the burial of Emperor Hadrian (S.H.A. *Hadr.* 25.7; see further d'Arms, *Romans*, 104–105 and bibliographical references in n. 154). Martial gives a parallel to Cicero's intent (1.114, 116), and the poet Silius Italicus, who owned one of Cicero's estates (probably that near Cumae), perhaps in the hope of inspiration bought, restored, and revered Vergil's tomb (Mart. 11.48, 49; Plin. *Ep.* 3.7.8: cf. Stat. *Silv.* 4.4.51–55).

[37] Cicero was exercised also by ensuring that what he constructed would be a shrine and not an extravagant funerary monument, for the latter would have been subject to taxation. For a guide to the labyrinth of plans and motives see D.R. Shackleton Bailey, *Cicero's Letters to Atticus*, 6 vols., Cambridge, 1965–67, V, 404–413.

[38] *Att.* 1.1.5, 3.2, 4.3, 5.7, 6.2, 7, 8.2, 9.2, 10.3, 11.3.

[39] Ibid. 2.3.2. See further Shackleton Bailey, *Atticus*, I, 356–357. Mention should be made also of a letter to M. Marius congratulating him on enjoying the scenery at his villa on the Bay of Naples, for "by making a hole" (window or gap in trees? the text is corrupt) he has opened up a view of Stabiae as of a stage (*Fam.* 7.1.1).

[40] *Rust.* 1.1.1–2.

[41] Ibid. 1.13.7: cf. ibid. 3.2.6.

[42] Ibid. 1.59.2: cf. Mart. 3.47; 3.58.45–51.

[43] *Rust.* 2.*Praef.*2.

[44] Ibid. 1.4.1–2: cf. ibid. 1.2.12; 3.3.1.

his manual for our purposes lies in its bountiful evidence of three features that were swiftly becoming essential to a rich man's estate.

At the beginning of the century, according to the Elder Pliny, P. Licinius, inspired by the artificial oyster beds invented by a contemporary, the Campanian speculator C. Sergius, built fishponds.[45] These could be a source of income,[46] but equally a mode of expensive ostentation, as has been seen already in Lucullus' massive engineering projects. Piscine passion rapidly grew rampant, Sergius and Licinius acquired cognomina for their services to society,[47] and Cicero inveighed against the "fishpond addicts."[48] Even the sober Varro grudgingly suggested to his wife that the running water of a pool for cattle could also pass between columns to serve as a sort of fishpond, if she so desired.[49] Other aristocrats lost their sense of proportion: some believed themselves in heaven if hungry fish came to the hand at sound of pipe or when summoned by name, a conceit entertained later in imperial circles and still celebrated in verse as late as the early sixth century A.D. at the Vandal court in North Africa;[50] Cicero's rival Q. Hortensius bought from Puteoli (Pozzuoli) to avoid eating his own fish, employed a host of fishermen catching sprats to feed them, lavished upon them every care, and wept at the death of one well-loved moray eel;[51] the orator L. Licinius Crassus went further, adorning his moray with earrings[52] and necklaces, and when reproved by his fellow censor Cn. Domitius Ahenobarbus for bewailing its death the bereaved enthusiast declared his moral superiority over Ahenobarbus who had not mourned the death of any of his three wives.[53]

The huge quantities of small birds required to satisfy upper-class Roman palates rendered an aviary a profitable rural enterprise not only through the sale of the birds themselves (we learn of no fewer than five thousand thrushes being sold from one estate in a single year[54]), but also through the use of the manure that they produced.[55] The invention of ornamental aviaries is credited to a friend of Varro, M. Laenius Strabo,[56] upon whose prototype he modeled his own on an estate at Casinum in southern Latium. Here an uncovered walk by the side of a stream led to an aviary 72 by 48 feet at the end of which was added a domed structure or tholos. The rectangular area consisted of a

---

[45] Val. Max. 9.1.1; Pliny *HN* 9.79.168; 9.80.170.

[46] Varro *Rust.* 3.2.17; Columella *Rust.* 8.16.5.

[47] Orata (Goldfish) and Murena (Moray) respectively (Varro *Rust.* 3.3.10; Columella loc. cit.).

[48] Cic. *Att.* 1.19.6; 1.20.3.

[49] Varro *Rust.* 1.13.3.

[50] Cic. *Att.* 2.1.7; id. *Paradoxa Stoicorum* 5.38; Varro *Rust.* 3.17.4; Pliny *HN* 10.89.193; Mart. 4.30.3–7; 10.30.22–24; Luxorius 5 Rosenblum (= *Anth. Lat.* 1.1.no.291).

[51] Varro *Rust.* 3.17.5–9; Pliny *HN* 9.81.172.

[52] Copied by Antonia Minor, wife of the Elder Drusus (Pliny loc. cit.).

[53] Ael. *NA* 8.4; Macrob. *Sat.* 3.15.4–5. For another verbal joust between these same colleagues over six luxuriantly shady nettle trees (*Celtis australis*) see Pliny *HN* 17.1.3–5.

[54] Varro *Rust.* 3.2.15: cf. ibid. 3.5.1–8; 3.6–11; Columella *Rust.* 8.1–15.

[55] The manure from thrushes and blackbirds is given preference above that of any other bird or animal by Varro (*Rust.* 1.38.2), while pigeon dung is chosen by Columella (*Rust.* 2.14.1).

[56] Varro *Rust.* 3.5.8; Pliny *HN* 10.72.141. Varro expressly refers to "ancient" profit-making aviaries, game preserves and fishponds (*Rust.* 3.3.6).

path between two fish basins enclosed by a peristyle of which the outer columns were of stone, while the inner were dwarf trees. This peristyle was netted with hemp, presumably planted with shrubs, and contained "all manner of birds" that were fed through the netting and watered by a rivulet. The pièce de résistance, however, was the tholos with an open colonnade netted with gut (less visible than hemp), behind which were carefully arranged trees lacking low branches so as to give shade from the sun without preventing light from entering the building. Within the colonnade were kept mainly songbirds such as nightingales and blackbirds, whose perches were formed by brackets attached to the columns, thus producing the auditorium of what Varro calls a "tiny avian theater." The colonnade surrounded a pool, linked to the basins mentioned before, for ducks and fish. From the middle of this pool rose a column that supported a revolving, horizontal, spoked wheel with in place of the felloe a broad rim to serve as a table for reclining guests, since this, despite Varro's stricture upon Lucullus, was a dining room. Its ceiling was a hemisphere that marked the time below by showing the movements of the morning star and the evening star (Venus), while above a pointer, connected to an external vane, indicated the direction of the wind.[57] Thus the diners, though protected from the direct rays of a fierce sun by the dome above their heads, could yet be refreshed by any breeze that chanced to blow as they simultaneously gazed through the spokes of their table at paddling ducks and darting fish and listened to the sweet songs of birds fluttering about their theater or perched upon its serried rows of seats.

Factitious may be these rural charms that Varro provided for his guests, but being a genuine countryman he did not succumb to the blandishments of natural perversion beloved by some of his contemporaries who taught birds human speech. The tragic actor Claudius Aesopus paid 100,000 sesterces for a single dish of such birds which in the next century earned him an accusation of cannibalism from the Elder Pliny.[58] Some birds, proving more adept than others, learned "to talk Greek and Latin, practising diligently and daily speaking new expressions in ever longer sentences." Avian pedagogy progressed apace, including among its crotchets the belief that acorn-feeding magpies develop the largest vocabulary,[59] and its longevity is attested by a Latin poem from Vandal North Africa.[60]

Game preserves were first built in the Roman world, according to the Elder Pliny, toward the middle of the first century B.C. by Fulvius Lippinus,[61] a man celebrated also for his introduction of segregated snail ponds,[62] and once more utility was combined

---

[57] Varro *Rust.* 3.5.9–17. For a discussion of the aviary see F. Fuchs, "Varros Vogelhaus bei Casinum," *Deutsches archäologisches Institut. Römische Abteilung. Mitteilungen*, 69 (1962), 96–105. The mechanism indicating the direction of the wind was copied from the *horologium* (so-called "Tower of the Winds") recently constructed in Athens by Andronicus of Cyrrhus, as Varro expressly states.

[58] *HN* 10.72.141–142.

[59] The locus classicus is Pliny *HN* 10.58.117–60.124.

[60] Luxorius 84 Rosenblum (*Anth. Lat.* 1.1.no.370). Lengthy poems on talking parrots had been written earlier by Ovid (*Am.* 2.6) and Statius (*Silv.* 2.4).

[61] Pliny *HN* 8.78.211. See further Varro on preserves for hares (*Rust.* 3.12) and the separate arrangements made for rearing dormice (ibid. 3.15).

[62] Pliny *HN* 9.82.173–174. For their construction see Varro *Rust.* 3.14.

with pleasure. Although Varro himself owned tamed boars and roebuck that came for food at the blowing of a horn, it was the orator Q. Hortensius who appreciated the inherent charms of such domesticity. According to Varro's account he possessed on his estate near Laurentum a walled forest of over thirty acres where he would dine with his guests at a table placed in a high spot. Upon command a slave accoutred as Orpheus with robe and lyre would blow upon a horn, at which a huge crowd of stags, boars, and other animals would gather, thus illusorily corroborating mythic tradition.[63] And again Vandal Africa can, six and a half centuries later, provide a parallel.[64]

Varro often mentions the luxurious appurtenances and extravagant actions of Hortensius,[65] but he does not indicate fully the catholicity of the latter's affections. It is from Macrobius that we learn how, eschewing water as the liquid refreshment of his plane trees, he pampered them with wine: indeed on one occasion during a legal case he begged Cicero to exchange positions of speaking with him so that he might return home to give a tree that he had himself planted its customary potation.[66]

The Republican poets have little specific to offer us.[67] Lucretius' work is thoroughly imbued with a love of nature, his master's delight in a garden being as it were ruralized. He castigates the man who races furiously between town house and country estate to find ennui in both,[68] a poetic and individualized treatment of the vernal diaspora from the city that is first attested by Cicero in 74 B.C.;[69] and he spurns the luxurious banquets in gilded chambers when instead one may recline beneath a lofty tree by running water on a greensward bedight with seasonal flowers,[70] but even this scene owes more to the Platonic topos from the *Phaedrus* than to a garden. Catullus, on the other hand, shows an appreciation of individual flowers, comparing a virgin with a prized bloom in a fenced plot[71] and a dilatory bride with a hyacinth in a rich man's garden.[72]

The Augustan Age shows a continuation of the trends more than adumbrated by Republican plutocrats who, in Sallust's judgment, had built cities rather than villas.[73] From Misenum to the Promontory of Minerva (Punta della Campanella) the Bay of Naples, which Cicero called "that Crater of Luxury,"[74] was now, apart from the towns,

---

[63] Varro *Rust.* 3.13. Strabo seems to suggest that Mithridates VI of Pontus had separate menagerie and hunting grounds on his estate at Cabeira (12.3.30 [C 556]. I am indebted for this reference to my student Miss K.D. Hargin-Reilly).

[64] Luxorius 6 Rosenblum (= *Anth. Lat.* 1.1.no.292). Tamed animals were also used in Rome for public spectacle (Stat. *Silv.* 2.5; Mart. *Spect.* 18; *Carm.* 1.14, 48, 104; 2.75; 5.31; 9.71), while Emperor Elagabalus (218–222) had lions and leopards trained to attend dinner in order to frighten guests (S.H.A. *Antoninus Elagabalus* 21.1).

[65] In addition to the passages already cited see *Rust.* 3.3.10; 3.6.6.

[66] *Sat.* 3.13.3: cf. Pliny *HN* 12.4.8; 16.91.242; Mart. 9.61.16.

[67] See, however, Grimal, *Jardins*, 368–377.

[68] 3.1060–1067.

[69] *Planc.* 26.65.

[70] 2.23–33.

[71] 62.39–47: cf. 11.21–24; 64.89–90.

[72] 61.87–90: cf. 61.21–22, 185–189.

[73] *Cat.* 12.3: cf. Sen. *Ben.* 7.10.5; *Ep.* 90.43.

[74] *Att.* 2.8.2. The area was commonly called "the Crater" (Strabo 5.4.3 [C 242]) from its volcanic nature.

an unbroken succession of estates[75] crowding the shoreline to the benefit of their owners' fishponds or commanding more extended prospects from a greater elevation such as that once owned by Julius Caesar near Baiae.[76] The emperor himself was more modest than many of his fellow citizens and actually had a villa of his granddaughter Julia razed to the ground for its opulence.[77] His own preferred retreats were at Lanuvium (Lanuvio), Praeneste (Palestrina), Tibur (Tivoli), and on the Bay of Naples. Suetonius gives us some idea of his personal taste: "he adorned his own villas not so much with decorative statues and pictures as with terraces, groves, and objects notable for their age or rarity, such as the colossal bones of monstrous sea creatures and wild beasts."[78] This cetaceous and possibly paleontological style of garden art, though of imperial inspiration, appears not to have set a fashion.

Early in the reign of Augustus Vitruvius compiled the only surviving ancient treatise on architecture, to which, despite the use of personal experience, a dependence upon Greek forerunners gives a Hellenistic flavor. It does not treat of gardens, but one passage relating to colonnades behind the theaters is of obvious relevance and may be summarized as follows: "the open-air spaces between the colonnades should be embellished with greenery because walks out of doors are very healthy, for the air from greenery is rarefied and removes the thick humor from the eyes, thus improving vision, as well as removing other humors from the body."[79] These promenades were to be kept dry and free of mud by the laying of a level of sand over porous charcoal and by the building of drains.[80]

The poets of the Augustan Age show in varying degrees a sensitivity to nature and by their frequent mention of flowers testify to the contemporary growth of floriculture on country estates at the expense of farming.[81] Specific information on gardens is, however, scanty. The Arcady of Vergil's *Eclogues*, albeit not untouched by gardens of the poet's time, is yet watered mainly by streams traditional and paradisiacal. His *Georgics*, though not a practical agricultural manual, glorify for urban ears a sturdy husbandry remote from "properties of pleasure": but a garden they do contain, and one that despite its poetic and almost mystical function does reflect contemporary reality in its combination of vegetables with flowers and trees, required here for an apiary.[82] Horace

---

[75] Strabo 5.4.8 [C 247].

[76] Sen. *Ep.* 51.11; Tac. *Ann.* 14.9.

[77] So states Suetonius (*Aug.* 72.3), but Augustus may have desired to obliterate remembrance of Julia whom he banished for adultery in A.D. 8. Similarly the villa left to him by Vedius Pollio he had razed so that no monument should be left to the man who while entertaining the emperor in this villa had desired a slave to be thrown to his moray eels for breaking a crystal goblet (Dio Cass. 54.23.2–6: cf. Sen. *Clem.* 1.18.2; *De Ira* 3.40.2–5).

[78] Suetonius mentions also "weapons of heroes" (*Aug.* 72.2–3).

[79] *De Arch.* 5.9.5.

[80] Ibid. 5.9.7. The sixth book, on private houses, contains much information on symmetry, alignment, and methods of construction that would be applicable to a villa.

[81] Horace expressly states this (*Carm.* 2.15). Italy was increasingly relying upon imported grain. For gardens in general in the Augustan poets see Grimal, *Jardins*, 379–409.

[82] *G.* 4.125–146: cf. ibid. 109–124. Pliny advises on the close relationship of flower garden and apiary (*HN* 21.41.70).

assails the sumptuous villas at Baiae, whose maritime extensions make even free-swimming fish feel cramped for space.[83] His prayers were for "a modest patch of land where there would be a garden and near the house a spring of never-failing water, and above these a little piece of woodland."[84] Blessed with Maecenas' gift of a Sabine villa, from which in summer he was reluctant to be torn away and to which he ever yearned to return when absent,[85] he did not cease to extol the charms of reclining on the grass beneath a shady tree by running stream in order to take a siesta, eat a simple meal, chat with friends, and, with garland over brow, quaff a favored wine.[86] His country estate was nature tamed by man, inhabited by gods, and made vivid for us by sympathetic description and particularization.[87] Tibullus in various poems joyously pictures a humble rustic life of toil, relaxation, and festivals in an interesting blend of realism and nostalgia for a Golden Age,[88] but he describes no gardens; "Lygdamus" in one passage spurns opulent villas containing "plantations that mimic sacred groves";[89] Propertius, more a lover of city life and more mystical in his attitude to nature than Tibullus, yet, as befits one who lived hard by the Gardens of Maecenas,[90] gives intimations of landscape architecture in his descriptions of both his grotto of poetic inspiration and the Tarpeian grove.[91] Ovid, who used to write his poetry in his garden,[92] indulges in a fondness for flowers and, especially in the *Metamorphoses*, clearly reveals man-made exemplars underlying many "natural" settings: indeed on one occasion he admits that "nature had imitated art."[93] Relegated to Tomis (Constantsa) he nostalgically recalls both farming and gardening on his own country estates,[94] activities that once he recommended as antidotes to love.[95] Finally, among Augustan poets may be mentioned parenthetically the authors of poems that found their way into the corpus of Vergil. These provide us with four descriptions of gardens, of which at least the last three, though not specifically pertaining to villas, are all consistent with known elements in the pleasure gardens of country estates. They are a small market garden, a wayside tavern's garden for its customers, a garden of alternating flowers set about a temple, and a shrine in the form of a grassy mound surrounded by polished marble and planted with numerous trees, shrubs, and flowers—mock heroic tribute to a deceased gnat.[96]

In the Julio-Claudian era the enthusiasm for villas continued, emperors themselves

---

[83] *Carm.* 2.18.20–22; 3.1.33–37.

[84] *Sat.* 2.6.1–3. The "garden" here is probably a kitchen garden.

[85] *Ep.* 1.7; 1.10; 1.14 etc.

[86] *Epod.* 2.23–28; *Carm.* 1.1.19–22; 2.7.17–25; 2.11.13–20; etc.

[87] Notably a tree rarely lacks its species, a wine its place of origin, a garland its constituent flowers.

[88] See esp. 1.1.1–44; 1.5.21–34; 2.1; 2.5.79–100.

[89] [Tib.] 3.3.15. Similarly the Elder Seneca says "people even mimic mountains and woods in their decaying houses" (*Cont.* 2.1.13) and "you enclose waters and groves within your buildings" (*Cont.* 5.5). Cf. Rut. Namat. *De Reditu Suo* 1.111.

[90] On the Esquiline (3.23.24; 4.8.1–2).

[91] 3.3.25–30 and 4.4.3–8 respectively.

[92] *Tr.* 1.11.37.

[93] *Met.* 3.155–162.

[94] *Pont.* 1.8.41–60.

[95] *Rem. Am.* 169–198.

[96] *Moretum* 61–91; *Copa; Ciris* 95–98; *Culex* 390–414 respectively.

procuring many by inheritance and confiscation, both often achieved through imperially encouraged suicide. The bravado of one victim, Valerius Asiaticus, has earned him a place in the affections of garden lovers, since before opening his veins he ordered that his funeral pyre be moved to prevent the possibility of damage to some shady trees in his garden.[97] Tiberius on his retirement to Capri in A.D. 26 was in possession of no fewer than twelve estates on the island;[98] and we are further told of his dining in a banqueting chamber that was built into a natural grotto near Tarracina in an area of huge caverns, some of which at that time accommodated "large and costly residences."[99] Caius was notorious for his extravagant estates, as he tunneled through rock, leveled hills,[100] and at his villa at Velitrae (Velletri) built a dining room for fifteen guests with servants in a plane tree, a large part of whose shade, the Elder Pliny contemptuously avers, he cast himself;[101] but his tour de force was the transformation of ships into floating gardens with baths, colonnades, dining rooms and "a great variety of vines and fruit-bearing trees" for his musical cruises along the Campanian coast.[102] Villas were again not distasteful to either Claudius or Nero, who in building his Golden House was doing nothing less than creating a country estate in the very heart of Rome.

During Nero's reign Columella, appalled by the decline in Roman agriculture,[103] published piecemeal a sane and painstaking treatise on the subject. At the insistence of the dedicatee, Silvinus, he accepted Vergil's invitation to deal with the garden in one book written in hexametric verse if not in poetry.[104] This takes the form of a lengthy catalogue of vegetables, flowers, shrubs, and trees encumbered with mythology but supported by practical information on soils. The rest of the work is too utilitarian to be of more than peripheral import to pleasure gardens, apart from much advice on aviaries, fishponds and game preserves[105] and the recommendation that a villa should be set back from the sea.[106]

[97] Tac. *Ann.* 11.3.2.

[98] Ibid. 4.67.3. Many of these must have passed to him from Augustus. He had himself the reputation of parsimony in building (ibid. 6.45.1: cf. 3.52.1) and a reluctance to inherit except from friends (ibid. 2.48.2).

[99] Strabo 5.3.6 (C 233). Tiberius' grotto was the scene of a famous accident when Sejanus shielded him from falling rocks (Tac. *Ann.* 4.59.1–2; Suet. *Tib.* 39). Of the extensive bibliography on this banqueting chamber see in particular E. Salza Prina Ricotti, "Forme speciali di triclini," *Cronache pompeiane*, 5 (1979), 130–149 and id., "The Importance of Water in Roman Garden Triclinia," in this volume.

[100] Suet. *Calig.* 37.2–3: cf. Philo *Leg.* 29.185; Joseph. *AJ* 18.249.

[101] *HN* 12.5.10.

[102] Suet. *Calig.* 37.2. This was doubtless inspired by the far more elaborate ship that Hiero II of Syracuse had built under supervision of Archimedes and that was the subject of a treatise by a certain Moschion (Athen. 5.206d–209e, esp. 207d-e).

[103] *Rust.* 1.*Praef.*11–20.

[104] Verg. *G.* 4.147–148; Columella *Rust.* 10.*Praef.*3–4; 10.1–5 (he later added a more utilitarian treatment of a kitchen garden's vegetables and herbs in prose [11.3]). A garden of primarily fruit trees but including flowers features also in the second *Eclogue* of Columella's contemporary Calpurnius Siculus, whose Astacus lauds its features in an amoebean singing match.

[105] *Rust.* 8.2–15; 8.16–17; 9.1 respectively.

[106] "It is always right for a villa to overlook the sea, when it is beaten and sprinkled by the spray, but it should never be on the edge but quite considerably removed from the shoreline; for it is better to be further from the sea than just a short distance because the air of the intervening space is heavier" (*Rust.* 1.5.5–6).

The Younger Seneca, Stoic philosopher and Nero's tutor, inveighs against the Roman partiality for scurrying from villa to villa[107] and vehemently assails ostentatious luxury. Men now expected baths with wide windows so that they might enjoy the scenery and acquire a tan while bathing,[108] or in natatorial perversity they built the foundations of their heated pools in the sea, while others employed artificial heating to worst winter in procuring the bloom of roses and lilies out of season or planted orchards and forests on the very rooftops,[109] a fancy first remarked by Seneca's father who recorded also fishponds.[110] Untouched by disapprobative annotations is, however, a description of the garden of Servilius Vatia's villa near Baiae which contained two massive and laboriously constructed grottoes—one sunny, the other shady—and, bisecting a grove of plane trees, a piscicultural stream that drew water from both the sea and Lake Acherusia.[111] One last excerpt from Seneca is of interest: no elderly man fails to plant for his successor's benefit.[112]

In the Flavian period (A.D. 69–96) men were able to enjoy their properties with peace of mind until confiscation was reintroduced by Domitian.[113] Under Vespasian the Elder Pliny published his encyclopedic *Natural History* which includes a very lengthy section on trees and other plants many of which were to be found on Roman country estates.[114] On several occasions he mentions dwarf trees in ornamental gardens and topiary work, the latter, he claims, invented by Caius Matius in the time of Augustus.[115] Vines could be trained round whole buildings,[116] cypresses clipped into thick hedges or prestigiously transformed into hunting tableaux and fleets of ships.[117] He discourses on the types of shade given by a variety of trees,[118] expatiates on the fragrances and hues of numerous flowers,[119] and catalogues the contrivances for raising water in a garden—wheel, windmill, and swing beam.[120]

---

[107] E.g., *Ep.* 2.1; 69.1; *Tranq.* 2.13. However, he did not always practise what he preached (see d'Arms, *Romans*, 133–134).

[108] A reflection elicited by a visit to the austere and fortified villa of the Elder Scipio at Linternum, which he briefly describes (*Ep.* 86.4–13: cf. 90.25).

[109] *Ep.* 122.8: cf. id. *Thyestes* 464–465; Mart. 8.14; 8.68. Other examples of the luxury of villas are noted by Seneca at *Ep.* 89.21; 90.7–10, 43.

[110] *Cont.* 5.5.

[111] *Ep.* 55.6. The natural look in artificial grottoes was effected by the use of pumice (Pliny *HN* 36.42.154: cf. Stat. *Silv.* 3.1.144–145).

[112] *Ep.* 86.14–15: cf. 12.1–2 where Seneca's bailiff, in addition to commenting on the age of the trees, seems to suggest the built-in obsolescence of the very structure of the house.

[113] Suet. *Dom.* 12.1–2 etc. Various villas of Domitian are listed by Martial (5.1.1–6). In contrast the unpretentious founder of the dynasty spent much of his childhood at his grandmother's villa (at Cosa [Ansedonia]), which he frequently visited when emperor and kept in its pristine, and presumably unostentatiously rustic, condition (Suet. *Vesp.* 2.1).

[114] They are listed by Grimal, *Jardins*, 459-461.

[115] *HN* 12.6.13; 12.11.22; 15.39.130–131; 16.28.70; 16.31.76 etc.

[116] Ibid. 14.3.11.

[117] Ibid. 16.60.140.

[118] Ibid. 17.18.89–91. He is concerned mainly with the extent to which they allow other plants to grow in their shade.

[119] Ibid. 21.10.14–40.69. He especially recommends the juxtaposition of roses and lilies, but his context here is garlands rather than gardens (21.11.22).

[120] Ibid. 19.20.60.

Among the divisions of epideictic oratory established by the rhetorical schools is the ekphrasis or description of an object. This serves as the framework for eight occasional poems in the *Silvae* of Statius (ca. 45–96), of which two are devoted to country villas. Statius' importance for us is further enhanced by his enthusiasm for the marvels of technology,[121] without which many of the illusions in Roman gardens could not have been created. In one poem he revels in the cool and beauteous peace of an estate above Tibur belonging to Manilius Vopiscus, an Epicurean littérateur, where he does admit that the charms of nature have outdone human skill.[122] The house itself was built on either side of the river Anio (Aniene) so that one could all but touch hands across the water,[123] courtyards faced the river or a stately ancient wood, one lofty tree had been allowed to remain within the house overtopping the roof, and the grounds contained shady pools and a bathhouse. The other poem describes the far more elaborate estate of the millionaire Pollius Felix at Surrentum (Sorrento) on the Punta della Calcarella.[124] Here the owner had truly tamed nature,[125] leveling hills, shaping and removing rocks, creating groves where there had been no soil before. On the shore near a shrine of Hercules stood the baths, fed by both fresh and seawater. From it a slanting and covered colonnade led up a cliff to a house so designed that each window afforded a different view, and, while some rooms were receptive to every sound of the sea, others were hushed in sylvan stillness. Elsewhere Statius sings in Horatian manner the praises of his simple estate at Alba (Albano),[126] for which Emperor Domitian had a watercourse built,[127] and spins an amorous etiological tale for a curiously shaped plane tree whose trunk bent over a pool before rising into the air on the estate of his friend Atedius Melior.[128]

The gilded society enjoyed by Statius was viewed from a proletarian position by Martial (ca. 40–ca. 104). In one poem he mocks an owner so intent on groves of laurels, planes, and pines and on his baths and a colonnade with alabaster floor that he had forgotten to leave room for eating and sleeping;[129] in another he at first glance offers

---

[121] This is most apparent in his description of the emperor's construction in A.D. 95 of the Via Domitiana from Sinuessa to Naples and its consequent benefits to users (*Silv.* 4.3). For a thorough treatment of the subject in general see Z. Pavlovskis, *Man in an Artificial Landscape: The Marvels of Civilization in Imperial Roman Literature*, Mnemosyne Suppl. 25, Leiden, 1973.

[122] *Silv.* 1.3.15–17, but contrast ibid. 7–8, 43–46. As befitted its owner, this estate was elegant and restrained rather than luxurious (90–94).

[123] Thus a sometimes unavoidable accident of humble housing (Mart. 1.86.1–2) became a deliberately designed feature of a rich man's mansion.

[124] *Silv.* 2.2 (cf. 3.1.91–104). Statius fleetingly mentions another Campanian estate of Pollius Felix at Pausilypon (Posillipo) that was called "Limon" (2.2.81–82: cf. 3.1.149).

[125] Cf. ibid. 1.2.154–157; 1.3.7–8, 43–46; 3.1.96–101 etc.

[126] Ibid. 4.5.1–28. Another poem (3.5) is, however, an apparently successful plea to his wife to accompany him in retirement to the Bay of Naples, whose manifold attractions he praises (see further d'Arms, *Romans*, 218–219).

[127] Ibid. 3.1.61–64.

[128] Ibid. 2.3. Of further peripheral interest in the *Silvae* are the descriptions of the Baths of Claudius Etruscus at Rome (1.5: cf. Mart. 6.42) and of the new temple of Hercules at Surrentum built near his own estate by Pollius Felix (3.1).

[129] 12.50. Toward the extravagances of Domitian, however, he is respectful.

the inconceivable, a simple and productive estate set amid the emulous self-indulgence of Baiae, but the eulogy of rusticity is soon rendered suspect by the inclusion among the poultry of peacocks, flamingos, pheasants, and similar delicacies of the table and among the farm workers of a voluptuous eunuch.[130] Martial was himself, like Horace, attracted by the simple country villa that yet did not lack its comforts. The gift of an estate upon his return to his native Spain in A.D. 98 elicited a summary of his rural delights: "this grove, these springs, this matted shade of the horizontal vine, this conduit of irrigating water, the meadows, the rose gardens which will not yield to Paestum that blooms twice a year, . . . the tame eel which swims in its enclosed waters, and the white tower which houses birds of similar hue (sc. doves). . . ."[131]

For over eight decades from the accession of Nerva to the death of Marcus Aurelius (96–180) Romans enjoyed uninterrupted security from arbitrary confiscation of estates. In the words of Trajan's eulogist: "You do not embrace in your huge holdings every marsh, every lake and even woodland pasture through dispossession of their former owners; rivers, mountains, seas are not now dedicated to the eyes of just one man; there are things for the emperor to see but not to own; at last the dominion of the *princeps* is broader than his personal acres."[132] Trajan indeed, following some restoration of property by Nerva, sold off various imperial estates, a process continued by Antoninus Pius.[133] Hadrian alone of the five emperors of this period is known to have constructed an outrageous new villa for himself, the huge complex at Tibur some of whose parts he named after philosophical schools, thus imitating Cicero, and places both known and unknown to sober geography.[134] Antoninus Pius and M. Aurelius show a return to moderation: both took delight in genuine rural pursuits, the latter describing to his mentor Fronto a day that they both spent on a farm in manual work, although the junior emperor did make time for reading Cato's agricultural treatise and hesitantly confesses in another letter that he felt bound to praise but not inclined to love a man whose estate was designed solely for profit at the expense of pleasure and beauty.[135] Eloquent testimony to the delights of country life possible at this period is afforded by the soldier C. Sulpicius Similis who, having obtained permission to resign his position of praetorian

---

[130] 3.58 (see further d'Arms, *Romans*, 212–213). It was probably still a *rara avis* in its area, if indeed it eschewed myrtles, planes, and ornamental box.

[131] 12.31: cf. 12.18. Before leaving Rome he had acquired a villa at Nomentum (Mentana) that he claims was quite unproductive (7.31; 9.60; 10.94: but contrast his invitation to dinner at 10.48). Of further interest among Martial's poems are 1.12; 1.49; 2.14; 4.25; 4.64; 6.43; 9.61; 9.90; 10.30; 10.96; 11.18; 12.72.

[132] Pliny *Pan.* 50.1–2. The whole chapter is important.

[133] Id. *Ep.* 7.31.4; Dio Cass. 68.2.1; Gromatici Veteres p. 239 Lachmann (Nerva, who also bought land for distribution to the poor); Pliny *Pan.* 50.5–7 (Trajan); S.H.A. *Antoninus Pius* 7.10 (Antoninus).

[134] The list of "provinces and places of great fame, such as Lyceum, Academy, Prytaneum, Canopus, Poecile, and Tempe" ends with the "Infernal Regions" (S.H.A. *Hadr.* 26.5). Cicero called two gymnasia at his Tusculan villa the Lyceum and the Academy (Cic. *Div.* 1.5.8; *Tusc.* 2.3.9 etc.). A parallel may be found also for the Canopus (westernmost mouth of the Nile) since the Nile and the Euripus were used as names for artificial streams by villa owners of the late Republic (id. *Leg.* 2.1.2, Sen. *Ep.* 83.5, and Pliny *Ep.* 1.3.1 show that the latter word became a regular term for an artificial watercourse on an estate).

[135] Fronto, *Ep. ad M. Caes. et invicem* 4.6.1 (cf. S.H.A. *Antoninus Pius* 11.2) and 2.7.1 respectively.

ANCIENT LITERARY EVIDENCE FOR PLEASURE GARDENS 23

prefect and retired to his estate for his remaining seven years of life, caused to be inscribed upon his tomb the words, "Here lies Similis, who existed so-and-so many years, but lived seven."[136]

The fullest surviving ancient descriptions of Roman villas come from the early part of this period. They were written by the Younger Pliny, a man who appreciated his country retreats for their salubrity[137] and peace-engendered encouragement of literary activity,[138] but who also took delight in things both natural and artificial and took pride when their harmonious union was of his own contrivance.

His Tuscan villa[139] lay on the gentle slopes of a hill in a natural amphitheater of rich cornfields and well-watered meadows sparkling with flowers that led through a belt of shrubs to serried vineyards and higher to forest-clad mountains, a setting of such beauty that it appeared to him rather a painted picture than real. Although justice cannot in brief be done to Pliny's description, a few points may be noted. Between the meadows and the south-facing colonnade of the house was a garden enclosed by a stone wall itself hidden from view by a box hedge. The garden contained various clipped shrubs within a broad walk, a bed of acanthus, and atop an incline a terrace fronting the colonnade. Its outstanding feature throughout was diversely clipped box, some of which were shaped into animals. At one side of the house was a walking area[140] where shady outer circuits were bordered by box and ivy-clad planes that were themselves enclosed by laurels. From the far end, by cypresses and rose beds, paths led past little lawns separated by box literally clipped to spell the names of gardener and owner, past further topiary work alternating with fruit trees, past an open area bordered by dwarf planes,[141] and finally, after some acanthus and more of the ubiquitous box, to an open-air dining room. This consisted of a curved seat of white marble, shaded by vines supported on four small columns of Carystian marble, and as table an artificially fed marble basin upon which floated plates in the shape of boats and birds. Nature was at the behest of the human artificer throughout: rooms of the house were designed to enjoy or overcome climatic conditions, to face ornamental ponds without or planted courts within; the grounds contained ever-changing vistas, all cunningly contrived, and for weary strollers many scattered seats, each with its own diminutive fountain. The style of the whole was summed up in one small pavilion near the open-air dining room: it contained

---

[136] Dio Cass. 69.19.2.

[137] *Ep.* 5.6.1–6, 45–46; 8.1.3. In one letter (5.19) he begs a friend for reasons of health to tend at the latter's villa at Forum Julii (Fréjus) an ill freedman.

[138] Ibid. 1.9.4; 1.22.11; 4.6.2; 9.10; 9.36.1–3 etc.

[139] Near Tifernum Tiberinum (Città di Castello) and described in *Ep.* 5.6. For reconstructions of this villa see H.H. Tanzer, *The Villas of Pliny the Younger*, New York, 1924, 108–135, and for commentary on the letter A.N. Sherwin-White, *The Letters of Pliny: A Historical and Social Commentary*, Oxford, 1966, 321–330.

[140] It was called a hippodrome for its shape, but was used mainly for walking (see Sherwin-White, *Pliny*, 327–328), although Pliny did take exercise also on horseback (*Ep.* 9.36.5). The circuits were measured to give a standard "constitutional" (cf. ibid. 3.1.4).

[141] This was described by Pliny as "an imitation of the countryside suddenly brought into a highly ornamental scene" (ibid. 5.6.35).

a bed in a closet with vine-shaded windows on all sides so that you could, in Pliny's words, "recline as in a wood, but not as in a wood feel the rain."

His Laurentine villa,[142] a little way south of Ostia, had a smaller and more limited pleasance since it lay on the shoreline. A formal walk surrounded by box and rosemary[143] encircled a garden thickly planted with mulberry and fig trees and, in the center, a shady pergola of vines, if the manuscripts are correct.[144] Another walking area, this one fragrant with violets, fronted a covered way[145] that led from a kitchen garden by the house to Pliny's prized personal addition to the villa, a garden-pavilion whose range of rooms with a diversity of views included a sun parlor and sleeping quarters. His other villas were at Comum (Como) where two delighted him especially. Both were on the lake and reminiscent of Baiae, "Tragedy" atop a small promontory, "Comedy"[146] curving around a bay: both possessed formal walks, but "Comedy" had the added attraction of enabling its proprietor to fish from his window almost without getting out of bed.[147]

Elsewhere Pliny postulates reasons for the regular ebb and flow of a spring near Comum, which ran through an artificial grotto and by which he would sometimes dine to marvel at this mysterious natural phenomenon,[148] and discusses with an architect the problems of repairing and extending a temple of Ceres on one of his properties.[149] Finally, he describes both his own daily regimen of four separate walks, one ride in a carriage or on horseback, and one bath at his Tusculan villa, and that of an admirable seventy-seven-year-old gentleman, Vestricius Spurinna, who kept fit on his estate with three walks, one of three miles, a carriage ride of seven miles, and, before his bath, lengthy and energetic exercise with a ball.[150]

Other writers of the period offer scant information. Juvenal, who assails the vices

---

[142] Ibid. 2.17. For reconstructions see Tanzer, *Villas*, 44–107 and for commentary Sherwin-White, *Pliny*, 186–199. The site of the villa has recently been identified; see Ricotti, "Roman Garden Triclinia," in this volume.

[143] Rosemary was used, as Pliny states, only as a stopgap in the box's failure to withstand direct exposure to wind and spray from the sea.

[144] See Sherwin-White, *Pliny*, 194.

[145] This had both seaward and landward windows so that temperature and air could be regulated (for the difficulties in ascertaining its exact position see Sherwin-White, *Pliny*, 195–198). The whole house was, like its Tuscan counterpart, designed to take maximum advantage of scenery and climate: its outstanding feature was a dining room so close to the sea as to be gently washed by spray in a storm.

[146] They were so called, as Pliny says in his description (*Ep.* 9.7), from the high boot and low shoe of actors in Greek tragedy and comedy respectively. With greater personal appropriateness the 2nd-century Lycian rhetorician Heraclides called his villa near Smyrna (bought with the proceeds of his profession) "Rhetoric" (Philostr. *VS* 2.26).

[147] Cf. Mart. 10.30.16–18. For an appreciative description from the 6th century of the natural delights of this lake and surrounding area see Cassiod. *Var.* 11.14.

[148] *Ep.* 4.30. The marvelous spring is mentioned also by his uncle (*HN* 2.106.232).

[149] *Ep.* 9.39. Note also a brief description of a friend's villa at Comum (ibid. 1.3) and an enthusiastic portrayal of a famous beauty spot, the source of the river Clitumnus (in Umbria) with its shrines, reminiscent of those in a private pleasure garden, and nearby riparian villas (ibid. 8.8).

[150] *Ep.* 9.36 (Pliny); 3.1 (Spurinna). They are not disconsonant with the medical advice given by Celsus (*Med.* 1.1–2). Pliny too at both his Laurentine and his Tuscan villa had a ball court (*Ep.* 2.17.12; 5.6.27).

of urban life in contrast with the traditional virtues of the countryside, derides the conceit of artificial imitation of nature in denying the verisimilitude of man-made grottoes.[151] Later Fronto praises to M. Aurelius the vigor of trees tended by man, mentions topiary work in myrtle and box, and alludes to the spectacular *catachanna*, a tree which being inoculated with various fruits testifies to the persistent Roman yearning to improve nature.[152]

From the accession of Commodus in 180 to the death of Carinus in 285 political anarchy and latterly barbarian invasions were accompanied by economic decline. Much of Italy lay untended, and as early as 193 Pertinax decreed that any man who brought back into cultivation wasteland, even if on imperial property, became legal owner with immunity from taxation for ten years;[153] but already Commodus had reintroduced confiscation of private estates for personal aggrandizement, a process that was vastly accelerated by Septimius Severus (193–211).[154] The Campanian coast had now lost its less than puritanical reputation. Septimius retired thither (and to his suburban estates) in 205 to protect his sons, singularly unsuccessfully in the case of the future emperor Caracalla, from the corruptive enticements of Rome,[155] and Severus Alexander (222–235) had a grand estate at Baiae,[156] but the area rapidly lost its popularity and had been almost completely abandoned by the wealthy when in 275 Tacitus emerged from his Baian villa to assume the purple.[157] From literary sources little is known of imperial taste in villas at this period: Commodus avoided the plague by staying on his Laurentine estate which was shaded by enormous groves of fragrant laurels,[158] and the Gordians (238–244) possessed a sumptuous retreat on the road to Praeneste,[159] while Elagabalus (218–222) introduced a novel style of landscape gardening in piling up a hill out of snow, if we can trust our scandal-loving source,[160] brought a flower garden into his banqueting chamber by means of a reversible ceiling that smothered his guests, some to

[151] *Sat.* 3.17–20.

[152] *Ep. ad M. Caes. et invicem* 1.3.7–8; *Laudes Neglegentiae* 4; *Ep. ad Antoninum Imp. de Orationibus* 2 respectively. The *catachanna* is mentioned also by M. Aurelius (Fronto, *Ep. ad M. Caes. et invicem* 2.6. Van den Hout = 2.11 Naber).

[153] Hdn. 2.4.6. Jones suggests that the crisis was only temporary following the plague that began in the reign of M. Aurelius (*Later Roman Empire*, II, 812), but there is little evidence of really substantial recovery. The problem of wasteland was, of course, not new and Pertinax' plan had been almost exactly anticipated about a century before in a speech put into the mouth of a Euboean landowner by Dio Chrysostomus (7.33–37).

[154] Dio Cass. 75.8.4; Hdn. 3.8.2; S.H.A. *Sev.* 12.1–5. Under Severus imperial holdings became extensive not only in Italy but also in Spain and his native North Africa. See further Frank, *Economic Survey*, V, 78–85; Rostovtsev, *Social and Economic History*, II, 702–703 (n. 34).

[155] Hdn. 3.13.1.

[156] S.H.A. *Alex. Sev.* 26.9–10. He was visited there by the historian Dio Cassius (Dio Cass. 80.5.2), who himself chose a villa near Capua, inland from the Campanian coast, as a quiet retreat for his literary toils (77.2.1).

[157] S.H.A. *Tacitus* 7.5–6.

[158] The fragrance of the trees was believed to combat the pestilence (Hdn. 1.12.2).

[159] S.H.A. *Gordiani* 32.2–3. Gordian II reveled in "gardens, baths, and the most charming groves" (ibid. 19.5), and Gordian III planned magnificent gardens in the Campus Martius at Rome (ibid. 32.6–8).

[160] "Aelius Lampridius" (S.H.A. *Heliogab.* 23.8).

death, in a cloudburst of violets,[161] and made fragrant his swimming pools with spices and roses,[162] only to be outdone by Carinus who swam amid apples and melons.[163]

From this period there survive no descriptions of actual gardens, and lost too are the "Georgics" of Decimus Claudius Albinus,[164] who was proclaimed Augustus but failed to overthrow Septimius Severus in 197. Literary evidence, however, is not entirely lacking, since fictional gardens were rooted in reality. The most abundantly portrayed of these is the productive pleasure garden on Lesbos in the pastoral romance "Daphnis and Chloë," which was written most probably in the third century. Here, encircled by a wall some 600 by 400 feet, is a decorative windbreak of tall trees with interlacing upper branches that protects fruit trees. Mentioned specifically are cypress, laurel, plane, pine, myrtle, apple, pear, pomegranate, fig, olive, vine. Within are the central feature of a shrine and altar to Dionysus, fountains and flower beds of roses, hyacinths and lilies, and patches of spontaneous violets, narcissi, and pimpernels. The same romance offers a second shady garden, own property of Eros, more vaguely described and containing many of the same plants and also poppies.[165] An earlier imaginary garden by the novelist Achilles Tatius includes interweaving trees garlanded with ivy and convolvulus and a basin of water set amid a flower bed to mirror roses, violets, and narcissi.[166] Elsewhere we find a beauteous grove with garden flowers as couch for the amorous ecstasy of Mars and Venus in Reposianus, an umbrageous and floriferous garden on a country estate as setting for an intemperate party of Alciphron, and a few hortulan glimpses from Pentadius, Flavius Philostratus, and his son-in-law; but in these fictional gardens allowance must always be made for the paradisiacal strain, of Homeric derivation, that may be seen also among earlier writers of the Roman Empire such as Dio Chrysostomus and Lucian.[167]

From the accession of Diocletian in 284 greater, though intermittent, political stability allied to a hesitant economic recovery brought about in the fourth century a slight amelioration of conditions in both city and country that was not completely obliterated by the chaos in the western half of the empire during the following century. Pleasure gardens precariously survived both the increasing fortification of villas, a process begun

---

[161] Ibid. 21.5. Nero had more moderately devised similar entertainment in his Golden House (Suet. *Ner.* 31.2: cf. Petron. *Sat.* 60). For further floral excesses see S.H.A. *Aelius* 5.7; idd. *Heliogab.* 19.7; 28.5; 29.8. Pliny gives a Greek origin for the more modest illusion of chandeliers in the shape of apples hanging on a tree (*HN* 34.8.14).

[162] S.H.A. *Heliogab.* 19.8; 21.6; 24.1.

[163] Idd. *Carus et Carinus et Numerius* 17.3.

[164] Idd. *Clod.* 11.7.

[165] 4.2–4; 2.3–6 respectively.

[166] 1.15 (cf. 1.1.2–6 for a similar scene).

[167] Reposianus *De Concubitu Martis et Veneris* (esp. 33–63) in J.W. and A.M. Duff, *Minor Latin Poets*, London-Cambridge, Mass., 1934, 524–539 (= *Anth. Lat.* 1.1.no.253), Alciphron 4.13 Schepers (1905 ed.), Pentadius *De Adventu Veris* in Duff and Duff, *Minor Latin Poets*, 546–549 (= *Anth. Lat.* 1.1.no.235), Flavius Philostratus *VA* 1.25; 2.8 (ostensibly not imaginary), Philostratus Lemnius *Imag.* 1.6.2 (attribution to this particular Philostratus not certain), Homer *Od.* 5.63-73 (Ogygia) and 7.112–131 (Phaeacia), Dio Chrysostomus 35.20–21 (contrast the brief description of a simple garden at 7.64–65), Lucian *Ver. Hist.* 2.11–16. Later a lush imaginary garden is portrayed by "Aristaenetus" (1.3), an erotic epistolographer of probably the second half of the 5th century.

in the third century, and the tendency of wealthy Romans to acquire vast tracts of land, in Italy and elsewhere, worked as their principal source of income in a quasi-feudal manner. The celebrated pagan Symmachus (ca. 340–ca. 402) and his father possessed not only three houses in Rome and one in Capua and for profit estates in Samnium, Apulia, Sicily, and Mauretania, but also for pleasure three suburban villas and twelve country villas, including, among six on the Bay of Naples, one at Baiae that had regained some of its former notoriety[168] (Symmachus moved frequently between his properties and is clearly not to be classed with the effete gentry castigated by the historian Ammianus Marcellinus for equating journeys to their estates with the marches of Alexander the Great[169]). The Christian Melania the Younger, who sold her property in 404 for the benefit of the poor, had owned land in Italy, Sicily, Spain, Africa, Mauretania, Britain, "and other countries,"[170] one of which estates contained a sumptuous villa and no fewer than sixty hamlets each with four hundred serfs.[171] Little immediately perceptible change was effected by the barbarian usurpation of power and Odoacer's deposition in 476 of the traditionally considered last Roman emperor in the West, Romulus Augustulus, who was relegated to a Campanian villa once owned by the Republican plutocrat L. Licinius Lucullus.[172]

Again for the fourth century specific literary information about pleasure gardens is sparse: Palladius' agricultural treatise is too practical to be of much value here;[173] of the palatial Dalmatian villa to which Diocletian retired in 305 all we learn is that he was very proud of its vegetables;[174] Symmachus is disappointingly uninformative apart from briefly expressed appreciation of his various villas' charm, salubrity, and peace,[175] although the last of these could pall.[176] About one of Melania's villas we do know a little: its outstanding feature was a pool from which bathers could enjoy the sight of both boats at sea and hunters in the forest.[177] The poets, however, have something to offer: Tiberianus evinces a genuine sensitivity to the beauties of nature in a description of a prattling stream passing through a fragrant, flowery grove that savors of a garden;[178] Ausonius (310–ca. 394) catalogues the merits of divers situations for villas along the

---

[168] Symmachus *Ep.* 5.93; 7.24. He does, however, comment on its isolation (ibid. 2.26). For details of Symmachus' properties see O. Seeck in *Monumenta Germaniae Historica, Auctores Antiquissimi*, VI.1, xlv–xlvi; d'Arms, *Romans*, 226–229.

[169] Amm. Marc. 28.4.18.

[170] *Vita S. Melaniae Iunioris Graeca* 11 (*Analecta Bollandiana*, 22 [1903], 14).

[171] *Vita S. Melaniae Iunioris Latina* 18 (op. cit., 8 [1889], 33).

[172] Marcellinus Comes, *Chron.* ad a. 476; Jordanes, *Romana* 344; *Getica* 46.242. Numerically the greatest known accumulation of property by a private individual is that of Bertram, bishop of Civitas Cenomanorum (Le Mans), who in the early 7th century left in his will nearly ninety properties, many of them villas (J.M. Pardessus, *Diplomata Chartae Epistulae Leges Aliaque Instrumenta ad Res Gallico-Francicas Spectantia*, Paris, 1850, no. 230). For a thorough survey of the whole subject see Jones, *Later Roman Empire*, II, 767–823.

[173] It does contain many scattered chapters on kitchen gardens and one (3.21) on the planting of flowers.

[174] *Epitome de Caesaribus* 39.6.

[175] E.g., *Ep.* 1.1; 1.5; 1.8; 3.50; 4.44; 6.81; 7.15; 7.26; 7.35; 8.23; 8.25.

[176] Ibid. 2.26.

[177] See above, n. 171 (cf. Symmachus *Ep.* 7.15).

[178] Duff and Duff, *Minor Latin Poets*, 558–561 (= *Anth. Lat.* 1.2.no.809).

banks of the Moselle, favoring those with broad prospects from their elevation,[179] and makes clear his preference for nature's subjugation to man;[180] Claudian (ca. 370–404) includes in his epithalamium of 398 to Emperor Honorius and his bride Maria a terrestrial paradise of Venus that owes something to gardens;[181] and the anonymous inspirator of Herrick's "Gather ye Rose-buds while ye may" strolls at dawn through a garden glimmering with hoarfrost.[182]

The fifth century is not entirely barren. Prudentius, who retired from an active administrative career in 405 to dedicate his remaining years to devotional poetry and thereby earned his sobriquet of "the Christian Horace," in one composition depicts the souls of the righteous singing hymns in a well-watered, fragrant, and flowery Roman pleasure garden, while in another he delights in the produce typical of a simple rural estate.[183] Rutilius Namatianus, probably in 417, chose to journey from Rome to his estates in Gaul by sea, since the roads were now in melancholy dilapidation. His consequent poem lauds the ever-vernal groves and their warbling birds within the confines of Roman mansions, a villa at Centumcellae (Civitavecchia) where a safe anchorage had been constructed within the house itself, a villa garden at Faleria (Porto di Faliesi) with a wood and spacious fishponds, and a villa built on an artificial peninsula at Triturrita (probably a little to the north of Livorno).[184]

References to country estates are frequent in the prose and verse of Sidonius Apollinaris (ca. 431–486), a Gallo-Roman aristocrat from Lyons who was appointed city prefect at Rome in 468 and bishop of the Auvergne in 471 before acquiring the ultimate and posthumous accolade of canonization. Although Sidonius admits his literary indebtedness to the Younger Pliny and to Statius,[185] his lengthy but frustratingly imprecise descriptions of his own villa at Avitacum (near Clermont-Ferrand) and that of a friend, Pontius Leontius, near Bordeaux must be rooted in reality. The former villa[186] lay between wooded hills, the foundations of its buildings sunk into the sandy bottom of a lake, which had shores either ugly with oozing slime and weeds[187] or winding and shaded by trees, while in the middle was an island and, for aquatic sports, a turning post on a pile of boulders, scene of many a gay collision. A noteworthy feature of the description is Sidonius' catalogue of the aural delights of his villa: at different times of

---

[179] *Mosella* 20–22, 283–286, 318–348.

[180] See Pavlovskis, *Artificial Landscape* (above, n. 121), 33–39. Note, however, Ausonius' rejection of excessive luxury (*Mosella* 48–54) and the description of his own very modest estate (*De Herediolo*). An extremely brief description of a garden appears at *Ep.* 31.242–244.

[181] *Epithalamium* 49–96. Note also the outrageous presence of terrestrial garden flowers at the marine seat of Neptune (ibid. 154–158).

[182] The poem is often included in the corpus of Ausonius (e.g., 22.2 Peiper = *Anth. Lat.* 1.2.no.646).

[183] *Liber Cathemerinon* 5.113–124; 3.21–80 respectively. See also *c. Symm.* 1.104–115.

[184] *De Reditu Suo* 1.111–114, 237–248 (cf. Pliny *Ep.* 6.31.15–17), 377–380, 527–540 respectively.

[185] *Ep.* 1.1.1; 4.22.2; 9.1.1 (Pliny); *Carm.* 22.*ep*.6 (Statius). On the nature of these debts see Pavlovskis, *Artificial Landscape*, 44–52.

[186] *Ep.* 2.2. Sidonius is at great pains to defend his villa against any possible charge of inferiority to Pliny's villas.

[187] This area may not have been on his property. The lake was about two miles long.

day and night he was enravished by distant piping of shepherds and bleating of their sheep, singing of nightingales, twittering of swallows, cawing of rooks, honking of swans and geese, chirruping of cicadas, and even vespertine croaking of frogs.[188] Two huge lime trees with interlacing branches provided shade for an open-air ball court, but there is no further vegetal detail. From another of his villas, however, Sidonius does list violets, marigolds, narcissi, hyacinths, saffron, cassia, thyme, and privet as well as an artificial grotto.[189] Leontius' estate, termed a *burgus* or fortress, was built on a hill and descended to a river.[190] It clearly contained open land and garden, for Sidonius mentions grain crops, laurels, and a spring issuing from rocks so naturally beautiful that, a rare tribute, they needed no artificial embellishment; but he expatiates on the buildings themselves that contained two inlets from the river, up one of which fish swam right into a dining room, while through the other in stormy weather boats were tossed into the baths to general merriment.

Since most barbarians were eager for Romanization, or at least its material manifestations, it is not surprising that Roman gardens long survived the fall of the empire in the West. The poems of Luxorius from the beginning of the sixth century show the Vandal absorption of Roman ways. One tells of a fish that fed from the hand when summoned; one of a boar that dined at table; one of a lofty pavilion adorned with a picture of its owner Fridamal slaying a boar and set amid a pleasure garden with trees, fountains, and a statue of Diana; one of an elaborate fountain, surrounded by statues, whose waters splashed over a marble step into a basin; one of a garden of lovely, never-failing foliage, ever-aromatic plants, mossy stream, and sweetly singing birds.[191] Toward the end of the century Venantius Fortunatus (ca. 540–ca. 600), a poet not immune to the beauties of nature, mentions sparkling and fragrant flowers, an elaborate fountain, and a fishpond in three brief poems in praise of three different Burgundian country villas.[192] For Italy itself there is the evidence of Cassiodorus (ca. 510–ca. 583), who held high office under a series of Ostrogothic rulers from Theodoric to Vitiges and after Justinian's conquest of Italy converted his estate at Scylacium (Squillace) in Bruttium (Calabria) into a monastery called "Viridarium" or "Garden." Here he offered anchorites "the sweet solitude of Mount Castellum" and their weaker brethren the coenobitic luxury of well-irrigated gardens and the "Gates of Neptune," the name he gave his own

---

[188] At the swimming pool, fed by water flowing through the mouths of sculpted lion heads, the noise of water from the falls was too great for easy conversation (cf. *Carm.* 18.5–6). Sidonius turns even this into an amusing and almost laudable feature.

[189] *Carm.* 24.53–74.

[190] Ibid. 22.101–230. Of peripheral interest are also ibid. 11.6–31; *Ep.* 2.10.4(poem); 4.21.5; 5.14.1; 8.4.1 and lines 33–41 of the poem at *Ep.* 9.13.5.

[191] 5, 6, 18, 34, 46 Rosenblum (= *Anth. Lat.* 1.291, 292, 304, 320, 332) respectively. Procopius mentions the shady and well-watered Vandal pleasure gardens at the time (A.D. 533) of Belisarius' conquest (*Vand.* 2.6.9). The existence of beautiful country villas in North Africa predates, of course, even the Roman occupation: Agathocles and his Sicilians in their invasion of 310 B.C. marched past numerous luxurious Carthaginian villas designed for pleasure as well as profit (Diod. Sic. 20.8.3–4), while Columella termed the Carthaginian writer Mago the "father of agriculture" (*Rust.* 1.1.13).

[192] *Carm.* 1.18, 20 (flowers), 19 (fountain and pond): see also ibid. 3.10.

excavation in "the bowels of the rocks at the foot of Mount Moscius" into which could swim "a school of fishes sporting in their free captivity" which "both refreshes the spirit with amusement and delights the eye with wonder. Eagerly they rush to the hand of man and before they become food they demand titbits: man feeds his darlings and, although he can catch them, frequently when well provided he lets them go."[193] But for the further survival and the development of the Roman pleasure garden and its appurtenances we must turn our gaze to Constantinople, the New Rome.[194]

---

[193] *Var.* 12.15 and *Institutiones* 1.29: cf. *Var.* 8.32. Further and often extensive descriptions of country estates and their delights may be found at *Var.* 8.31; 11.10; 11.14; 12.22.

[194] The distinction between Roman and Byzantine is notoriously hard to make. Perhaps the 6th-century garden poems of the *Greek Anthology* (9.663–669) should be accounted Roman. An even more difficult case is that of the *Geoponica*, in its present form a 10th-century reworking of a probably 7th-century compilation of largely earlier material with an eastern Mediterranean bias.

Recently Excavated Gardens and Cultivated Land of the Villas at Boscoreale and Oplontis

WILHELMINA F. JASHEMSKI

The eruption of Vesuvius in A.D. 79, which tragically destroyed Pompeii, Herculaneum, and the many villas in the surrounding area, preserved detailed information about Roman gardens and cultivated land that can be known from no other sites (Fig. 1). The lower slopes of Vesuvius and the surrounding Campanian plain were dotted in antiquity with a multitude of thriving villas. Through the years many of these have been hurriedly, too often partially, sometimes even clandestinely, excavated, and then they were often hastily covered over again so that the precious soil could be returned to cultivation. Three villas, which are today being carefully excavated and will become permanent archaeological sites, give us our first detailed information about villa gardens and the crops raised on the cultivated land. These three villas are discussed in this paper.

The dominant feature of the landscape today is the barren cone that has been building up in the low, wide crater formed in A.D. 79 when Vesuvius erupted (Fig. 2). But in antiquity, as the poet Martial tells us, Vesuvius was "green with viny shades; here had the noble grape loaded the dripping vats. These ridges Bacchus loved more than the hills of Nysa."[1] The words of the poet are vividly illustrated by the artist on a lararium (household shrine) found in the House of the Centenary (IX.viii.6)[2] at Pompeii. Scholars believe that this painting[3] suggests the appearance of Vesuvius before the eruption in A.D. 79.[4] Vines grow on the slopes in quincunx formation. Bacchus stands on his favorite mountain, clothed in huge grapes (Fig. 3). The poet goes on to say that Vesuvius was also the haunt of Venus. This was quite appropriate, for the Italian Venus was the goddess of growing things and of gardens long before she became identified with the Greek goddess of love, Aphrodite.[5] But more about Venus later, when we stop briefly at Pompeii at the end of this paper. For Venus was also the tutelary goddess of Pompeii.

At the rustic villa of L. Crassius Tertius at Oplontis (modern Torre Annunziata), on

---

Support for my excavations was provided by Dumbarton Oaks and the Soprintendenza of Pompeii. My work was greatly facilitated by the generous cooperation and gracious hospitality of Dr. Giuseppina Cerulli Irelli, Superintendent of Pompeii, Dr. Stefano De Caro, Director of Excavations at Pompeii, Dr. Antonio D'Ambrosio, in charge of the *deposito* at Pompeii, Ferdinando Balzano, assistant at Torre Annunziata, and Vincenzo Matrone, assistant at Boscoreale. Nicola Sicigiano was our able foreman.

[1] Mart. 4.44. All abbreviations for ancient authors and their works are those found in N.G.L. Hammond and H.H. Scullard, eds., *The Oxford Classical Dictionary*, 2nd ed., Oxford, 1970, ix–xxii.

[2] Sites in Pompeii are easily located by the system introduced by Giuseppe Fiorelli, who became director of the excavations in 1860. He divided the city into nine regions; each region was subdivided into numbered insulae or blocks, and each entrance in each insula was assigned a number. Thus each door has an address of three numbers.

[3] Now in the Museo Archeologico Nazionale at Naples, inventory no. 112286.

[4] E. Cocchia, "La forma del Vesuvio nelle pitture e descrizioni antiche," *Atti dell'Accademia di Archeologia, Lettere e Belli Arti*, 21 (1899), 47–56; A. Rittman, "L'eruzione vesuviana del 79: Studio magmalogico e vulcanologico," in *Pompeiana. Raccolta di studi per il secondo centenario degli scavi di Pompei*, Naples, 1950, 474.

[5] For Venus as a garden deity at Pompeii, see Wilhelmina F. Jashemski, *The Gardens of Pompeii, Herculaneum and the Villas Destroyed by Vesuvius*, I, New Rochelle, N.Y., 1979, 124–130.

the coast, a short distance from Pompeii, no garden has yet been found.[6] When the columns of a portico began to come into view, there was the possibility of a peristyle garden. But the area enclosed by a portico on three sides was not a garden; the courtyard area was crudely paved. The villa, however, has yielded significant information about what was grown on land nearby. In a room opening off the south portico several cubic meters of carbonized plant material were found (Fig. 4). It had apparently fallen from the upper story where it had been stored. This material is slowly being separated, studied, photographed, and identified by Professor Massimo Ricciardi, of the Institute of Botany at the University of Naples Agricultural College, at Portici, and Dr. Francis Hueber, Curator of Paleobotany at the Smithsonian Institution in Washington, D.C.

The large quantity of grapevine leaves, tendrils, and small branches, some of which clearly showed the cut where they had been pruned, indicates that this material was hay that had been collected in a vineyard.[7] Oak, olive, and *Prunus* leaves were also present. But in the vineyards that I have excavated at Pompeii it was not at all unusual to find trees. The majority of the plants identified were legumes or grasses such as would have been found growing under the vines. Among those identified are the vetch (*Vicia sativa* L.), fenugreek (*Trigonella foenum-graecum* L.), alfalfa, lupines, and clovers, including the red clover (*Trifolium pratense* L.), all of which would have made good hay. And of course there were weeds and wild flowers. Among these were sorrel, chickweed, mustard, mint, buttercup, wild geranium (*Geranium rotundifolium* L.), mallow, hypericum, wild carrot, wild chrysanthemum, bramble, and the bracken fern. It was not surprising to find the little red corn poppy (*Papaver rhoeas* L.), which is a wild flower. There was also a seedpod of another poppy (*Papaver setigerum* DC.).[8] Blossoms of the violet (*Viola arvensis* Murray) were also found. The abundance of flax (*Linum usitatissimum* L.) in the hay indicates that this crop was raised nearby and had escaped into the vineyard (Fig. 5). The importance of this material is shown by the fact that of the 111 taxonomic entities that Professor Ricciardi had identified in 1978, sixty-seven species, thirty-one genera, and one family have been added to the list of 408 plants probably known in the first century B.C.[9] More

---

[6] This villa, located on the Via Murat, is at the rear of the Scuola Media "G. Parini," where it was discovered by chance during the construction of the school. For a map showing the location of this villa and also that of the luxurious villa at Oplontis on the Via Selpolcri, see Jashemski, *Gardens*, I, fig. 497 on pl. 322.

[7] M. Ricciardi and G. G. Aprile, "Preliminary Data on the Floristic Components of Some Carbonized Plant Remains Found in the Archaeological Area of Oplontis near Naples," *Annali della Facoltà di Scienze Agrarie dell'Università di Napoli in Portici*, ser. 4, vol. 12 (1978), 204. Additional information was obtained in conversation with Prof. Ricciardi.

[8] This seedpod was originally identified by Ricciardi and Aprile ("Preliminary Data," 205) as that of the opium poppy (*Papaver somniferum* L.), but now, based on more recent study, they identify the pod as that of *Papaver setigerum* DC. For the characteristics of *Papaver setigerum* DC., see V. La Valva, S. Sabato, and G.S. Gigliano, "Morphology and Alkaloid Chemistry of *Papaver setigerum* DC. (Papaveraceae)," *Taxon*, 34(2) (1985), 191–196.

[9] See Ricciardi and Aprile, "Preliminary Data," 204–212, for a complete list and discussion of all the plants that had been identified by Prof. Ricciardi by 1978.

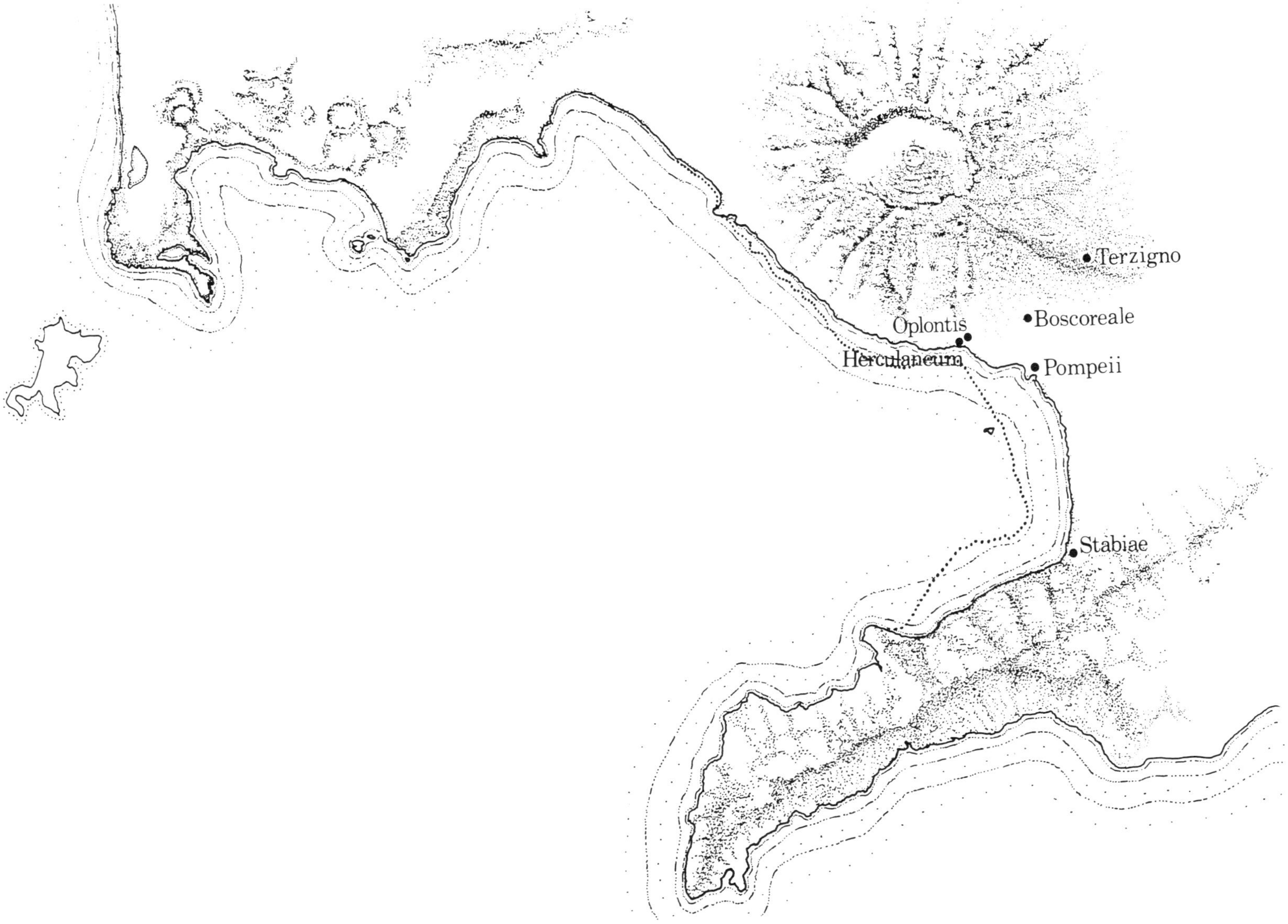
Terzigno
Boscoreale
Oplontis
Herculaneum
Pompeii
Stabiae

1. Map of the Vesuvian area (Deborah Auten)

2. Vesuvius dominates the Campanian plain; Pompeii in the foreground (air photo: Pompeii Tourist Bureau)

3. Painting on household shrine showing Bacchus standing on Mount Vesuvius as it appeared before the A.D. 79 eruption (photo: Stanley Jashemski)

4. Collecting carbonized hay in the villa of L. Crassius Tertius at Oplontis
(photo: Stanley Jashemski)

5. Carbonized flax capsule (*Linum usitatissimum* L.)
(SEM photo: Francis Hueber)

6. Carbonized minute brown scavenger beetle (*Microgramme ruficollis* Marsham, family Lathridiidae)
(SEM photo: Francis Hueber)

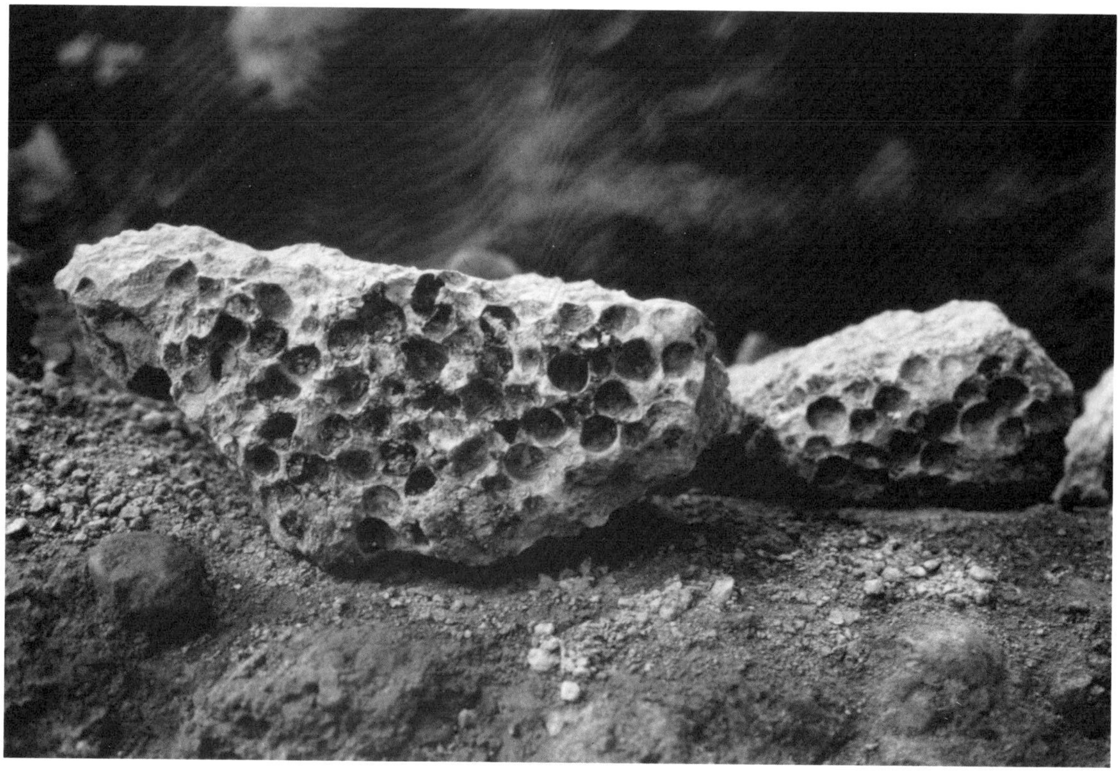

7. Imprints of filberts (*Corylus avellana* L.) stored in the villa of L. Crassius Tertius (photo: Francis Hueber)

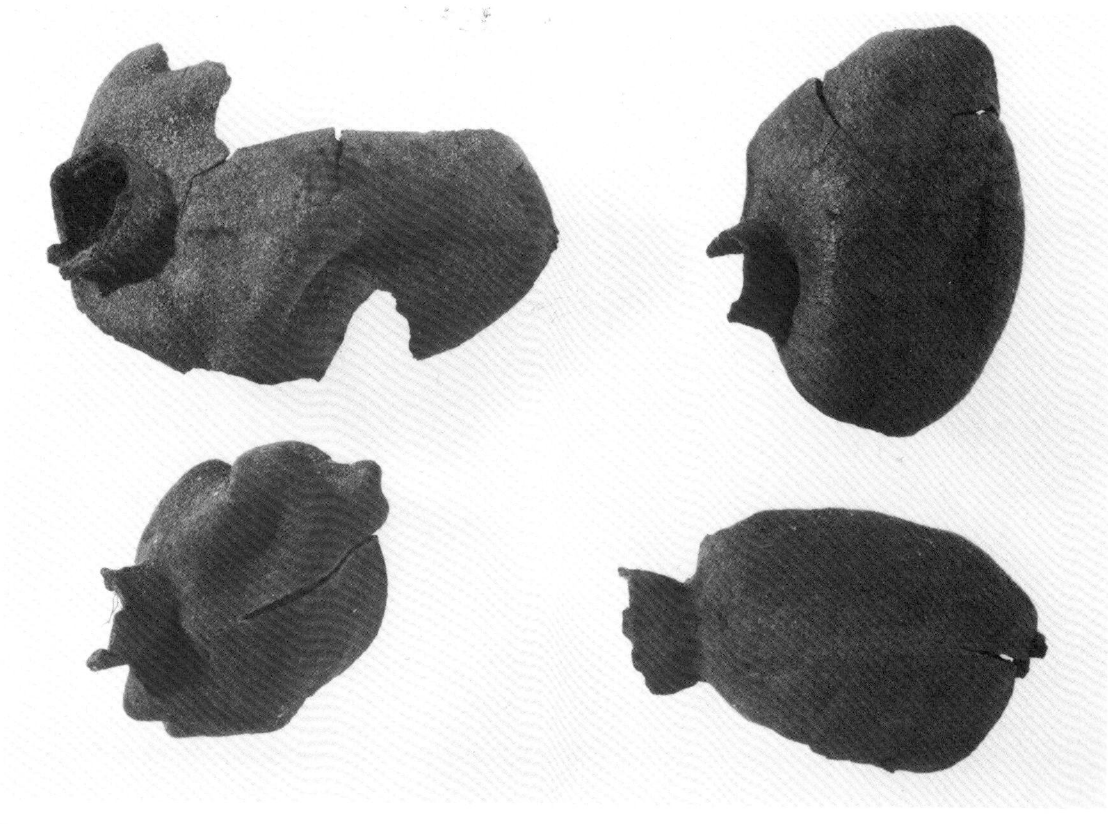

8. Carbonized pomegranates (*Punica granatum* L.) stored in the villa of L. Crassius Tertius (photo: U.S. Department of Agriculture)

9. Niche lararium (household shrine) in the portico of the *villa rustica* at Boscoreale (photo: Henry Ferry)

10. Bacchus found in the lararium of the *villa rustica* at Boscoreale (photo: Henry Ferry)

11. Cast of winepress in the *villa rustica* at Boscoreale
(photo: Francis Hueber)

12. Restored winepress in the Villa of the Mysteries at Pompeii
(photo: Stanley Jashemski)

13. Altar and lararium in the pressing room in the *villa rustica* at Boscoreale (photo: Henry Ferry)

14. *Cella vinaria;* embedded dolia in which wine was fermented in the *villa rustica* at Boscoreale (photo: Francis Hueber)

15. Hearth and oven in the kitchen in the *villa rustica* at Boscoreale (photo: Francis Hueber)

16. Shelves in the temporary kitchen in the *villa rustica* at Boscoreale (photo: Henry Ferry)

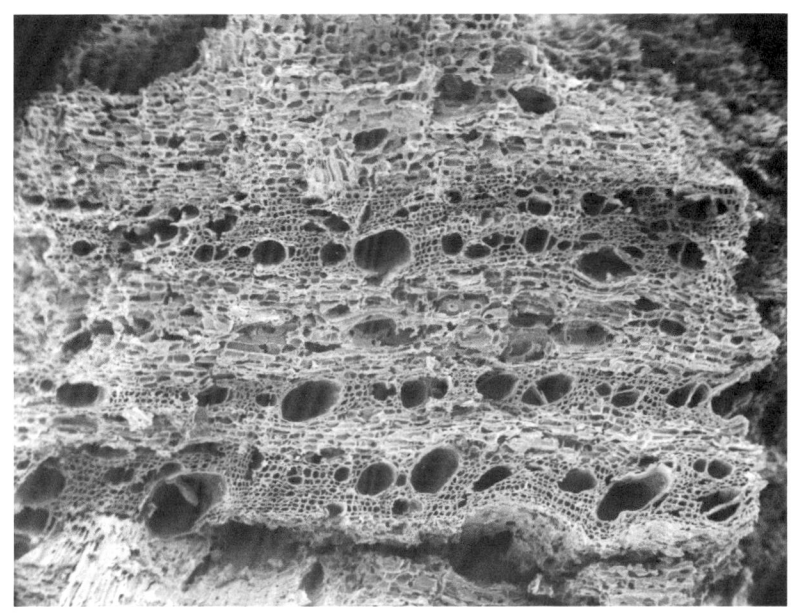

17. Detail of grape stem (*Vitis vinifera* L.) cross section
    (SEM photo: Francis Hueber)

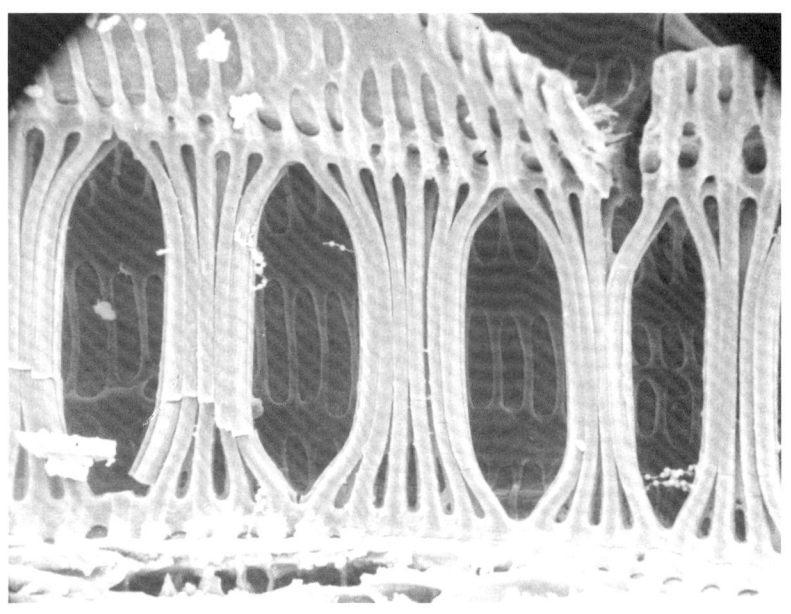

18. Detail of grape stem longitudinal section
    (SEM photo: Francis Hueber)

19. Replanted vineyard at *villa rustica* at Boscoreale; stratification of volcanic material clearly visible in cut at edge of excavated area (photo: Henry Ferry)

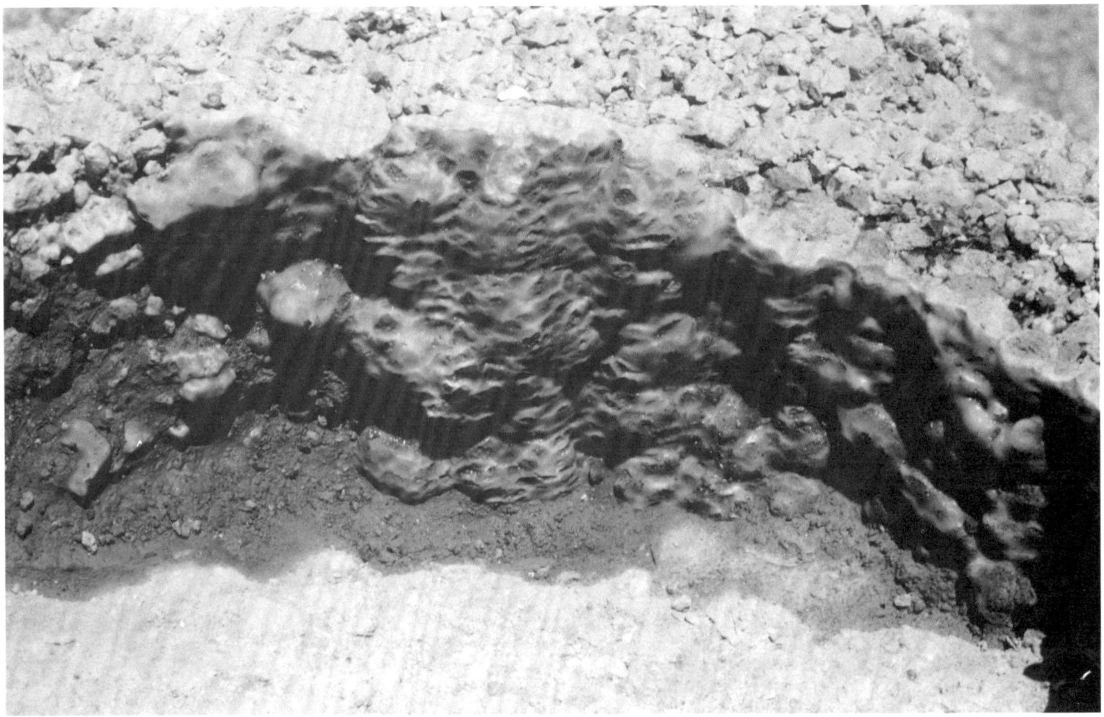

20. Calcium carbonite deposit lining tree trunk cavity (photo: Stanley Jashemski)

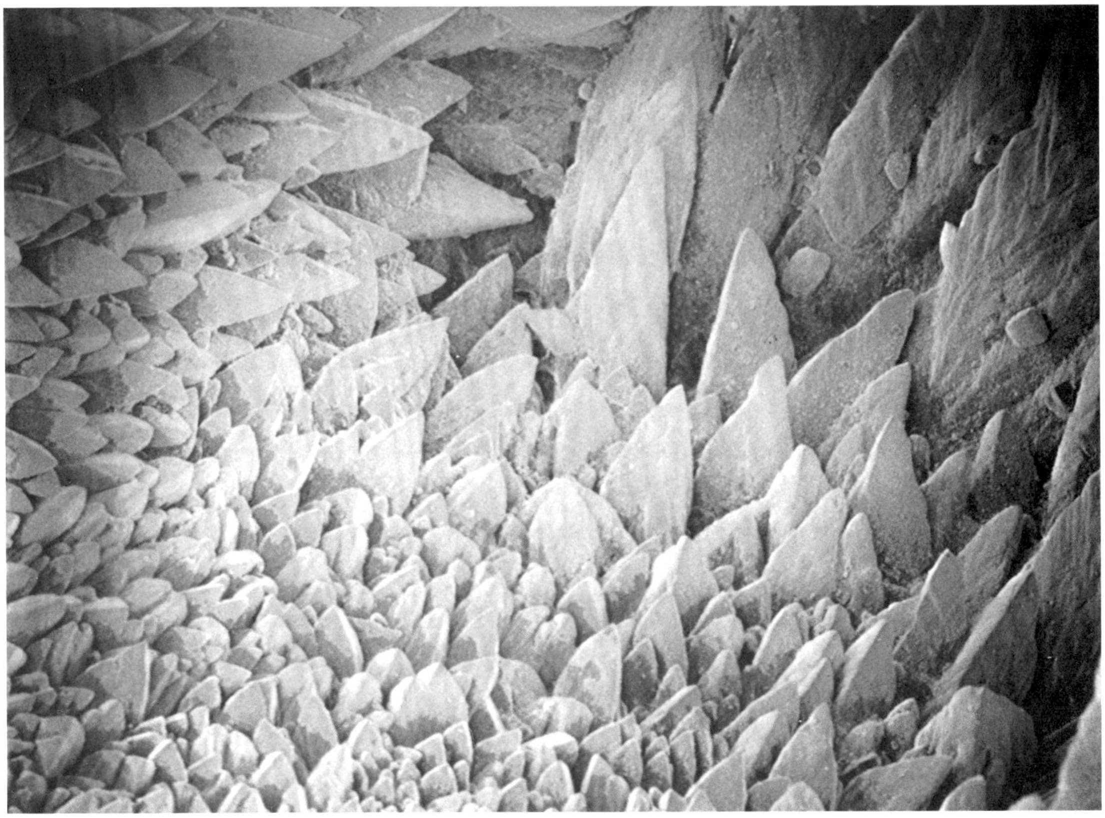

21. Calcium carbonite crystals (SEM photo: M.E. Taylor)

22. Country road in front of *villa rustica* at Boscoreale; cavity of tree root 29 (photo: Sarah Gladden)

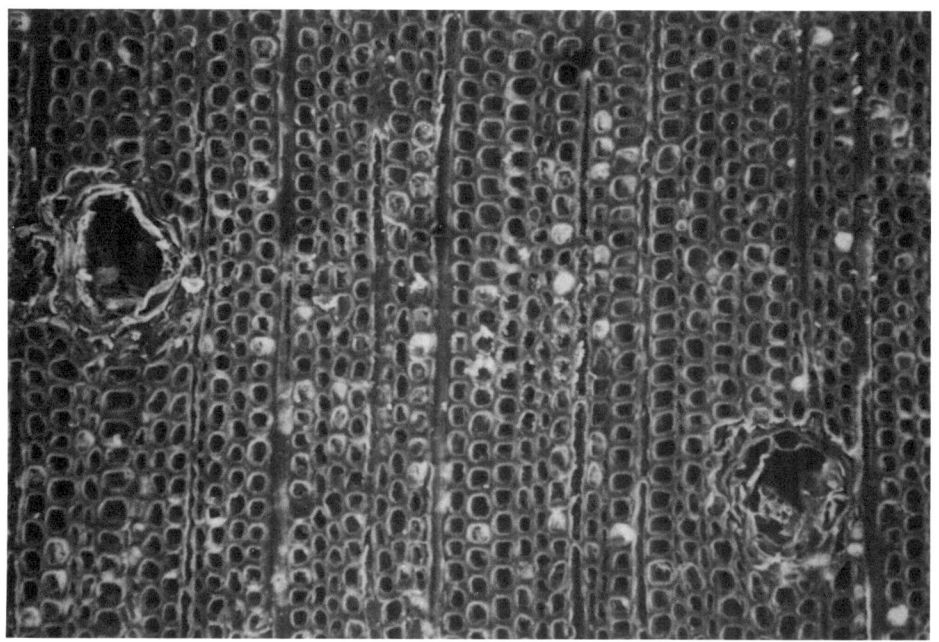

23. Detail of cross section of tree root 29; identified as umbrella pine (*pinus pinea* L.) (SEM photo: Francis Hueber)

24. Detail of radial longitudinal section of tree root 29; identified as umbrella pine
(SEM photo: Francis Hueber)

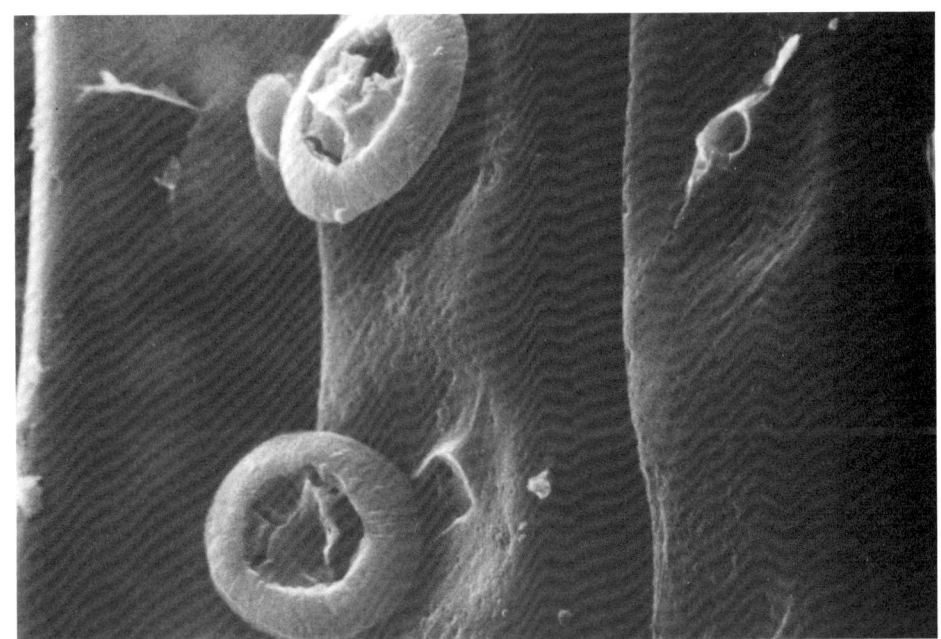

25. Detail of oblique longitudinal section of tree root 30; identified as umbrella pine
(SEM photo: Francis Hueber)

26. Country road in front of *villa rustica* at Boscoreale, showing casts of tree roots along the road (photo: Francis Hueber)

27. Cast of tree root 29; identified as umbrella pine (photo: Francis Hueber)

28. Vegetable garden at *villa rustica* at Boscoreale
    (photo: Francis Hueber)

29. Cast of pig at *villa rustica* at Boscoreale
(photo: Arlando Nazzareno)

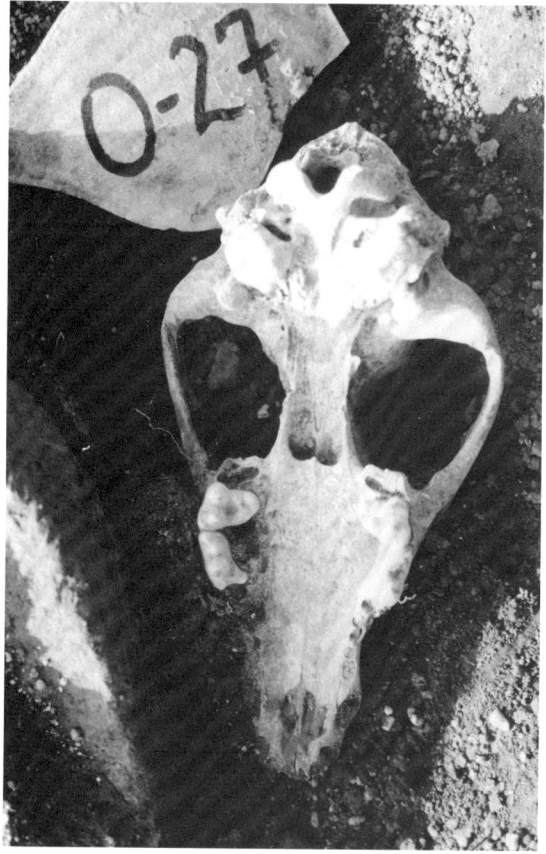

30. Skull of dog found at *villa rustica* at Boscoreale
(photo: Sarah Gladden)

31. Portrait of dog in *caupona* (I.xii.3) at Pompeii (photo: Stanley Jashemski)

IV
VIII
XVII
VII
I
II
III
hearth
IX BIS
IX
VI
settling basin
cistern
XII
XIV
X
XI
V BIS
XVI
broken dolium
cistern
boundary stone
boundary stone
country road
VILLA RUSTICA IN LOCALITA'
VILLA REGINA DI BOSCOREALE
10 m

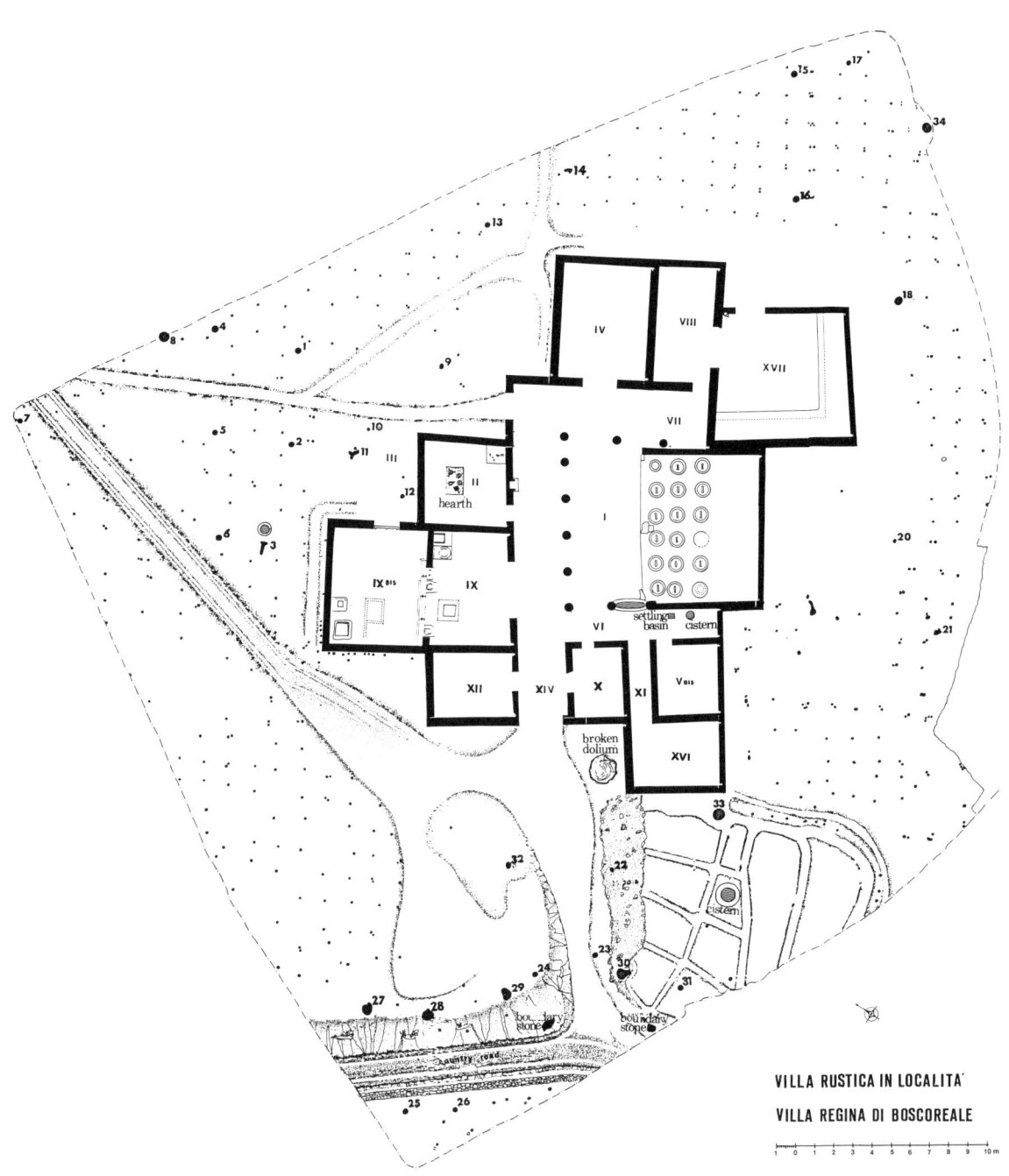

32. Plan of *villa rustica* at Boscoreale (E. Salza Prina Ricotti)

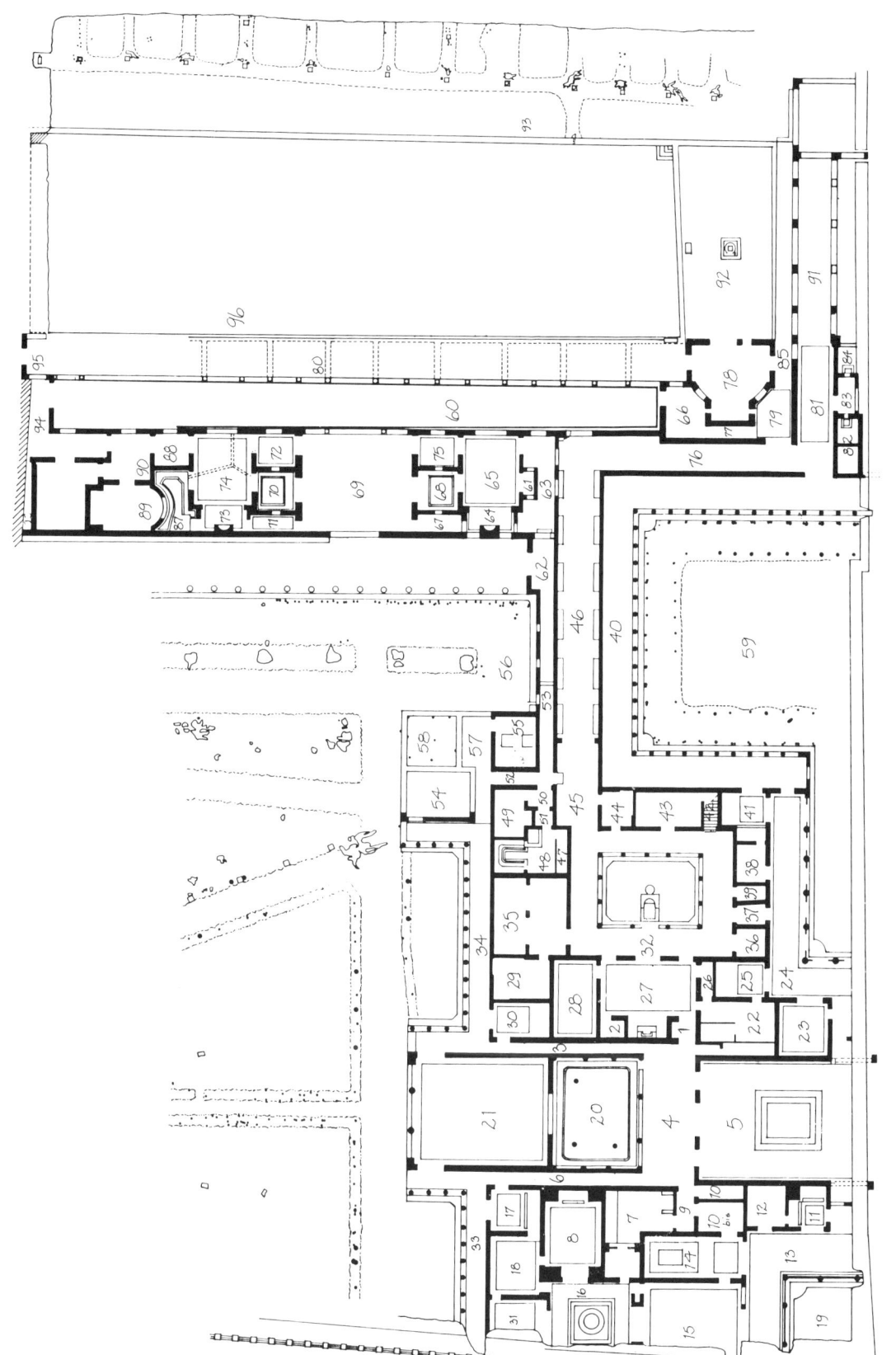

33. Plan of the villa of Poppaea at Oplontis (Soprintendenza alle Antichità della Campania-Napoli; garden details by Stanley Jashemski)

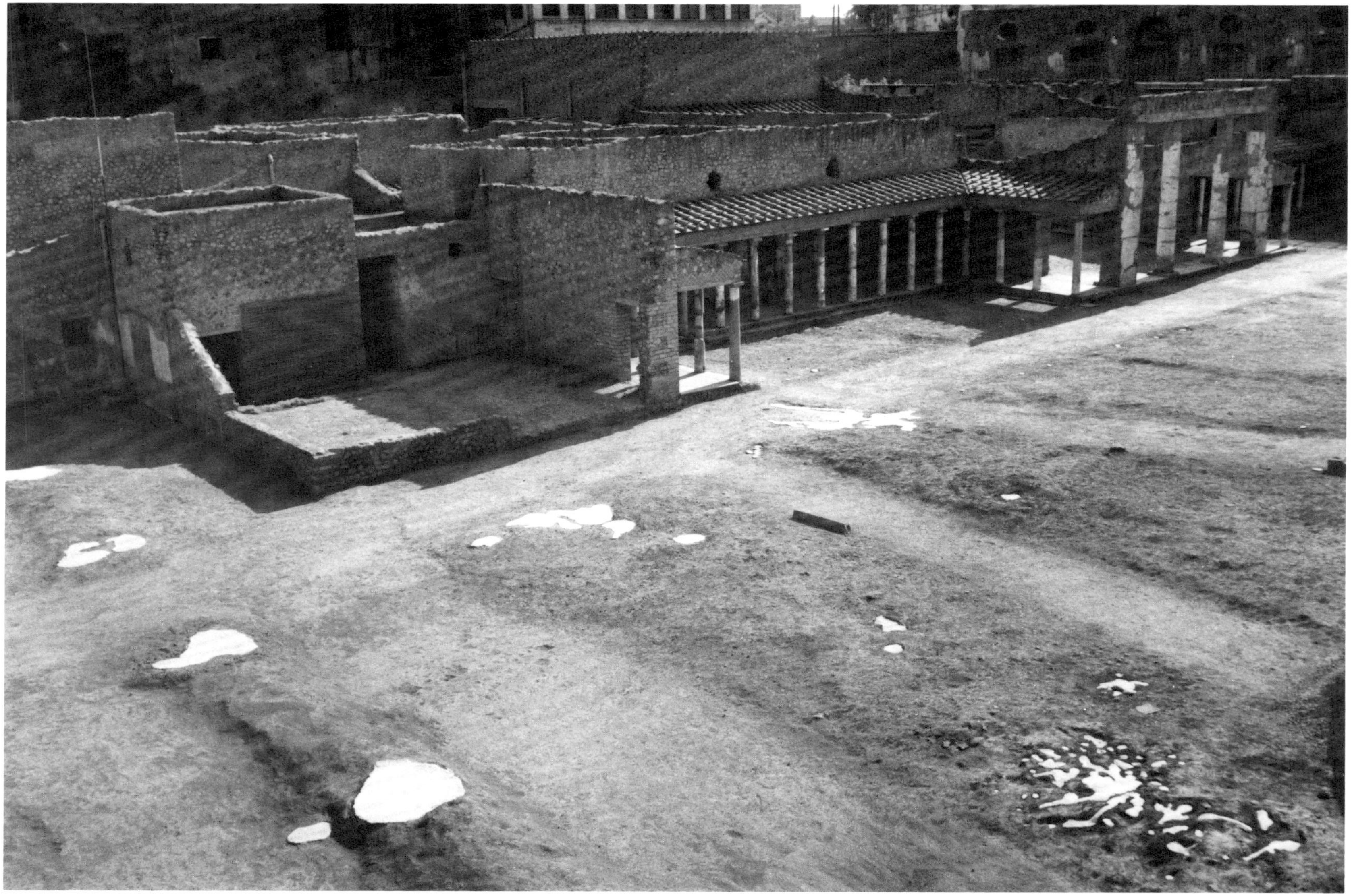

34. North garden of the villa of Poppaea at Oplontis; casts of row of large trees on left, clumps of bushes in next two beds (photo: Stanley Jashemski)

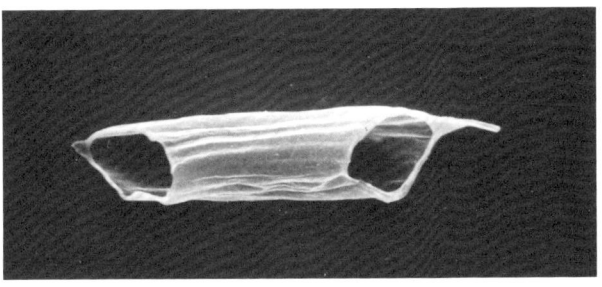

35. Wood cell from large olive branch (*Olea europaea* L.) (SEM photo: Francis Hueber)

36. Detail of garden painting in north courtyard garden (70) at Oplontis; centaur fountain on west wall, crater fountain and peacock on north wall (photo: Stanley Jashemski)

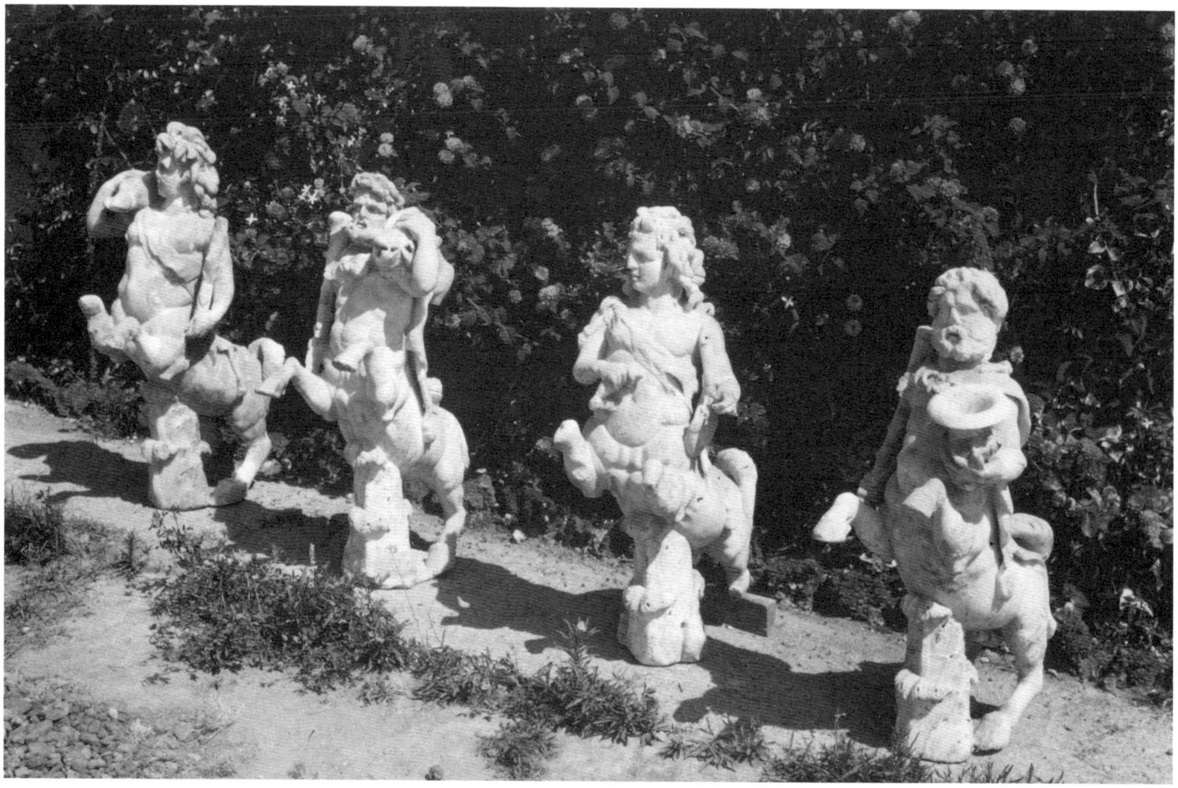

37. Four centaur fountains at the villa of Poppaea at Oplontis (photo: Stanley Jashemski)

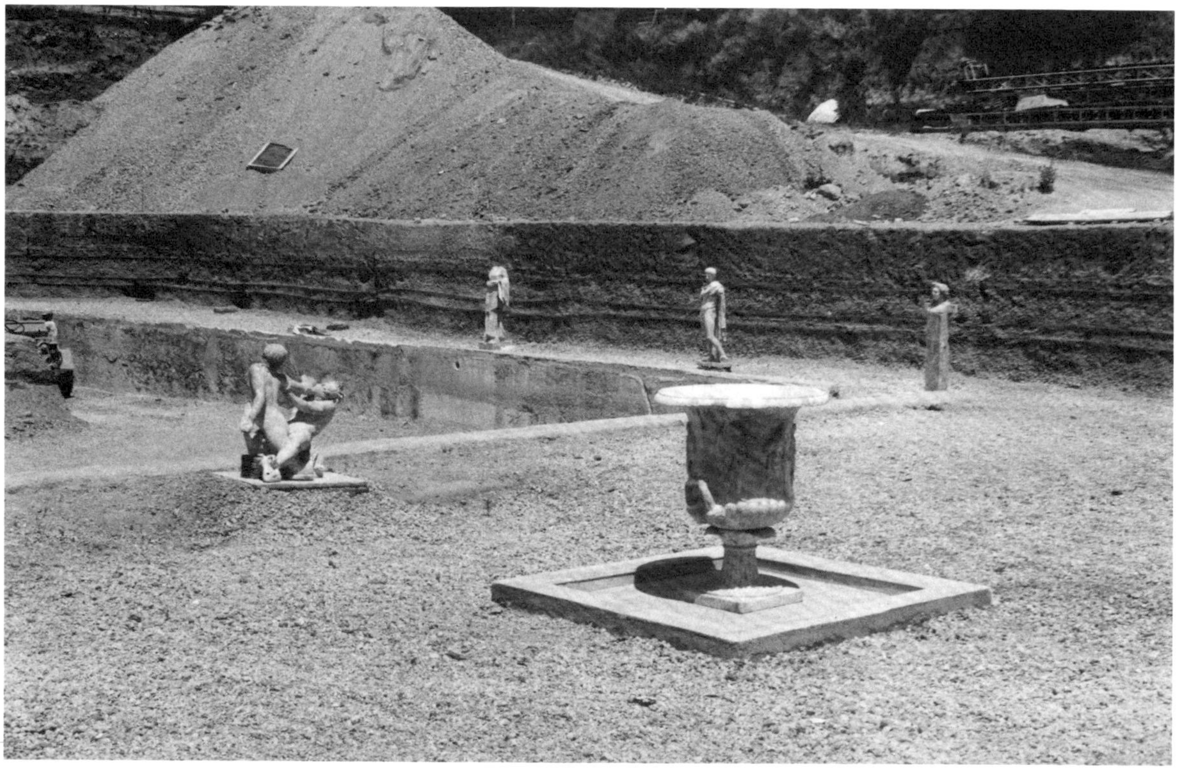

38. Crater fountain at south end of large swimming pool in east garden; statuary amid plantings along east edge of pool (photo: Stanley Jashemski)

39. East wing of villa opening on large swimming pool; sculpture garden on right, view toward north (photo: Francis Hueber)

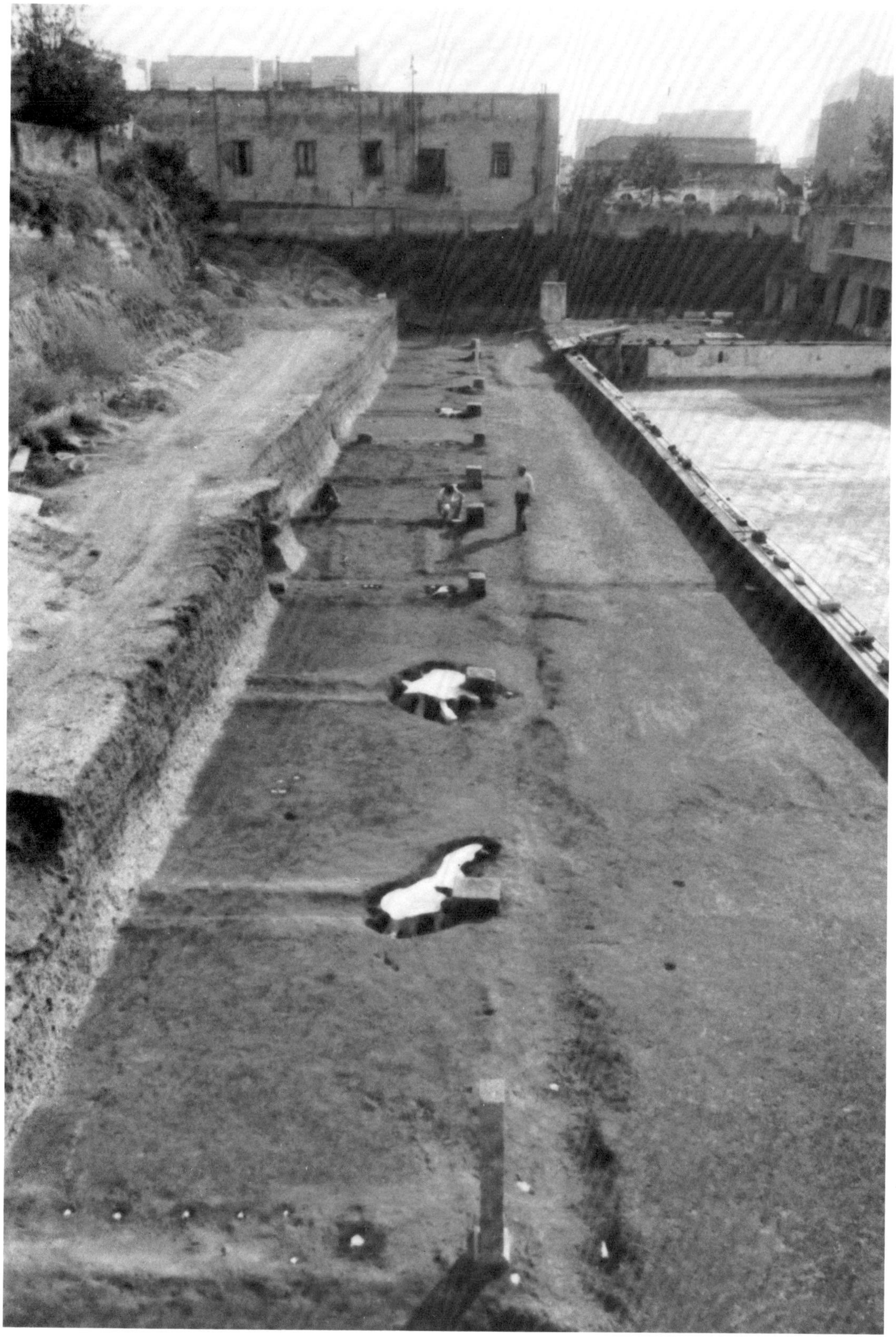

40. Contoured beds and casts of plantings in sculpture garden along pool, view toward south (photo: Francis Hueber)

41. Cast of tree root behind statue base 10 in sculpture garden
    (photo: Francis Hueber)

42. Cast of tree root behind statue base 11 in sculpture garden
    (photo: Francis Hueber)

43. Cast of root of lemon tree (*Citrus limon* (L.) Burm. f.) behind statue base 8 in sculpture garden (photo: Francis Hueber)

44. Air-layering lemon tree today at Boscoreale (photo: Francis Hueber)

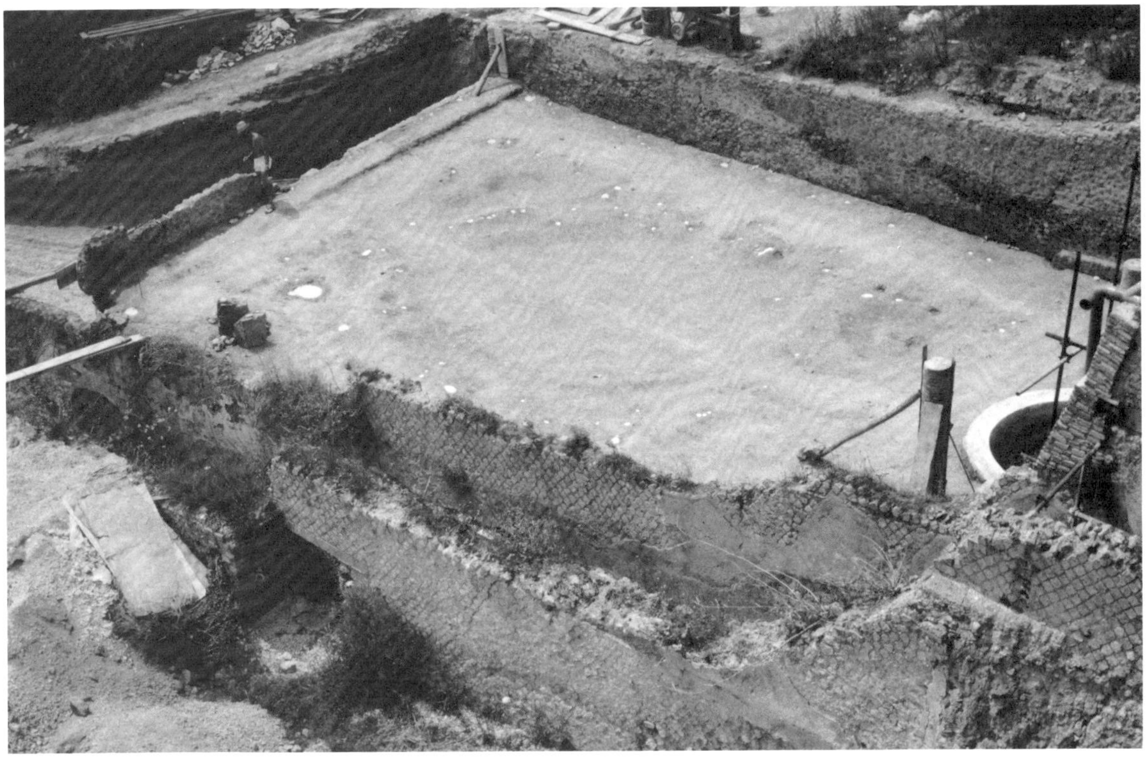

45. The garden of the House of the Wedding of Alexander, view toward the northwest (photo: Sarah Gladden)

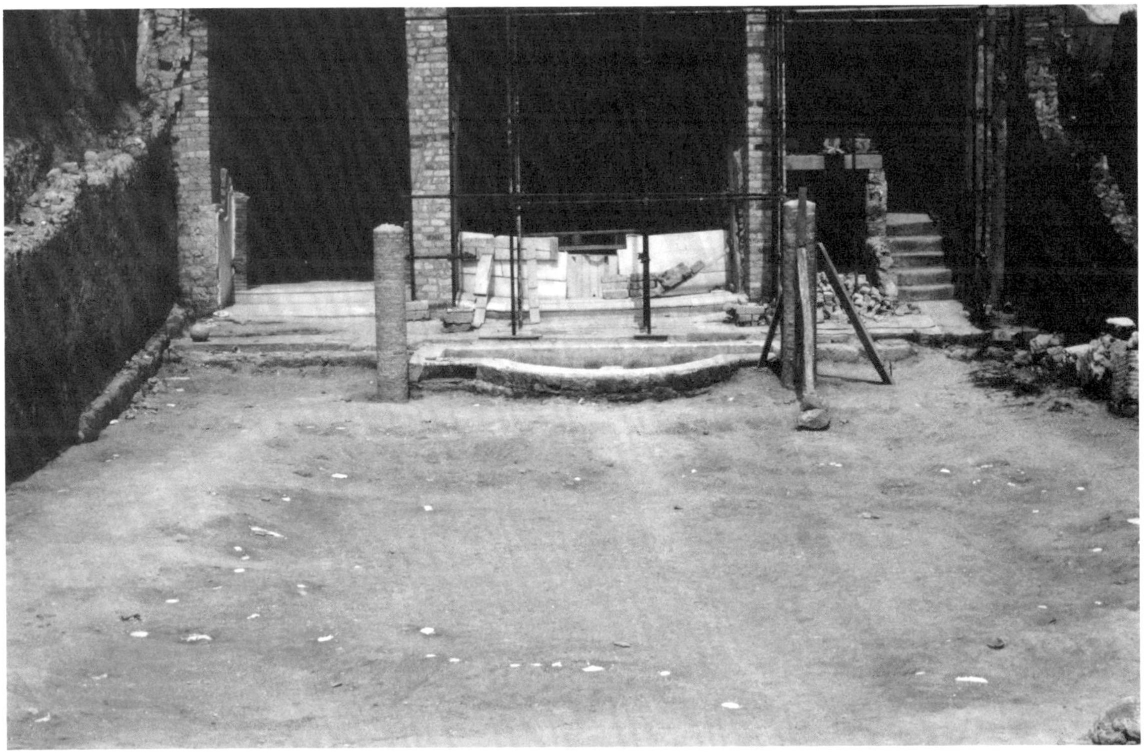

46. The House of the Wedding of Alexander, view toward east from garden; garden room on left, middle room, water triclinium, pool at edge of garden (photo: Sarah Gladden)

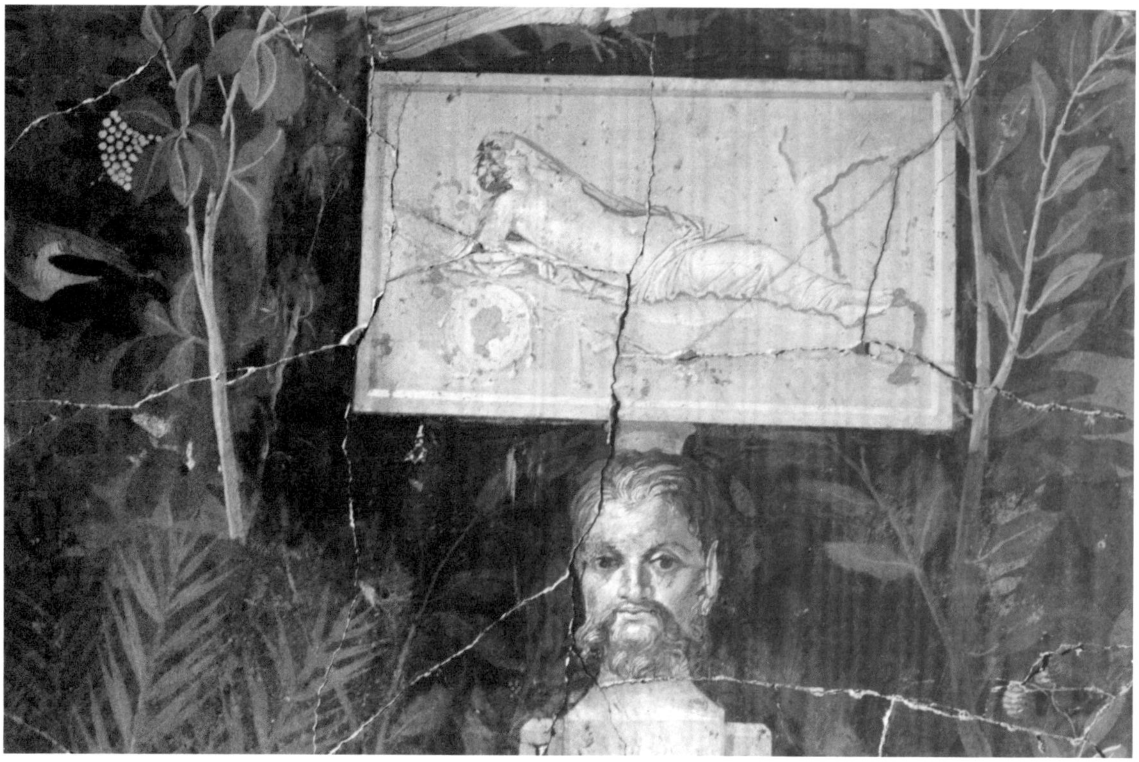

47. Detail of garden painting with faun herm in front of pinax decorated with painting of reclining woman (photo: Fotografia Foglia)

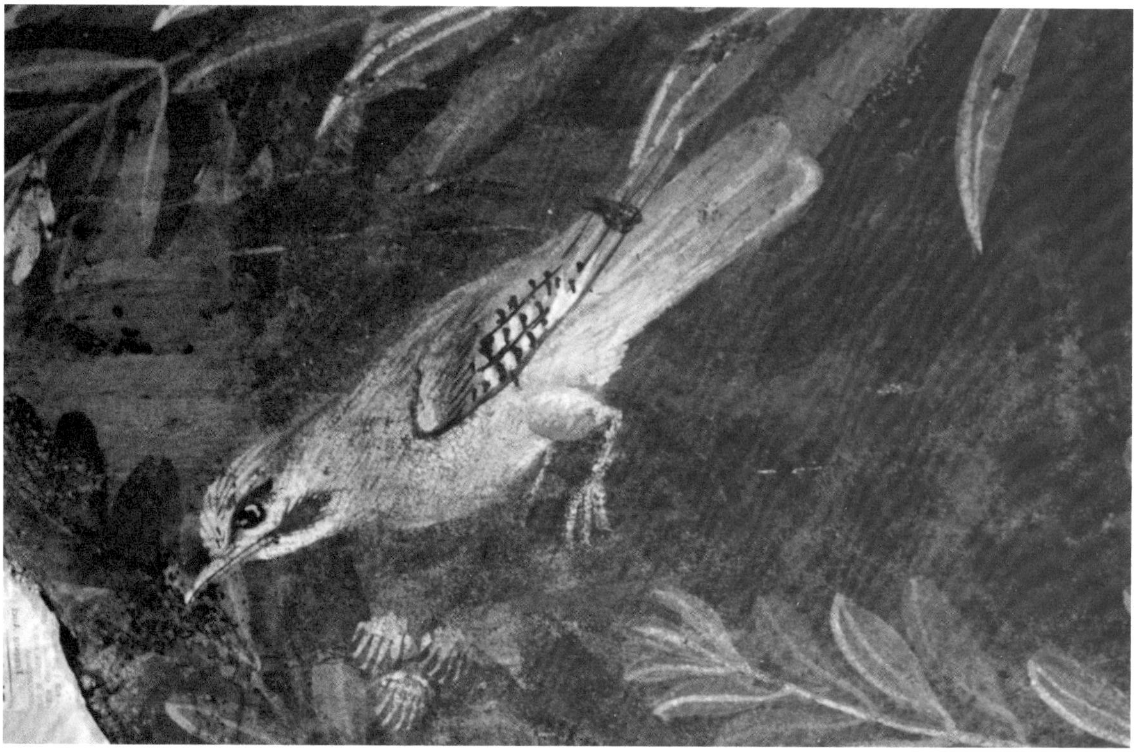

48. Jay (*Garrulus glandarius* L.) (photo: Fotografia Foglia)

49. Detail of garden painting with madonna lilies (*Lilium candidum* L.), opium poppies (*Papaver somniferum* L.), a young date palm (*Phoenix dactylifera* L.), and large white morning glories (*Calystegia sepium* L.) (photo: Fotografia Foglia)

50. Warbler perching on hollow reed that stakes rosebush (photo: Fotografia Foglia)

recently Dr. Hueber has identified still more plants in this hay.[10] Carbonized pollen grains and insects (Fig. 6) were also found in it.

The villa has yielded other significant evidence regarding the crops raised. The imprints of filberts (*Corylus avellana* L.) that had been gathered and stored in the villa were found perfectly preserved, even though the nuts had completely disintegrated (Fig. 7). In the spring of 1984 a most surprising discovery was made: over a ton of pomegranates (*Punica granatum* L.) had been carefully stored between layers of straw (Fig. 8). They were obviously gathered before August 24, at which time they would not yet be ripe. This raises the interesting question as to the intended use of a ton of green pomegranates. According to Pliny, green pomegranates were used in tanning leather,[11] but no evidence of this activity has been found thus far in this villa. Pomegranates were also used in making wine.[12]

In the past various ancient villas have been temporarily excavated in the area occupied by the modern cities of Boscoreale and Boscotrecase on the lower slopes of Vesuvius. Recently, however, when in the course of building a new apartment complex at Boscoreale, just a kilometer north of Pompeii, eighty large cement pillars were put in the ground and evidence was found of an ancient rustic villa, the villa and the land immediately surrounding it were fortunately declared a permanent archaeological zone. The villa building was excavated in 1977–80 by Dr. Stefano De Caro, Director of Excavations at Pompeii.[13]

This site is an unusually important one, for it is the first time in the entire Vesuvian area that there has been an opportunity to excavate farmland attached to a villa. I began excavating the land attached to the villa during the summer of 1980. It was our good fortune to uncover almost immediately an ancient country lane that led directly to the entrance of the villa. The ruts left by the wheels of the cart traveling over this path were still clearly visible. They were exactly the same distance apart (132 cm) as the wheels of the cart found within the villa. A footpath led to the rear entrance into the portico of the peristyle. As we continued our excavations, the size, shape, and location of the root

---

[10] A complete list and discussion of all the plants identified by both Prof. Ricciardi and Dr. Hueber will be the subject of a chapter in a volume edited by Wilhelmina F. Jashemski and Frederick G. Meyer entitled *The Natural History of Pompeii and the Other Vesuvian Sites*, New Rochelle, N.Y. (forthcoming).

In June 1983 an extraordinary discovery was made by Dr. Elena Menotti, who is excavating a *villa rustica* at Terzigno, found higher on the slopes of Vesuvius, where volcanic material was being quarried for sale. In a room in this villa another quantity of carbonized hay was found, which now awaits study and identification.

[11] Pliny *HN* 13.113.

[12] Ibid. 14.103; Dioscorides *Materia Medica* 5.26. Dr. Joan Frayne suggested to me that "on the whole these wines seem to have been made by adding the pomegranates as a flavoring to must. This would mean that unripe fruit could be used if necessary, because the fruit sugar would be supplied by the must." It is hoped that further excavation will throw light on the intended use of the green pomegranates.

[13] Nineteen large round cement pillars were found in the area set aside as an archaeological zone. Eighteen were removed. The nineteenth, which was found adjacent to the east wall of the villa, where it had miraculously missed destroying the wall, was left standing.

and stake cavities that we found showed that the area had been planted in a vineyard. There were also eight tree root cavities. With special tools we emptied all the root and stake cavities of the lapilli that had filled them when the roots and stakes decayed, measured the cavities, reenforced the large ones with wire, and filled all the cavities with cement. The vineyard had been informally staked with the vines supported by both stakes and trees, as is true in many vineyards in the area today. The small root cavities along the wall of the villa were perhaps those of rosemary.

The front door of the villa leads into the west portico of the peristyle where there is a niche lararium (Fig. 9), in which there appropriately was found a small marble head of Bacchus, the god who presided over vineyards (Fig. 10). In the two rooms (IX and IX bis) in which the grapes were pressed, the cavity left by the beam of a huge press was preserved, and a cast was made of this (Fig. 11).[14] The restoration of a similar winepress, found in the Villa of the Mysteries at Pompeii, makes clear the working of such a press (Fig. 12). Juice was emptied into the container embedded to the left of the altar in front of the lararium in the pressing room (Fig. 13). Columella tells us of the religious ritual at the time the grapes were pressed. Sacrifices were offered in greatest piety and purity to the vessels of the winepress and to the deities of wine, Bacchus and his female counterpart, Libera.[15] After the juice was extracted it was fermented in the eighteen dolia embedded in the peristyle courtyard (I), today protected by a roof (Fig. 14).

Also off the west side of the portico was a kitchen (II), with a hearth in the middle of the kitchen floor and an oven in the corner (Fig. 15). This kitchen, however, was not in use at the time of the eruption. The room (XII) to the left of the pressing room served as a kitchen. A shelf in this room throws helpful light on the controversy about the so-called cross at Herculaneum (Fig. 16). A. Maiuri was sure that the imprint left in the wall in a room in the Casa del Bicentenario at Herculaneum was that of a Christian cross.[16] Other scholars maintained that the cross was not used as a Christian symbol this early and said that the imprint had been left by a shelf. At Boscoreale we have such a shelf preserved.

Any root material still preserved in the root cavities and all bits of carbonized plant remains still on the surface of the soil were carefully collected and their findspots noted. When the carbonized material was sectioned and photographed with a scanning electron microscope by Dr. Hueber, he found, not surprisingly, a large number of identifiable grape stems (*Vitis vinifera* L.) (Figs. 17, 18). There were also many carbonized grape seeds. Most of the roots, however, had been badly destroyed by fungal activity.

The stratification of the volcanic debris that covered Boscoreale is different from that found at Pompeii (Fig. 19). First there was a substantial air fall of pumice, up to a thickness of 1.45 meters. Next a brief ground surge, made up of coarse pumice and

---

[14] Dr. Hueber examined carbonized bits of the huge beam that were still preserved and determined that the beam had been made of oak.

[15] Columella *Rust.* 12.18.4.

[16] A. Maiuri, *Ercolano—I nuovi Scavi 1927–1958*, Rome, 1958, 237 and fig. 186.

sandy ash, traveled on the ground at high velocity and bent over the limbs of trees, preserving their cavities. This was followed by another air fall of pumice and stone fragments. Then came a second ground surge followed by an extended fall of 0.52 meters of pumice and stone fragments. There were six ground surges in all; the fifth, significantly more powerful and destructive, sheared off the tops of trees and the top of the villa building. The sixth surge was the thickest of all, but the trees had been destroyed before this surge.[17]

Because of the way in which Boscoreale was covered, the cavities left by several decaying tree trunks were preserved. These cavities were lined by an unusual hard substance (Fig. 20). We chopped off a piece of this material and brought it to Dr. M.E. Taylor at the University of Maryland for analysis. A scanning electron microscope photograph shows the beautiful crystals of calcium carbonate that had been leached out by rain falling through the volcanic fill (Fig. 21). This material provides valuable information for Professor John Foss, the agronomist who is studying the soil at the A.D. 79 level and trying to determine the extent to which the soil at that level today has been changed through the years by leaching.[18]

When I returned in 1982 to continue the excavation of the villa land, I found that the portion of the vineyard excavated thus far had been replanted (Fig. 19). In 1982 we excavated the area to the rear and to the east of the villa. In the stratification of the east cut a dark area was clearly visible where early excavations had taken place in the fourth or fifth century A.D. and the lapilli replaced by soil. This excavation, which can be dated by lamps found in the replaced soil, fortunately did not reach the A.D. 79 level and disturb our root cavities.

In 1983 we continued work toward the front of the villa. We found that although the country lane running through the vineyard led to the entrance of the villa, the ruts continued to a sizable area to the left and below the tree (32) to the left of the entrance. This area, which was unplanted, was perhaps a place to park wagons when they were not in use. There was also a roadway which led down from the entrance of the villa leaving a raised area around the tree (32). For some strange reason this area had been used as a trash heap. Perhaps items broken by the earthquake of A.D. 62 were hurriedly cleared out and thrown by the front door. But other people's trash is the archaeologist's treasure. When we found the fragment of a lamp decorated with grape leaves, we thought that this was an appropriate lamp to be used in this villa. The fragment of a terra sigillata dish decorated with daisies reminded us of the corn marigold (*Chrysanthe-*

---

[17] I am indebted to Prof. Haraldur Sigurdsson, of the Graduate School of Oceanography, Narragansett Bay Campus, of the University of Rhode Island, who visited our excavations and discussed the nature of the volcanic deposits at Boscoreale with me. I was also privileged to consult H. Sigurdsson, S. Carey, W. Cornell, and T. Pescatore, "The Eruption of Vesuvius in A. D. 79," *National Geographic Research* (Summer 1985).

[18] For the results of the studies of the soil in gardens at Pompeii and Oplontis made by Prof. Foss see Jashemski, *Gardens*, I, 254–256 and Table B.

mum segetum L.) that covered the villa site. The fragment of a terra sigillata bowl had the stamp of the potter ΛΛ or VV in planta pedis, which we had found before.[19] Much hard carbon was found in this trash, which we carefully removed. It was obvious that this was a place where trash was burned. Much of the carbon was so compacted that it had to be separated by flotation. The identification of the carbonized material by Dr. Hueber has only just begun.

One day in late June a severe thunderstorm began before lunch and continued for several hours. Lightning struck uncomfortably close to the ancient villa building in which we were taking shelter. It was obvious why the roadway from the entrance sloped noticeably downward. Otherwise the water would have poured in the front door where we were standing. We suddenly had considerable help with our flotation, as we collected charcoal that had been washed down by the torrent of water in the road leading down from the entrance of the villa.

We were especially concerned about the rainstorm, for we had found the most interesting soil contours around the cistern we had discovered at the right front of the villa. We did not want the contours destroyed, for it was obvious that the vineyard did not continue in this area. We had found here an entirely different planting pattern.

One of our most exciting discoveries was the country road that ran in front of the property.[20] The two boundary stones can be seen in Figure 22. The road is unusually deep but the same width (132 cm) as, but quite unlike, the lane that ran through the vineyard on the villa property.

The neighboring property on the opposite side of the public road was also planted in a vineyard. In the limited area available for excavation we found seven vine root cavities, perhaps four stake cavities, and the root cavities of two small trees. At the back of the property, near the decaying wall that marked the boundary, was an amazing collection of trash. But more about that later.

A row of huge trees bordered the public road on the side adjacent to the villa, continuing across the roadway leading from the villa to the public road. The root cavities of these trees were very large and quite different from the tree root cavities found in the vineyard. From the root cavities (29 and 30) on each side of the roadway approaching the villa we were able to salvage a considerable amount of root material which Dr. Hueber was able to identify. A knot of perfectly preserved wood full of natural resin was found in the root cavity of tree 29 (0.50 × 0.55 m at ground level and 0.90 m deep). The scanning electron microscope photographs of a cross section of this wood, showing general cell structure plus the resin canals (Fig. 23), and of a radial longitudinal section,

---

[19] Found in the gardens of I.xi.6 and III.vii.11 at Pompeii. Prof. Comfort tells me that this stamp with toes pointed to the left or right and reading either VV or ΛΛ are both to be associated with the stamp in A. Oxe and H. Comfort, *Corpus vasorum Arretinorum: A Catalogue of the Signatures, Shapes, and Chronology of Italian Sigillata*, Bonn, 1968, no. 906.

[20] The cross section of a similar country road is dramatically visible on two sides of the quarry, near the *villa rustica* at Terzigno, when one stands on the level where volcanic material has been quarried down to the prehistoric level and looks up about halfway to the A.D. 79 level.

showing typical bordered pits in the cell walls (Fig. 24), definitely identify this tree as the beautiful umbrella pine (*Pinus pinea* L.). The wood in the root cavity of tree 30 (0.56 × 0.80 m at ground level and 0.78 m deep) was less well preserved, having been almost completely destroyed by fungi. The scanning electron microscope photographs of an oblique longitudinal section show little buttonlike casts, which are the resin casts of pit cavities of bordered pits typical of pines (Fig. 25). This makes it possible to identify this tree too as the umbrella pine. The two other large trees along the public road (cavity 27: 0.55 × 0.65 m at ground level and 0.46 m deep; cavity 28: 0.52 × 0.58 m at ground level and 0.80 m deep) were definitely deciduous trees, but the root material analyzed so far has been too damaged to make it possible to identify their species. But both the shape and size of the root cavities suggest that these trees were probably plane trees (*Platanus orientalis* L.), which still today are planted along country roads. Casts show the shapes of the roots of the trees along the road (Figs. 26, 27).

A survey of this site at the end of our 1983 season showed that most of the land immediately surrounding the villa had been planted in a vineyard. At the end of three seasons we had found a total of approximately 250 vine root cavities and 120 stake cavities. At thirty-eight locations it was difficult to tell if the cavities were those of vine roots or of stakes. Sixteen cavities appeared to be those of herbs, three were probably those of weeds. There were thirty-four trees. Most of the trees were in the vineyard. The longest dimension at ground level of the root cavities of these trees ranged from 0.10 to 0.98 meters, the median longest dimension of ground level being 0.20 meters. Only four had a longest dimension over 0.42 meters.

Root material was found in only a few of the root cavities, but this material had been so destroyed by fungal activity that it was of little value for identifying the trees. Other evidence, however, gives helpful information. The carbonized olives (*Olea europaea* L.) and almonds (*Prunus dulcis* (Mill.) D.A. Webb) found in the vineyard help identify several trees. These were identified by Dr. Frederick Meyer, Research Botanist at the U.S. National Arboretum in Washington, D.C., who, among his many contributions to the project through the years, has identified the carbonized fruit, nuts, and seeds found in our excavations. The shape and size of the tree roots are also helpful in identifying the trees. After the cement has hardened we pull away the soil from the cast revealing the shape of the ancient root. Dr. Carlo Fideghelli of the Istituto di Frutticoltura, Ministero dell'Agricoltura at Rome, who has made a study of the shapes of modern fruit and nut tree roots in this area, examined both the cavities and the casts that we made of each cavity. He found that the casts of cavities 3, 11, and 19 had the appearance of the roots of a fig tree (*Ficus carica* L.). He also pointed out that fig trees are always found near the house. These cavities were the three largest cavities in the vineyard, having a largest dimension at ground level of 0.52, 0.69, and 0.98 meters. Root cavity 33 was also large, but it was adjacent to the house and badly damaged during the restoration of the villa, so that it was impossible to measure it. Dr. Fideghelli believed that this was also a fig, for the fig is always the tree close to the house. This was undoubtedly a self-planted tree that grew very large. Fig trees in this location, he pointed out, are very common. Seeds take root easily.

Dr. Fideghelli believed that tree 1 (0.25 × 0.32 m at ground level), tree 8 (0.30 × 0.30 m at ground level), and tree 34 (0.20 × 0.25 m at ground level) were walnuts (*Juglans regia* L.). The cavities of the trunks of these trees were preserved in the volcanic fill, and it was possible for the Soprintendenza to make casts of them. A cast was also made of tree 32, to the left of the entrance (Fig. 26). This tree could have been a walnut or a cherry (*Prunus cerasus* L.). Dr. Fideghelli pointed out that other fruit trees would not have a central leader so tall. An apple tree (*Malus domestica* Borkh.) would have a larger trunk for the height. A walnut grows tall rapidly. Tree roots 5 (0.10 × 0.12 m at ground level) and 10 (0.08 × 0.10 m at ground level) had the appearance of those of apricots (*Prunus armeniaca* L.). A peach tree would have a more spreading root. Tree root 21 (13 × 17 m at ground level) had the appearance of a peach root (*Prunus persica* L.). All of these trees are found in the vineyards in the Vesuvian area today.

Upon completing the excavation of the area to the right of the main entrance of the villa, we discovered that the unusual soil contours were those of a small vegetable garden (Figs. 26, 28). The cistern in the middle of the garden furnished the necessary water. Here were undoubtedly raised the choice cabbages and onions for which the Pompeii area was so famous in antiquity.[21] The soil contours were the same as those in modern vegetable gardens in the area today. The garden was divided into small plots separated by irrigation channels, which also served as paths.

But more than vines, trees, and vegetables were grown on the land connected with this villa. The threshing floor (XVII) attached to the villa (on the east) is evidence of diversification. The floor may have been used for drying and/or threshing fava beans (*Vicia faba* L. var. *minor* (Peterm. & Harz) Beck), a very popular crop in antiquity,[22] or for drying hay or threshing grain.

We wondered if the contents of the amphoras or other containers found in the kitchen might reflect crops raised in the villa. To determine the contents, scrapings were made. After preparation, each sample was viewed in the scanning electron microscope, and an energy dispersive spectometer X-ray was performed by Dr. Taylor at the University of Maryland. The results, studied by Dr. Taylor and Dr. Franz Kasler, Professor of Chemistry at the University of Maryland, showed that the contents included wine, oil, and garum. Wine was produced on the villa. Olives were raised on the villa, but no press has been found in the area excavated. Garum, a popular fish sauce, would certainly be found in any well-stocked kitchen.[23]

But there is still other evidence of diversification. Cement, poured into a cavity in

---

[21] Pompeii gave its name to a special variety of onion, *Pompeiana cepa*. Columella *Rust*. 12.10.1 gives directions for preserving it. For the Pompeian cabbage see Pliny *HN* 19.140 and Columella *Rust*. 10.135.

[22] According to Pliny *HN* 18.117, this bean had the highest place of honor among the leguminous plants. It was used in a variety of ways for all kinds of beasts and especially for man. See Frederick G. Meyer, "Carbonized Food Plants of Pompeii, Herculaneum, and the Villa at Torre Annunziata," *Economic Botany*, 34, no. 4 (1980), 407-408.

[23] For the importance of garum in the Roman diet see Robert Curtis, "The Production and Commerce of Salted Fish Products in the Roman World," *Aufstieg und Niedergang der römischen Welt*, 2.11, Berlin (forthcoming).

the ash, preserves the appearance of a pig raised on the villa (Fig. 29). Dr. Henry Setzer, mammalogist emeritus at the Smithsonian Institution, who identified the bones that we found scattered in the vineyard, says that there is no doubt that pigs were raised on the villa, for he has identified the bones and teeth of several pigs. There were also various bones that were those of either sheep or goats, which are almost impossible for the specialist to distinguish. The bones of a cow were also found. Dr. Setzer also identified the bones of an ancient toad or frog, the first that we have found in our excavations. And there was the almost perfectly preserved skeleton of a tiny lizard. But even though it was found in the A.D. 79 level, and completely covered by undisturbed fill, the bones were not ancient. The little lizard had easily made its way through the cracks in the lapilli and there met his end.

It was not surprising to find a dog's skull (Fig. 30), for we have found the bones of dogs in every large garden that we have excavated. Most were large watchdogs, but there was one small dog.[24] The Pompeians were very fond of dogs. One proud owner had painted a portrait of his dog, with jeweled collar, on the wall of his *caupona* (tavern; I.xii.3). It appears to be the same breed as the dog in this villa (Fig. 31).

I had always hoped that we would find some bird bones in our excavations, for birds were such an important aspect of the ancient garden and are always prominently pictured in garden paintings,[25] but chickens were the only birds that we found. It is of course obvious that the birds would have flown away when Vesuvius erupted. We found our first bird bones at Boscoreale. These were identified by Dr. Storrs L. Olson, Curator, Department of Vertebrate Zoology at the Smithsonian Institution. The breast bone of a coot (*Fulica atra* L.) was found in the trash pile outside the villa entrance, which included debris from meals. The leg bone and a portion of a breast bone of a rail (*Railus aquaticus* L.), another water bird, was found in the debris on the south side of the country road, where debris from meals and other trash was thrown. Only the bill of a chaffinch (*Fringilla coelebs* L.) was found in the same place. Small songbirds were considered table delicacies. Various bones of a dormouse (*Mus cardinus avellanarius* L.), also considered a table delicacy, were found in the same debris. More difficult to explain are the bones of a little ermine or weasel (*Mustela erminea* L.) and the bones of a martin (*Martes martes* L.). There was also the partial skeleton of a pine vole (*Pitymys savii* de Selys Longchamps), a rodent about the size of a large mouse, and the almost complete skeleton of a snake, not yet identified.

The excavation of the original area set aside as an archaeological site at Boscoreale has now been completed (Fig. 32), but there is still some unfinished work. A new area to the west of the area excavated has been set aside by the commune of Boscoreale for

---

[24] Jashemski, *Gardens*, I, 103, 217, 242, 247, 254, 279. The skull of a dog was found in the large rear garden of the Villa of Poppaea at Oplontis.

[25] For the birds in the garden paintings see Jashemski, *Gardens*, II, app. 2, which gives a description, with bibliography, of every garden painting that has been found in the Roman Empire. The birds in these paintings are identified by Dr. George Watson, Chairman of the Department of Zoology at the Smithsonian Institution, an ornithologist specializing in Mediterranean birds.

a museum, and the intervening land can now be excavated. The soil samples taken for pollen analysis are still to be studied—a long and laborious process. And Dr. Hueber hopes to find that some of the material taken from the root cavities can still be identified, but this material is so damaged that I suspect it will make only our fungus and bacteria specialists happy. But we now know much about life on this ancient *villa rustica*.

And now for a very different type of villa, a second villa at Oplontis located on the Via Sepolcri in modern Torre Annunziata. It is a most luxurious villa, believed to have belonged to Poppaea, the wife of Emperor Nero. Thus far the villa has thirteen remarkable gardens, which I have excavated. (See plan, Fig. 33.) It provided the first opportunity to excavate villa gardens scientifically using the most recent archaeological techniques. This villa, also for the first time, gives us archaeological evidence for the great exterior gardens onto which the villa opened—the parklike settings pictured in the many small paintings of seaside villas found in Pompeian wall decoration.

I began work at this site in 1974, in the large garden at the rear of the villa. In the volcanic debris that covered Oplontis there was less pumice but voluminous fine-grained surge and pyroclastic flow material.[26] As we uncovered the garden we discovered that its formal architectural layout reflected the plan of the villa itself. From its entrance the perspective through the atrium continued through an enclosed garden and the grand salon, with its monumental entrance at the rear, to a landscaped pathway on the central axis of the villa. On either side of this pathway we found contoured beds that extended to the east-west passageway along the rear of the villa. The small root cavities in the ridges that outlined each side of these two pathways were those of shrubs, perhaps box. There were also a few larger root cavities of trees.

At the edge of the garden were two parallel passageways separated by a row of huge trees arranged in two mounded beds. The longest dimension of these cavities at ground level ranged from 1.45 to 2.13 meters, and they were up to 1.57 meters in depth. A group of specialists from the Ministero dell'Agricoltura at Rome who studied these cavities and casts believed that the trees were probably plane trees.[27] A large group of cavities (with longest dimension at ground level 3.45 m) at the corner of the colonnade, a similar group of cavities directly to the east, and a third better-preserved group of cavities to the north each appeared to be those of a thicket of twenty to twenty-five oleanders. (See plan, Fig. 33, and Fig. 34.)

The diagonal passageway to the east of the central one was obviously balanced by a similar one on the opposite side (today under the street), the two meeting at the passageway on the central axis of the villa at some point under the still unexcavated lapilli. Four masonry statue bases were found along the edge of the diagonal passageway on the east. On these had been mounted the marble shafts that supported the sculptured

---

[26] For a description of the volcanic deposits at Oplontis, see H. Sigurdsson, S. Cashdollar and S.R.J. Sparkes, "The Eruption of Vesuvius in A. D. 79: Reconstruction from Historical and Volcanological Evidence," *American Journal of Archaeology*, 86 (1982), 42–43.

[27] If plane trees, they would be about a hundred years old. See Jashemski, *Gardens*, I, 297–300 and figs. 444, 450–452.

white marble heads that were found nearby. There was a head of Aphrodite, a portrait of a Julio-Claudian woman, one of a Julio-Claudian child, and a head of the child Dionysos (recently stolen).[28] These herms were set in the midst of clumps of plants, some larger than others, but the shapes of the cavities suggested that the plants were probably oleanders.

Flanking the central passageway we found the bases of three of the four marble centaur fountains that had been stored in the rear west portico (33) of the villa. This proved that the final location of the fountains had been on each side of the central passageway, but there was no evidence of pipes, so the centaurs were not used as fountains at the time of the eruption. Two of the centaurs were male, two were female.

A large branch (1.80 m long) of a tree found in the volcanic ash at the height of about 2.50 meters, at the north edge of the excavated area, had the appearance of fresh wood, and specialists believed that the tree could easily be identified. But when they made sections they found that the cellular structure had been almost totally destroyed. Finally, in order to isolate individual cells Dr. Hueber treated the wood samples with chromic and nitric acid in combination. He finally found a sample that yielded several cells which showed that the large tree was an olive (Fig. 35). The cavities left by the spreading branches of this huge tree, which grew in the as yet unexcavated part of the garden, can be seen in the cut in the volcanic fill, as well as the branches of other large trees, which may be part of a row of olives. In this connection it is interesting to note that separated from the early villa, but connected with this property, was a rustic building (rooms 82, 83, 84, and probably 81) with a *torcularium*.

A balloon photograph taken at the end of our 1977 season shows the architectural layout of this garden. It is obvious that the large and complex portico, which stretched across the back of the villa, looked out on a parklike garden, the dimensions, design, and plantings of which we are only beginning to discover.

In the east wing of the villa, which was built later (in the Julio-Claudian period), we were to find four spectacular little gardens, the walls of each one decorated with paintings of gardens to make the small gardens appear larger.[29] The painted gardens contained fountains, large bushes, and trees—too large to be accommodated in these little gardens. On either side of a large open exedra (69) was a small courtyard garden (68 and 70). It is interesting to note that in the garden paintings in these two gardens we find centaur fountains (Fig. 36) similar to the sculptured centaurs in the rear garden (Fig. 37). The painted centaurs, however, support basins, as do painted sphinxes. Crater fountains are also found in these garden paintings. The third garden (61), a charming, very tiny raised garden recessed into the south wall of the room (65) to the south of the south courtyard garden, is unlike anything that has been found thus far in the Vesuvian area. Balancing this garden, in the north part of the east wing, was the fourth garden (87), the excavation of which has just been completed. This garden had a large bay

---

[28] For a detailed discussion and interpretation of the sculptures found in this villa, see Stefano De Caro, "Sculpture Found at the Villa at Oplontis," in this volume.

[29] For detailed descriptions of these garden paintings see Jashemski, *Gardens*, II, app. 2.

window in the north wall, and a window in the south wall, through which there was a splendid vista through the two courtyard gardens (70 and 68) to the small raised garden beyond.

The east wing of the villa looked out on a large swimming pool 17 meters wide and 60 meters long and, to the south of the pool, on an attractive garden (92) which could be enjoyed through the open windows of a beautiful *diaeta* (room 78). To the south of the pool, on its longitudinal axis, was a small shallow square marble pool, in which was the base of the large crater fountain of Pentelic marble (Fig. 38), which had been stored in the rear portico of the villa at the time of the eruption. This fountain is similar to the crater fountains pictured in various garden paintings (Fig. 36) in this villa.[30] Near the center of the south edge of the swimming pool was a sculptured white marble group of a hermaphrodite and a satyr.

Along the east side of the swimming pool, and on a slightly lower level than garden 92, was a large and impressive garden, the limits of which are not yet known, in which a row of thirteen statue bases has thus far been discovered (Fig. 39). The symmetry of the garden indicates that there would have been one more statue base, but this would be under the modern street and beyond the limits of the area available for excavation. Directly behind each statue base we found a root cavity, which we emptied of lapilli, measured, studied, and made a cast of (Fig. 40). Counting from the south, root cavities 1, 2, 4, 5, 10, and 11 (longest diameter at ground level 0.75–1.42 m) were all those of large trees. The size and shape of the root cavities led the specialists to identify these trees as probably plane trees (Figs. 41, 42). Only root cavity 13 seems to depart from the symmetry of the plantings. Instead of a plane tree in this location, which symmetry would suggest, this tree left a single root cavity which has the same diameter (0.24 × 0.27 m) down to a depth of 0.78 meters, at which point it divided into five large roots, the longest 0.57 meters. The root cavity has the appearance of a cypress and suggests that at the north end of the pool the garden may have made a transition to another planting pattern.

The four statue bases 6–9 were directly opposite the large open exedra (69), and the plantings behind these statue bases were carefully planned to provide a splendid picture when viewed across the water from this room. Remnants of a branch of a small tree (which had a root cavity 0.22 × 0.26 m at ground level) behind base 6 made it possible to identify this tree as an oleander (*Nerium oleander* L.).[31] The root cavity behind base 9 was similar in size (0.25 × 0.32 m) and also appears to be an oleander. Examination of the woody material from the tree behind statue base 8 indicated that this could only be a laurel (*Laurus nobilis* L.) or a lemon tree (*Citrus limon* (L.) Burm. f.). But when we excavated the root cast (0.20 × 0.20 m) we found that this tree had been air-layered in a pot (Fig. 43). Laurels root easily and are never started in this way. Lemon trees are

---

[30] Crater fountains were pictured in the garden paintings in the courtyard garden (20) in the original villa, as well as in the two small courtyard gardens (68 and 70) in the east wing.

[31] See Jashemski, "The Campanian Peristyle Garden," *Ancient Roman Gardens*, Dumbarton Oaks Colloquium on the History of Landscape Architecture, 7, Washington, D.C., 1981, 47–48 and figs. 35–36.

air-layered. When we excavated the "pot" we found that a broken amphora had been used; the root was growing out of the mouth of the amphora. Lemon trees are still air-layered today, but cast-off plastic containers or tin cans take the place of broken amphoras. At Boscoreale, above our excavations, we found lemon trees being air-layered in this way (Fig. 44). The cavity behind statue base 7 was similar in size and shape and appeared to be that of a lemon tree root. The four statues in the center of the garden would have made a beautiful picture from the large exedra, with the two oleanders behind the statues on the edges framing the picture and with lemon trees behind the two statues in the middle.

At a distance of approximately 4.50 meters behind statue bases 6 and 9 we found a low base, and behind each of these bases we found plentiful remains of the branches of a woody shrub, which have not yet been analyzed. Water channels with raised borders perpendicular to the rear of each tree suggest the arrangement of this space in planting beds (Fig. 40). The complexity and beauty of this impressive garden will only become clearer with further excavation.

So far six of the white marble statues that were displayed on the statue bases in this sculpture garden have been recovered. Beginning at the south, there was a head of Hercules on the marble pillar on statue base 3, next an ephebe, and then a large statue of Nike. Balancing these in corresponding positions along the north end of the pool was another Nike, from statue base 10, a statue of Artemis(?) still standing on the statue base in front of root cavity 11, and next a head of Hercules on the marble pillar on the base in front of root cavity 12.[32]

In conclusion, we stop briefly at Pompeii, the city of Venus Pompeiana, for Venus was the chief deity at Pompeii. Dr. De Caro has now finished excavating an impressive house at Pompeii (VI. Ins. Occid. 39–41), which we might call a city villa. It was three stories high, one of the houses built over the city wall when the wall was no longer needed for protection after Pompeii became a Roman city. The house had a perfect little jewel of a formal garden which I excavated in 1983 (Fig. 45). At the east end of the garden was a pool, painted blue inside, with a fountain rising in the middle and twenty-eight jets along the edges. The middle room on the ground level was a water triclinium, which was dominated by an apsed mosaic fountain with water steps down which the water fell, passing between the marble couches and eventually emptying into the pool. To the north of the water triclinium was a beautiful, high, vaulted garden room, a place for taking the siesta while looking out on the lovely formal garden and listening to the music of the many jets. This room was cool, even on the hottest summer day, for the sun never reached the rear of the room, where the bed was placed (Fig. 46).

The walls of this garden room were decorated with a magnificent garden painting, the most beautiful one yet found, as if to suggest that the room was a continuation of the actual garden. In the center of the garden pictured on each side of the long walls is a bubbling fountain with a charming herm painted on each side—one, a red-haired,

[32] See De Caro, below, 102–112.

mustached faun (Fig. 47), the first such found, the other herm, a round-faced girl with a braid down her center part. The lush garden is full of beautifully and accurately painted birds (Fig. 48), trees, and flowers, many pictured for the first time.[33] Behind each fountain is a hawthorn tree (*Crataegus monogyna* Jacquin), found for the first time in a garden painting.

On the east wall, and prominently visible from the garden, is the most beautiful and accurately painted madonna lily (*Lilium candidum* L.) yet found at Pompeii (Fig. 49). Next is an opium poppy (*Papaver somniferum* L.), the first to be found in a Campanian garden painting. The small white daisylike flowers with yellow centers could be either the wild camomile (*Chamomilla recutita* (L.) Rauschert) or the very similar corn camomile (*Anthemis arvensis* L.), both of which are found in the area today. Then come a carefully painted young date palm and a spectacular group of four large white morning glories (*Calystegia sepium* (L.) R. Brown), the first found in a garden painting. One of the most beautiful details in the entire room is found on the south wall. A pert warbler perches on a hollow reed, which stakes a thorny rosebush with three lovely red roses, Venus' own flower (Fig. 50). At the base of the rosebush are more white camomiles, also some larger yellow corn marigolds.

In 1980 fragments of this painting were found in the lapilli, where they had fallen from the wall, and the fragments were put together like the pieces of a jigsaw puzzle. In 1983 the lower part of the room was excavated, and here the painting was found still on the wall. This has now been removed in large sections, and the entire room is in the process of being restored. The paintings will be backed with a new, costly aluminum honeycomb, which will protect and preserve them forever, when they are displayed in the newly rebuilt Antiquarium with its temperature and humidity controls.

As soon as all the laboratory tests have been completed and the pollen, soil contours, carbonized fruits, nuts, seeds, and the bits of charcoal have yielded their secrets, the gardens and vineyards that we have excavated will be replanted, and modern visitors can enjoy them as did the ancient owners and their guests.

---

[33] For colored plates of this painting and a detailed description of the birds and plants found for the first time in this garden painting, see Jashemski, *Gardens*, II, app. 2.

The Sculptures of the Villa of Poppaea at Oplontis: A Preliminary Report

STEFANO DE CARO

INTRODUCTION

I shall start with a description of the buildings and the geographical context of the largest villa at Oplontis,[1] in Torre Annunziata near Naples, as a preliminary to a discussion of the sculptural decoration. This is a brief but necessary account in view of the exceptional nature of the complex and of the close relationship in Roman culture between architecture and sculpture.

Buried by the eruption of Vesuvius in A.D. 79, the villa was partially explored in the nineteenth century by excavating tunnels,[2] the method employed at Herculaneum in the previous century. In the last twenty years the site has been completely and carefully excavated by the Soprintendenza of Naples and later of Pompeii. The villa, which is on the lower slopes of Vesuvius (Fig. 1, no. 5), where the Tabula Peutingeriana, an ancient map of the Roman world, locates Oplontis,[3] is sited a short distance from the sea and probably not far from the coast road that, since archaic times, must have connected the settlements of the southern part of the Gulf of Cumae. It seems significant that up to now only evidence for villas has been found in the Oplontis area,[4] whether situated on the seashore as *villae maritimae*, like those in the area of the modern bathing establishments (Fig. 1, nos. 1–2), or further back on the slopes of the volcano, like the one located near the E. Cesaro school building (Fig. 1, no. 8).

The area around our villa (Fig. 1) is particularly rich in discoveries: there are remains of several other buildings in the neighboring Fattorusso property (6), near the building of the Salesian Fathers (7), in the area of the Parini school (10), and in the area of the housing development (11; dolia, perhaps of a *villa rustica*).

The Soprintendenza of Pompeii is now doing an exploration of the area of the Parini school where the so-called villa B is located. This site is particularly interesting because its first phase dates to the second century B.C., showing that Oplontis was already occupied in late Samnite times before being a settlement of villas in the Roman period. Sometimes these villas are rather scattered; sometimes they are closely grouped

---

[1] On the villa at Oplontis see A. de Franciscis in *Fasti archaeologici*, 18–19 (1963–64), 7420; idem, "La villa romana di Oplontis," *La parola del passato*, 153 (1973), 453 ff; idem, "La villa romana di Oplontis," in *Neue Forschungen in Pompeji*, ed. B. Andreae and H. Kyrieleis, Recklinghausen, 1975, 1 ff; S. De Caro, "Sculture dalla villa di Poppea ad Oplontis," in *Cronache pompeiane*, 2 (1976), 184–225; C. Malandrino, *Oplontis*, Naples, 1977; A. de Franciscis, "Beryllos e la villa 'di Poppea' ad Oplontis," in *Studies in Classical Art and Archaeology. A Tribute to P.H. von Blanckenhagen*, ed. G. Kopcke and M.B. Moore, Locust Valley, N.Y., 1979, 231–233; idem, "La dama di Oplonti," in *Eikones. Festschrift H. Jucker, Antike Kunst*, suppl. 12, Bern, 1980, 115–117; W.F. Jashemski, *The Gardens of Pompeii*, I, New Rochelle, N.Y., 1979, 289–314. For the volcanological aspects of the A.D. 79 eruption in the Oplontis area see now H. Sigurdsson, S. Carey, W. Cornell, and T. Pescatore, "The Eruption of Vesuvius in A.D. 79," *National Geographic Research* (Summer 1985), 332 ff, especially 353–357 and figs. 26–29.

All abbreviations below for ancient authors and their works are those found in N.G.L. Hammond and H.H. Scullard, eds., *The Oxford Classical Dictionary*, 2nd ed., Oxford, 1970, ix–xxii.

[2] See M. Ruggiero, *Scavi di antichità nelle provincie di terraferma*, Naples, 1888, 99 ff (20 April 1833; 2 March 1839–9 October 1840).

[3] See K. Miller, *Itineraria romana*, Stuttgart, 1915.

[4] See Malandrino, *Oplontis*, 32 ff.

and connected, leading one to suspect that there was an urban pattern something like a *pagus* of Pompeii. This would explain the presence of a specific place name in the Tabula Peutingeriana.[5] The archaeological evidence confirms, in any case, the description of this part of the Gulf of Naples given in the Augustan Age by the geographer Strabo (5.4.8): "Here, then, the gulf that is called the 'Crater' comes to an end, being marked off by two capes that face the south, namely, Misenum and Athenaeum. And the whole of the gulf is garnished, in part by the cities which I have just mentioned, and in part by the residences and plantations, which, since they intervene in unbroken succession, present the appearance of a single city."[6]

The villa to be discussed, the so-called villa of Poppaea, was built, to judge by the construction and decoration, around the middle of the first century B.C., after the conquest of Samnite Pompeii by Lucius Sulla and the establishment of the Roman colony. The conquest must have led to the rearrangement and improvement of the road that leaves Pompeii through the Herculaneum Gate (the ancient Salt Gate) and goes in the direction of Oplontis; the new path of the road cut through private properties and was, undoubtedly, an official act of the newly established Colonia Cornelia Veneria Pompeianorum. On the one hand, the new road may be considered a result of the policy to develop the Roman road system as a means of military and civil control of Italy; on the other hand, it must be related to the investments of the Roman ruling classes in real estate on the Campanian coast from Baiae to Surrentum (Sorrento).[7] This fact, as well as a preliminary observation of the size of the villa in its first phase, supports the hypothesis that it was a Roman property from the beginning and not that of a member of the local Samnite aristocracy, humiliated by the military conquest of Pompeii and dispossessed of his estates by colonial expropriations.

In its first phase the villa (Fig. 2) had a compact plan, with a central rectangular section consisting of a large atrium (5), an inner garden (20), and a large hall, probably a triclinium (21); these last two structures belonged to a later renovation. On the sides of this central section are two nearly square wings. The western part, reserved for entertaining and for the owners' residence, has a central hall (15), a triclinium (14), some *cubicula,* and *diaetae* (11, 12), decorated with 2nd style wall paintings; in the northern part of this wing a bathing complex was built later around a little portico (16) with a kitchen-*praefurnium* (7), a *calidarium* (8), a *tepidarium,* and other bathing rooms (31, 17) decorated in 4th style.

The eastern wing is mainly a service quarter. It is organized around a central peristyle (32) with an inner garden and a little cascade fountain. It includes a large hall with

---

[5] On the place name see de Franciscis, "Villa romana" (1973); see also G. Alessio, "Oplontis," *Studi etruschi*, 33, ser. 2 (1965); on the topographical problem see A. Maiuri, "Note di topografia pompeiana," *Rendiconti dell'Accademia di Archeologia, Lettere e Belle Arti di Napoli,* 34 (1959), 81 ff.

[6] μέχρι μὲν δεῦρο ἔχει τέλος ὁ κόλπος ὁ Κρατὴρ προσαγορευόμενος, ἀφοριζόμενος δυσὶν ἀκρωτηρίοις βλέπουσι πρὸς μεσημβρίαν, τῷ τε Μισηνῷ καὶ τῷ Ἀθηναίῳ. ἅπας δ᾽ ἐστὶ κατεσκευασμένος τοῦτο μὲν ταῖς πόλεσιν, ἃς ἔφαμεν, τοῦτο δὲ ταῖς οἰκοδομίαις καὶ φυτείαις, αἳ μεταξὺ συνεχεῖς οὖσαι μιᾶς πόλεως ὄψιν παρέχονται. (Trans. H.L. Jones, *The Geography of Strabo*, Loeb ed., London, 1928.)

[7] See J.H. d'Arms, *Romans on the Bay of Naples. A Social and Cultural Study of the Villas and Their Owners from 150 B.C. to A.D. 400*, Cambridge, Mass., 1970; idem, "Ville rustiche e ville d'otium," in *Pompei 79: Raccolta di studi per il decimonono centenario dell'eruzione vesuviana,* ed. F. Zevi, Naples, 1979, 65–86.

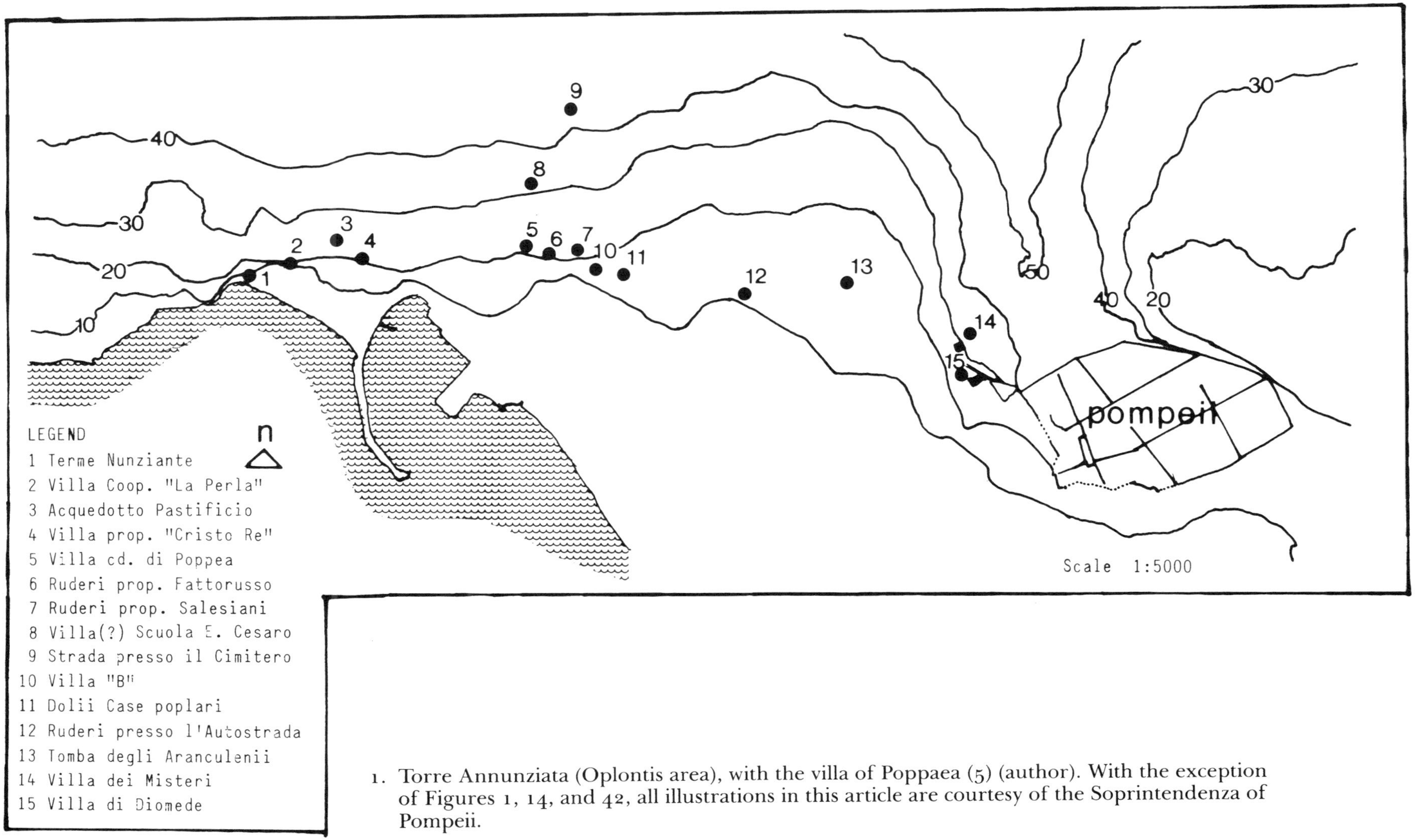

LEGEND
1 Terme Nunziante
2 Villa Coop. "La Perla"
3 Acquedotto Pastificio
4 Villa prop. "Cristo Re"
5 Villa cd. di Poppea
6 Ruderi prop. Fattorusso
7 Ruderi prop. Salesiani
8 Villa(?) Scuola E. Cesaro
9 Strada presso il Cimitero
10 Villa "B"
11 Dolii Case poplari
12 Ruderi presso l'Autostrada
13 Tomba degli Aranculenii
14 Villa dei Misteri
15 Villa di Diomede
n
pompeii
Scale 1:5000

1. Torre Annunziata (Oplontis area), with the villa of Poppaea (5) (author). With the exception of Figures 1, 14, and 42, all illustrations in this article are courtesy of the Soprintendenza of Pompeii.

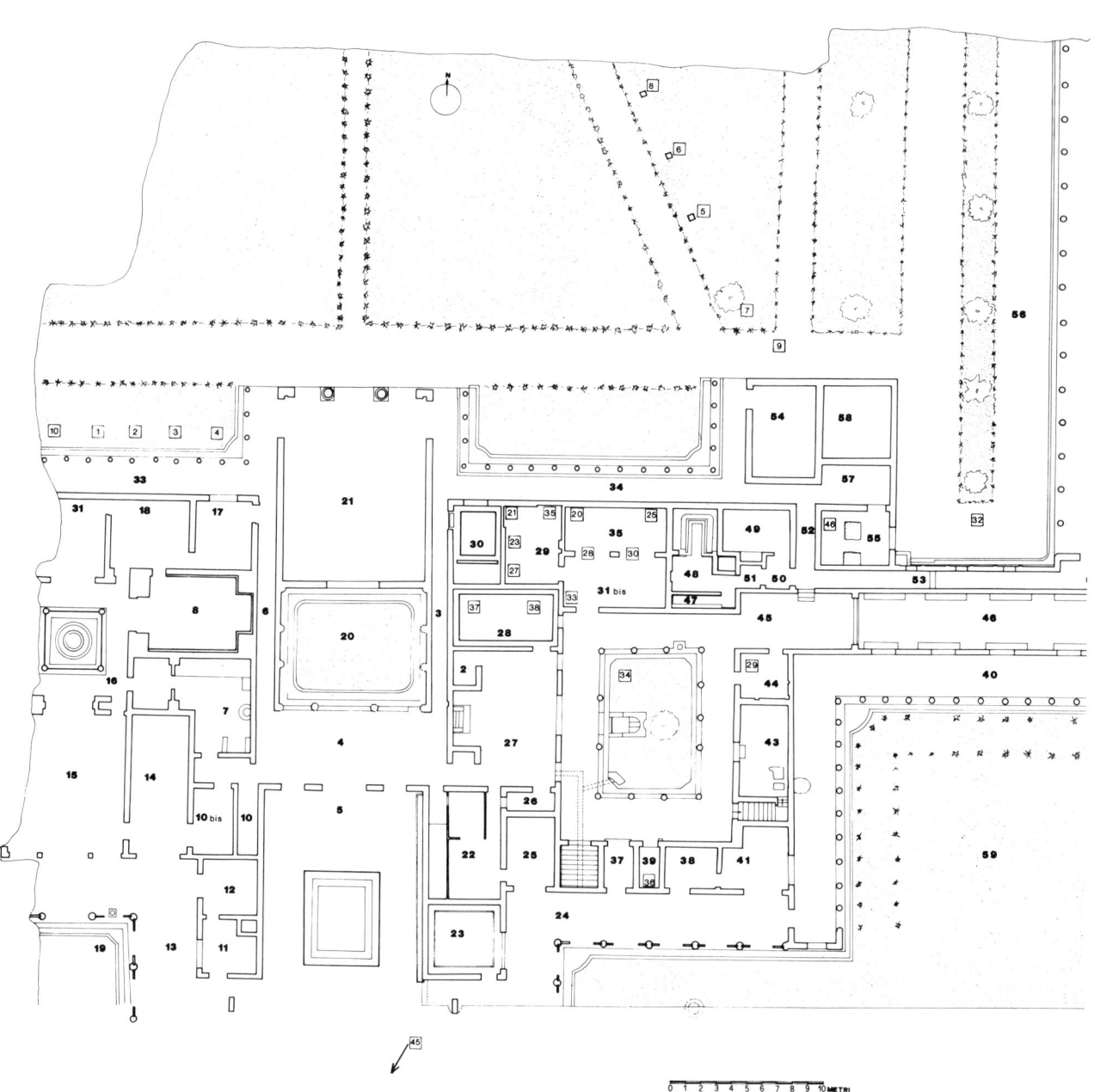

2. Plan of the villa of Poppaea at Oplontis with the findspots of the sculptures

94
91
92
39
89
87
88
24
74
73
71
70
72
22
69
80
56
67
68
75
60
47
64
65
32
61
63
53
62
46
40
59
NATATIO
14
19
18
17
16
15
13
66
78
76
77
79
12
11
42
44
43
81
86
82
83
84

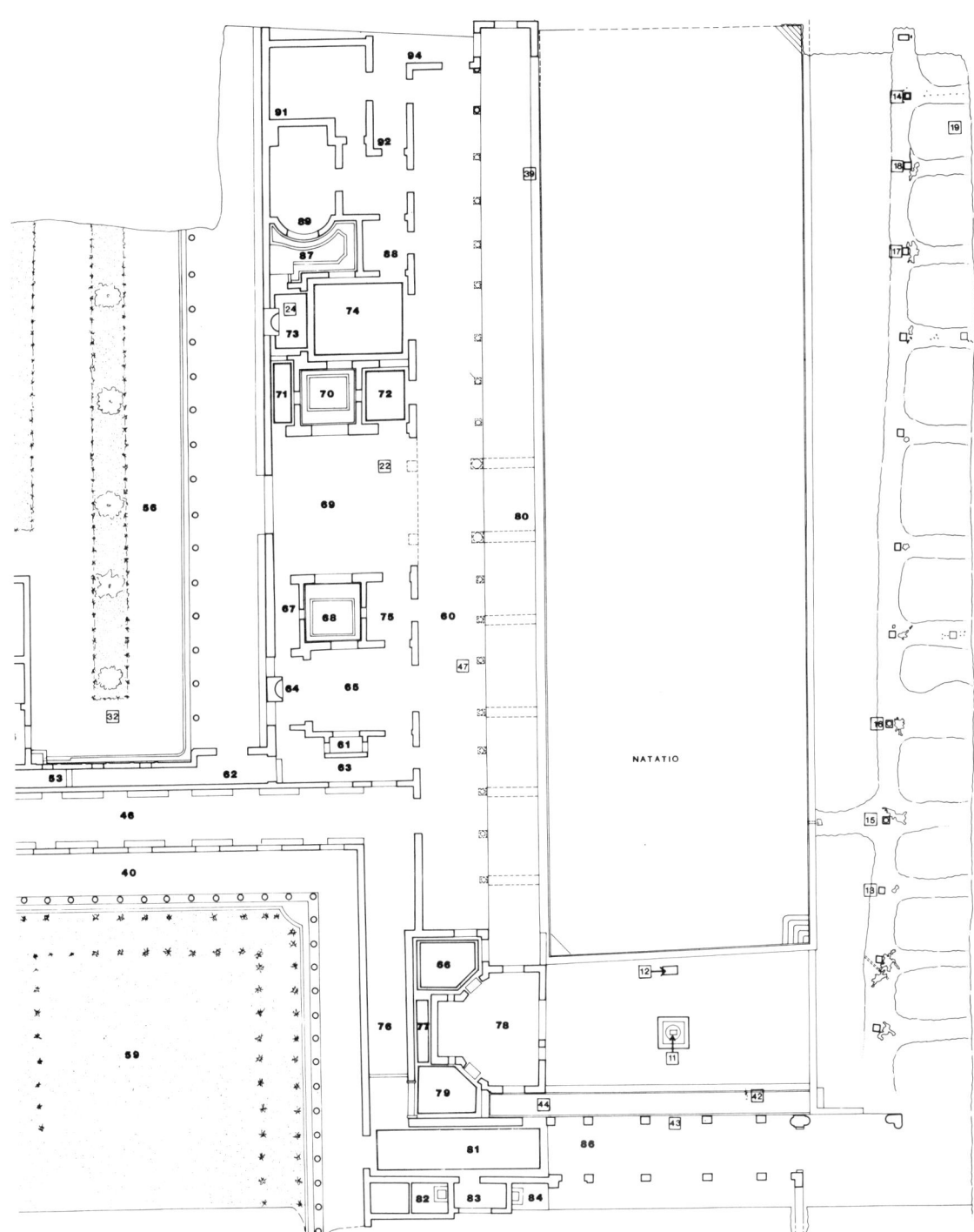

a *lararium* (27), many storerooms (35, 44, 43), and rooms for slaves on the upper floor. The rooms looking outward (23, 37, 38, 41, 30, 29) must be considered part of the owners' residence since they were used for walks in the porticoes. The residential sections—the portico and the rooms opening onto it—are decorated with mosaics and elegant wall paintings in 2nd and later 3rd and 4th styles. The service rooms, on the contrary, have terrazzo floors, and the walls are covered with a coarse plaster or a stripe decoration, well known at Pompeii where it is used in minor rooms such as in the passages in the Villa Imperiale or in the *latrina* of the Stabian Baths. The arrangement of the northwestern corner is particularly interesting, with a small but functional bath consisting of a *latrina* (47–48) and a little *calidarium* (49).

It is not certain whether the northern (33–34) and southern porticoes (13) belonged to the first phase since they now have wall paintings in 4th style. Nevertheless, the corner position of rooms 12, 13, and 23, all painted in 2nd style, makes one think that at least the southern portico (7) could date to the first phase. It is certain that in this first phase the outer wall of the villa was the eastern line of rooms 49-54-44; a perimeter wall was found under the floor of room 45. Separated from this block, but dependent on it, was a *pars rustica* in rooms 82-83-84 (and probably 81) with a *torcularium* probably linked with a *praedium*, cultivated with vines or olives, at an unknown distance from the villa.

At the time of the 3rd style (the Augustan–Julio-Claudian period) the villa saw some alterations such as a redecoration with new paintings in rooms 25 and 10. These alterations are to be regarded as simple maintenance work rather than a new phase.

The second phase in the architectural development of the villa saw the construction of a large new quarter east of the first nucleus around a *natatio*, a big swimming pool about 60 meters long (east side, 58.32 m; west side, 59.27 m) and 17 meters wide. This pool forms the central element of the addition and was, without doubt, at first even wider (to the edge of portico 60) and probably longer (to the *ambulatio* with pergola 91); afterward some problems of stability with the columns made it necessary to narrow the pool and build reinforcements against the foundations of portico 60. Around the piscina one can recognize two architectural nuclei, both used solely for entertainment and recreation. The northern one, placed between two porticoes (60 and the west one), is balanced by the large living room 69; this is nearly an exact duplicate of hall 21 but still more luxurious, with a rich floor in *opus sectile*. The room is situated also on the middle transverse axis of the *natatio*, a position made more prominent by the wider intercolumnation and by the greater height of the correspondent columns in portico 60. Two companion rooms with apses (65 and 74), probably both triclinia, serve as pendants on the sides of hall 69. Between these rooms four little inner gardens opened as light shafts, with their real and painted floral backdrops, along a continuous visual axis of appropriately placed windows.

The second nucleus in the southwestern corner of the *natatio* concludes portico 60 in the same way that rooms 54, 57, and 58 conclude portico 34; but here we have to note a greater complexity of conception in the elaborate plan of room 78, with windows opening onto the waters of the *natatio* and with magnificent decorations—wooden paneling on the walls and *opus sectile* of colored marbles on the floor. This section, if compared with the similar *diaetae* of the villa at San Marco in Stabiae (Castellamare), bears evidence of belonging to a distinct architectural type, probably connected with porticoed *natationes*. Unfortunately we have not yet uncovered the end of this eastern quarter either on the south side, where there is an *ambulatio* with a pergola supported by pillars, or on the north and east sides where the garden appears to continue. Thus for the time being it is very difficult to reconstruct a picture of the whole complex and its general logic. To judge from the wall paintings, this section can be dated to middle-late 4th style, A.D. 50–70 (the white-ground wall painting of the portico is very close to room 7 in the House of the Centenary, IX.viii.6, in Pompeii). The style of the Corinthian capitals of the portico also agrees with this date or with a slightly earlier one. Almost all the painted wall decoration of the other rooms seems to date to this time, preceding the earthquake of A.D. 62 which in this part of the villa caused the collapse of the western brick portico and that of portico 60, as is shown clearly by the columns and capitals stored in hall 21 during the cleanup period after the earthquake.

There are also two other quite distinct quarters: an older one, of the later Sullan period, and a newer, Neronian one. They are connected by a gallery (46), a service passage (62), and a portico (40): a good solution for the practical connection of the two parts, but not such a good one for the problem of an organic architectural connection. The date of this connecting section must be assigned to before the earthquake of A.D. 62, since bricks of old columns to be reused and decorative pieces such as a neo-Attic crater (below, no. 11) damaged by the earthquake were found in passage 62. We must also deduce that portico 40, evidently unfinished in A.D. 79, was already under construction in A.D. 62 and that the earthquake interrupted the work when its floor had not yet been laid and when an old pit was still under the west wing.

On the other hand, restoration work must have been undertaken after the earthquake, even if slowly and late. In fact, in addition to certain elements such as columns and capitals which had been moved, indicating that clearing operations had been undertaken in A.D. 79, we have evidence of some construction work shown by the heap of potsherds for flooring found in portico 40.

The layout of the gardens, extremely important to the whole conception of the villa's architecture, is discussed by W.F. Jashemski.[8] It suffices for me to mention the design of the northern garden, a real masterpiece of topiary art, with a north-south path aligned on the central axis of the villa[9] and two diagonal paths on the sides, probably all leading to a central fountain, the real focus of the perspective from the atrium. The same function of completing the architecture of the porticoes was played by the east-west path along portico 34 and by the two north-south ones in area 56 along the west portico; likewise in area 59 by the plants along portico 40 and by the path along

---

[8] "Recently Excavated Gardens and Cultivated Land of the Villas at Boscoreale and Oplontis," in this volume.

[9] For the motif of the northern *porticus triplex* and comparisons with Pompeian wall paintings see A. Boethius, *The Golden House of Nero*, Ann Arbor, 1950, 113–114.

the eastern side of the *natatio*. Before concluding this rapid description of the main problems of the architecture I should like to give an idea of the size of the villa. It extends for about 130 meters in length and 110 in width, smaller only than the magnificent Villa of the Papyri in Herculaneum[10] which is about 260 meters long and about 70 meters wide. A clearer picture is provided by comparing the built-up surface areas excluding green areas. First in size is the Villa of the Papyri with about 5,600 square meters, as opposed to about 5,000 for the villa at Oplontis, about 4,000 for the Villa of the Mysteries[11] in Pompeii, and at least as many for the villa at San Marco in Stabiae.[12] To give some idea of how this compares with town houses, one of the largest in Pompeii, that of the Faun, is about 3,050 square meters including, however, the large open garden areas.

The choice of these examples is not casual: all four of these villas belong to the pseudo-urban type[13] and seem to have received their primary arrangement (or the decisive one in the case of the Villa of the Mysteries) in the Late Republican period; moreover, they closely resemble each other in plan, for instance, in the position of the atrium between two symmetrical side sections.[14] Finally, the comparison among the Oplontis, Papyri, and San Marco villas is particularly interesting as regards the incoherence of the connection between the older nuclei around the atrium and the later ones, in which the *natatio*[15] is the dominating feature.

At present forty-four, perhaps forty-five, sculptures have been found in the villa, including a marble crater and many other fragments, smaller sculptures, and reliefs. This large number of pieces ranks the villa as one of the richest in sculptural furnishings in the Roman world, second only in Campania to the Villa of the Papyri. As will be clear from the excavation report, the findspot of the sculptures in several cases was not the original position in which they had been displayed, but was completely accidental because of their displacement and storage. The storing of other materials, such as lamps and pottery, also bears witness to this. The list of sculptures is certainly incomplete, as other pieces must still be buried in the unexcavated areas. After these preliminary remarks I shall present the individual sculptures with brief descriptions.

---

[10] See D. Comparetti and C. De Petra, *La villa ercolanense dei Pisoni, i suoi monumenti e la sua biblioteca*, Naples, 1972 (reprint); and, recently, *La villa dei Papiri*, ed. D. Mustilli et al., 2nd suppl. to *Cronache ercolanesi*, 13 (1983).

[11] See A. Maiuri, *La villa dei Misteri*, Rome, 1931.

[12] See O. Elia, "Le coppe ialine di Stabia," *Bollettino d'arte*, 42 (1957), 97–103; idem, *Pitture di Stabia*, Naples, 1957; A. Maiuri, *Pompei, Ercolano e Stabia*, Novara, 1961; O. Elia, "Stabiae," *Enciclopedia dell'arte antica, classica, e orientale*, Rome, 1958–66, VII, 459–463; A. de Franciscis, *Ercolano e Stabia*, Novara, 1974.

[13] See D. Mustilli, "La villa pseudourbana ercolanense," in *Villa dei Papiri*, 14–15 and nn. 37–38 on the well-known passage of Vitruvius (6.5.3): "in urbe atria proxima januis solent esse, ruri autem pseudourbanis statim peristylia, deinde tunc atria habentia circum porticus pavimentatas spectantes ad palaestras et ambulationes."

[14] The comparison between the Villa of the Mysteries and that of the Papyri is in Mustilli, "Villa pseudourbana," 16.

[15] The *natatio* of the Villa of the Papyri is 66.76 m long and 7.14 m wide; for such large pools Mustilli recalled the passage of Pliny (*Ep.* 5.25) describing his Tuscan villa: "si natare latius . . . velis, in area piscina est."

1. Centaur with a club and a little boar on his shoulder[16] (Inv. no. OP. 68). *Fig. 3*

The statue, of blue-veined white marble perhaps from Aphrodisias, is half-size (h. 90 cm). Its function as a fountainhead is shown clearly by the vertical hole that pierces the entire sculpture so water could spout from the boar's mouth. The statue is a Roman copy of the first century A.D., deriving from a second-century B.C. original inspired by a group, probably Pergamene, of the third century B.C. Other replicas of the sculptures are in the Cinquantenaire Museum in Brussels (the former Somzée Collection).[17] The piece was found in February 1970 under portico 33. The acanthus support (Inv. no. OP. 649) was found later in the north garden, a fragment of the centaur's hip (Inv. no. OP. 402) in hall 21 behind one of the columns stored along the wall, and a fragment of the club (Inv. no. OP. 832) in storeroom 35.

The following three male and female centaurs (nos. 2–4) belong to the same group as no. 1; they were found together with it and some capitals of portico 60.

2. Centaur with a club and a crater (Inv. no. OP. 70). *Fig. 4*

Size and marble same as no. 1. In this statue there is a fountain hole running from the plinth to the centaur's mouth. A replica, from the Somzée Collection, is in the Neder-over-Heembeck Museum in Belgium with an ox head instead of the crater.

3. Female centaur with a club and a lyre (Inv. no. OP. 55). *Fig. 5*

Size and marble like nos. 1 and 2. Here too a fountain hole runs from the plinth to the mouth. It is to be noted that the female centaurs wear a *nebris*, or fawn skin, while the male centaurs wear a *pardalis*, or panther skin.

4. Female centaur with a club and a fawn on her shoulder (Inv. no. OP. 71). *Fig. 6*

Size and marble like nos. 1, 2, and 3. In this case the water spouted from the fawn's mouth. A fragment of hair was found in storeroom 35.

Other fragments belonging to this group are (1) a horse's hoof (Inv. no. OP. 427), found in room 44 (a *cubiculum* used in later times as a storeroom), showing an iron pin and plaster traces from an ancient restoration and (2) a horse's knee, found in portico 34,[18] showing similar iron pins from an ancient restoration.

Before their storage under portico 33, these centaurs, which form a well-balanced group with two males and two females and thus probably complete, must have been positioned in the north garden on both sides of the central path, where three of the statues' bases have been found still in situ. However, the lack of water pipes around the bases indicates that the position of these fountain statues was not their original one; they must be imagined originally on a basin, a fountain, or something similar, probably at the end of the path as the focal point of the north-south central axis of the complex.

---

[16] The centaur group is published by De Caro, "Sculture," 198–219; see also Jashemski, *Gardens*, 304, fig. 466.

[17] F.A. Furtwängler, *Sammlung Somzée*, Munich, 1897, 32 ff; cf. also S. Reinach, *Répertoire de la statuaire grecque et romaine*, Paris, 1897, t. II, vol. II, 823, 1, 2, 3; A. Cumont, *Catalogue des sculptures et inscriptions antiques des Musées Royaux du Cinquantenaire*, Brussels, 1913, no. 23; for the Pergamene prototypes cf. J. Schäfer, "Kentauren aus dem Asklepieion von Pergamon," *Pergamon Gesammelte Aufsätze*, Berlin, 1972, 185 ff, figs. 27–30.

[18] The confusion with which the fragments of these and of other sculptures of the villa were scattered in various places can only be explained as cleanup work done in a hurry and by unskilled workers; they seem to have started work soon after the sculptures were damaged, carrying the fragments to the several rooms allotted for their storage, without bothering to collect all the pieces of the same statue in one place but mixing them indiscriminately.

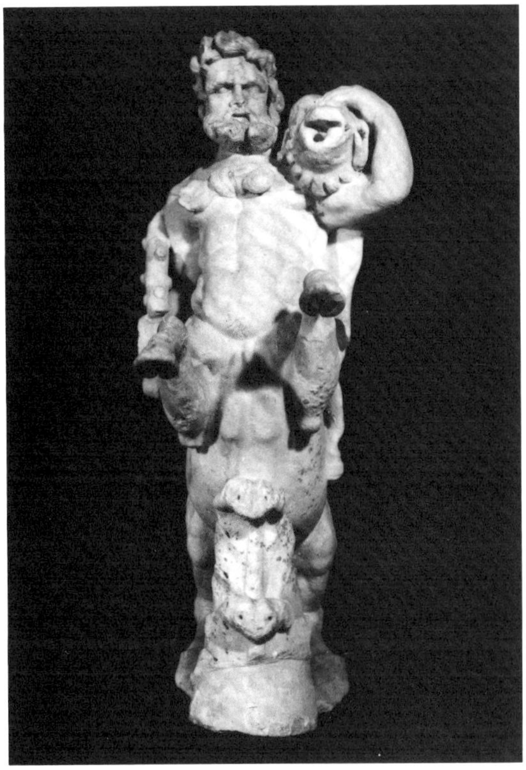

3. Centaur with a boar (no. 1)

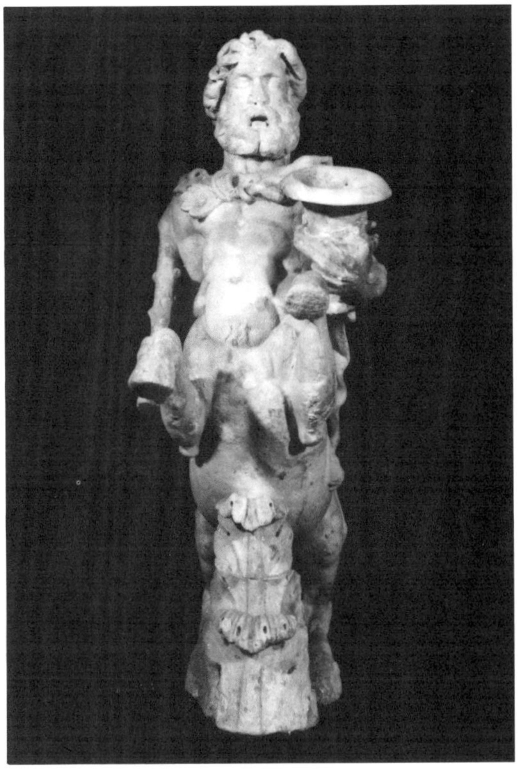

4. Centaur with a crater (no. 2)

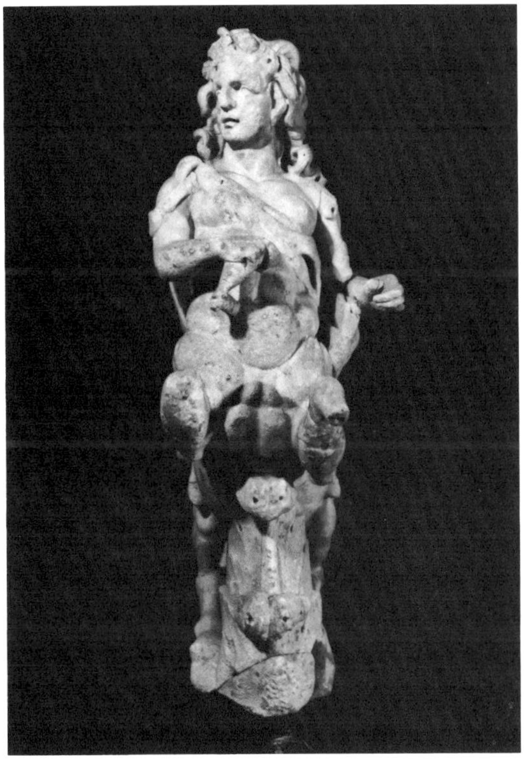

5. Female centaur with a lyre (no. 3)

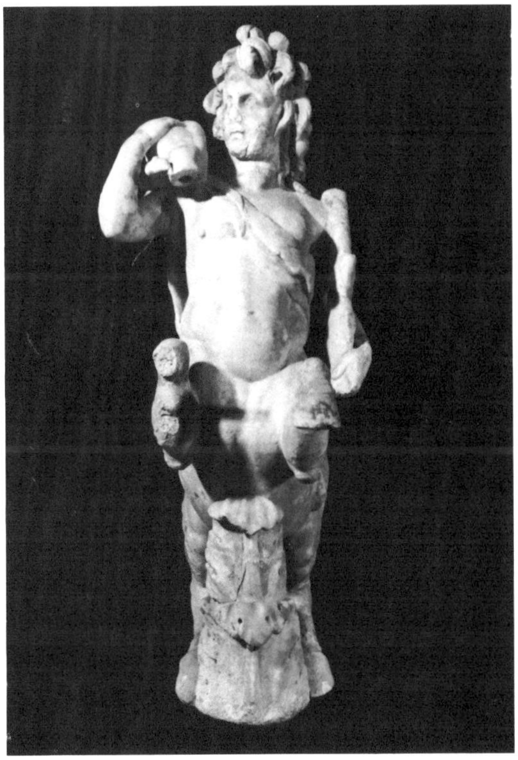

6. Female centaur with a fawn (no. 4)

5. Aphrodite head (Inv. no. OP. 1321). Fig. 7a, b

The head,[19] of white marble (h. 36 cm), was found without its pillar on 12 June 1974 at the beginning of the east diagonal path in the north garden. It was probably just slightly displaced from its original position on the path, like the portrait of the Roman lady (below, no. 7). The head faces forward and is cut under the neck where it has a cuneus to be inserted in a pillar. A cipollino marble pillar has in fact been found, a little displaced, in the same area. The head probably represents Aphrodite. This identification is supported by the characteristic hairstyle with long locks on the sides of the head ending in a massive chignon at the nape of the neck; moreover, the butterfly chignon set with a diadem above the forehead is typical. Rather frigid in execution, the head is a Roman copy of a type of the second century B.C. characterized by a post-Praxitelean shading of insular or Alexandrian type.[20] The hairstyle, deriving from Hellenistic Aphrodites, is rather unusual and lies between the type with the hair separated on the forehead and wound in a ribbon (such as the Venus of Milo) and the type with the butterfly knot (such as the Aphrodite by Doidalses). This hairstyle is found also on Hellenistic terracottas from Myrina and Troy[21] assigned to the second century B.C. and representing similar female heads with shaded surfaces.

6. Portrait of a boy (Inv. no. OP. 2518). Fig. 8a, b

The head,[22] of white marble (h. 28 cm), was found on 28 September 1976 on the diagonal path where it was set in line with no. 5. The sculpture was supported by a herm of African marble with the two usual side appendages of white marble (h. 97 cm). The pillar was set on a plinth of blue-gray marble (21 × 22 × 13 cm) which in turn was set on a brick base. The sculpture, of good quality, represents in a sensitive way a boy of about ten to twelve years of age with a slightly wide face, full cheeks, large eyes, a thin nose, and a small mouth with opened lips. The hair consists of long locks starting radially from the top of the head. On the forehead the locks are separated and inserted between others curled in the opposite direction on the temples. The rendering of the hair is coarser on the back of the head, evidently because it was not in view. The hairstyle and facial features are strongly influenced by the official portraiture of the young Julio-Claudian princes, but the absence of other imperial portraits in the villa leads me to conclude that the boy represented here is not a prince; he is probably just an anonymous private individual interpreted according to the dominant style of dynastic representation. From a physiognomic point of view, the closest comparison is a head, once in the Guthmann-Zimmermann Collection, of the

---

[19] Unpublished; see only Jashemski, *Gardens*, 301, fig. 459.

[20] Cf., for example, the heads in P. Arndt, W. Amelung, and G. Lippold, *Photographische Einzelaufnahmen antiker Skulpturen* (hereafter *EA*), Munich, 1893 ff, nos. 901–903 (see also W. Amelung "Dell'arte alessandrina," *Bullettino della Commissione Archeologica Comunale di Roma*, 25 [1897], 115 and fig. 4), no. 4988 (head in the Welz Collection, Fulda), no. 5049 (art market); for the hairstyle see *EA*, no. 1565. For similar Aphrodites see also V. Scrinari, *Sculture romane di Aquileia*, Rome, 1972, 48, no. 135, fig. 135. The head is close to the taste of the Medici Aphrodite (cf. G.A. Mansuelli, *Le sculture della Galleria degli Uffizi*, I, Rome, 1958, no. 45, fig. 45); it is, therefore, likely that for heads like this one, decorative pieces, we are not dealing with copies deriving from a famous prototype but with works "in the manner of" a whole stylistic current.

[21] See S. Mollard Besques, *Musée National du Louvre. Catalogue raisonné des figurines et reliefs en terre-cuite grecs, étrusques et romains*, II, Paris, 1954, 182, fig. 218 (a–i) from Myrina; D. Burr Thompson, *Troy. The Terracotta Figurines of the Hellenistic Troia*, suppl. Monog. 3, Princeton, 1963, 42 ff.

[22] Unpublished; see only Jashemski, *Gardens*, 301, fig. 461.

7 a, b. Aphrodite head (no. 5), front and profile views

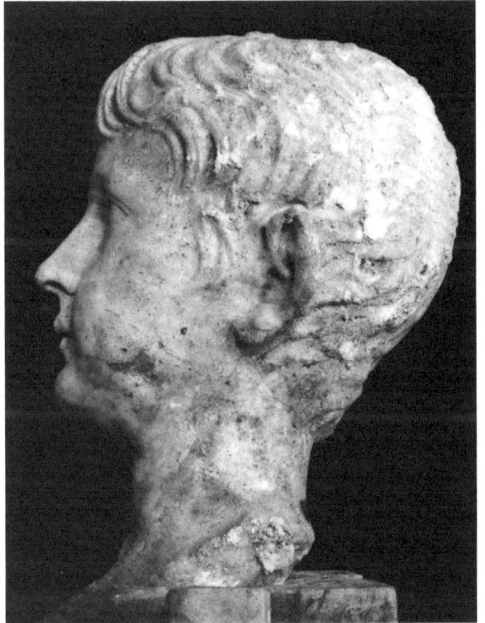

8 a, b. Portrait of a Julio-Claudian boy (no. 6), front and profile views

same type as the Lucius Caesar of Corinth, according to K. Gebauer.[23] Moreover, one must recall the head in the Vatican Museum representing the same boy, which has been identified as Gaius Caesar by Z. Kiss.[24] Another comparison can be seen in a porphyritic head in Karlsruhe,[25] while others exist in Mainz, Pesaro, Torraco, Genoa, Pozzuoli, and Berlin,[26] this last being very close to the Oplontis head. Another very similar head, in Copenhagen,[27] has been interpreted by F. Poulsen as a young Nero, an enticing suggestion that I prefer not to accept here, bearing in mind the caution necessary in this difficult task of the attribution of juvenile portraits.

The style of the sculpture, characterized by a sensitive rendering of the facial features, agrees with a Tibero-Claudian date.

7. Portrait of a lady[28] (Inv. no. OP. 1442). *Fig. 9a, b*

The head, of white marble (h. 32 cm), was found on the ground on 1 July 1975 near the same diagonal path where it must have been set in line with nos. 5 and 6, probably on a brick base recently found at the south end of the path. The head lay near its pillar, which is of gray-blue veined marble (h. 108 cm, base 18.5 × 17.5 cm), and once had the two usual side appendages of which only traces of the iron connecting pins remain. The possibility of an identification with a member of the imperial family seems to be excluded by the facial features, which are very distinctive: the aquiline nose and the lips are set in an unusual way, with the center of the upper lip slightly overlying the lower; this feature gives a sulky look to the face,[29] so different from those of the Julio-Claudian ladies, except perhaps for Agrippina the Younger. As for the hair, in which there are still traces of red color, its style belongs, as recognized by A. de Franciscis, the first publisher of the piece, to the type of Antonia the Younger.[30] So the portrait must date to the same period as no. 7.

8. Crowned head of the child Dionysos[31] (Inv. no. OP. 2517). *Fig. 10a, b*

Recently stolen, the head, of white marble (h. 28 cm), was found on 24 September 1976 with its small pillar of the same African marble as that of no. 6 (h. 93 cm, base 15 × 16.5 cm). Both were situated with nos. 5, 6, and 7 along the east diagonal path in the north garden at the perimeter of the excavation. The pillar was set on a plinth of blue-veined marble reworked from an old pillar decorated with plant motifs, broken and used as a support (23 × 25 × 10 cm). This plinth in turn was set on a brick base.

---

[23] Cf. *EA*, XIV A, nos. 3913–3914 (K. Gebauer); for the head from Corinth cf. E.H. Swift, "A Group of Roman Imperial Portraits at Corinth," *American Journal of Archaeology*, 25 (1921), 337, pl. 11.

[24] Cf. Z. Kiss, *L'iconographie des princes Julio-Claudiens au temps d'Auguste et de Tibère*, Warsaw, 1975, figs. 31a–b, 37; G. von Kaschnitz-Weinberg, *Le sculture del Magazzino del Museo Vaticano*, Vatican City, 1936–37, 262, no. 620, pl. xcviii.

[25] Cf. Kiss, *Iconographie*, figs. 56–57.

[26] Ibid., figs. 58–59, 66–67, 74–75, 88–89, 93, 94–95.

[27] Cf. F. Poulsen, *Les portraits romains. Glyptothèque Ny-Carlsberg*, I, Copenhagen, 1962, 98–99.

[28] Published by de Franciscis, "Dama di Oplonti"; see also Jashemski, *Gardens*, 301, fig. 458.

[29] See the profiles of the portrait in Copenhagen, no. 636 (Poulsen, *Portraits*, 97–98, no. 63, pl. cvi), and of that in the Museu da Citade in Faro (Portugal) (W. Trillmich, "Ein Bildnis der Agrippina Minor von Milreu/Portugal," *Deutsches archäologisches Institut. Abteilung Madrid. Madrider Mitteilungen*, 15 (1974), 184 ff, pls. 36–37, 38; cf. K. Polaschek, *Studien zur Ikonographie der Antonia Minor*, Rome, 1973, pl. 1.

[30] See above, n. 28.

[31] Unpublished; cf. only Jashemski, *Gardens*, 301, fig. 460.

9 a, b. Portrait of a Julio-Claudian lady (no. 7), front and profile views

10 a, b. Head of the child Dionysos (no. 8), front and profile views

The sculpture represents the god as a smiling child with his hair gathered up into a plait on his head and with a crown of berries tied by a taenia falling down onto his shoulders. The taenia was painted blue. Behind the crown there is a deep drill hole, probably for the insertion of a metal diadem. On the back the treatment of the head is coarser, evidently because it was rarely in view. The identification of the figure with Dionysos is supported by a comparison with a similar head from Pompeii[32] which forms part of a double herm in which an adult, bearded Dionysos is the counterpart to the child. The type of the laughing boy with an open, smiling mouth revealing the teeth was created in the second century B.C. in the Rococo phase of Hellenistic art (see, for instance, the Nymph head in the "Invitation to Dance" group).[33] Also, the theme of the crowned boy, Eros or Dionysos, was one of the most loved of the contemporary terracottas of the numerous Asia Minor productions (Myrina, Troy, Delos).[34] The popularity of the theme in the decoration of Roman gardens is confirmed, in addition to the many sculptured herms, by a new wall painting in a Pompeian house in the Insula Occidentalis, in which a boy is represented, perhaps also Dionysos, against a background of oleanders such as those hypothesized by Jashemski behind the Dionysos head of Oplontis.[35]

9. Herm[36] (Inv. no. OP. 1455). *Fig. 11*

Unfortunately only the lower part of the white marble pillar (h. 86 cm) and the gray-blue marble plinth (h. 22 cm) of the herm, found on 5 March 1973 north of the east end of portico 34, have been preserved. On the face of the plinth there is a small cavity for the insertion of the phallus; on the top of the pillar, on each side of the chest, there are two long curls, while on the back there are remains of long hair styled with thin curls gathered into a flat mass. These few preserved features are enough to identify the statue as a bearded Dionysos of archaistic style, a much-loved subject in garden decoration[37] and to be connected with the preceding child Dionysos (no. 8).

10. Boy with a duck[38] (Inv. no. OP. 56). *Fig. 12*

The sculpture is of white marble, nearly life-size (max. h. 46 cm), and represents a child struggling with a duck. The small statue was used in a fountain; the water spouted from the duck's mouth. The sculpture is a copy, probably of the beginning of the first century A.D., of a second-century B.C. original and is one of the many variants on the theme of the celebrated "Boy with the Goose" by Boethos

---

[32] From the House of M. Lucretius in the Via di Stabia (IX.iii.5); see E.J. Dwyer, *Pompeian Sculpture in Its Domestic Context: A Study of Five Pompeian Houses and Their Contents*, Rome, 1982, pl. XIV, nos. 52–54; for other similar herms with two Dionysiac heads see Dwyer, *Sculpture*, 74, figs. 36–38, also from the House of M. Lucretius; E. Paribeni, *Sculture greche del V secolo. Museo Nazionale Romano*, Rome, 1953, 43, no. 67; *EA*, nos. 4496–4497, formerly in the Gallatin Collection, probably from Pompeii; O. Waldhauer, *Die antiken Skulpturen der Ermitage*, I, Berlin-Leipzig, 1928, 67 ff, pl. XXIII, no. 52.

[33] Cf. A.W. Lawrence, *Later Greek Sculpture*, New York, 1969, 19, pl. 31; the motif of the smile is found in other types of the same period: cf. *EA*, no. 2247 (Rome, Lateran, see W.H. Helbig, *Führer durch die öffentlichen Sammlungen klassischer Altertümer in Rom*, 3rd ed., Leipzig, 1913, II, no. 1232), no. 2735 (Rome, Villa Borghese, Casino, see Helbig, *Führer*, 2nd ed., Leipzig, 1899, no. 968).

[34] For Myrina see Mollard Besques, *Catalogue*, II, pls. 39f, 44a, 47d, 53e, 54c, 107f, etc. For Troy see Burr Thompson, *Troy*, pls. LI–LIV, nos. 258–278. For Delos see A. Laumonier, *Exploration archéologique de Delos. Les figurines de terre cuite*, XXIII, Paris, 1956, nos. 835–841, 849–850, 853–855, 899 (with the crown low on the forehead), and 212 ff; cf. also the mask, 265, no. 1235 and pl. 94).

[35] Cf. Jashemski, *Gardens*, 306, fig. 409.

[36] Unpublished.

[37] Cf. Dwyer, *Sculpture*, 43–44 and n. 1, pls. X–XI, figs. 36–41.

[38] Published by De Caro, "Sculture," 187 ff; see also Jashemski, *Gardens*, fig. 467.

11. Herm (no. 9)

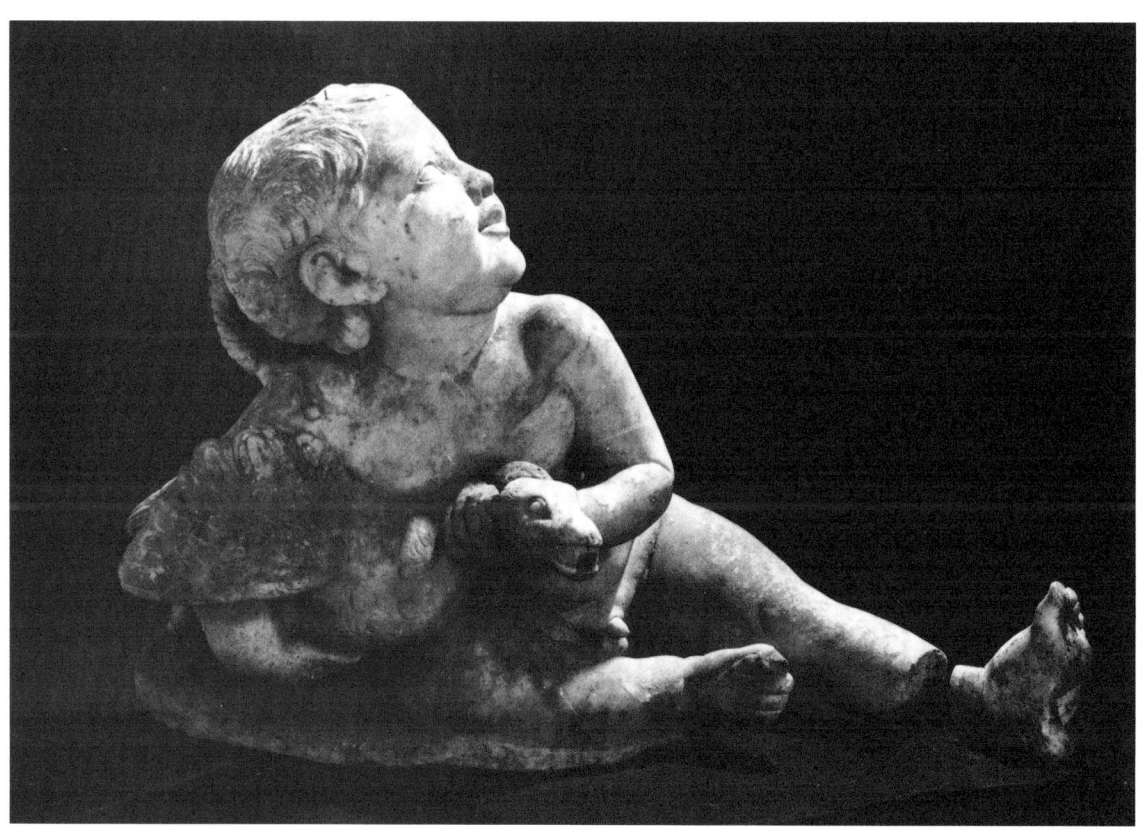

12. Boy with a duck (no. 10)

of Chalkedon.[39] Other replicas of the Oplontis statue are in the Galleria Borghese,[40] in the Vatican Museums,[41] and in the Hermitage.[42] The piece was found in February 1970 below portico 33 together with the centaurs group (nos. 1–4). The head of the duck and the left foot of the boy were found some years later, in storeroom 35 (Inv. no. OP. 830–831), while the base with the carved motif of a shell, not in situ, was found in the newly excavated room 89 in the area of the *natatio*. The sculpture, probably broken during the earthquake, was clearly displaced, its original position having probably been on the fountain of peristyle 32, in the shade of the big tree discovered by Jashemski, or on the fountain that I have hypothesized at the north end of the north-south path.

11. Neo-Attic bell crater with "Waffentanzer"[43] (Inv. no. OP. 1406). *Figs. 13, 14*

The crater is of white Pentelic marble (h. 109.5 cm; mouth 94 cm; base 48 × 48 × 6.2 cm). The foot of the vase consists of a square plinth from which springs a fluted cone-shaped support; this is decorated by a fillet and ends with a crown of tongues in relief which supports the body of the vase carved from a single marble block. The lip is decorated with pearls and an egg-and-dart motif. The fluted handles bear heads of Sileni at their point of attachment. The lower part of the body has a decoration of tongues in relief recalling the motif of the support. The decoration around the body consists of six naked male figures bearing swords and shields and wearing helmets; they are represented as dancing, three on each side of the vase (Fig. 14), with a couple facing each other (F. Hauser's types 47 and 50)[44] and one isolated. Remnants of color are still visible on the edge of the shields, on the helmets (red), on the sword blades (blue), and on the radiating crown decorating the center of the shields (gold).

The crater was used as a fountain, as is clearly shown by the hole piercing the bottom. It was found, broken in about sixty fragments, in April 1975 in passage 53 together with a heap of column tiles probably placed there after the earthquake of A.D. 62. A fragment of the lip has been found (Inv. no. OP. 2724) in the open area 56 north of passage 53. Many traces of an ancient restoration are evidence that the vase had already been broken into

---

[39] An essential bibliography is in L. Laurenzi, "Boethos 1," *Enciclopedia dell'arte antica*, II, 118–120; see also M. Bieber, *The Sculpture of the Hellenistic Age*, New York, 1955, 81.

[40] Cf. H. von Steuben in Helbig, *Führer*, 4th ed., Tübingen, 1963–73, II, 275; see also R. Calza, *Catalogo del Museo Borghese*, Rome, 1957, 11, no. 83.

[41] Cf. W. Amelung, *Die Skulpturen des Vatikanisches Museums*, Berlin, 1903, I, 444, no. 194, pl. 46, the first left in the highest row.

[42] R. Herzog, "Das Kind mit der Fuchsgans," *Österreichisches archäologisches Institut. Jahreshefte*, 6 (1903), 235, fig. 208.

[43] Unpublished. For the shape cf. the craters of Mahdia (A. Merlin-L. Poinssot, *Cratères et candélabres de marbre trouvés en mer près de Mahdia*, Tunis-Paris, 1930, pls. 10, 19); those of the Naples Museum (E. Pernice, *Die hellenistische Kunst in Pompeji. Gefässe und Geräte aus Bronze*, Berlin-Leipzig, 1925, pl. XI, 37); and other vases in many museums (see W. Fuchs, *Die Vorbilder der neuattischer Reliefs*, Deutsches archäologisches Institut. *Jahrbuch*, 20. Ergänzungsheft, Berlin, 1959, passim).

[44] See F. Hauser, *Die neuattischen Relief*, Stuttgart, 1889; Fuchs, *Vorbilder*, 41 ff.

13. Neo-Attic crater with "Waffentanzer" (no. 11)

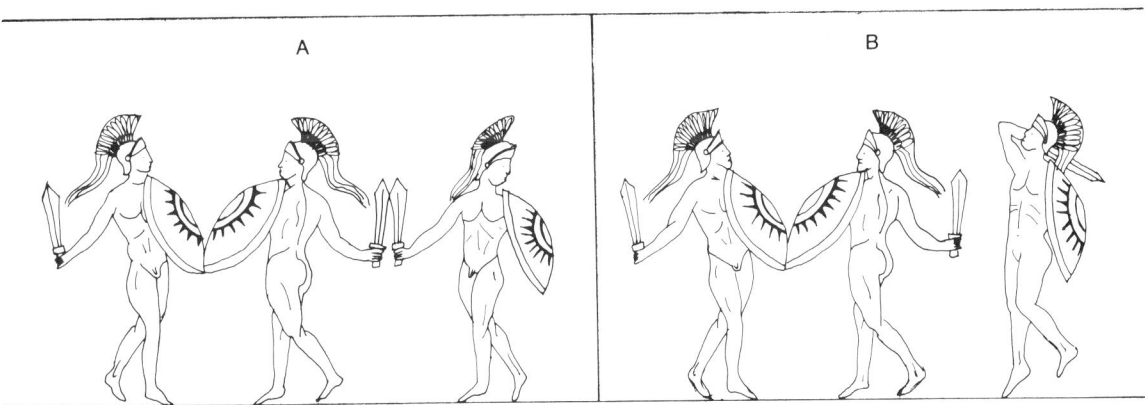

14. Neo-Attic crater, sketch of the decoration: sides A and B (author)

about twenty fragments[45] and badly restored. Bronze pins had been used for the smallest fragments and big iron pins embedded externally for the largest ones, which caused the mutilation of several figures. Similarly the handles, originally carved from the same block of marble, were restored, piecing together some original fragments but coarsely replacing others. A similar substitution is evident in the mouth where a lost fragment of the lip was replaced by a coarse imitation in bluish-white marble. The original position of the crater is certain thanks to the discovery, in November 1977, of the base (Inv. no. OP. 2799) still in situ in a square marble pool in the center of area 92.

The crater was situated on the longitudinal axis of the *natatio* (cf. Fig. 45) and, at the same time, on the axis of pergola 91 and of *diaeta* 78. Such a position is similar to that of the marble crater in the villa at San Marco in Stabiae and may be compared to many garden paintings where the fountain crater is one of the most popular elements. Painted craters also appear in the Oplontis villa in the small inner gardens of the wing facing the *natatio*.

As for the decoration of the crater, we are in the fortunate position of knowing the exact prototype from which the neo-Attic decorations (a fragment of another crater, two amphoras, a slab relief) derive. The original was a base found on the Acropolis of Athens which is decorated with identical figures of naked dancing youths armed with swords and shields and wearing Attic helmets. Luckier still, this Athenian base was inscribed with a dedication made by Xenokles, a personage known as gymnasiarch in 346/45 B.C. and agonothete in 307/6 B.C. G. Lippold[46] was thus able to study the relationship between the prototype, dated by him to around 330 B.C. and assigned to the atelier of Leochares, and the neo-Attic derivations. These appear more or less varied and corrupt or differing from the original in the relationship between the figures or in their sizes. Relationship and size were in fact adapted to the objects on which the neo-Attic sculptor was to employ the motif. A new variation is shown by the Oplontis crater in the introduction of a new type of dancer deriving from the beloved repertory of the dancing Maenads, following Hauser's type 25 of the *chimarophonos* Maenad. The date of our crater, to judge from the weakness in the rendering of the musculature, must be set at the end of the first century B.C. or at the beginning of the first century A.D.

12. Satyr and Hermaphrodite[47] (Inv. no. OP. 2800). *Figs. 15a, b; 16a, b*

The sculpture is of white marble (h. 1 m) and is set on a rectangular marble plinth (91 × 58 cm). It was found on 12 November 1977 on the south edge of the *natatio*. Other fragments belonging to it had already been found in storeroom 35 (August 1973; Inv. no. OP. 741) and in room 44 (August 1973; Inv. no. OP. 1154), and a foot was found very recently near a statue (below, no. 18) along the *natatio*. The sculpture had been restored with iron pins (like the crater). A bronze pin in the fragment with the crossed feet can be assigned to another restoration phase or interpreted as an inserted plug. Other fragments are still missing, and, in the hope that they may turn up, the restoration of the statue awaits the end of the excavations.

---

[45] The existence of extensive restorations, carried out before the last damages to this piece and to several other of the villa's sculptures, lead one to suspect that, in addition to that of A.D. 62, another earthquake occurred in the Vesuvian area not long before the eruption of A.D. 79. The same hypothesis was advanced by K. Schefold: "La peinture pompéienne. Essai sur l'évolution de sa signification," *Latomus*, 108 (1952), 246; "Pompeji unter Vespasian," *Deutsches archäologisches Institut. Römische Mitteilungen* (hereafter *RM*), 60–61 (1953–54), 114, n. 32, 116; "Zur Chronologie der Dekorationen im Haus der Vettier," *RM*, 64 (1957), 152 f; *Vergessenes Pompeji*, Bern, 1962, 133, 183; "Probleme der Pompejanischen Malerei," *RM*, 72 (1965), 124, n. 48; *Archaiognosia*, 1 (1980), 95. Naturally, if this hypothesis is confirmed, a large part of the last construction phase of Pompeii (and of the villas in its vicinity) must be reviewed.

[46] Cf. G. Lippold, *Die griechische Plastik*, Munich, 1950, 271, pl. 94,3.

[47] Unpublished.

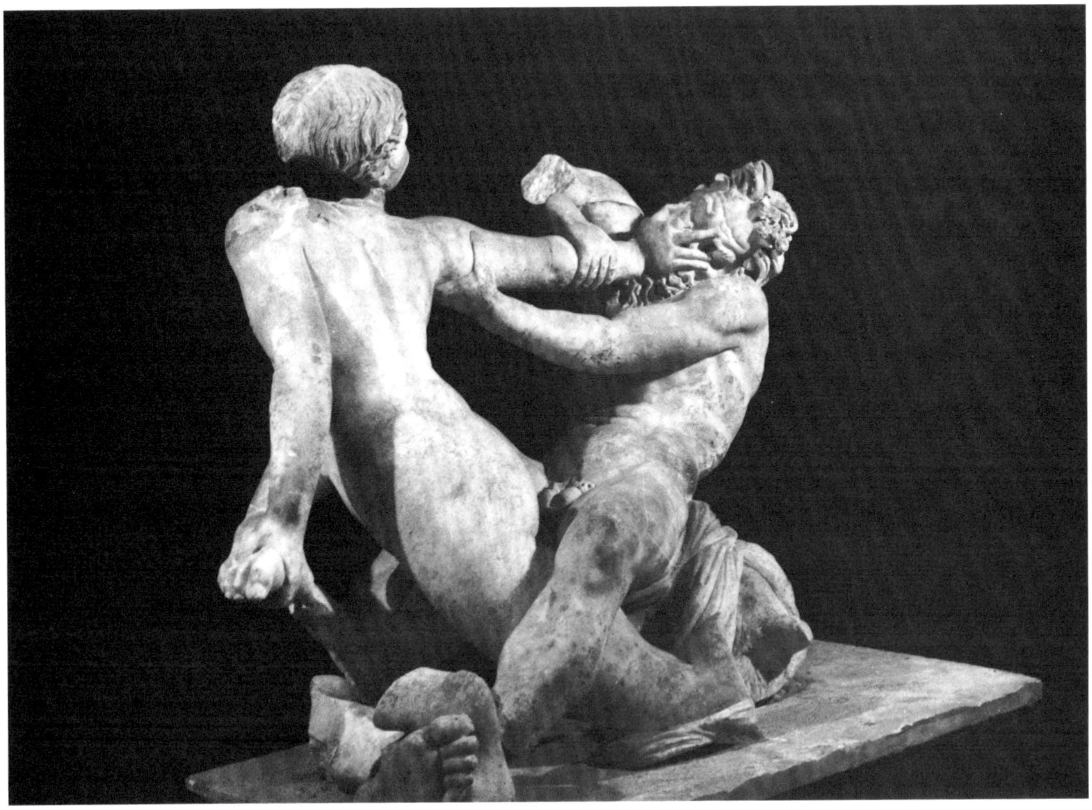

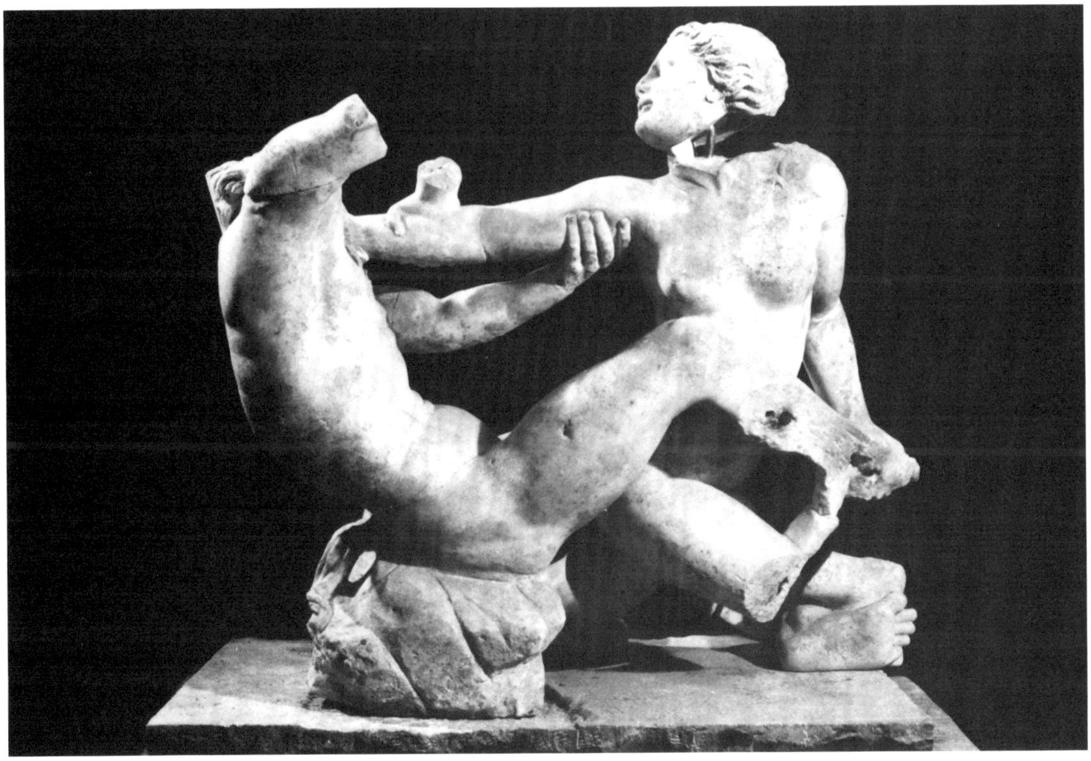

15 a, b. Satyr and Hermaphrodite group (no. 12)

The group represents, slightly less than life-size, a Satyr trying to embrace a reluctant Hermaphrodite; the Satyr clasps his legs from behind and catches him by an arm while at the same time trying to free his face from the Hermaphrodite's hand.

We know nineteen other replicas of the group in marble both life-size and smaller. The group is also represented by two small bronzes, a wall painting from Pompeii, a gem, and two mosaics from Antioch.[48] It was thus a widely esteemed type, as were other famous *symplegmata* (the Pan and Daphne, the sitting Hermaphrodite with the young Satyr, the crouching Satyr and Nymph). The old proposal by Hauser identifying this group as the *opus nobile* mentioned by Pliny the Elder[49] as executed by Kephisodotos, son of Praxiteles, a sculptor working in the first half of the third century B.C., has been rejected by many scholars (B. Ashmole, W. Klein, P. Marconi, G. Krahmer, M. Bieber, E. Pfuhl, L. Laurenzi) who considered the rhythm of the sculpture and the Rococo theme as characteristic of the second century B.C.

Other scholars (such as A.W. Lawrence, D. Mustilli, and D. Levi), recalling that the literary sources speak of *pornographoi* painters working in the generation before Alexander the Great, reverted to the earlier chronology and to its identification with the work of Kephisodotos.[50] We may observe that we have no idea as to the rhythm of the "pornographic" paintings of the fourth century B.C. and that it is difficult to conceive of so complex and, at the same time, so mischievous, refined, and decorative a work in early Hellenistic times. I therefore prefer to date this group, the most violent of all the *symplegmata*, second only to the "Pan with the Goat" of the Naples Archaeological Museum, to the second century B.C.[51] The large number of replicas shows that the group met with great favor, both because of the theme, in which the violence of the Eros is dissolved in an ironic vein of sensuality (Fig. 16a, b), and because of the complex composition which was rich in correspondences, intersections, and breaks. The position of the Oplontis group on the edge of the swimming pool (cf. Fig. 45), between the green of area 92 and the water of the *natatio*, enhanced all the sculpture's qualities whether through the bucolic environment, natural to both creatures, or through the possibilities of appreciating the complicated motifs of form and content from many points of view, by going around the figures, looking at their reflections in the water, or even by swimming under them in the pool.

---

[48] Cf. P. Hermann, "Hermaphroditus," *Lexikon der griechischen und römischen Mythologie*, ed. W.H. Roscher, Leipzig, 1884–1937, I, cols. 2337 ff; P. Marconi, in *Bullettino della Commissione Archeologica Comunale di Roma*, 51 (1923), 227; E. Schmidt, "Über einige Fälle der Übertragung gemalter Figuren in Rundplastik," in *Festschrift Paul Arndt*, Munich, 1925, 142, n. 2; B. Ashmole, *Ancient Marbles at Ince Blundell Hall*, Oxford, 1929, 19 ff, no. 30, pl. 21, n. 130. The complete list is in H. Brunn and F. Bruckmann, *Denkmäler griechischer und römischer Skulptur* (text by P. Arndt and G. Lippold), Munich, 1932, no. 731, n. 1; D. Levi, *Antioch Mosaic Pavements*, Princeton, 1947, I, 183 ff; II, pl. XL. For the painting in the Naples Museum from the *tablinum* of the House of the Dioscuri (inv. no. 110878) see H. Roux and L. Barré, *Herculanum et Pompéi. Musée secret*, Paris, 1862, 91, pl. 17,1 (the same painting is in Schmidt, "Einige Fälle," 101, fig. 9, and is quoted by W. Helbig, *Wandgemälde der vom Vesuv verschütteten Städte*, Leipzig, 1868, no. 552).

[49] "Cuius laudatum est Pergami symplegma nobile digitis corpori verius quam marmori impressis" (Pliny *HN* 36.24).

[50] For the whole history of the attributions see L. Laurenzi, "Ermafrodito," *Enciclopedia dell' arte antica*, III, 423.

[51] I would think of a date in the third quarter of the century; cf., for example, the late 2nd-century B.C. terracotta from Centuripe (Centorbi, Sicily) with Pan and a Nymph and the marble group of Aphrodite and Pan (ca. 100 B.C.) in W. Fuchs, *Die Skulptur der Griechen*, Munich, 1979, 376–377 and figs. 417–418.

16 a. Satyr and Hermaphrodite group (no. 12), detail of Satyr's face

16 b. Satyr and Hermaphrodite group (no. 12), detail of Hermaphrodite's face

13. Herakles herm (Inv. no. OP. 2742). Fig. 17a, b

The sculpture, a herm of white marble provided with the usual side appendages attached with an iron pin, was found on 29 November 1977 on the third brick base from the south along the east side of the *natatio* (cf. Fig. 45). The sculpture (h. 42 cm, base w. 27.1 cm) is cut at the breastbone and rests on a cipollino marble pillar still in situ. It represents a young head, slightly turned toward the left, in a pathetic expression with the lips opened and the eyes looking up under deeply hollowed orbital eyebrows. The hair is rendered with locks starting radially from the top of the head; on the forehead, two series of twisted and raised locks form a shadowed frame around the forehead. Around the head there is a crown of white poplar leaves tied in pairs to a taenia; this is knotted at the nape of the neck and falls down with two overlaid ribbons on each side of the chest. The sculpture, an excellent work, is missing the crown of the head, which was probably made from the beginning as a separate piece or had been broken and was awaiting a replacement.

14. Herakles herm (not yet inventoried). Fig. 18a, b

The sculpture, found on 8 March 1984 near the twelfth pillar along the *natatio*, is a replica of no. 13 also in size (h. 44 cm; base w. 27.1 cm), in the type of marble, and in the shape of the herm (the appendages are also missing). It is better preserved because the head, partially missing in the other example, is complete. Even though identical in type, this head is remarkably different from the other, not only in the position of the head, here turned slightly to the right, but also in its expression. In fact, because of the horizontal cut of the eyebrows, the face almost completely lacks the pathos of the other copy and seems to have a rather formal look, rather like an idealized portrait "in the manner of" Herakles.

These Oplontis twin heads belong to one of the most popular types of representations of Herakles, certainly an *opus nobile*. B. Graef, who published the earliest study of the series,[52] knew no less than twenty-three examples of replicas and variants, not counting the several Hellenistic and Roman portraits inspired by the same model.[53] Recently another scholar, A.F. Stewart,[54] has again associated twenty-three pieces with the series while excluding some of the sculptures accepted by Graef. At the time when the sculptures of the Temple of Athena Alea in Tegea had not yet been discovered, the type was thought to be a Praxitelean work.[55] Graef was the first to associate this variant, called the Genzano type from the herm from Genzano in the British Museum, with Skopas. He also suggested identifying the head with that of the famous statue of Herakles worked by the Parian master for the gymnasium in the agora of Sikyon (Pausanias 2.10.1). The same scholar furthermore rejected the identification, proposed by A. Furtwängler,[56] of the body with that of the Lansdowne Herakles type;[57] this type, Graef argued, had of course an almost similar head but lacked some of the typical features such as the poplar crown that seems to be a constant characteristic of the series. The problem has been much discussed during the last eighty years, becoming one of the thorniest problems of the history of Greek sculpture to which various solutions have

---

[52] Cf. B. Graef, "Herakles des Skopas und Verwandtes," *RM*, 4 (1889), 189–226.

[53] Cf., for example, the portrait of Alexander I Balas in a terracotta from Delos (Laumonier, *Figurines*, pl. 38, no. 7); the portrait of Ptolemaeus of Mauritania (Helbig, *Führer*, 3rd ed., no. 1829 A–B, Villa Albani); and the portrait of Domitian in Boston (C. Vermeule, *Iconographic Studies*, Boston, 1980, 20–21, figs. 6–7).

[54] Cf. A.F. Stewart, *Skopas of Paros*, Park Ridge, N.J., 1977, 139–140, app. 4, A.

[55] See P. Wolters, "Praxitelische Köpfe," *Deutsches archäologisches Institut. Römische Abteilung. Jahrbuch*, 1(1886), 54 ff.

[56] A. Furtwängler, *Masterpieces of Greek Sculpture*, London, 1895, 515 ff.

[57] For the Lansdowne Herakles see S. Howard, "The Lansdowne Herakles," *J. Paul Getty Museum Publication* 1 (1978), 2nd ed.; see also P.E. Arias, *Skopas*, Rome, 1952, 1 and pl. 1, 3, 4.

17 a, b. Herakles herm (no. 13), front and profile views

18 a, b. Herakles herm (no. 14), front and profile views

been proposed.⁵⁸ Some have confirmed the attribution of the Genzano head to the Lansdowne Herakles identified as the Herakles of Sikyon; others have related only the Genzano head to the Herakles of Sikyon; still others have associated only the Lansdowne Herakles with the Skopasian school and possibly with the statue of Sikyon.

Without recounting the whole history of the problem, I shall review only the most recent and, I believe, convincing opinions expressed by Stewart:⁵⁹ the heads of the Genzano type belong to a statue, different from the Lansdowne type, preserved in a unique complete copy of the Antonine Age in the Los Angeles County Museum where it arrived from the Hope Collection. Actually this statue has a Genzano-type head and holds in the left hand the apples of the Hesperides and in the right the club. A chlamys hangs from the figure's left arm, exactly like the image of a statue on a Sikyonian coin of the period of Geta which, probably, represents the Skopasian statue, one of the most celebrated monuments of that town. According to Stewart, the work was executed by Skopas around 370 B.C., at the beginning of his sculptural career. He also attributes the Lansdowne Herakles⁶⁰ to Skopas but of a later date and executed perhaps for a private patron in Athens. In comparing the several existing copies of the Genzano type Stewart has reconstructed a type with the face looking over the left shoulder, crowned by white poplar,⁶¹ a taenia falling down from the hair onto the shoulders, the locks parted above the right eye, and with short twisted curls over the left forehead.

Compared with this reconstruction, the twin replicas of Oplontis appear to be—at least the first one—among the finest preserved and certainly the most "Skopasian." In comparison the heads of the Museo Capitolino and of the British Museum look like frigid, academic sculptures, for which reasons C. Picard did not accept their association with Skopas: ". . . ici la figure se nuance surtout de douceur, de rêve, voire de mélancolie."⁶² These difficulties seem to fade in the first of the newly discovered Oplontis replicas. Above all, the eyes and the expression, softened in the other replicas, are here emphasized, sunken in the orbits under the weight of the eyebrows cut in an oblique line closing the nose line with a sharp angle. We cannot ascribe these features to the copyist, and furthermore they agree perfectly with the Skopasian style. On the other hand, we have to note that the motif of the twin replicas inverted in their movement is classicistic and decorative, completely unrelated to the original conception of the statue.

15. Ephebe (Inv. no. OP. 2818). *Fig. 19a, b, c*

The statue, of white marble, superficially corroded, was found on 19 May 1978 on the fourth pillar along the *natatio* (cf. Fig. 45). It represents in life-size (h. 1.54 m; base 1.60 m) a standing youth, completely naked except for a chlamys that covers his back; the chlamys crosses the upper part of the chest horizontally from a knot on the right shoulder to the left shoulder behind which it hangs. The figure rests its weight on the right leg (behind which there is a support) and bends the left leg with the foot slightly back. The left arm is raised with the hand open to hold a missing object (there are holes for pins). The right arm is extended along the right leg with the

---

⁵⁸ For the literature see Arias, *Skopas*, 104–108, sect. I, 3–57; Stewart, *Skopas*, 90–91, 98–99, and app. 4; R. Stupperich (review of Stewart's book) in *Gnomon*, 52 (1980), 283.

⁵⁹ Stewart, *Skopas*, 90–91 and n. 7.

⁶⁰ Ibid., 98–99.

⁶¹ Oak or ivy leaves can be variants; we don't know the symbolic meaning of the white poplar, but it was probably connected to some local religious tradition. Thus, for instance, only white poplar timber could be used in a ceremony in the Altis at Olympia (Pausanias 5.13.3): see H. Gossen, "Pappel," in *Paulys Real-Encyclopädie der classischen Altertumswissenschaft*, XVII, 8 (1949), 1082.

⁶² See C. Picard, *Manuel d'archéologie grecque. La sculpture*, III, 1, Paris, 1948, 707.

19 a. Ephebe (no. 15), front view

19 c. Ephebe (no. 15), back view

19 b. Ephebe (no. 15), side view

fingers closing around a missing cylindrical object, probably a spear. The head, of a white marble clearer and more translucent than that of the body, is slightly turned to the right; it is round in shape with the hair very coarsely executed on the top and a line of short curls parted on the forehead. Around it there is a taenia drawn with engraved lines.

W. Trillmich has recently made a detailed analysis[63] of the iconographic type, starting with a statue in Cartagena. Among the many replicas[64] listed by Trillmich, the statue in Cartagena is one of the closest to the Oplontis figure. The main lines of the sculpture are indeed the same: the weight resting on the right leg with the left one bent and the chlamys positioned horizontally. There are, on the other hand, some differences, such as the position of the left arm which here is reaching out, while in the Cartagena statue it is held at the side; the right shoulder, covered by the chlamys in our statue and naked in the Cartagena one; the position of the support, behind the leg in Oplontis and at its side in the Cartagena statue; and the movement of the chlamys' folds. The other statues cited as comparisons by Trillmich in Copenhagen, Dresden, Paris, Rome, and Benevento,[65] all close in their main lines to the Cartagena-Oplontis couple, differ in the *ponderatio* of the figures, the weight resting on the left leg instead of the right one. This and other variations, in the position of the arms and the rendering of the chlamys, induced Trillmich to suggest that in the case of this and of other similar series it would be absolutely useless to search for a prototype; we are rather in the presence of statues conceived "in the manner of," so to speak. That is to say that, given a certain theme and a style to reproduce, one or more copyists did not make an exact copy of a celebrated statue but *imitationes* of the images carried out on that theme by the school or the stylistic moment chosen as model.[66] The moment to which the statues of the Oplontis-Cartagena group are to be referred is clearly that of the end of the fifth and the beginning of the fourth century B.C. and the artistic style that of the Polykleitan school. These statues of ephebes, a little bit too elegant and slender, lack the energy of the vigorous athletic ideal of the Polykleitan style; and also, from the stylistic point of view, the *ponderatio* and the anatomical rendering are referred to types dating just to the beginning of the fourth century B.C.,[67] such as those represented by Attic red-figured-vase painters working in the manner of Meidias. This chronological analysis carried out by Trillmich is now brilliantly confirmed by the Oplontis statue which, alone in the series, still preserves the head. The reference to the Polykleitan models is confirmed by the massive structure of the skull and the styling of the hair combed with short round locks starting from the top

[63] W. Trillmich, "Eine Jünglingsstatue in Cartagena und Überlegungen zur Kopienkritik," *Deutsches archäologisches Institut. Abteilung Madrid. Madrider Mitteilungen*, 20 (1979), 339 ff.

[64] For the relationship of the concepts of copy, replica, variant, *imitatio*, see Trillmich, "Jünglingsstatue," passim.

[65] Copenhagen: Ny Carlsberg Glyptotek, no. 397; P. Arndt, *La Glyptothèque Ny-Carlsberg*, Copenhagen, 1912, 86–99, pl. 55; Trillmich, "Jünglingsstatue," 348, no. 1, with other literature. Dresden: Skulpturensammlung; Trillmich, "Jünglingsstatue," 348, no. 92, with literature, pl. 57a. Paris: Louvre, no. 3067; Arndt, *Ny-Carlsberg*, 86, fig. 47; Trillmich, "Jünglingsstatue," 349, no. 3, with literature. Rome: Vatican, Galleria dei Candelabri, no. 2395; E. Ghislanzoni in *Notizie degli scavi*, 1911, 287, fig. 1; Trillmich, "Jünglingsstatue," 349, no. 4, with literature. Benevento: Museo del Sannio, no. 291; Trillmich, "Jünglingstatue," 349, no. 5, with literature, and pl. 57b.

[66] Still in the 3rd century A.D. the type, elaborated as an Apollo with a quiver and a griffin, was used for a portrait in the Museo Nazionale Romano (see *Il Museo Nazionale Romano. Le sculture*, I, 2, Rome, 1981, 31, no. 23); for a discussion of the problem of the copies and an argument against the trend to recognize too close derivations from single prototypes see M. Bieber, *Ancient Copies. Contribution to the History of Greek and Roman Art*, New York, 1977, 5 ff.

[67] Cf. Trillmich, "Jünglingsstatue," 350 and n. 22 which cites a statue in Dresden (F. Hiller, *Formgeschichtliche Untersuchungen zur griechischen Statue des späten 5. Jahrhunderts v. Chr.*, Mainz, 1971, 17, n. 23, pls. 4,6).

of the head:[68] the Dioskophoros, the Hermes, even the Doryphoros for the structure of the skull, and above all the Athlete of Dresden also for the general conception of the figure. Also the style of the head confirms the general character of the Oplontis-Cartagena series as a free imitation of the theme and of the taste of the Polykleitan style, probably without any exact connection with a definite prototype of that time. As for the meaning of the Oplontis statue, the lack of attributes does not permit any identification: in the series of statues cited above only the example in Copenhagen has been interpreted as Paris awaked by Eros, based on the childlike hand on his leg and by comparison with a neo-Attic relief in Naples.[69] In the Oplontis statue and in all the others of the series there is no trace of this hand, and the type is used many times (for instance, in Pompeian paintings) for ephebes or young heroes such as Hippolytos, Narkissos, Meleagros, and so on. Considering also the individual features of the Oplontis figure, one would even think of a generic figure of an ephebe.

16. Nike (Inv. no. OP. 2798). *Fig. 20a, b, c*

The statue was found on 10 February 1978 on the fifth pillar east of the *natatio* (cf. Fig. 45). The sculpture (h. with base 1.76 m) is of white marble, the head being of a marble clearer and more translucent than the body. It is attached to a square cipollino base (side 40 cm; h. 16 cm) by a large cylindrical dowel inserted in an appropriately carved attachment. The sculpture represents a life-size standing female figure in a chiton with fine folds fitting closely around the body. The mantle worn over the chiton is draped around the waist with large horizontal folds and falls down in a curve covering the body to the knees. Over

20 a. Nike (no. 16), front view

the chiton the goddess wears two belts crossing over the breastbone and tied with a large knot. The figure is conceived as suspended in the air, flying down toward the onlooker. The feet are raised above the ground and positioned close together in the old archaic iconography of flight, while the garments, pressed against the front of the body, are blown back by the wind. Two attachments on the shoulders and two iron pins in the back testify to missing wings probably in bronze. The Nike, as we must identify the figure, raises outstretched arms with half-opened hands to hold missing attributes (certainly a crown and another object). The head is looking down, the mouth slightly smiling. The hair is rendered as long locks starting from the top of the head, where they are tied by a ribbon, and two large rolls on each side starting from a snail-chignon on the forehead and ending in a long tail on the neck.

[68] Cf. P.E. Arias, *Policleto*, Milan, 1964, passim and fig. 86.

[69] Naples, Museo Archeologico Nazionale, inv. no. 6682; *Guida Ruesch*, no. 268; Fuchs, *Vorbilder*, 137 ff; Bieber, *Sculpture*, 3rd ed., New York, 1961, 653.

17. Nike (not yet inventoried). *Fig. 21*

The statue was found in July 1983 on the tenth pillar east of the *natatio*. The sculpture is an exact twin of no. 16 in both size and execution. In some details it shows a more careful rendering. Thus the knot at the crossing of the belts in this copy is decorated with a *gorgoneion*, while the same belt bears in relief little knots conceived as metallic. The sculpture lacks the head, wings, right arm, left hand, and both feet, fragments that will probably be found in further excavations.

Twelve more replicas of these statues exist in the Pergamon Museum in Berlin,[70] in Paris,[71] Florence,[72] Alexandria,[73] Oxford,[74] London,[75] Cyrene,[76] Rome,[77] and Leningrad.[78] The type has long been interpreted as an *opus nobile* because of the abundance of the Roman replicas and of some "classic" features recalling, for instance, the Nike on the hand of the Pheidian Athena Parthenos in the general conception of the figure and of the cloak. H. Bulle[79] compared the style of the drapery and the motif of the strips crossing on the breast with the Athena Nike of the balustrade of the homonymous temple and suggested that the type had to be dated to the same period. He further identified it with a famous bronze statue, an *agalma chalkoun* representing Nike, that the Athenians raised on the Acropolis after the victory at Sphacteria in 425 B.C. (Pausanias 4.36.6). This hypothesis was accepted by C. Blümel,[80] who published the statues in Berlin and confirmed the stylistic analysis of Bulle. In 1941, while studying the problem of the Zeus of Pheidias, H. Schrader[81] reexamined all the replicas and proposed the Nike standing on the hand of Zeus in Olympia, dated by him to the decades 470–50 B.C., as the prototype. This identification, widely accepted, raised the doubts of B. Schweitzer because of the frigid style of the statues. M. Robertson concurred: "A Nike in Berlin has been associated with that of Zeus, perhaps rightly, but it is a singularly characterless work."[82] A revision of the series has been carried out recently by A. Gulaki[83] in the context of research on Classical and classicistic representations of Nike.

[70] C. Blümel, *Römische Kopien griechische Statuen des fünften Jahrhunderts v. Chr.* (catalogue of the Berlin Museum), Berlin, 1931, 42–45, pls. 74–76, K 181–183.

[71] Jacquemart-André Museum: cf. Blümel, *Kopien*, 43, fig. 9; Louvre, no. 1776; cf. W. Froehner, *Notice de la sculpture antique du Musée Impérial du Louvre*, Paris, 1869, 478.

[72] Cf. Mansuelli, *Galleria degli Uffizi* (above, n. 20), I, 40, no. 14 (inv. no. 1006).

[73] Cf. H. Schrader, "Das Zeusbild des Pheidias in Olympia," *Deutsches archäologisches Institut. Jahrbuch*, 56 (1941), 21, no. 5, figs. 29–31.

[74] Ashmolean Museum: cf. B. Ashmole, book review in *Journal of Hellenic Studies*, 52 (1932), 136; Schrader, "Zeusbild," 22, no. 6, figs. 33–36.

[75] In the Wellcome Historical Medical Museum: C. Vermeule and D. von Bothmer, "Notes on a New Edition of Michaelis: Ancient Marbles in Great Britain," *American Journal of Archaeology*, 63 (1959), 332, pl. 78, fig. 2.

[76] Cf. E. Paribeni, *Catalogo delle sculture di Cirene*, Rome, 1959, 28, no. 38, pl. 41.

[77] Vatican, Museo Chiaramonti, XXX, 9: Amelung, *Vatikan*, I, 200, pl. 47; Schrader, "Zeusbild," 24, no. 8 and figs. 39, 40, 43, 44; Lateran, X, 561: Arndt and Amelung, *EA*, nos. 2209–2210; Schrader, "Zeusbild," 24, no. 9, figs. 45–48.

[78] Waldhauer, *Sculpturen*, III, no. 352, fig. 105.

[79] In Roscher, ed., *Lexikon*, III, 338.

[80] Blümel, *Kopien*, 42.

[81] Schrader, "Zeusbild."

[82] For this problem see G. Becatti, *Problemi fidiaci*, Milan-Florence, 1951. Schweitzer's critique is in his review of Becatti's book in *Gnomon*, 28 (1956), 567; he found in the Berlin type "ausgesprochene Frontalität und strenge tektonische Gebundenheit der Figuren" and, excluding the hypothesized function, suggested that of an acroterion. As for the style, it has nothing to do, continued Schweitzer, with Pheidias. For other discussions see G. Becatti, "Fidia," *Enciclopedia dell'arte antica*, II, 653–654; P.E. Arias, *Problemi di scultura greca*, Bologna, 1965, 353; and M. Robertson, *A History of Greek Art*, Cambridge, 1975, 320.

[83] Cf. A. Gulaki, *Klassische und klassizistische Nikendarstellungen. Untersuchungen zur Typologie und zur Bedeutungswandel*, diss., Univ. of Bonn, 1981, 218 ff.

20 b, c. Nike (no. 16), side and back views

21. Nike (no. 17)

Rejecting the arguments of Schrader, she recognized the classicizing character of the type and assigned it to the Roman period, around the middle of the first century B.C. The prototypes that inspired it are of around the late fourth century B.C., but they are eclectically interpreted with mannered archaistic features typical of that Roman period (*aemulationes*).

The new Oplontis replicas are from many points of view certainly among the best of the series. If we look at the rendering of the drapery of the horizontal cloak in frontal view and compare it with the same element in one of the best replicas in existence up to now, the Berlin statue K 181, we notice on the Oplontis statues an execution and arrangement of the folds that is richer and softer than the deep grooves, all rigidly parallel, cutting the cloak of the Berlin copy.[84] The main difference between the Oplontis statues and the others is in the head preserved up to now in only two replicas. It probably refers back to the prototype as far as the general position is concerned: in fact both in the Berlin statue K 182[85] and in the Wellcome Historical Medical Museum example we find the same long tail of hair falling onto the neck and other archaistic features such as the hair styled with waves around the forehead and on top of the head, the slightly smiling face, and the downward inclination of the head. The prototypes of such a face seem to be works such as the so-called Penelope, dating to 460–50 B.C.[86] As for the forelock, it must be explained as in the same taste of archaizing neo-Classicism.[87] In a different version another copyist gave the statue in Paris a fine butterfly knot in the fashion of Hellenistic Aphrodites.

18. Artemis(?) (not yet inventoried). *Fig. 22.*

The statue was found on 21 July 1983 on the eleventh brick base east of the *natatio*. The sculpture, of white marble (max. h. pres. 1.15 m), rests on a square plinth of the local so-called Sarno limestone. The statue, which lacks its head, represents a young standing female figure, with the weight of the body gravitating on the left leg and with the right leg bent. A support is close to the left leg. The figure wears a sleeveless chiton with clinging folds revealing the legs above the knees. At the waist the chiton is wound into a *kolpos* tied by a belt. A second belt crosses the breast from the left hip to the right shoulder, probably to hold a quiver. The maiden raises her right arm, now missing and sharply cut with an iron pin for the attachment; the left arm was extended along the hip, and the hand, lacking the fingers, held in its palm an object attached with other pins and now missing. The feet, now detached and lacking the toes, have open sandals. One of the feet of the Satyr-Hermaphrodite group (no. 12) was found near them.

---

[84] The lower fidelity of the Berlin copy is shown by a detail of the same folds. The upper fold in the Oplontis statues falls down close to the left arm, a detail lacking in the Berlin copies but appearing in the sculptures in the Jacquemart-André Museum and at Oxford.

[85] Cf. Schrader, "Zeusbild," figs. 8–10.

[86] Cf. B. Sismondo Ridgway, *The Severe Style in Greek Sculpture*, Princeton, 1970, passim; see also D. Pandermalis, "Sul programma della decorazione scultorea," in *Villa dei Papiri* (above, n. 10), 38, fig. 31.

[87] For similar variants in severe style sculptures cf. P. Zanker, *Klassizistische Statuen*, Mainz, 1974, 84–85 and pls. 64–65.

22. Artemis or Amazon (no. 18)

We know of few rather coherent replicas of the statue, in Florence,[88] in Copenhagen,[89] in Villa Doria Pamphilij in Rome,[90] in Ince Blundell Hall,[91] and in the Museo Nazionale Romano,[92] as well as a couple of variants. As was noted by E. Paribeni, the last scholar to study the copy in the Museo Nazionale, the identification of the huntress is doubtful. In fact she could be either an Artemis, an Atlanta (whose iconography is often the same as that of the goddess), or an Amazon who is frequently represented with a naked breast (but not always, as shown by the Doria Amazon in Villa Doria Pamphilij in Rome). And the still-possible discovery in the villa at Oplontis of the figure's attributes—a bow or a quiver—would probably not aid in its identification. As for its stylistic position, in the *ponderatio* and in the *chiasmus* of the body the statue seems to derive from the Polykleitan Amazon but lacks its force and is dissolved in slenderer and more elegant forms. We have observed a similar derivation in the statues of the ephebes of the beginning of the fourth century B.C. coming from the ideal of the Doryphoros. On the other hand, the existence in this series of statues along the *natatio* of a figure of a late Polykleitan-type ephebe as companion to this statue (exactly like the couple Amazon-Doryphoros in the Villa of the Papyri) influences the identification of this maiden. For, if in the young ephebe we see a hero, not a god, this huntress must be identified as a heroine (Atlanta or Amazon) rather than as the hunter-goddess.[93]

19. Portrait of a boy (not yet inventoried). *Fig. 23a, b*

This piece was found on 2 March 1984 between the eleventh and twelfth bases on the east side of the *natatio*, although it certainly does not belong to either of the bases. The head, of white marble (h. 27 cm), is cut under the neck with a small part of the chest and has a dowel to be inserted in a pillar with an iron pin. The sculpture represents a boy, of about seven to nine years of age, his head slightly turned toward the left. The hair in long curly locks starts from the top of the head and is parted on the forehead in the usual Julio-Claudian hairstyle. The eyes are distanced beneath the large forehead, the nose is thin, the cheeks full, the mouth with fleshy lips is slightly opened in a serious manner.

This find is recent, and time did not allow me to make a careful study and to verify hypotheses as to possible identifications. One may, nevertheless, observe that the portrait could be dated around the late period of Augustus or Tiberius, as it is similar to a portrait from Settecamini in the Museo Nazionale Romano.[94]

---

[88] Cf. *EA*, no. 326, Garden of the Palazzo Corsini; W. Amelung, *Führer durch die Antiken in Florenz*, Munich, 1897.

[89] F. Poulsen, *Catalogue of Ancient Sculpture in the Ny Carlsberg Glyptotek*, Copenhagen, 1953, 88, no. 86, pl. VII, 86.

[90] B. Palma, in *Le antichità di Villa Doria Pamphilj*, ed. R. Calza et al., Rome, 1977, pl. LXXIII, no. 113.

[91] Ashmole, *Ince Blundell Hall*, no. 23, pl. 6.

[92] E. Paribeni, *Museo Nazionale Romano. Le sculture*, I, 2, 282, no. 7 (inv. no. 693).

[93] We cannot exclude the possibility that the statue of the ephebe may represent Apollo, as shown by the portrait statue in the Museo Nazionale Romano (see above, n. 66), in which case the Artemis pendant would be very appropriate.

[94] Cf. B.M. Felletti Maj, *Museo Nazionale Romano. I ritratti*, Rome, 1953, 76–77, no. 132, fig. 132.

23 a. Portrait of a boy (no. 19), front view

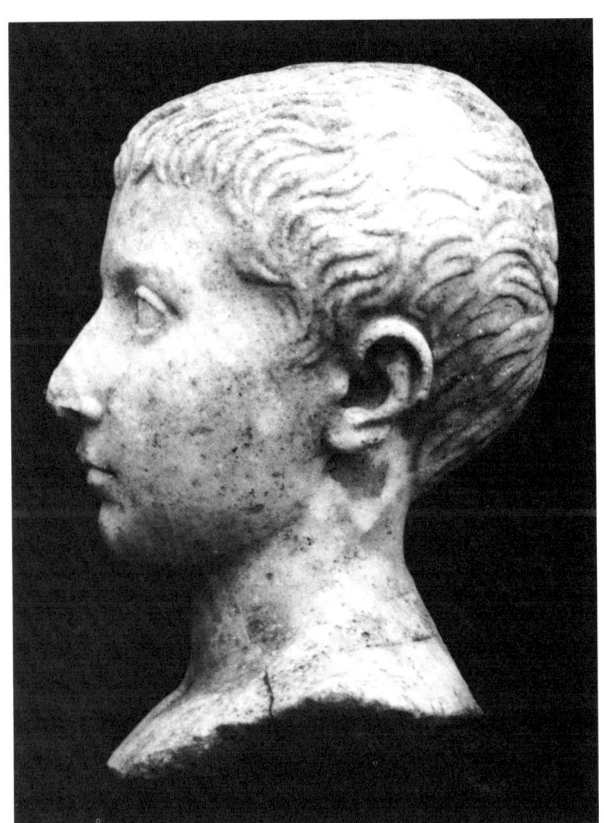

23 b. Portrait of a boy (no. 19), profile view

20. Aphrodite unlacing her sandal[95] (Inv. no. OP. 1252). *Fig. 24*

The statuette, of white Dokimian or Parian marble (h. 52.5 cm), supported by a round base, represents the goddess completely naked preparing to bathe. She raises her left foot to remove her sandal and rests her left forearm on a small statue standing on a high base. A tiny Eros is below her foot. The goddess' head is decorated with a diadem; the hair is parted on the forehead and gathered up in a lock at the nape of the neck. Two holes in the ears testify to the existence of earrings which are now missing; they were probably gold, like those of similar Pompeian statuettes.[96] She holds an apple in her left hand—the prize of the beauty contest. Traces of color show that the statuette was painted with a simple polychromy: yellow on the hair of the goddess and of the Eros, red on the sandals and on the cloak of the Eros.

The statuette is one of the very many examples, about seventy in various materials, belonging to a type[97] greatly esteemed in antiquity because of the elegance and unusualness of the spiral movement of the figure. The replicas differ, however, in size, in accompanying figures, and, several times, in the dress of the goddess. In the well-known "Venus in bikini" from Pompeii[98] Aphrodite wears an exiguous, bikini-like harness, a necklace, armbands, a bracelet, and gilded sandals; under her forearm is a small figure of the god Priapus.

Scholars[99] have suggested that the prototype of this series was created in the eastern Greek world between the end of the third and the beginning of the second century B.C. together with a companion piece where the goddess was completely dressed. As for our piece, it could be dated to around the end of the first century B.C.

The Oplontis statuette was found in September 1973 in room 35, a storeroom in the service quarter, stored with a statuette of a seated Fortuna (below, no. 25) and broken fragments of other sculptures (the Boy with a duck, no. 10, and the Centaurs, nos. 1–4). The findspot clearly shows that the piece had been moved from its original location, which may have been in one of the apses of rooms 64 or 65.

21. Base with horse hooves (Inv. no. OP. 109). *Fig. 25*

The base, of white marble, was found on 27 September 1971 in room 29, used as a storeroom. Unfortunately only the base of the statuette put together from fragments remains, preserving a rocky support and three hooves of an animal, perhaps an equine. On the basis of their number and position one may hypothesize that the animal's right leg was raised. I have no hypothesis to suggest as to the original location of this statuette (l. 34 cm; max. h. pres. 6 cm); however, this is a garden statuette like the animal figures that so frequently appear in Pompeian gardens.[100]

---

[95] De Caro, "Sculture," 219 ff, figs. 30–34.

[96] Cf. J.B. Ward-Perkins and A. Claridge, *Pompei A.D. 79*, catalogue of the London exhibition, London, 1976, no. 219.

[97] Bieber, *Sculpture*, 91, nn. 74–75, figs. 394–395, 606–607.

[98] *Pompeji: Leben und Kunst in den Vesuvstädten*, catalogue of the exhibition held at Villa Hügel, Essen, Recklinghausen, 1973, 142, no. 199.

[99] R.A. Higgins, *Greek Terracottas, British Museum*, London, 1967, 108, 119, pls. 50f and 59e.

[100] Cf., for example, Dwyer, *Sculpture*, pls. XIII–XXII, 82, XXXVII.

24. Aphrodite unlacing her sandal (no. 20)

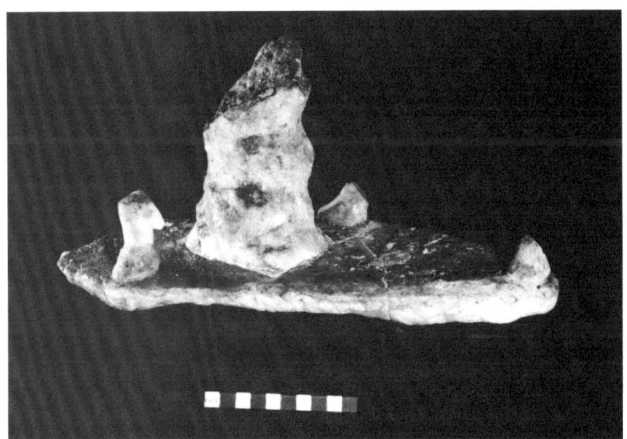

25. Base with horse hooves (no. 21)

22. Base with a crab (Inv. no. OP. 1517). *Fig. 26*

Found on 3 January 1976 in the large hall 69 facing the *natatio*, this rectangular base of white marble (32 × 18 cm) lacks a corner. Two depressions are carved into it; a crab[101] preserving traces of red color is set into one of them. An animal statuette or a figurine, for instance a fisherman forming a group with the crab, must have been set into the other, larger depression. The sea theme is very appropriate for a fountain or for the *natatio*.

23. Fragment of a female figure in archaistic style (Inv. no. OP. 493). *Fig. 27*

The fragment, of white marble (max. h. pres. 9.4 cm), was found on 27 September 1971 in storeroom 29 together with base 21. It preserves both feet with the open sandals of a female figure about half-size in a parallel pose with the left foot advancing. The figure wears a chiton or a tunic in fine material with subtle folds falling down to the feet which are half uncovered. The lower part of a mantle worn over the tunic is preserved on the back.

The position of the foot reveals the iconography of the kore evidently reinterpreted in the neo-Attic archaizing style very popular with Romans in the first century A.D. The sculpture is too poorly preserved for the represented figure to be identified; nevertheless, we may note the resemblance of the pose, and of the style, to the Isis from the Temple of Isis in Pompeii.[102]

24. Fortuna (Inv. no. OP. 2660). *Fig. 28*

The statuette, of blue-veined white marble (h. 20.5 cm; diam. of base 9.3 cm), was found in area 73 belonging to the apsidal room 74 in the wing west of the *natatio*. It is an interesting example of an unfinished piece, probably worked on in the days preceding the eruption. The sculpture was only roughed out: it was to have represented the goddess Fortuna, easily identified by the standing female figure holding a cornucopia in her right arm and leaning her left arm on a rudder. The sculptor had already engraved the lines of the face and hair, though he had not worked the legs, still connected in the marble with the rudder. We may note the holes of the hand drill by which he had just begun to detach the elements. In the same way the head is still connected with the cornucopia, and the back is still rough.

It is, nevertheless, easy to see that the sculptor, intending to make a copy of one of the most common types of statuettes in the Roman world,[103] would not have achieved very good results. Even in this rough state we can see that the arms, which are too long, and the mistaken proportions of the limbs reveal an unskilled craftsman, perhaps the same who substituted a fragment of the lip of the neo-Attic crater with the same marble.

25. Seated Fortuna (Inv. no. OP. 1324). *Fig. 29*

Found on 8 November 1973 in storeroom 35 together with the Aphrodite unlacing her sandal (no. 20), this statuette, in very corroded

---

[101] Cf. the sea crab from the garden of Julia Felix in Jashemski, *Gardens*, 49, fig. 85.

[102] Ward-Perkins and Claridge, *Pompei A.D. 79*, no. 202.

[103] Cf. M. Floriani Squarciapino, "Fortuna," *Enciclopedia dell'arte antica*, III, 726.

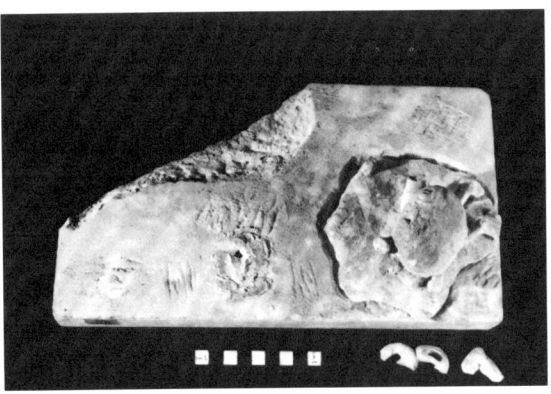

26. Base with a crab (no. 22)

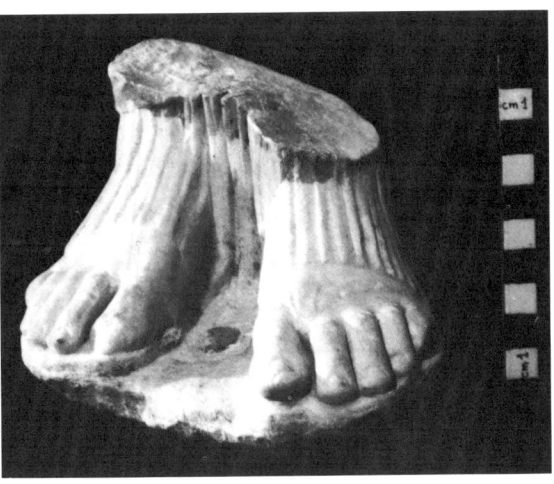

27. Fragment of an archaistic statue (no. 23)

28. Unfinished Fortuna statuette (no. 24)

29. Seated Fortuna statuette (no. 25)

alabaster-like marble, once set on a base of the same material (h. 20.5 cm; base 10.5 × 8.5 × 6 cm), represents the seated goddess Fortuna. In spite of the corrosion we can recognize the conventional type of the goddess wearing a richly draped harness and holding the cornucopia in her left hand as in a celebrated small bronze from the House of the Fortune in Pompeii.[104] The roughness of the back and the small size of the figure lead us to think that it may have been a lararium statuette.

26. Fragment of a shoulder bust (Inv. no. OP. 719). *Fig. 30*

The fragment, whose findspot and date are unknown, is of white marble (base 13.2 × 13 cm) and preserves the right part of a male shoulder bust, perhaps of a young figure. A vertical hole probably testifies to its function as a fountain element. Because of the poor state of preservation it is impossible to form a hypothesis on the personage represented.

27. Fragment of a right hand (Inv. no. OP. 494).

Found on 27 November 1971 in room 29 together with other sculpture fragments, this piece, of white marble (l. 4.5 cm), must belong to a small statuette.

28. Fragment of a knee (Inv. no. OP. 737).

The fragment (10.5 × 6 cm) was found on 8 November 1973 in room 35.

29. Fragment of a statuette leg (Inv. no. OP. 1162).

The fragment (max. h. pres. 8.1 cm) was found on 20 August 1973 in room 44 together with a fragment of a centaur and many of the villa's implements. The right leg, probably from the figurine of a child, must have belonged to a small statuette, already restored in antiquity, as shown by the hole in the upper side.

30. Fragment of a head with locks of hair (Inv. no. OP. 336).

The fragment, of white marble (7.1 × 6.6 cm), was found on 8 November 1973 in storeroom 35 together with other sculpture fragments. Because of the poor state of preservation it is impossible to reconstruct the piece to which it might belong.

31. Fragment of a wild beast skin (Inv. no. OP. 1015).

The fragment, of white marble (l. 6 cm), is probably part of an animal skin, a *nebris* or a *pardalis* of a centaur or similar creature.

32. Fragment of a club (Inv. no. OP. 2720).

The fragment, of white marble, was found in the area of garden 56 on 9 July 1977.

33. Base of a fountain statuette(?) (Inv. no. OP. 333).

Found in storeroom 35 on 8 November 1973, the piece, of white marble (diam. 24 cm), has a cornice molding and a central hole convenient for a fountain statuette.

34. Sundial (Inv. no. OP. 1257). *Fig. 31*

Found in garden 32 on 7 September 1973, probably not far from its original location,[105] this sundial (h. 34 cm; base w. 27 cm) is of white marble and still preserves the original bronze gnomon. Compared with the simpler Pompeian sundials, often of tufa, this sundial is clearly richer: one may note the articulated moldings of the base and the decoration with

---

[104] Cf. Dwyer, *Sculpture*, 70–71, fig. 80.

[105] For sundials in Pompeian gardens cf. Jashemski, *Gardens*, 112, fig. 183.

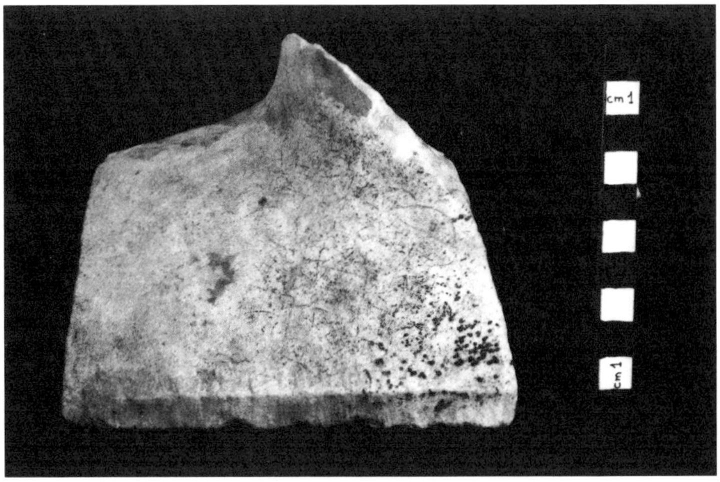
cm 1
cm 1

30. Fragment of a shoulder bust (no. 26)

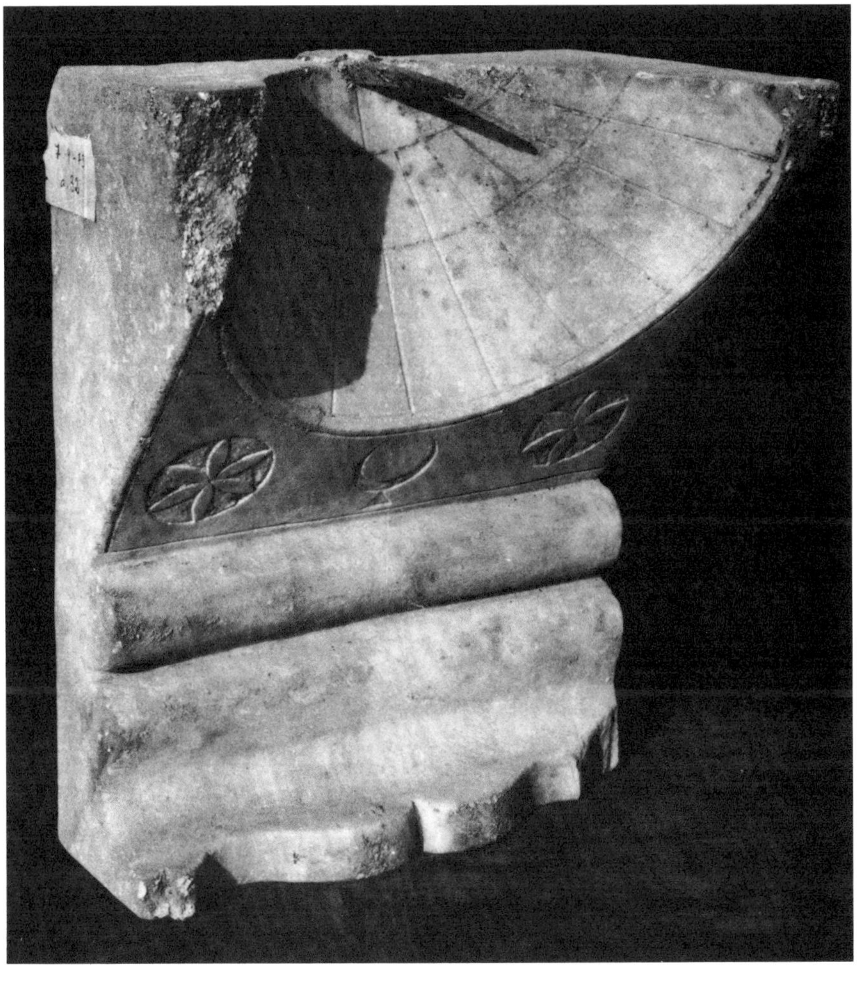

31. Sundial (no. 34)

two rosettes and a crescent moon originally painted in red. A similarly elaborate sundial was set up in the precinct of the Pompeian Apollo sanctuary. The spherical bowl is divided into the canonical cunei of the Roman day and into the three curves of the winter solstice, the equinoxes, and the summer solstice[106] more carefully than the majority of the twenty-nine Pompeian sundials found to date.

35. Fragment of a little column with plant carvings (Inv. no. OP. 728). *Fig. 32*

Found on 27 November 1971 in room 29, used as a storeroom. Only a vertical fragment decorated with tendrils having large, scattered leaves is preserved. The column (h. 40 cm) has a central hole probably for a fountain.

36. Fragment of a little column with plant carvings (Inv. no. OP. 518). *Fig. 33*

Found on 4 July 1973 in room 39, a staircase leading up to the slaves' rooms, the cone-shaped column is preserved in its lower part (h. 59 cm; diam. of base 10.7 cm). The base is decorated with acanthus leaves from which tendrils with ovoid leaves and berries grow.

The taste for such columns decorated with plants and executed in an almost toreutic style is very widely diffused in the Roman world. There are many examples in Pompeii, for instance, in the peristyle of the House of the Vettii, as herms or statuette supports[107] or in paintings, particularly 3rd style.[108]

37. Fragment of a little pillar with plant carvings (Inv. no. OP. 729). *Fig. 34*

The fragment was found stored in room 28, north of the lararium on 20 January 1972. The parallelepipedal pillar, of cipollino marble (h. 62 cm; w. 14 cm; d. 6 cm), is decorated in front with shoots of branches and leaves with little birds, and on the sides by a simpler motif of leaves. The back was meant to be leaned against something. On the upper side there is an iron pin from an ancient restoration.

The execution of the figured motif, with sharp angles, very closely recalls the fragment, deriving from another small pillar, reused as the base of the head of the child Dionysos (no. 8). Both can perhaps be dated to the Tiberian period.[109]

38. Fragment of a little pillar (Inv. no. OP. 1358). *Fig. 35*

Found together with no. 37, this parallelepipedal pillar, of very corroded cipollino marble (h. 58 cm; w. 28 cm; d. 10 cm), is decorated on three sides: on the first by a torch inserted in a frame, on the opposite side by leaves, and on the third side by simple moldings.

---

[106] Cf. J. Drecker, *Die Theorie der Sonnenuhren*, Berlin-Leipzig, 1925; S.L. Gibbs, *Greek and Roman Sundials*, New Haven-London, 1976; D. Giorgetti, in *Studi romani*, 24, 3 (1976), 369 ff; cf. also the simpler piece in *Catalogo del Museo Nazionale Romano*, I, 3, Rome, 1982, 185, VII, 11.

[107] Cf. V. Spinazzola, *Le arti decorative in Pompei e nel Museo Nazionale di Napoli*, Milan, 1920, 67; P. Gusman, *La ville impériale de Tiburs. Villa Hadriana*, Paris, 1904, pl. 251, fig. 413; Jashemski, *Gardens*, 35, fig. 54 and 37, fig. 59. For items in the Museo Nazionale Romano cf. *Catalogo*, I, 3, 47; II,15; for a column of larger size see ibid., I, 2, no. 32.

[108] Cf. Spinazzola, *Arti decorative*, 93.

[109] For similar small pillars in the Museo Nazionale Romano cf. *Catalogo*, I, 3, 173; VII, 1; VII, 2, with literature and comparisons. See also *Marmora Lunensia Erratica*, Sarzana, 1983, 215, no. 79, 218, no. 219, 221 (Archaeological Museum of La Spezia).

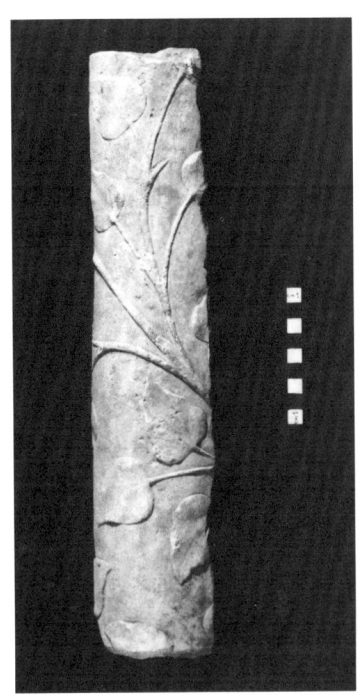

32. Fragment of a little column (no. 35)

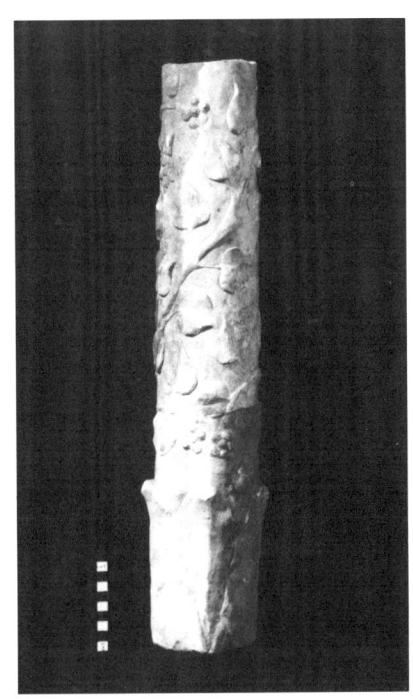

33. Fragment of a little column (no. 36)

34. Fragment of a little pillar (no. 37)

35. Fragment of a little pillar (no. 38)

36 a, b. Fragments of an architectural slab (nos. 39 a, b)

39 *a, b.* Two fragments of an architectural slab with scrolls (*a:* Inv. no. OP. 2815; *b:* not yet inventoried). *Fig. 36a, b*

Fragment *a* was found on 14 March 1978 reused and overturned to form the marble edge of *ambulatio* 90, totally built of reused fragments. Fragment *b* was found on 23 October 1984 in the south garden area behind the little brick pillars east of the pool. The slab, of white marble (*a:* l. 32 cm; h. 22 cm; *b:* l. 27.3 cm; h. 18.2 cm), is decorated with scrolls in which are inserted a crouching Eros and a lizard (Fig. 36a) and another Eros, a crab, and a butterfly (Fig. 36b).[110] On the sides of the slab, once set vertically, there are moldings, one of which is badly cut. The piece, of modest quality, dates to the first half of the first century A.D.

40. Fragment of an architectural slab with scrolls (Inv. no. OP. 2816). *Fig. 37*

Found with no. 39 *a, b* and decorated with scrolls and a flower, the slab, because of its size, seems to have belonged to a different frieze or to another slab. It is of white marble (l. 24 cm; h. 11 cm).

41. Fragment of an architectural slab with scrolls (Inv. no. OP. 2646). *Fig. 38*

Found in portico 60 on 2 March 1976, this piece, of white marble, decorated with scrolls and flowers, also seems to have belonged, because of its size (h. 13 cm; l. 16 cm) and of the molding of the cornices, to a different slab from nos. 39 and 40.

---

[110] Cf. J.M.C. Toynbee and J.B. Ward-Perkins, "Peopled Scrolls: An Hellenistic Motif in Imperial Art," *Papers of the British School at Rome*, 18 (1950), 1 ff; see also T. Kraus, *Die Ranken der Ara Pacis. Ein Beitrag zur Entwicklungsgeschichte der augusteischer Ornamentik*, Berlin, 1953.

SCULPTURE FOUND AT THE VILLA AT OPLONTIS

37. Fragment of a slab with scrolls (no. 40)

38. Fragment of a slab with scrolls (no. 41)

39. Cast impression of a slab with scrolls (no. 42)

42. Another fragment of a slab with scrolls. *Fig. 39*

Found with nos. 39 and 40 in *ambulatio* 90, this fragment (h. 22 cm; l. 1.48 m) is preserved as a cast impression on the plaster that attached the slab to the wall. The absence of the slab, if due to the earthquake of A.D. 62, could testify that the monument from which fragments 39–42 came had been destroyed even before the earthquake. The following two pieces might also be assigned to this hypothesized monument.

43. Fragments of a marble slab with an inscription (Inv. no. OP. 2791). *Fig. 40*

Found overturned as a threshold between two pillars in *ambulatio* 91, the slab (h. 20 cm; l. 79 cm) still preserves good red-painted and engraved letters: .... M. AEDICVLAM.... The size and quality of the letters seem to indicate that it may have belonged to a public inscription, perhaps once in Pompeii.

44. Fragment of a slab (Inv. no. OP. 2789). *Fig. 41*

This slab, of white marble (46 × 18 × 3 cm), was found on 15 November 1977 reused as a socle of one of the walls in passage 85. Rectangular and framed by moldings, it shows in its central frame an Eros offering a fruit to a cock. The workmanship is very poor.

45. Athena. *Fig. 42*

To this list of marble sculptures must be added another one said to have been found at the end of the nineteenth or the beginning of the twentieth century in the area of the modern building occupying the southwest corner of the villa. The sculpture is now lost. It is said to have been exported abroad, but there is a photograph of the piece used on the label of the mineral water that springs up near the findspot. The water was called "Minerva," deriving its name from the sculpture. To judge from the very poor photograph, the sculpture was a herm on a pillar. The goddess, if we accept the traditional identification, is represented facing forward with a large mass of hair dressed in the snail fashion of the archaic style.

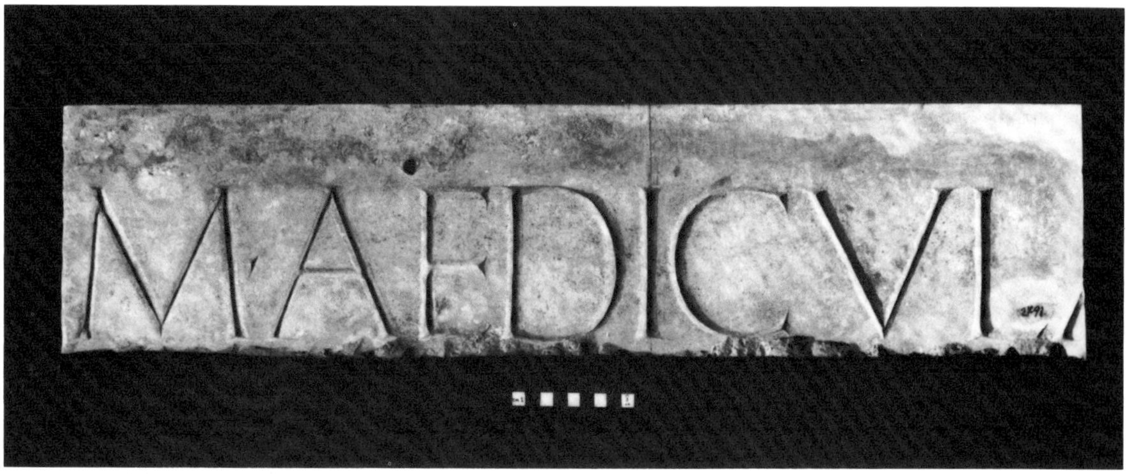
M AEDICVL

40. Fragment of an inscription (no. 43)

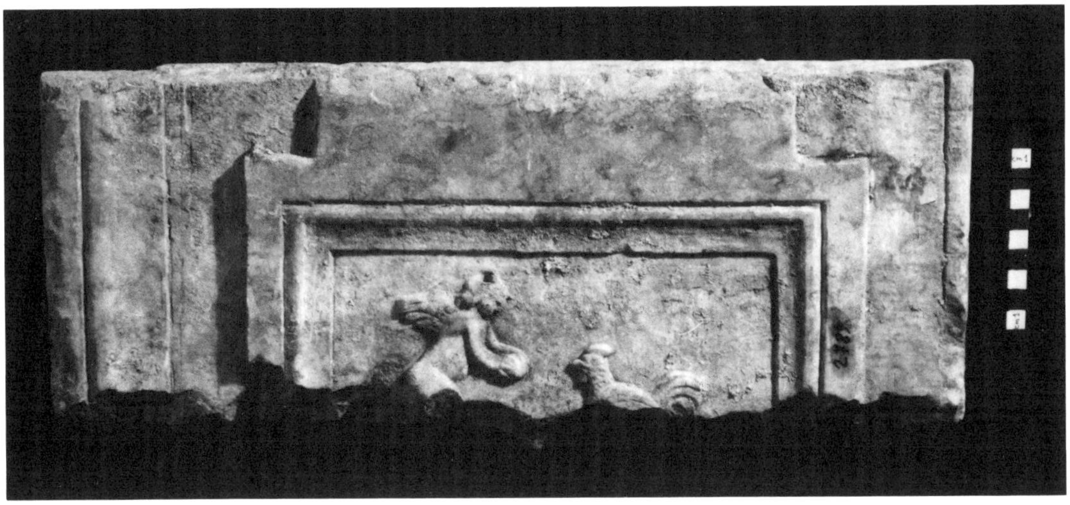

41. Fragment of a slab with an Eros and a cock (no. 44)

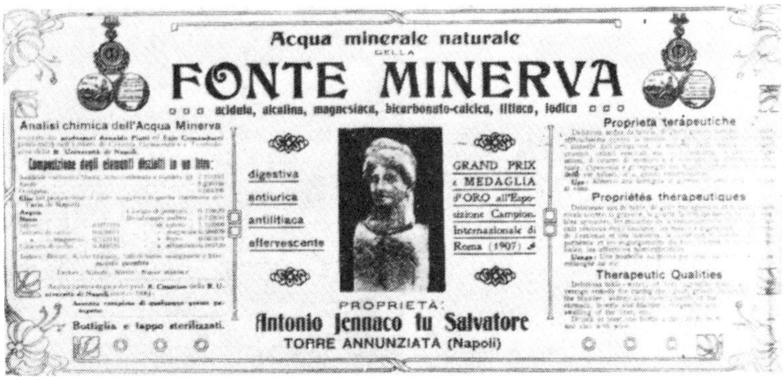
Acqua minerale naturale
DELLA
FONTE MINERVA
acidula, alcalina, magnesiaca, bicarbonato-calcica, litiaca, iodica
Analisi chimica dell'Acqua Minerva
Proprietà terapeutiche
digestiva
antiurica
antilitiaca
effervescente
GRAND PRIX e MEDAGLIA d'ORO all'Esposizione Campionaria Internazionale di Roma (1907)
Propriétés thérapeutiques
Therapeutic Qualities
Bottiglia e tappo sterilizzati.
PROPRIETÀ:
Antonio Jennaco fu Salvatore
TORRE ANNUNZIATA (Napoli)

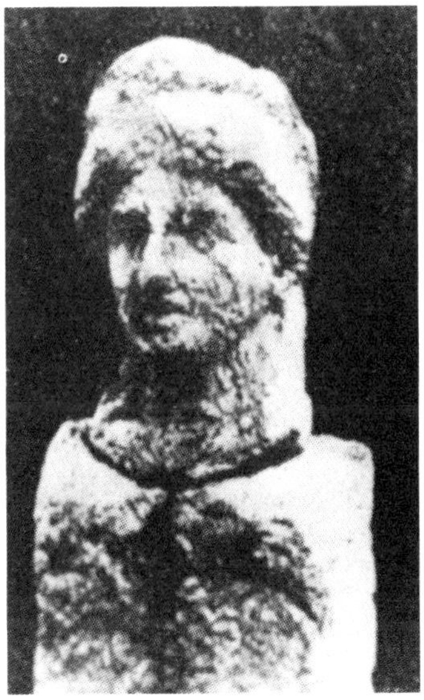

42. Athena herm (no. 45), from an old photograph used as a label (Archeoclub Oplontis)

43. Terracotta bust of a goddess (no. 46)

44. Fragments of a terracotta figure (no. 47)

Before concluding the catalogue I want to mention two terracotta sculptures because, owing to their size, they also played a role in the decoration of the villa, even if unfortunately we do not know their original locations and their relationship to the marble sculptures.

46. Shoulder bust of a goddess (Inv. no. OP. 521). *Fig. 43*

The sculpture was found on 11 January 1974 in many pieces in a hole in the pavement of room 55, excavated and still open at the time of the eruption. The goddess wears a chiton richly folded and tied tightly under the breast by a belt knotted in the center. A mantle covers the shoulders and the back. The head, facing forward, has the archaistic features of large almond-shaped eyes, closed mouth, and hairstyle. There are traces of white-colored slip and of colors. The bust (h. 31 cm; l. 26 cm) is similar to one, smaller in size but very close in style, found in the central peristyle of the House of the Citharist in Pompeii (I.iv.5.25).[111]

47. Fragments of a female bust (or statue) (Inv. no. OP. 2784). *Fig. 44*

The fragments (22 × 21 cm) were found in portico 60 on 20–29 April 1977. Since many of the pieces are still missing, it has been impossible to reconstruct the figure. We can, however, say that it was life-size and wore a chiton in the style of Hellenistic-type maidens.

---

[111] Dwyer, *Sculpture*, 97, XXIV, fig. 164. Such busts are very common in the Hellenistic world; see, for example, J. Raeder, *Priene. Funde aus einer griechischen Stadt*, Berlin, 1983, 36, no. 32, figs. 16, 17a. As for the Gulf of Naples area, see strict comparisons in the Neapolitan ex-votos from a sanctuary on the acropolis: M.R. Borriello and A. De Simone, "La stipe di S. Aniello," in *Napoli Antica*, catalogue of the exhibition, Naples, 1985, 159 ff, especially 163–164, nos. 26, 14.

CONCLUSIONS

Having concluded this brief catalogue of the sculptures, one must now try to understand if in this remarkable sculpture collection there was a logic that led to the choice of these pieces by the owner and to their placement in the villa. First of all, we may note the great difference between the sculptural furnishings in a villa like this and in the houses of Pompeii. It is enough to glance through the last work of E.J. Dwyer on some sculptural groups from Pompeian houses to see how much richer the villa is in both the number and, above all, in the importance of its pieces than any Pompeian house. There *oscilla*, small animals, herms, and Dionysiac figurines are dominant; here, in addition to the bucolic theme and to the garden pieces (the centaurs, the fountain statuettes, the boy with a duck, the crab, and so on), there is a true gallery of sculptures of celebrated moments of Greek art: Skopas, the Polykleitan school, *opera nobilia* (either copies, *imitationes*, or *aemulationes*), which Pompeii lacks almost totally and which provide a measure of the provincial level of the artistic culture of the town and, at the same time, of the Roman-urban cultural level of this villa.

In the second place, as for the function, we recall that almost all the sculptures found until now in the villa are garden pieces.[112] This is clear because of the subjects of the sculptures (centaurs, satyr, and so on) as well as the actual location in which they have been found. On the other hand, none of the rooms of the villa bears any trace of bases testifying to the display of sculpture on the interior, unlike the Villa of the Papyri where statues were set in the atrium, in the upper portico, and in many other rooms. The only inner areas where we can hypothesize sculptural decoration are the apses of rooms 65 and 74, suitable for statuettes such as the Aphrodite unlacing her sandal or the lararium for the little religious statues such as Fortuna. The sculptural decoration is essentially conceived as a garden decoration, and primarily for the two main gardens of the villa, the one north of the old nucleus and the one east of the *natatio*.

The north garden had, as we have seen, the four centaurs and female centaurs group, originally perhaps around a fountain possibly located on the axis of the central path. Afterward they were placed on the sides of that same path, creatures peopling the vegetation of the garden in the same way as satyrs, Sileni, and wild and small woodland animals were immersed in the green of the gardens of Pompeii, conferring on them an atmosphere of mythic and epigrammatic vitality. Remarkable, on the other hand, is the subtle counterpoint that distinguishes the centaurs bearing objects of human use, like the crater and the lyre, from those with the game or wild animals—an antithesis between wild nature and civilized nature probably already present in the Hellenistic prototypes which were also created for garden decoration.

One must recognize a different significance in the row of heads and portraits along the diagonal path in the same garden: two heads of gods, an Aphrodite and the boy

---

[112] For sculpture in Roman (and Greek) gardens: Jashemski, *Gardens*, passim; Dwyer, *Sculpture*, passim; H. Döhl, "La scultura," in *Pompei 79* (above, n. 7), 201 ff; D.K. Hill, "Some Sculpture from Roman Domestic Gardens," in *Ancient Roman Gardens*, Washington, D.C., 1981, 81 ff; B. Sismondo Ridgway, "Greek Antecedents of Garden Sculpture," ibid., 7 ff.

45. View of the south side of the *natatio* with some of the sculptures (nos. 13, 15, 16, 11, 12) replaced in their findspots

Dionysos, and two portraits, probably of the owner's family, a lady and a boy. Despite the caution necessary because the excavations are not yet concluded (other sculptures must be under the northern scarp and others near the opposite west diagonal path), I think that the combination of gods and humans is not casual. Though not a more or less explicit deification, nevertheless the sequence of a human child and a child-god, of a human woman and a goddess could not but suggest to the people walking in the garden gratifying comparisons—and that without the pomposity of an exhibition in an atrium or a *tablinum* but with the casualness of a walk in the park. The correspondence gods-humans (and the flattering allusion) becomes even more pertinent if we accept the identification of the portraits as those of a mother and her son: the same mother-son relationship could then be suggested, according to a well-accredited version of the myth, between Aphrodite and Dionysos.

As for the crater and the group of the Satyr and the Hermaphrodite on the south side of the *natatio* (Fig. 45), they create no difficulty: I have already spoken of the use of the craters in *natationes*; I now suggest the possibility that the Oplontis vase originally stood in the center of an apse, as in the villa of San Marco in Stabiae, which would give a greater significance to its original function as a fountain. As for the *symplegma*, it must be compared to the other erotic group, wilder still, of Pan and the goat, which stood on the edge of the *natatio* of the Villa of the Papyri, or with the group of the boar attacked by dogs from the basin of the House of the Citharist in Pompeii, echoes of a world of satyrs and animals, of a wild nature evoked in the cultured order of a garden. In the east garden of the *natatio* the sequence of the statues leaning against the trees formed in itself an architectural movement that was a natural counterpart to the colonnade on the opposite side of the pool: an open-air gallery which could be enjoyed as a whole by the people walking along portico 60 beyond the narrow sheet of water or individually by people walking near the sculptures.

Moreover, we may note that the statues are in a slightly oblique line in relation to the edge of the pool and that the divergence of these lines proceeds from north to south. This is probably because the diagonal line of trees on whose roots the brick bases of the statues are built existed before the pool. Nevertheless, it is possible that the decision to respect the line of the trees and not a parallelism with the side of the pool was also made so that the statues would not overlap but appear all together in a fanlike arrangement. Probably the optical cone was intended to highlight the southern end of the basin with the background of the pergola and, beyond it, of the sea.

The complex of statues is then in some ways comparable to that of the Villa of the Papyri, but on a smaller scale. The superiority of the Herculanean villa's statuary is shown not only by the number of statues and the intrinsically greater value of the many bronze sculptures found there and totally lacking in this one, but also by the wider range of subjects such as statues of Hellenistic kings, philosophers, and other personages lacking in the villa at Oplontis. So while in the Villa of the Papyri the interplay of correspondences is more articulated with couples, groups, and twin figures, here in Oplontis the statues are more regularly placed in a row, at regular distances, with the constant rhythm of the trees against which they were set. The couples that the twin statues of Herakles and Nike evidently formed are opened to set up more distant correspondences in a discourse that, in spite of the incompleteness of the series (the sculptures of pillars I, II, VI, VII, VIII, and IX are missing), I believe it is possible to reconstruct. In the succession (from the south) Herakles, Ephebe, Nike, and Nike, Amazon, Herakles, we find clearly a sequence of the type A, B, C .... C, B, A: one would expect to find in the central empty spaces another two couples of twin statues completing the symmetry. If this is true and not only an entirely coincidental occurrence, the choice of the figures too cannot be casual or only imposed by symmetry: the clue, in my opinion, lies in the two figures of the Ephebe and the Artemis. In fact they both represent the Greek athletic ideal, the first one in the male, the second one in the female version, in whichever mythic figures they could be identified. A well-known passage of Pliny the Elder confirms that the Romans had no sense of the exact identification of such figures, appreciated as gymnasium symbols: "Placuere et nudae tenentes hastam ab epheborum e gymnasiis exemplaribus quas Achilleas vocant." ("They also appreciated naked figures of youths holding a spear, from the statues of the ephebes in the gymnasia, and they called such figures Achilleans.")[113] In this description we must recognize the sculptures of the Polykleitan and late Polykleitan ephebes, from the most famous of all, the Dory-

---

[113] Pliny *HN* 34.18.

phoros, to our Oplontis ephebe. Athletic statues are represented in the same way in stucco in the apses of the *natatio* of the villa at San Marco in Stabiae.[114] The heads of the Skopasian Herakles also receive a perfect explanation from the perspective of the athletic ideal and of the gymnasium atmosphere, and all the more so if it was that of the gymnasium of Sikyon; and, in the same way, the Nike can be explained as the goddess of Victory in the contests. Thus this is a collection of γυμνασιώδης sculpture that transforms the whole area into a Greek-style gymnasium in which the large pool is perfectly explained as an actual *natatio*, a swimming pool in which Roman youths could compete over a distance of 200 (Roman) feet or run on the path alongside it under the eyes of the Protector Gods and Heroes.

This is in complete harmony with both the Hellenizing tendencies of Roman Republican culture and with the main lines of the Augustan policy toward youth which expressed itself in institutions like games and associations and in monuments like the large palaestras (for instance, those of Herculaneum and Pompeii), where the new youth of the Principate could train both the spirit and the body for the future formation of the perfect *civis romanus*. And it would not be inappropriate for this Oplontis villa gymnasium if the lost Athena head (no. 45) could be proved to come from there, the same goddess of wisdom to whom were sacred, in the Roman conception of the Greek paideia, the gymnasia. Let us recall the well-known passage of the first letter of Cicero to Atticus: "Hermathena tua valde me delectat et posita ita belle est, ut totum gymnasium eius ἀνάθημα esse videatur." ("I am highly delighted with your Hermathena, and have found such a good position for it, that the whole class-room seems but an offering at its feet.")[115]

I believe that even this partial reconstruction of the decorative program at Oplontis is coherent, yet the progress of the exploration has very recently shown a greater complexity; a start of a second row of pillars for statues and possibly of a second path east on the east side of the *natatio* have been found, while the new portrait of the Julio-Claudian boy (no. 19) seems to enrich this sector of the villa with a new figural theme.

---

[114] Ward-Perkins and Claridge, *Pompei A.D. 79*, no. 251.
[115] Cic. *Att.* 1.1; trans. E.O. Winstedt, Loeb ed., London-New York, 1912.

APPENDIX[116]

I have already mentioned the difficulties involved in attempting to determine the ownership of the villa at Oplontis during the first phase of its existence. This attempt becomes even more difficult for the succeeding phase in the imperial era. However, for that period we do have some clues, which allowed de Franciscis to propose a convincing hypothesis:[117] the discovery in the villa of an amphora of the Julio-Claudian period with an inscription painted in red, "(. . .)cundo Poppaeae," which, on the basis of a graffito on the bottom of an Italic platter in *terra sigillata*, he proposed to complete as "(Se)cundo Poppaeae," that is, "To Secundus, slave of Poppaea." De Franciscis has identified the owner of the villa as Poppaea Sabina, from A.D. 62 consort of Nero and, from A.D. 63, Augusta who, according to the evidence of a Herculanean wax tablet, was owner of a pottery in the Pompeian suburbs ("in Pompeiano in figlinis Arrianis Poppaeae Aug[ustae]").[118] Other arguments in support of de Franciscis' hypothesis are the discovery of a wine-jar stamp, "C. Arriani Amphionis," which recalls the "figlinae Arrianae" of the Herculanean tablet,[119] and a graffito, μνησθητι Βηρυλλος (may Beryllos be remembered), which has been connected with Beryllos, a freedman of Nero mentioned by Flavius Josephus.[120] This seems sufficient evidence to accept de Franciscis' theory. The grandioseness of the villa in its second phase precludes, even more than in the first phase, the possibility of a local owner, and, if we accept the validity of the date of the inscription on the amphora, we cannot then propose some Pompeian Poppaea of the local *gens* Poppaei, but think only of Poppaea Sabina Augusta.

M. Della Corte had already suggested identifying the *gens* Poppaea of Pompeii with the family that sent two consuls to Rome in A.D. 9, the *consul ordinarius* Q. Poppaeus Sabinus and the *consul suffectus* Q. Poppaeus Secundus.[121] In addition, he had proposed identifying the Pompeian Olii with the *gens* of T. Ollius, briefly husband of the daughter of Q. Poppaeus Sabinus, Poppaea Sabina, famous for her beauty (and it would seem for her behavior), the mother of Poppaea Sabina, later Augusta. The arguments of Della Corte, echoed by C. Giordano[122] (inscriptions that include names of the Poppaei and acclamations in honor of Nero), are perhaps not enough to establish the Pompeian origins of the Poppaei; one need only recall the total absence of the two consular Poppaei in the public inscriptions of that city. Nevertheless, a connection remains between the city of Pompeii and the Roman Poppaei; Nero's visit to the Temple of Venus in

---

[116] Translated from the Italian by E.B. MacDougall.

[117] Cf. de Franciscis, "Villa romana" (1975) (above, n. 1), 15–18.

[118] Cf. V. Arangio-Ruiz and G. Pugliese Carratelli, "Tabulae Herculanenses," *Parola del passato*, 34 (1954), 56 ff.

[119] Normally it should have been "in figlinis Arrianiis," with two *i*'s, if it was connected with C. Arrianius Amphio: nevertheless, a single *i* is also possible.

[120] Cf. de Franciscis, "Beryllos e la villa 'di Poppea' ad Oplontis" (above, n. 1).

[121] M. Della Corte, *Case e abitanti di Pompei*, 3rd ed., Naples, 1965, 293 ff.

[122] C. Giordano, "Iscrizioni graffiti e dipinti nella casa di C. Giulio Polibio," *Rendiconti dell'Accademia di Archeologia, Lettere e Belle Arti di Napoli*, 50 (1975), 29 ff.

Pompeii, which brought a donation of "millia milliorum pondera auri,"[123] was emphatically recorded in a graffito in the House of Julius Polybius together with another that reports a gift by Poppaea (Augusta) of a beryl and two pearls to the same goddess ("Munera Poppaea misit Veneri sanctissimae berullum helencumque; unio mixtus erat"), gifts that testify to the generosity of the two Augusti to the city after the earthquake of A.D. 62 and in any case to Poppaea's special concern for Pompeii.

The Pompeian Poppaei seem to have been, to judge from the political rank they achieved (the aedileship in A.D. 61),[124] most probably former freedmen and agents (*procuratores*) of the Roman Poppaei and those proprietors of the lead-pipe workshops and perhaps of a villa at Puteoli (Pozzuoli), as we saw in "figlinae," related without doubt to a farm at Pompeii, as well as a property at Stabiae, now known from some recently discovered inscriptions. And that these properties were already relatively old is shown by the fact that the *sponsor* of the little tablet displayed *in Pompeiano* in the "figlinae Arrianae" was P. Cornelius Poppaeus Erast(us), probably given the function of a sponsor, the superintendent of the pottery. The name of this person testifies that he or his father was an ex-slave of the Poppaei adopted by one P. Cornelius: this association is explained by the fact that Poppaea Sabina *mater*'s second husband, following her marriage to T. Ollius, was P. Cornelius Lentulus Scipio (*cos. suffectus* in A.D. 24). The slave belonging to the Poppaei, therefore, became the property of P. Cornelius Lentulus as part of his wife's dowry and was freed by him. The fact that the "figlinae Arrianae" were inherited by Poppaea Sabina Augusta and not by her half-brother, P. Cornelius Scipio Asiaticus, demonstrates that they were really part of the Poppaei estate, that is, belonging to Poppaea Sabina *mater* and before that to the father, Q. Poppaeus Sabinus, *consul ordinarius* in A.D. 9.

If the "figlinae Arrianae" of Poppaea Sabina Augusta can be linked with the Poppaea estate in Pompeii and the Oplontis villa is one of its properties, there is then the possibility that the ownership of the villa could go back to Q. Poppaeus Sabinus who having attained "principum amicitia consulatum ac triumphale decus," and having governed "maximis provinciis per quattuor et vigenti annos,"[125] could have acquired either by purchase or inheritance such a property and the others in Campania. But since his estate was inherited by his daughter at his death in A.D. 35, apparently without other heirs, it is more likely that her husband, P. Cornelius Lentulus Scipio, who was a member of the highest senatorial aristocracy, was responsible for the extensive enlargement of the western part of the villa, perhaps as a continuation of a project already initiated by Poppaeus Sabinus. At the death of the mother, who committed suicide in A.D. 47 (the head, cat. no. 7, might be her portrait), the villa then passed with the hereditary estate of the Poppaei to the daughter, Poppaea Sabina, then a young girl (between fifteen and seventeen years of age), perhaps not yet married to her first husband, Rufrius Crispinus

---

[123] Ibid., 22, n. 5.
[124] *Corpus Inscriptionum Latinarum*, X, 827.
[125] Tac. *Ann.* 6.39.

(praetorian prefect in A.D. 47). The death of Poppaea in A.D. 65 would then explain the slowness of the repairs at the villa.

If this string of hypotheses is true, then one may ask whether the silver treasure discovered in the House of Menander in Pompeii[126] might not have belonged to the villa at Oplontis. It consists of 121 pieces of finely decorated tableware, the most precious service ever found at Pompeii, certainly inappropriate for the Pompeian house, which, although beautiful, is not exceptional among the private buildings of Pompeii. That the Poppaei owned the house is confirmed by the discovery of the "signaculum Erotis, Q(uinti) Poppaei," which names the overseer in charge of the house. We could, therefore, suppose—although it is clear that this is purely conjecture—that the silver had been taken from the villa, for whose spacious and sumptuous triclinia a similar service would have been appropriate, to await the completion of the villa's renovations at the safer city property under the care of the faithful superintendent.

[126] Cf. A. Maiuri, *La Casa del Menandro*, Rome, 1932.

The Importance of Water
in Roman Garden Triclinia

EUGENIA SALZA PRINA RICOTTI

The role played by water in Roman open-air triclinia has fascinated me ever since, long ago, I read a letter of Pliny the Younger[1] describing his Tuscan villa and its garden. Among other things he spoke at length of an open-air triclinium placed in a secluded part of his estate—a park called the Hippodrome. The description was very detailed, and it was easy to visualize the triclinium[2] (Fig. 1). In the middle of the Hippodrome there was a vine trellis (Fig. 1,a) supported by four columns. Under that pergola a marble *stibadium*,[3] a semicircular tricliniar couch (Fig. 1,b), was set at the edge of a pool. Guests reclined on this couch, and servants standing on the other side of the basin (Fig. 1,c) put the heavy trays on its edge and floated toward the diners the food which was in special vessels shaped like ships and birds. It was a very attractive setting.

Behind the servants another pool spouted a jet of water (Fig. 1,d) high into the air. The perspective was closed by a marble pavilion composed of two rooms: the first one (Fig. 1,e), the larger, had another fountain in it and, very likely, chairs and settees to sit on; the other (Fig. 1,f), an alcove or *zoothecula* as Pliny calls it, was furnished with a comfortable bed.[4] The rays of the sun flowed through its windows, subdued and filtered by the leaves of the vines, and gave a fresh, green, restful illumination to this recess.

In his letter Pliny also describes in detail the charms of the Hippodrome, a delightful garden with many shaded walks, boxwood hedges, topiary bushes cut in interesting shapes, pools, fountains, and marble settees for tired strollers. But we must concentrate on the open-air triclinium that was so original and so pleasant. We can enumerate its distinctive characteristics and establish a typology: the *stibadium* under a canopy of vines; the pool on which the food was floated and which substituted for the usual little table;[5] a place just in front of the pool where the servants could stand when serving and where they could lay the heavier trays; another pool under the open sky, all shining and blue, just in the center of a smooth carpet of fresh, green grass; an agreeable path on which one could stroll at leisure; places to rest and sit in the park; and, to complete the charms

---

[1] Pliny *Ep.* 5.6. All abbreviations for ancient authors and their works are those found in N.G.L. Hammond and H.H. Scullard, eds., *The Oxford Classical Dictionary*, 2nd ed., Oxford, 1970, ix–xxii.

[2] Many people were so fascinated by the letters in which Pliny describes his villas that they tried to reconstruct their plans. Many of these drawings have been collected in a book: H.H. Tanzer, *The Villas of Pliny the Younger*, New York, 1924.

[3] The *stibadium* was a particular form of tricliniar couch that came into fashion around the end of the 1st century A.D. Martial mentions it (Mart. *Epigrammata* 10.48.6; 14.87).

[4] We can deduce from another of Pliny's letters, the one about his Laurentinum (Pliny *Ep.* 2.17), that the *cubiculum*, at least for Pliny, was larger than the *zoothecula*. In fact speaking of the Laurentinum he describes a pavilion with a *cubiculum* and a *zoothecula* in which he used to retire when he wished to be left alone. From what he says one can draw the conclusion that while the *cubiculum* was a regular room, even a large one (in fact it was used as a drawing room), the *zoothecula* was an alcove furnished only with a bed and two chairs.

[5] The table that was placed among the tricliniar couches was nearly always very small and easy to move around. It was just a support for trays. There was no need to have a real table like the ones we use today, ample stands for individual plates, because Romans did not use them and ate with their fingers.

of the place and add to its comfort, a marble pavilion where one could relax lulled by the soothing sounds of crystal-pure waters gushing in the fountains, by the rustle of leaves stirred by a gentle breeze, and by the songs of birds.

I was fascinated by this description. So I did a reconstruction of the *stibadium*, put it in my files, and forgot all about it. I had other research to do at that time. In fact I was very much involved in solving the main problem of the grotto at Sperlonga, and in 1969 I finally succeeded in being the first to find the original position of the Polyphemus group (Fig. 2,a) and in attempting its probable reconstruction.[6] But while I was drawing the plan of the grotto I got interested in one of its triclinia[7] because it was very similar to Pliny's *stibadium*, a dining arrangement that by now I had begun to call a "water triclinium" or a "triclinium with a water *mensa*." The water triclinium of Sperlonga was set on an island in the center of a rocky fishpond and was both a functional and a decorative element of this nymphaeum (Fig. 2,e). Moreover, at that time it was the only example of a water triclinium known from archaeological evidence.

Today the water level in the Sperlonga grotto is much lower than it was originally, and the water triclinium's islet rises more than two feet above the fishpond's surface (Fig. 3); but we can plainly see that in Roman times the top of the island was nearly level with the water in the fishpond. In fact two rows of holes built into its walls as a refuge for the fish in this piscina[8] are now completely out of the water (Fig. 4), while originally they would have been totally submerged. Unfortunately the whole tricliniar island is in very bad shape. Luckily we can still see the small pool of the water triclinium on the grotto side of the island and the little footbridge that served as a place for the slaves to stand while serving the food.

In Roman times the mouth of the grotto extended over the front part of the triclinium. It was here in fact that the accident occurred that endangered Tiberius' life while he was dining in the "praetorium cui speluncae nomen est," as Tacitus[9] and Suetonius[10] relate in their chronicles. It could not have happened elsewhere, for it was the only place where the mouth of the grotto could have collapsed, as it did during that ill-fated banquet. It is easy to reconstruct what happened: in ancient times the mouth of the grotto had to start from the ship's prow sculpted in the last spur of the rocky cliff on the northern side of the nymphaeum. It is the only logical way to explain the existence of this plastic decoration and its abrupt ending in broken and badly jagged bare rock (Fig. 5). On the opposite side the mighty natural arch was buttressed by the steep slope of the cliff. The scars left on the cliff face by the first-century A.D. landslide are still visible, and now the rocks, devoid of all trace of vegetation, form a whitish frame around the nymphaeum entrance (Fig. 6). If we draw the projection of the ancient

---

[6] E. Salza Prina Ricotti, "Il gruppo di Polifemo a Sperlonga," *Rendiconti della Pontificia Accademia Romana di Archeologia* (hereafter *RendPont*), 42 (1969–70), 117–134.

[7] Idem, "Forme speciali di triclinii," *Cronache pompeiane* 5 (1979), 102–149.

[8] L. Jacono, "Note di archeologia marittima," in *Neapolis*, Naples, 1913, 3–4; Columella *Rust.* 8.17.6.

[9] Tac. *Ann.* 4.59.

[10] Suet. *Tib.* 39 in *De vita duodecim Caesarum*.

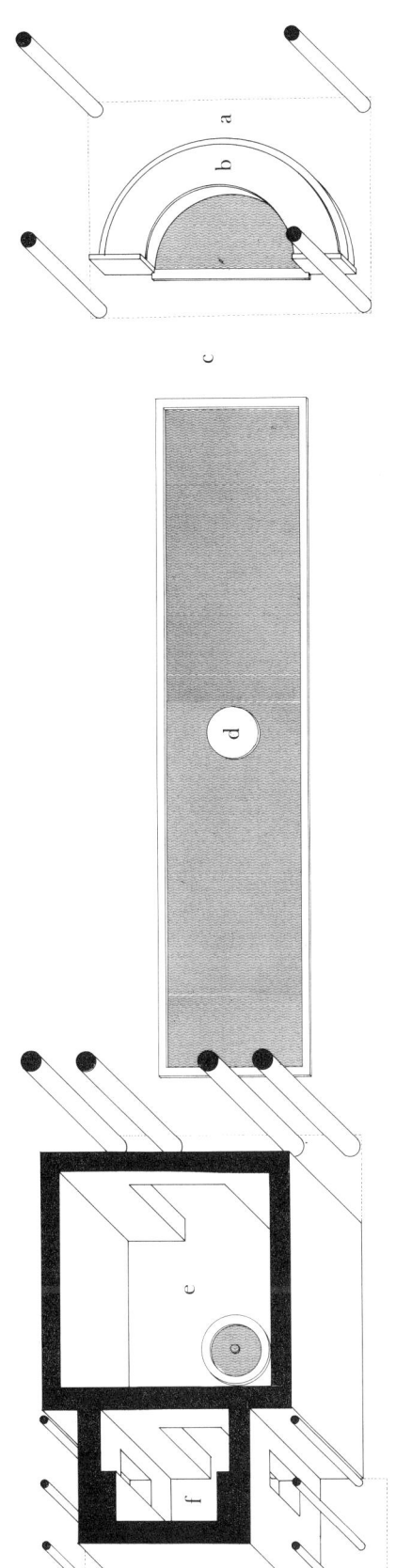

1. Reconstruction of Pliny's *stibadium* (author)

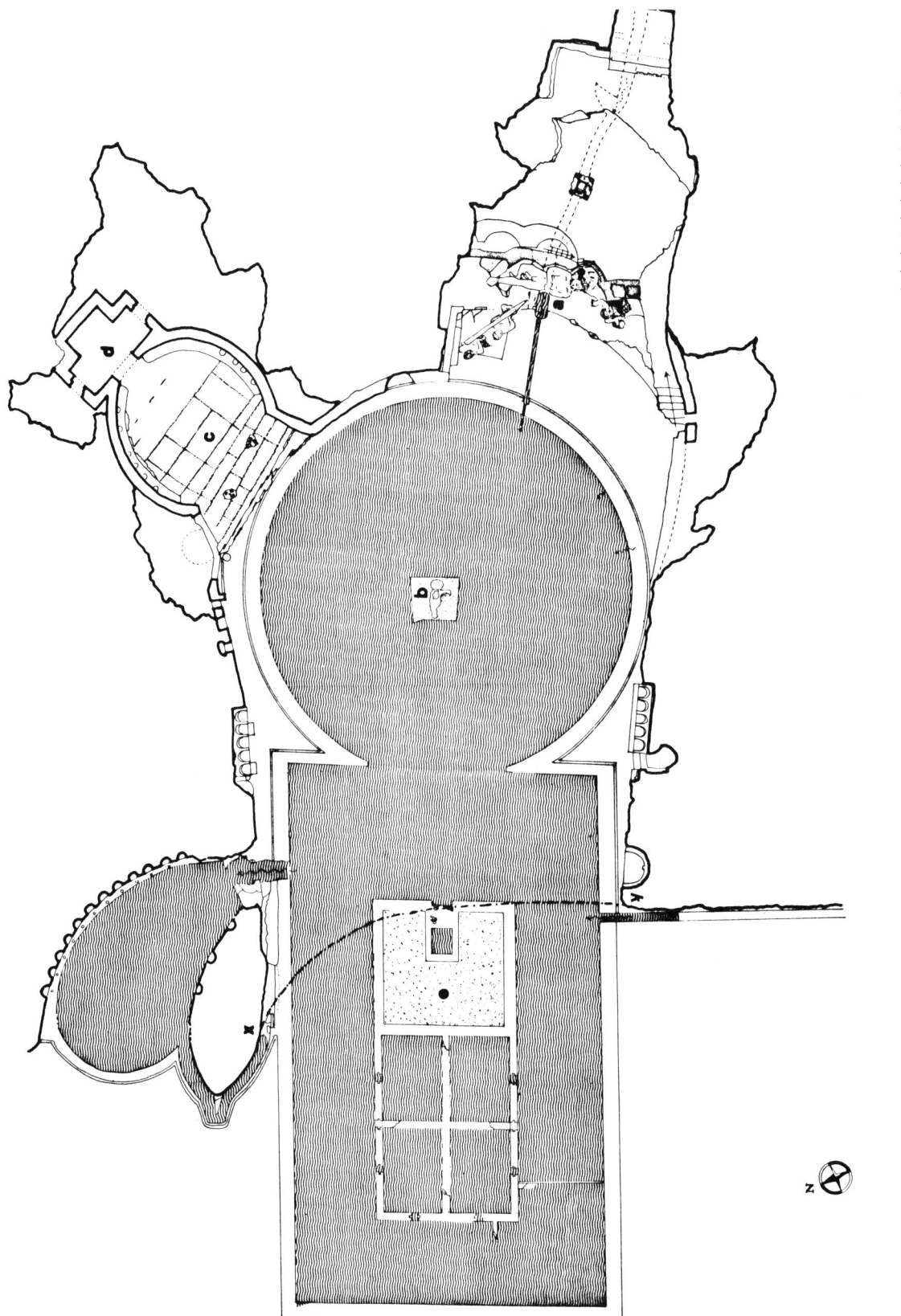

2. Plan of nymphaeum at Sperlonga with the water triclinium (author)

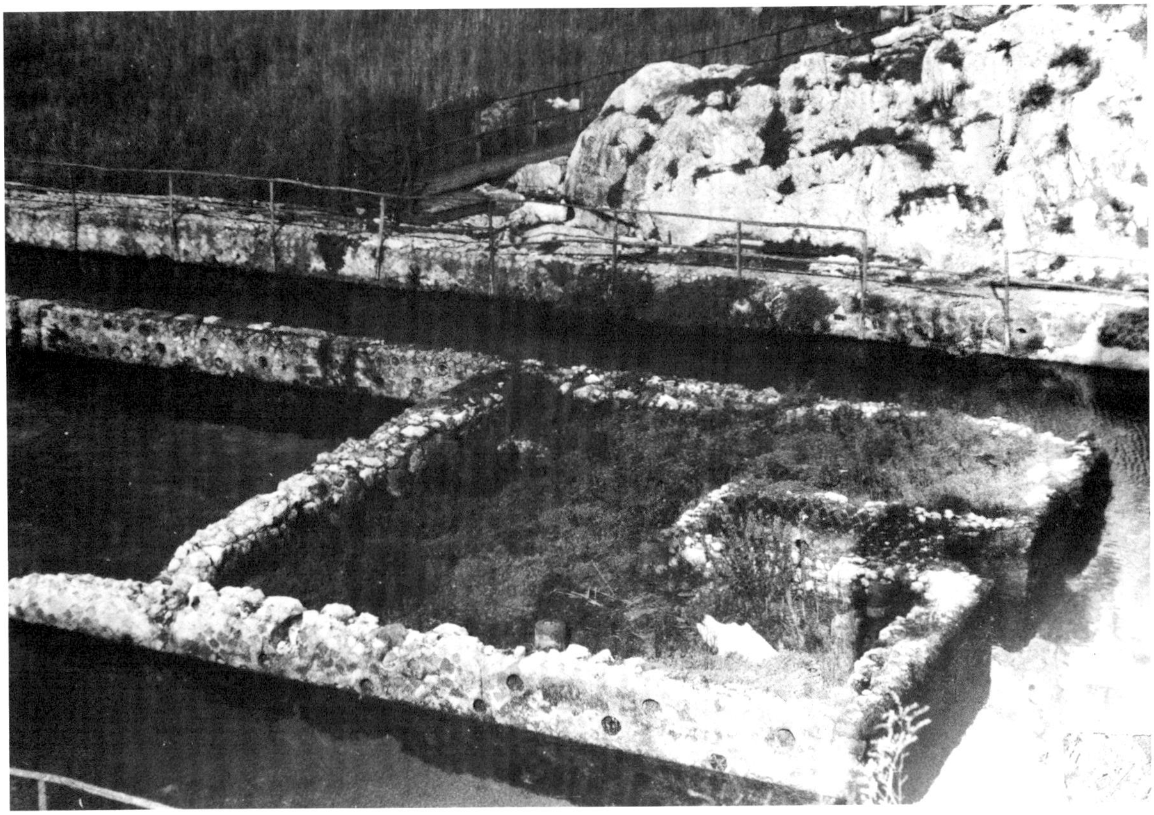

3. Water triclinium of Sperlonga (photo: Germanicum)

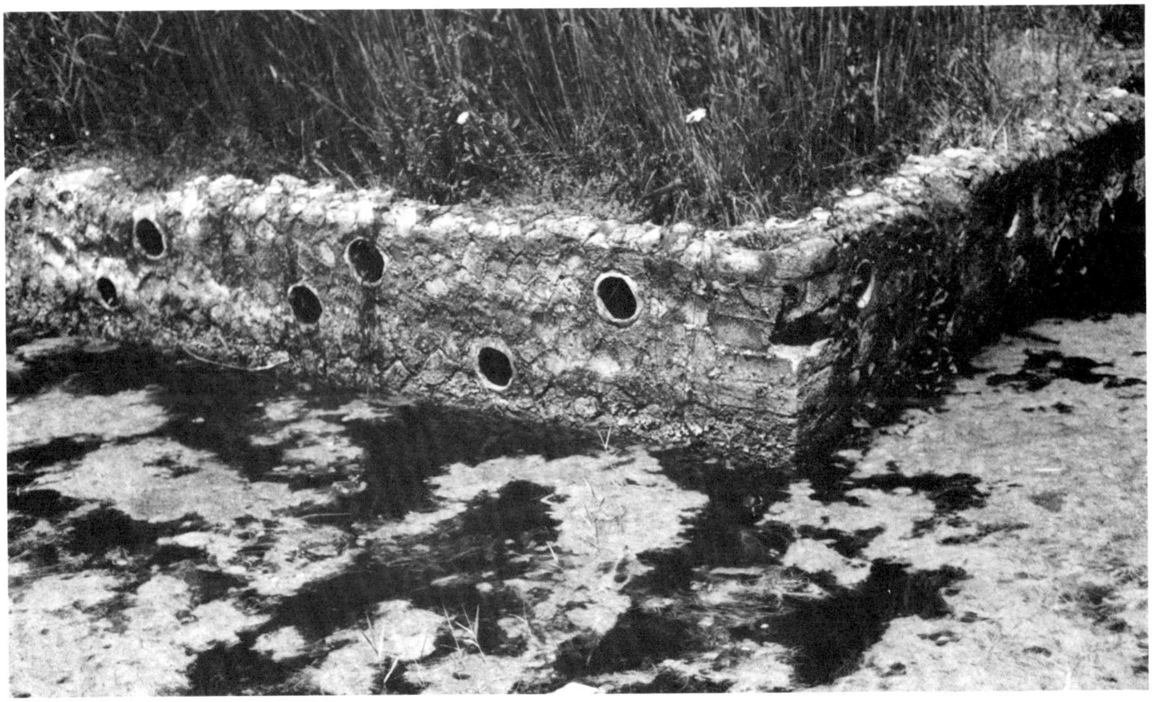

4. Holes for rock fish in the walls of the water triclinium (photo: author)

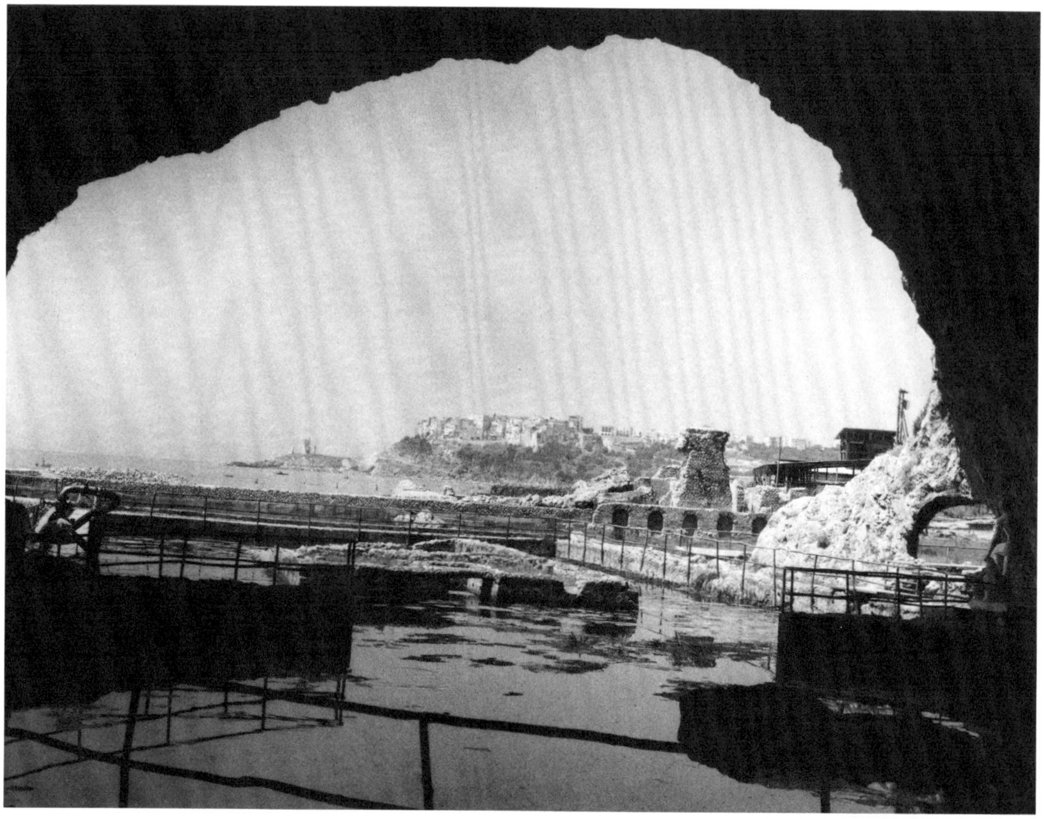

5. Ship's prow, Sperlonga (photo: Germanicum)

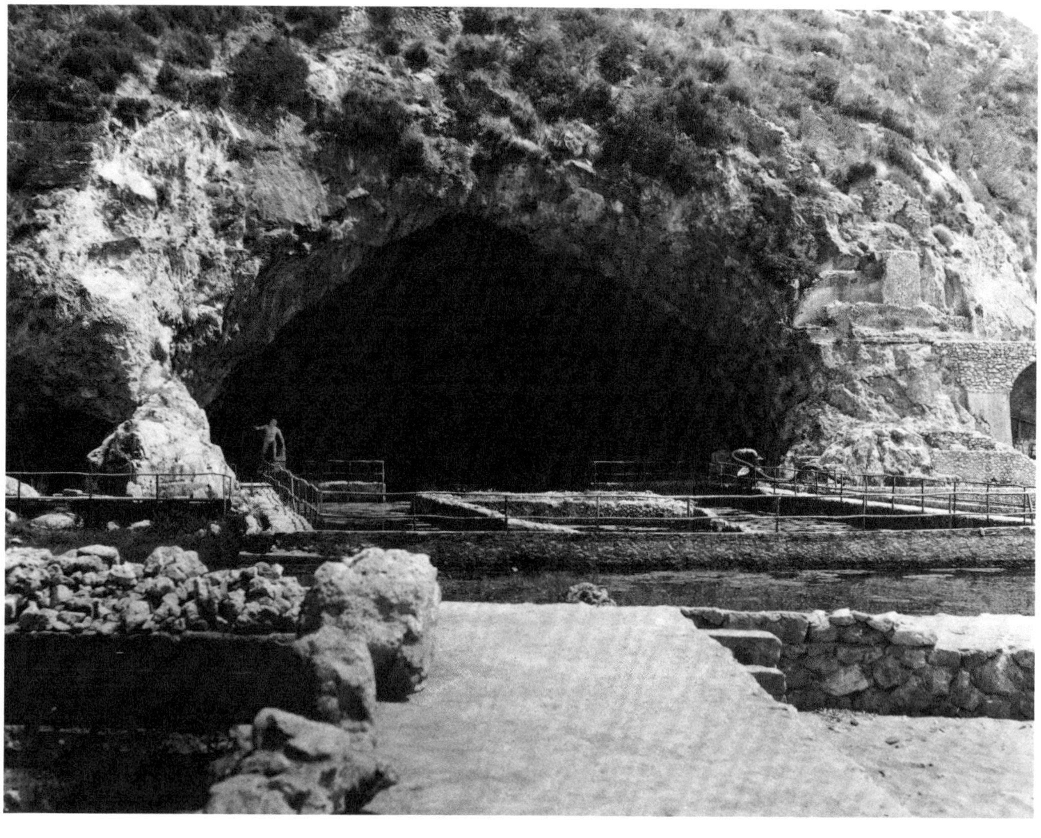

6. Landslide marks on the hillside, Sperlonga (photo: author)

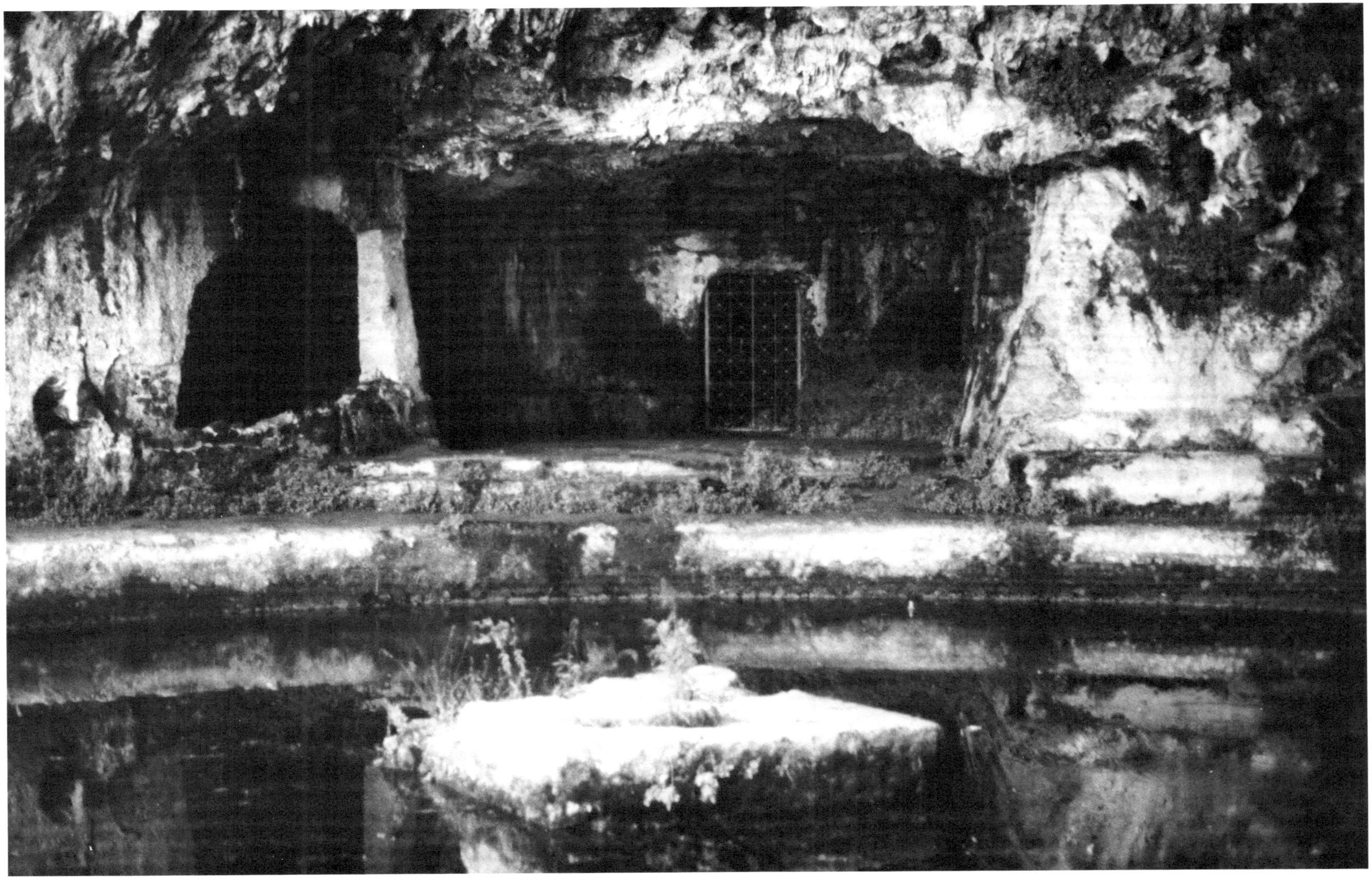

7. Lateral grotto of nymphaeum at Sperlonga (photo: author)

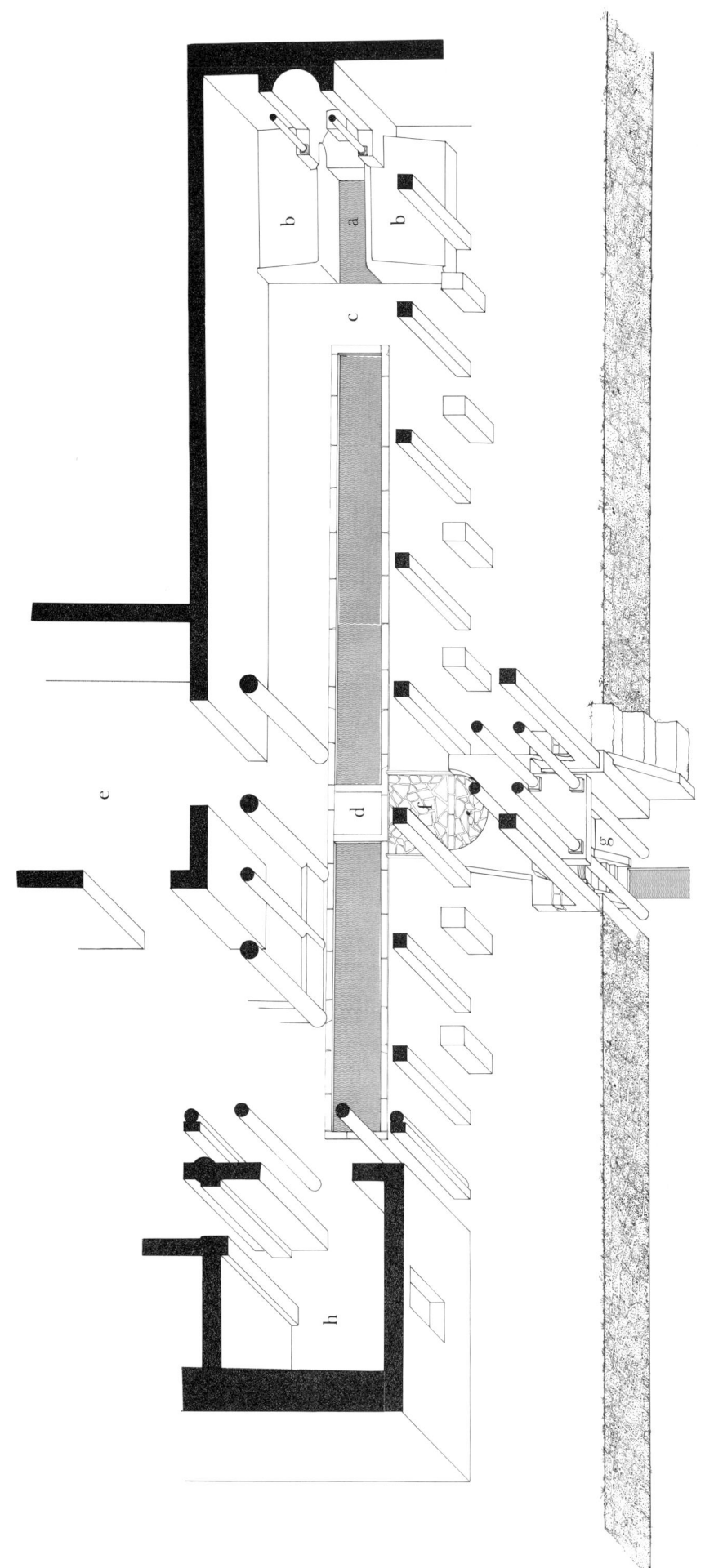

8. Axonometric view of the water triclinium in the House of Loreius Tiburtinus, Pompeii (author)

9. Terrace of the House of Loreius Tiburtinus, Pompeii
(photo: Soprintendenza of Pompeii)

10. Nymphaeum in the garden of the House of Loreius Tiburtinus, Pompeii
(photo: Soprintendenza of Pompeii)

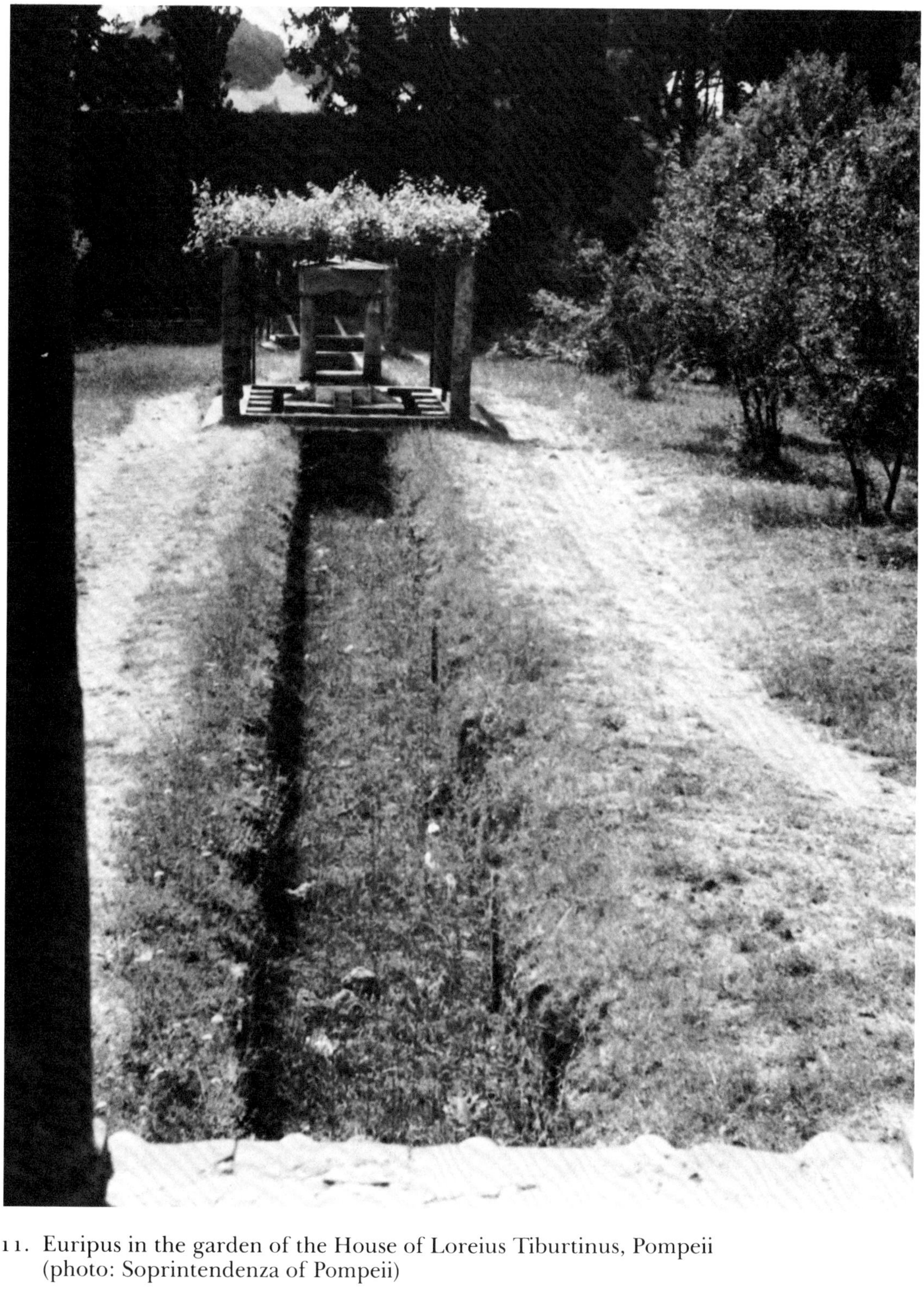

11. Euripus in the garden of the House of Loreius Tiburtinus, Pompeii (photo: Soprintendenza of Pompeii)

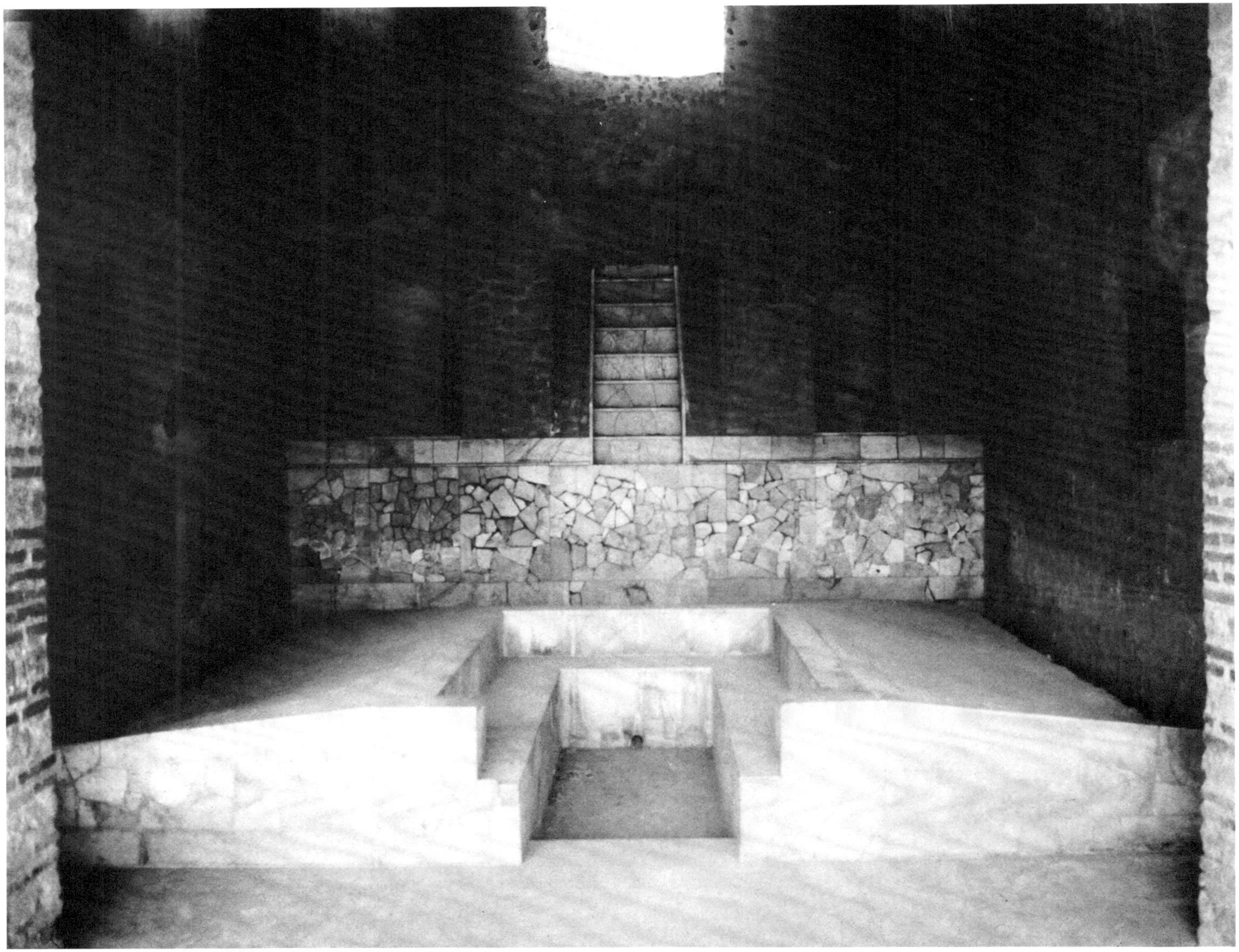

12. Triclinium in the exedra of the peristyle garden in Iulia Felix's praedium, Pompeii (photo: author)

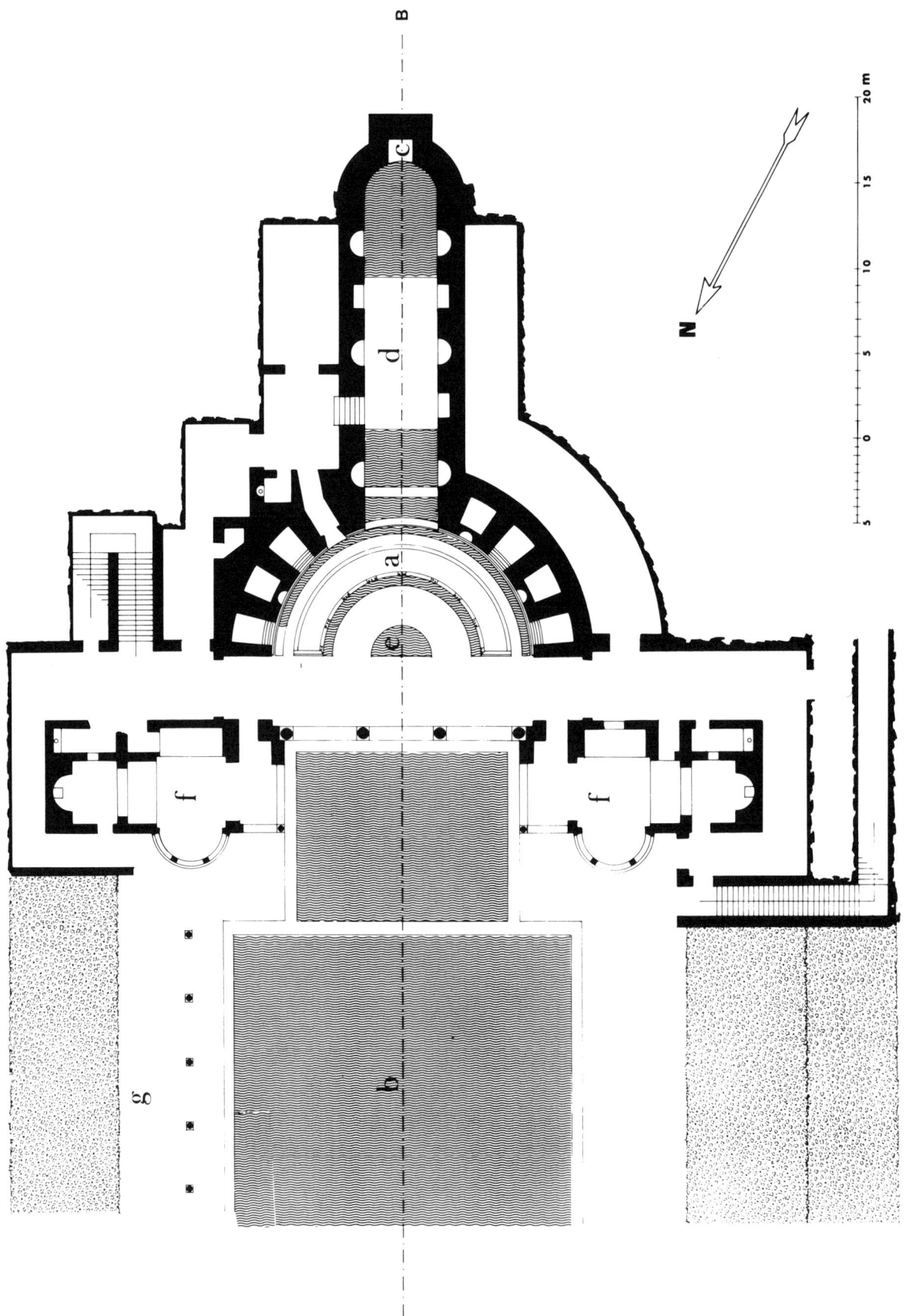

13. Plan of the Canopus of Hadrian's villa (author)

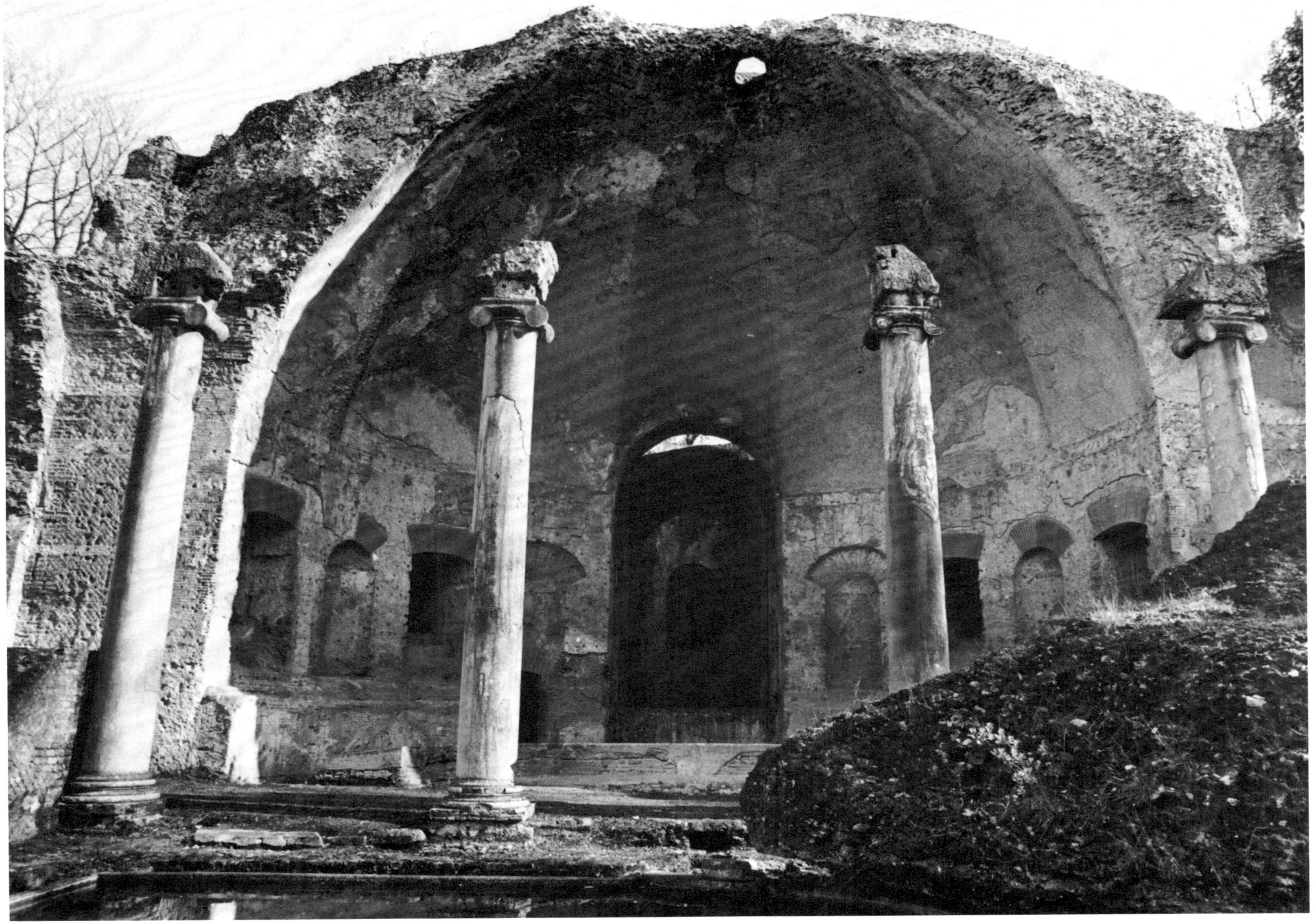

14. Exedra of the Canopus (photo: F. Luciolli)

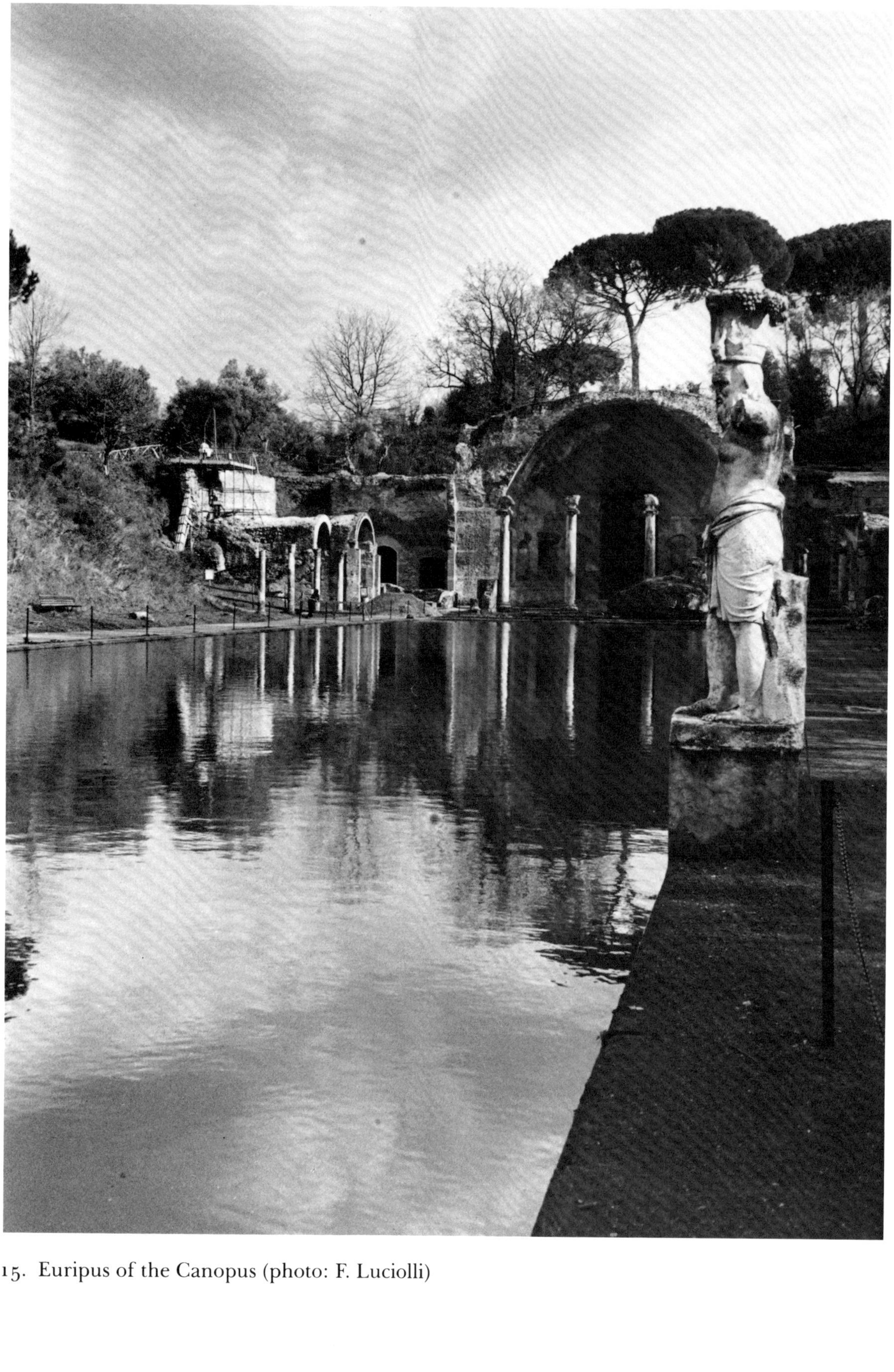

15. Euripus of the Canopus (photo: F. Luciolli)

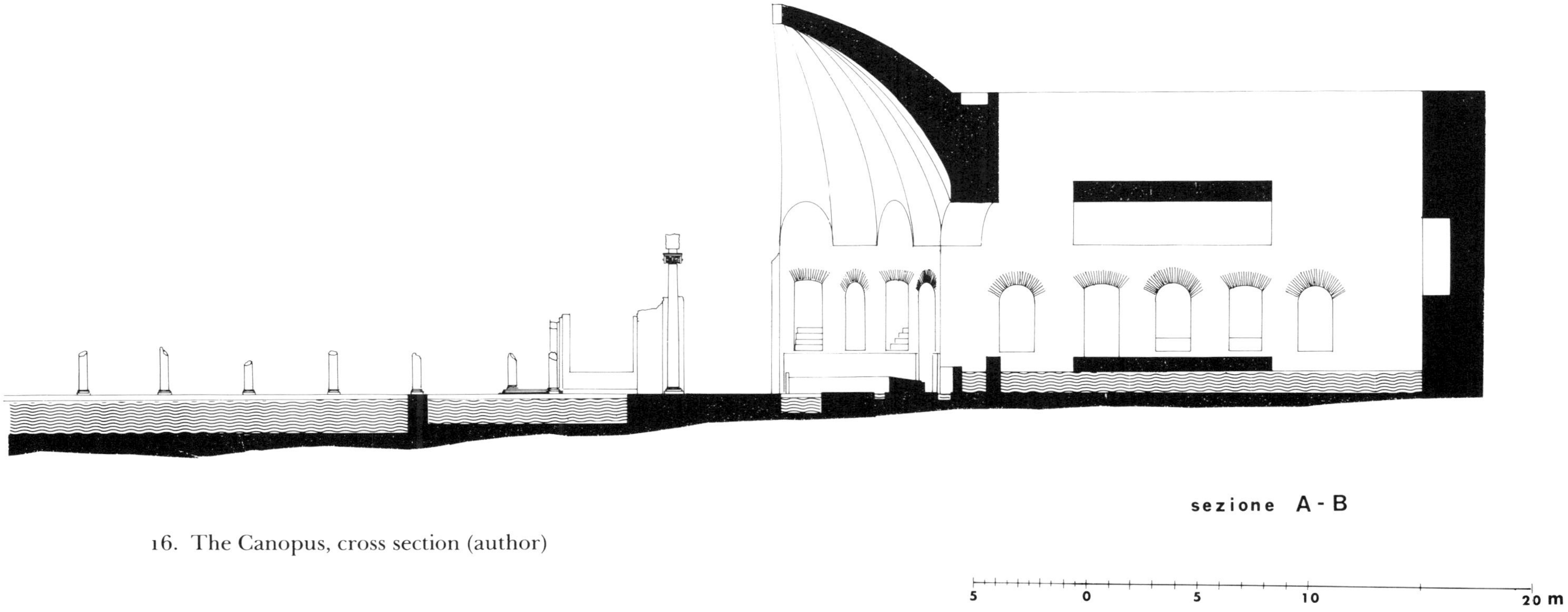
sezione A - B
5
0
5
10
20 m

16. The Canopus, cross section (author)

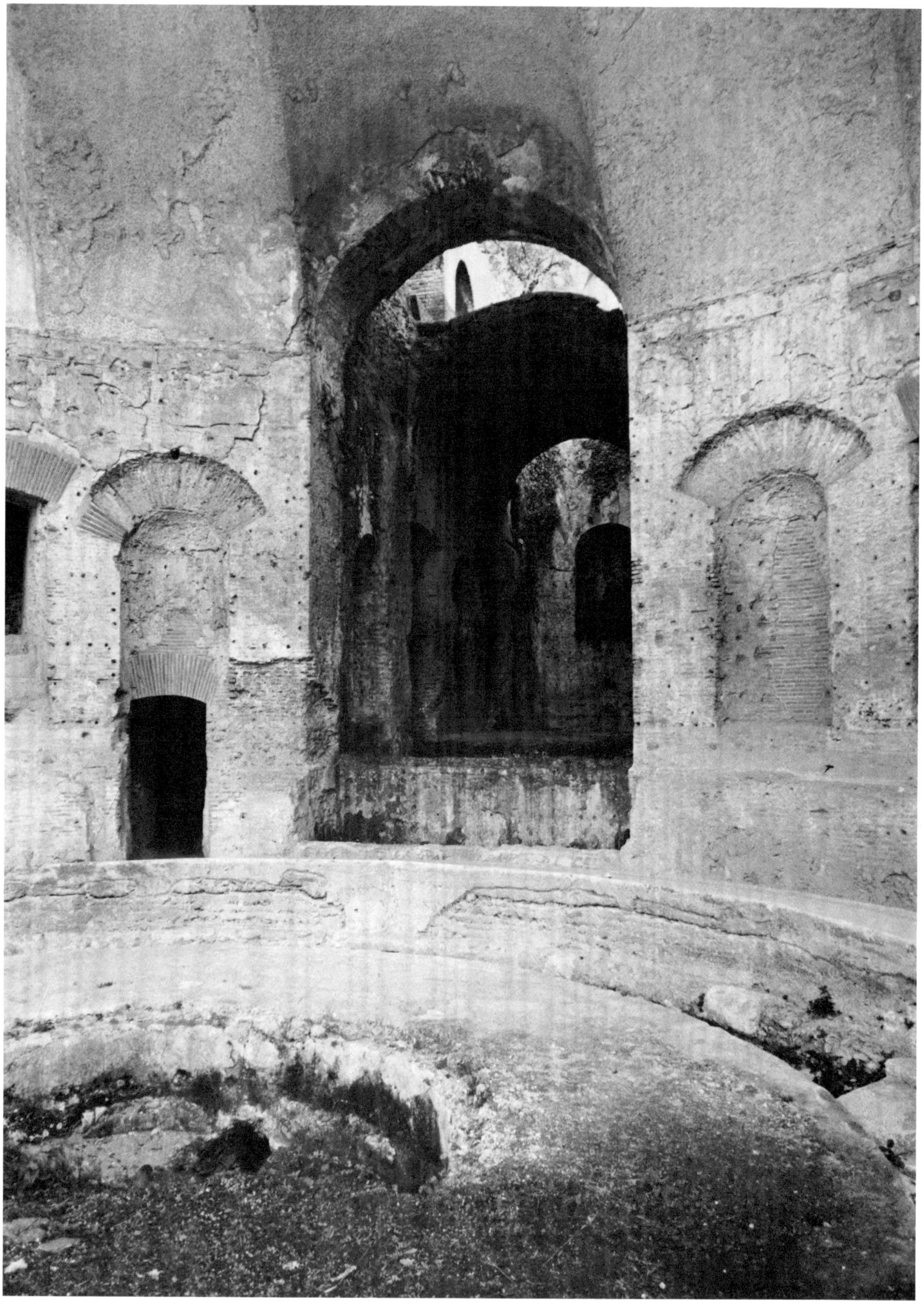

17. The water triclinium of the Canopus (photo: F. Luciolli)

18. Reconstruction of the exedra of the Canopus prepared for a banquet (author)

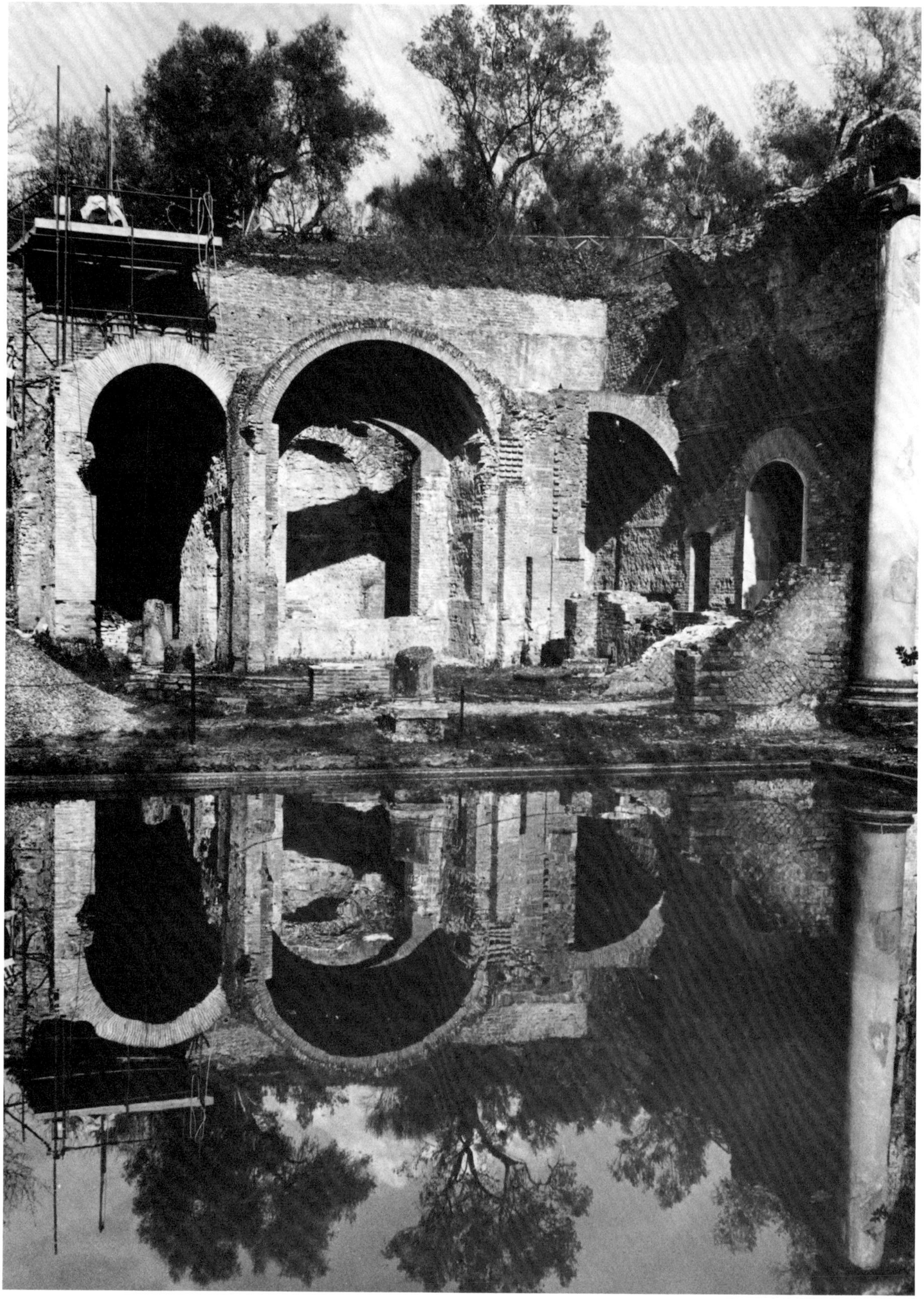

19. Lateral pavilion of the Canopus (photo: F. Luciolli)

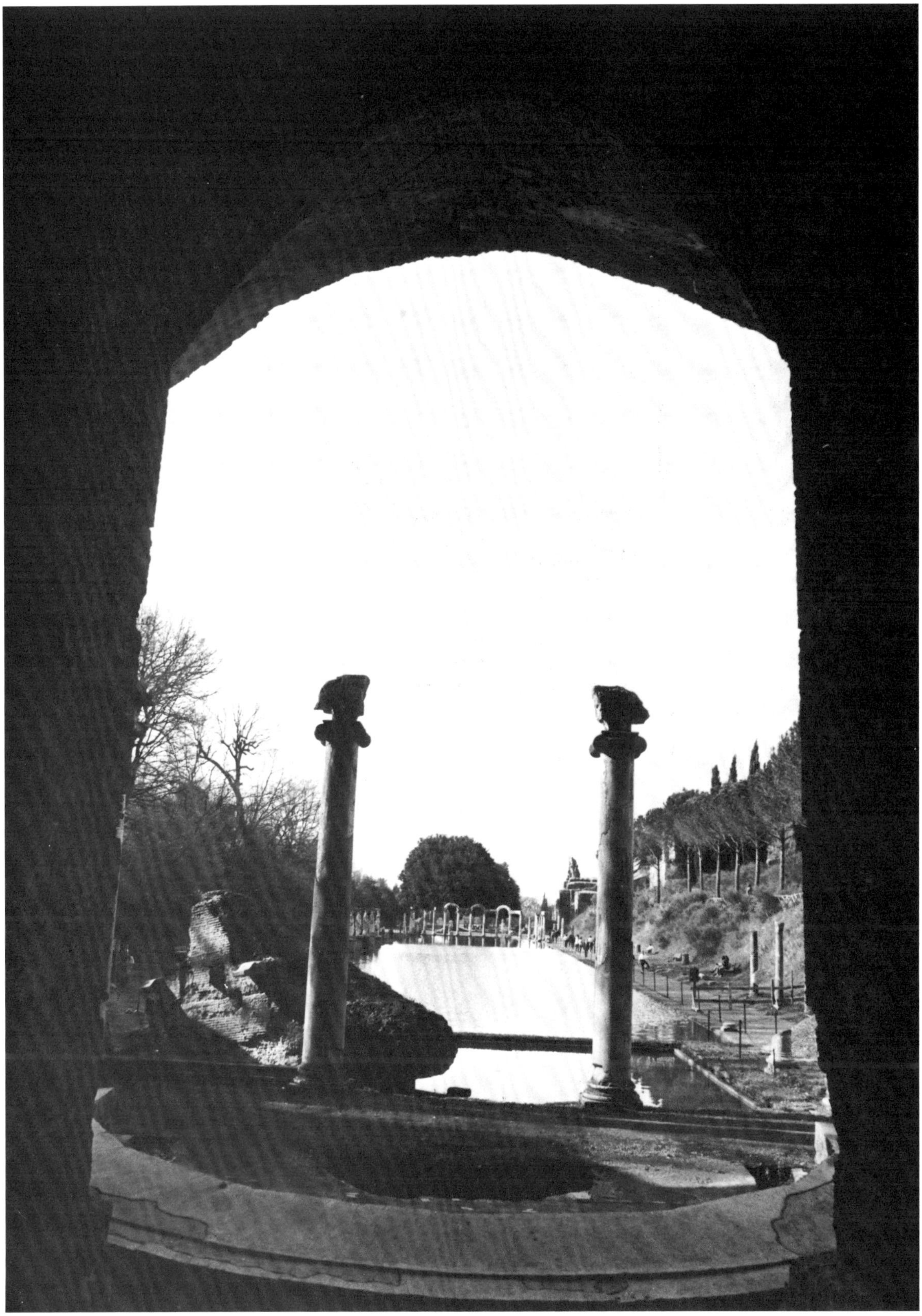

20. The Canopus: banks of the euripus (photo: F. Luciolli)

m
m
n
m
j
j
j
i
f
e
g
h
d
d
c
d
d
d
d
a
b
N
5 0 5 10 15 20 25 m

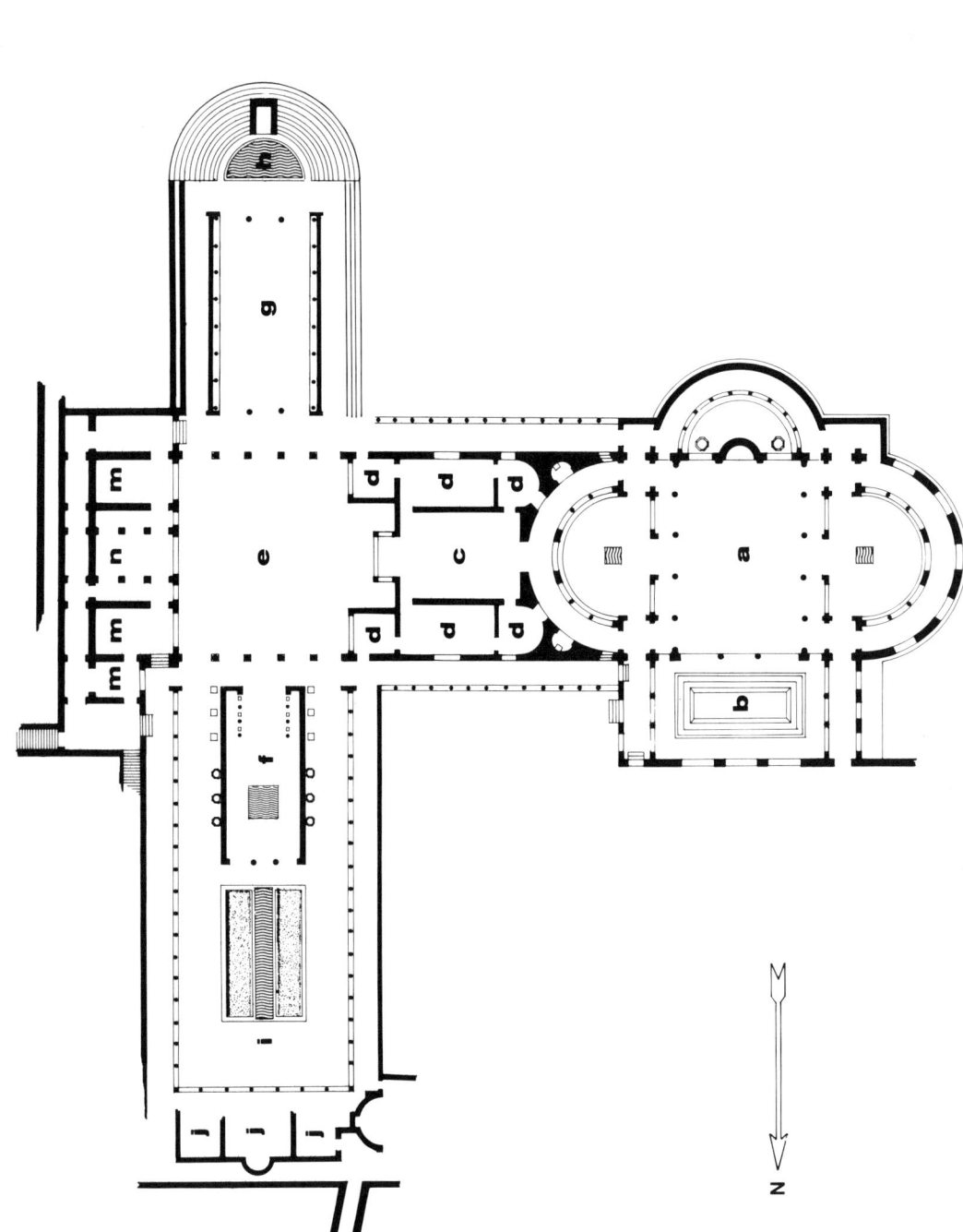

21. Plan of the Stadium complex (author)

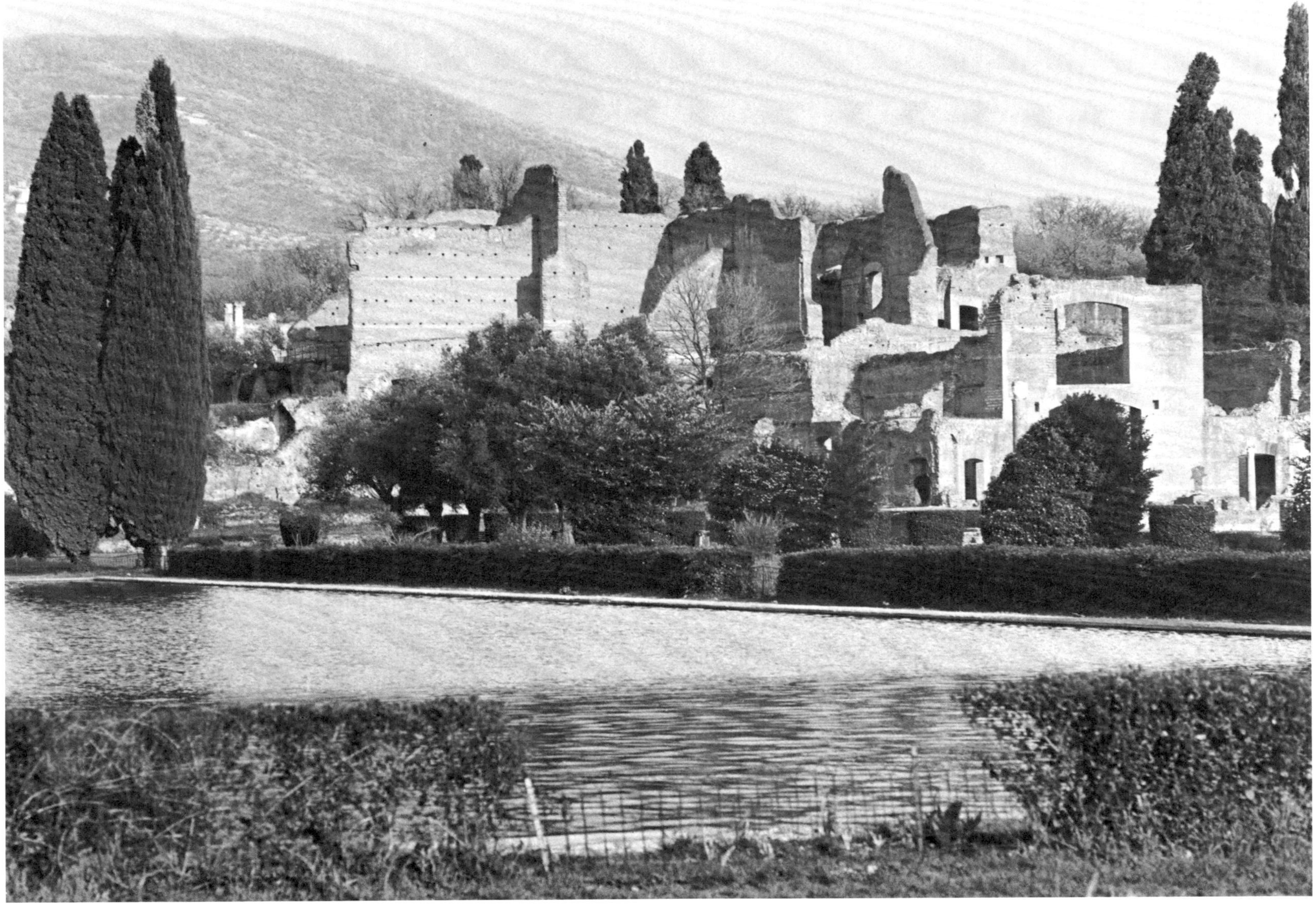

22. The Stadium complex seen from the Poecile (photo: F. Luciolli)

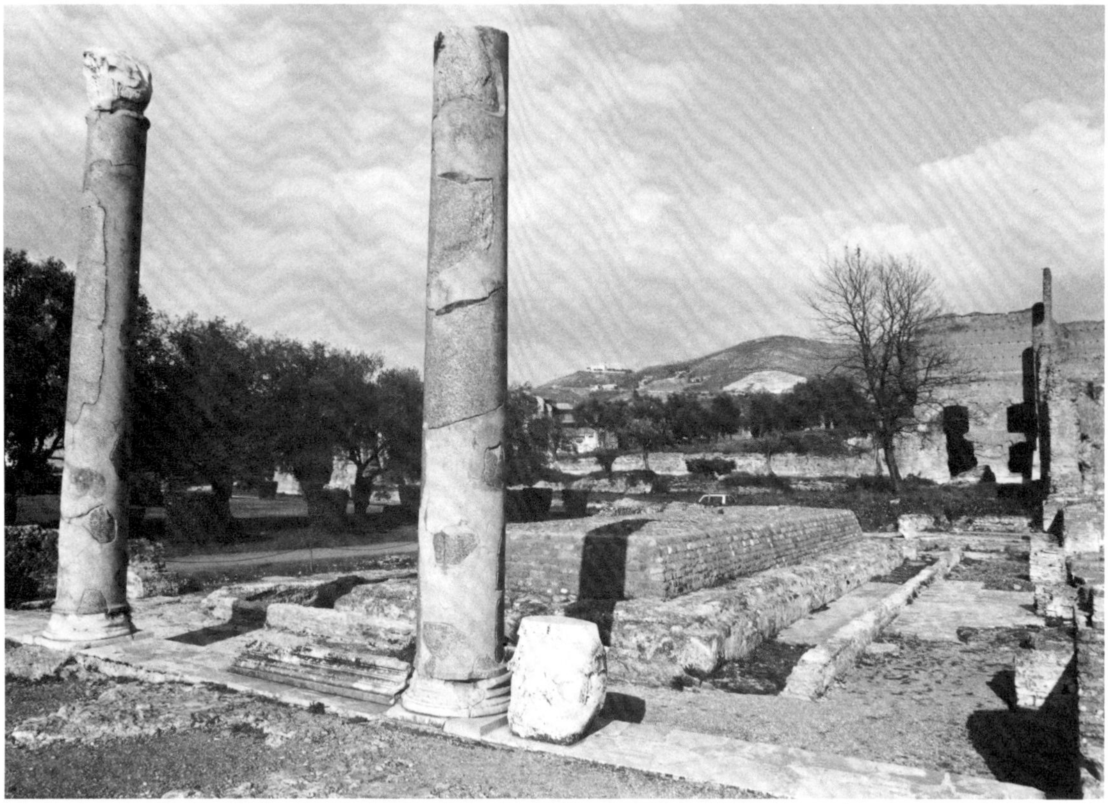

23. The great fountain of the Three Exedras building (photo: F. Luciolli)

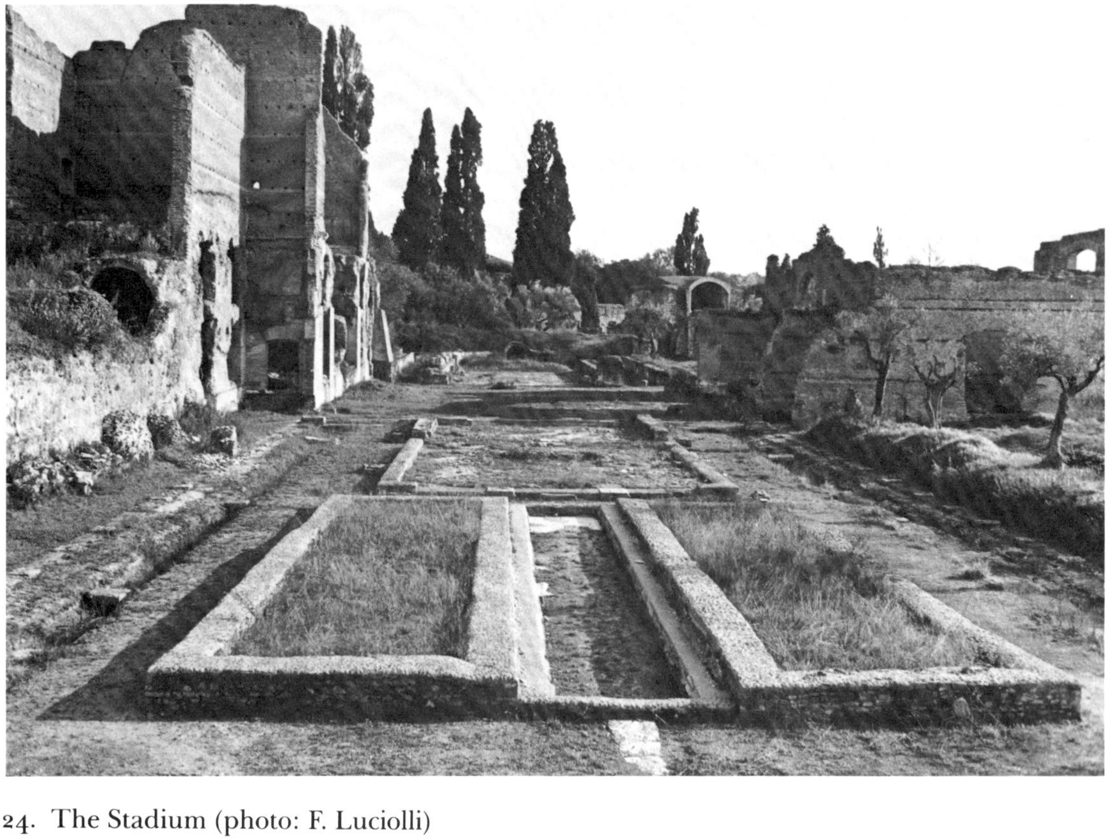

24. The Stadium (photo: F. Luciolli)

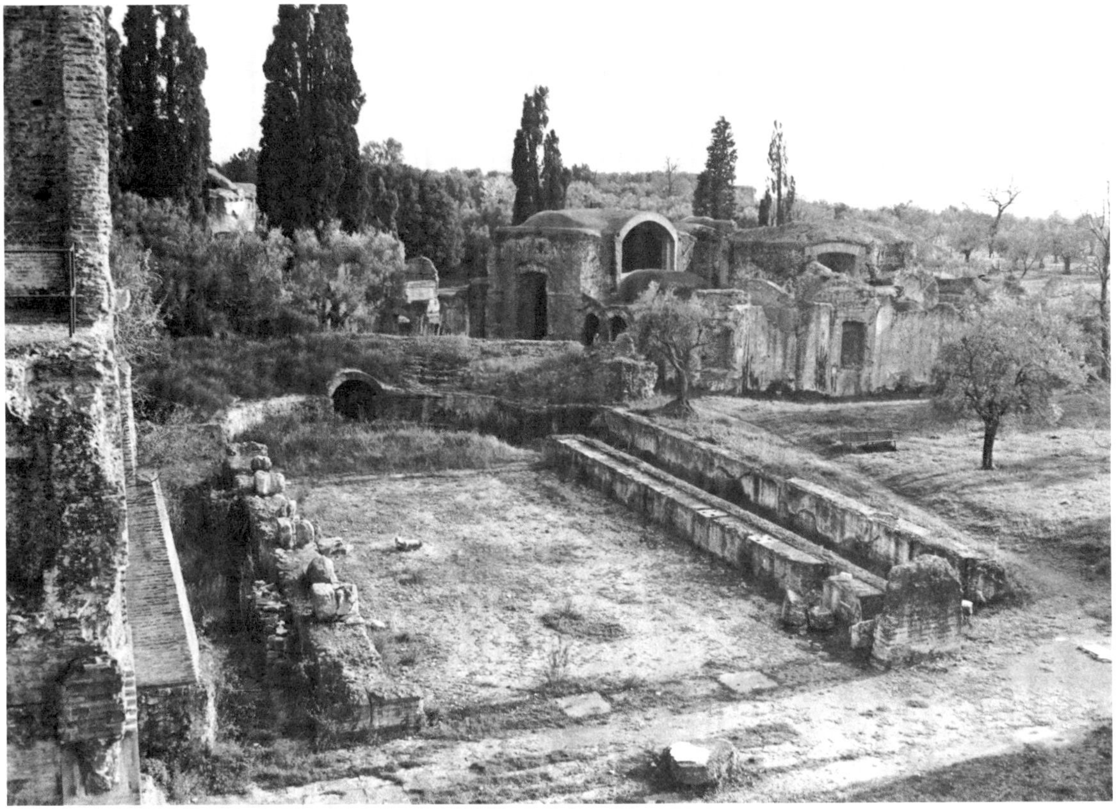

25. The Stadium nymphaeum (photo: F. Luciolli)

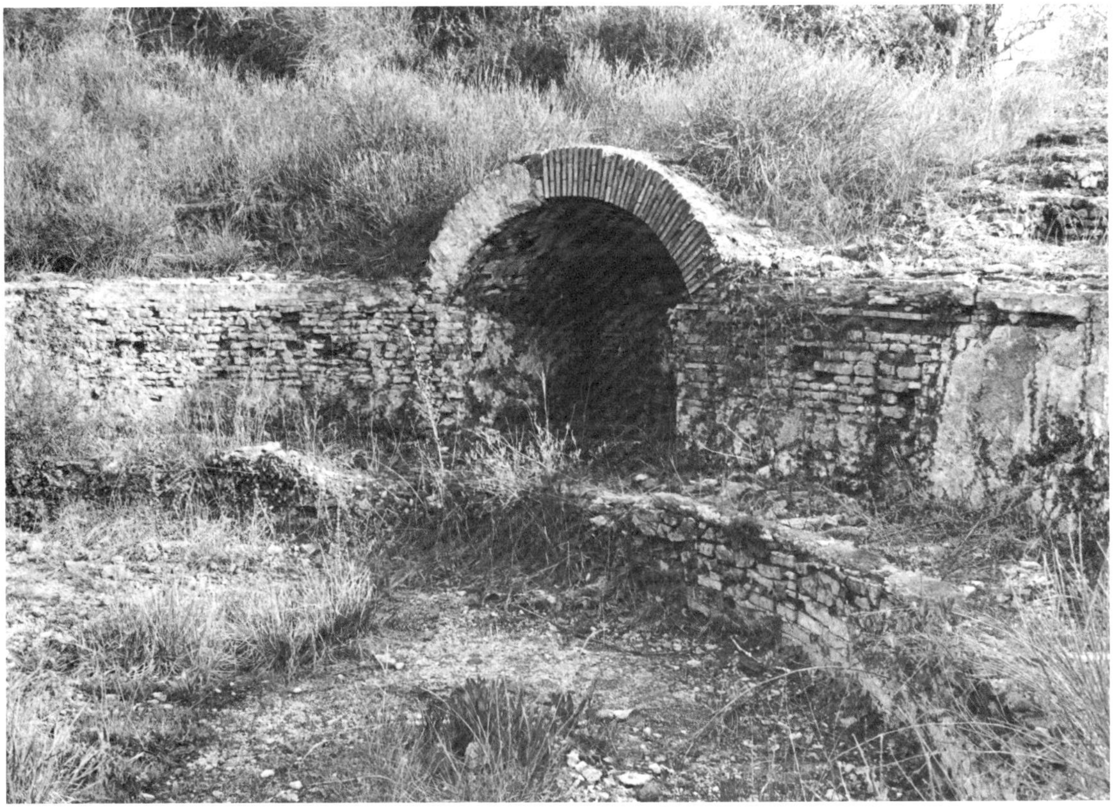

26. The grotto in the Stadium nymphaeum (photo: F. Luciolli)

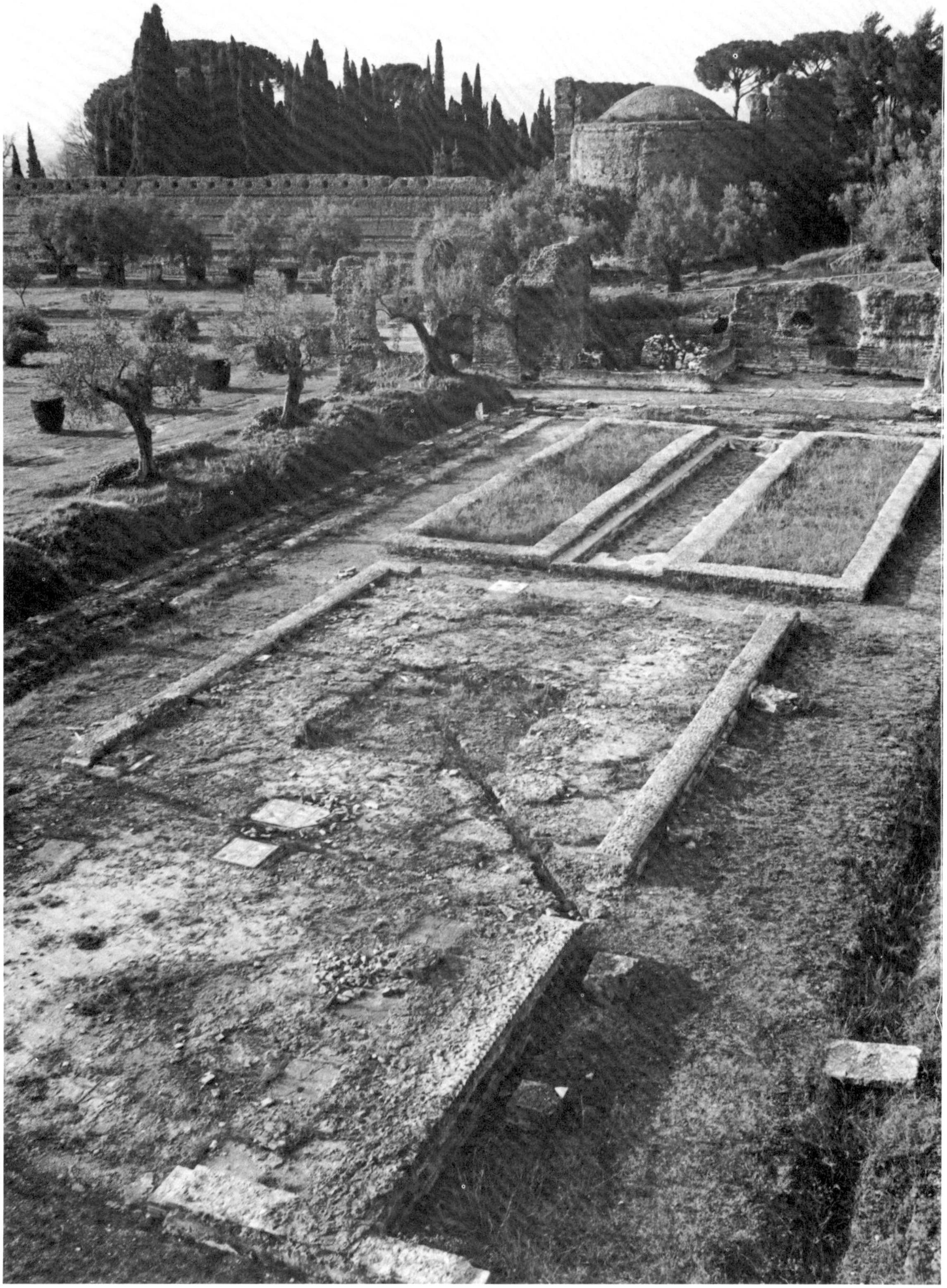

27. The north pavilion in the Stadium complex (photo: F. Luciolli)

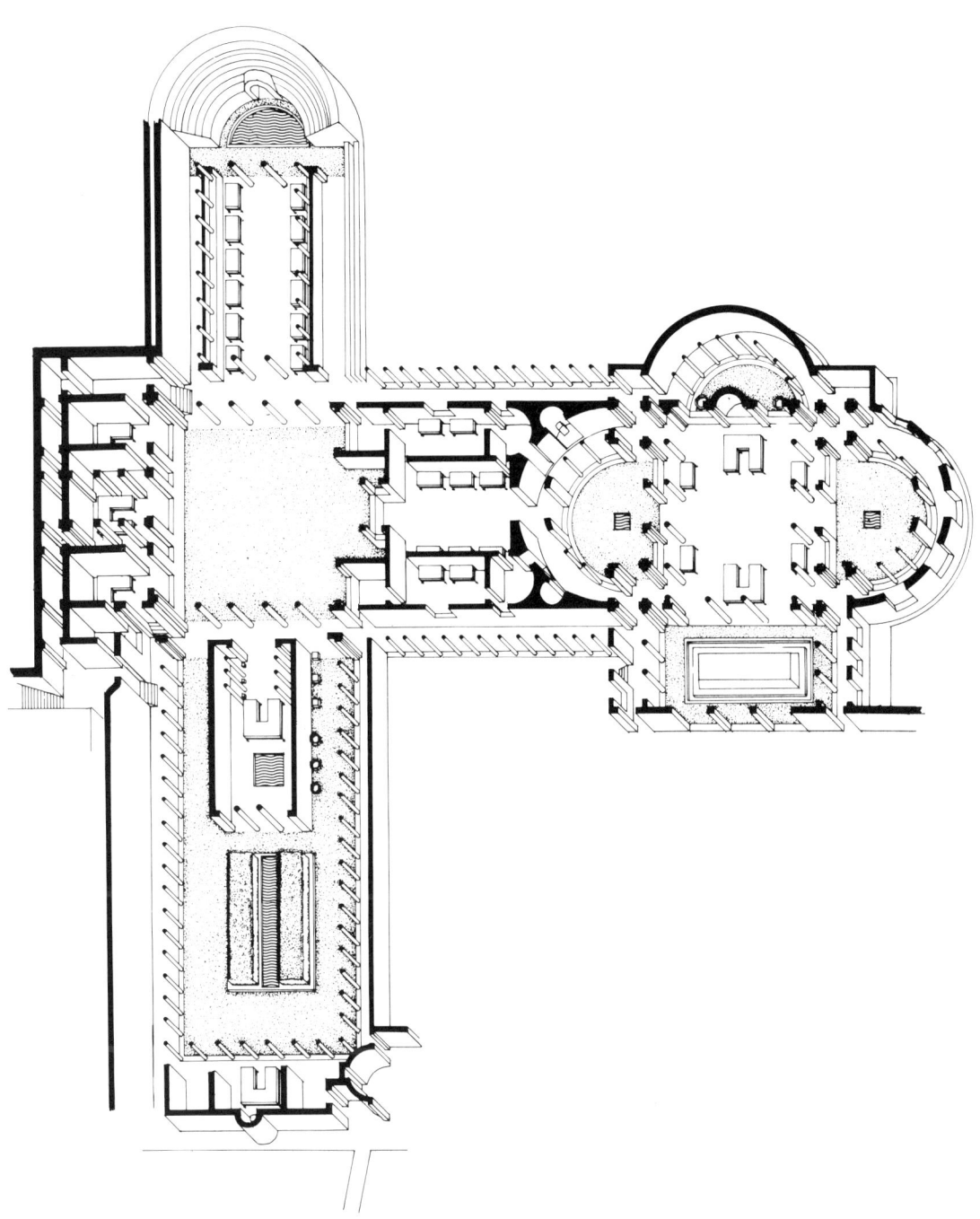

28. Axonometric reconstruction of the Stadium complex with tricliniar couches (author)

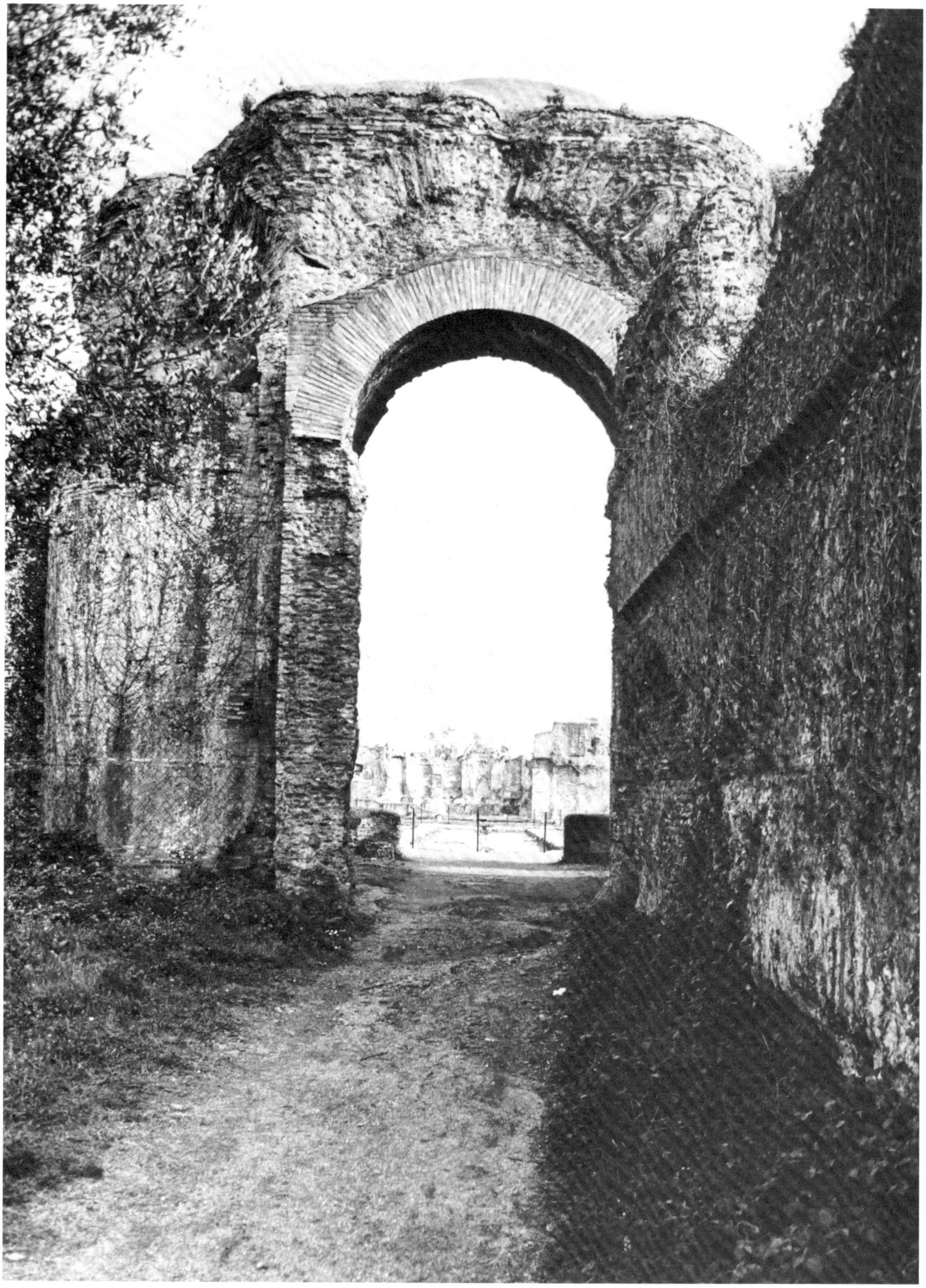

29. The Piazza d'Oro entrance hall (photo: F. Luciolli)

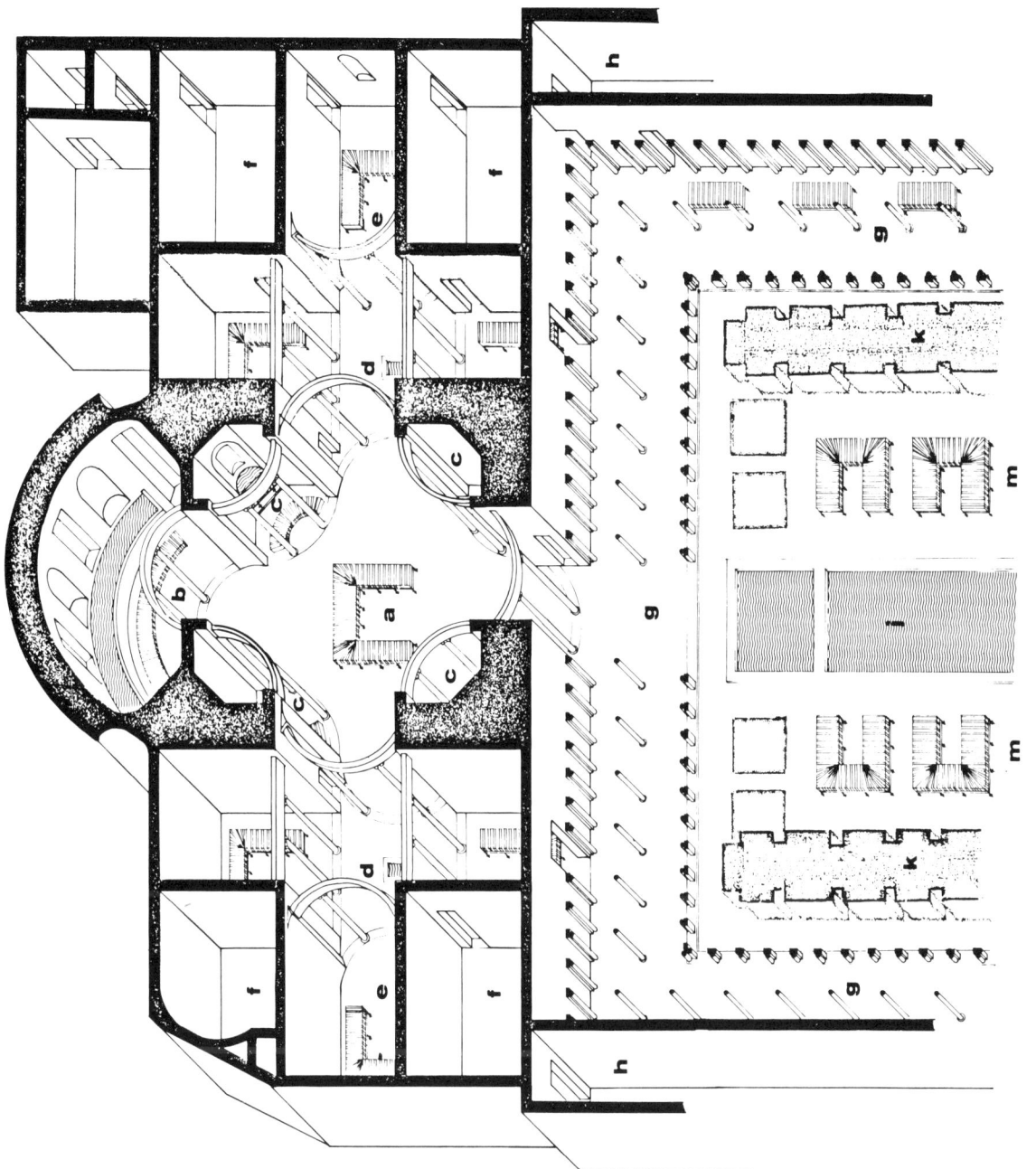

30. Axonometric reconstruction of the main pavilion in the Piazza d'Oro (author)

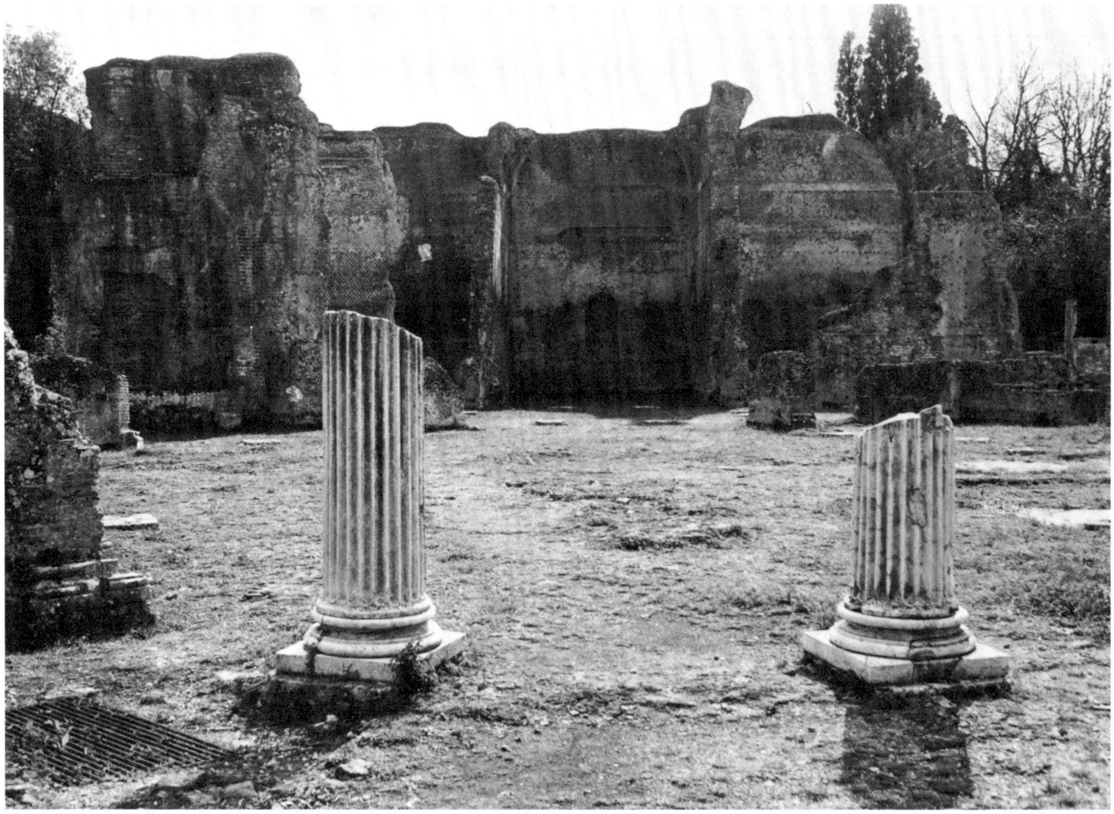

31. The principal axis of the main pavilion in the Piazza d'Oro (photo: F. Luciolli)

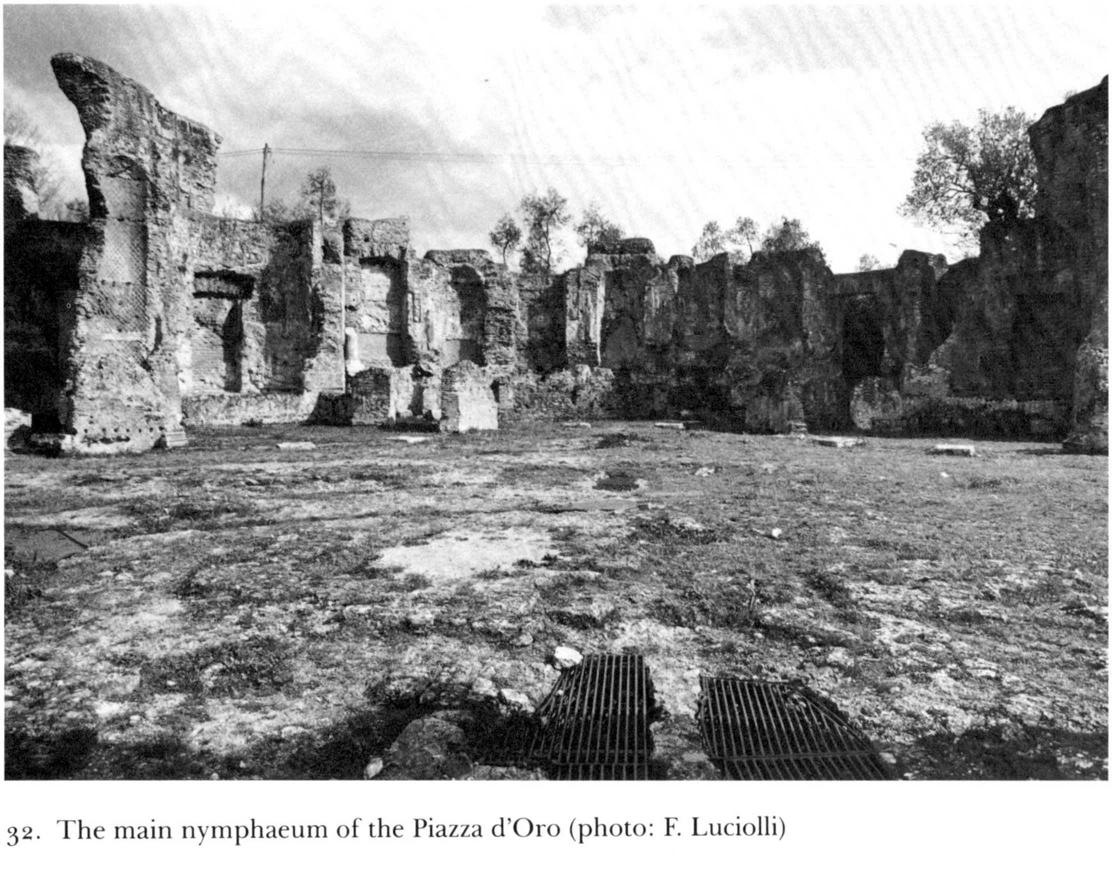

32. The main nymphaeum of the Piazza d'Oro (photo: F. Luciolli)

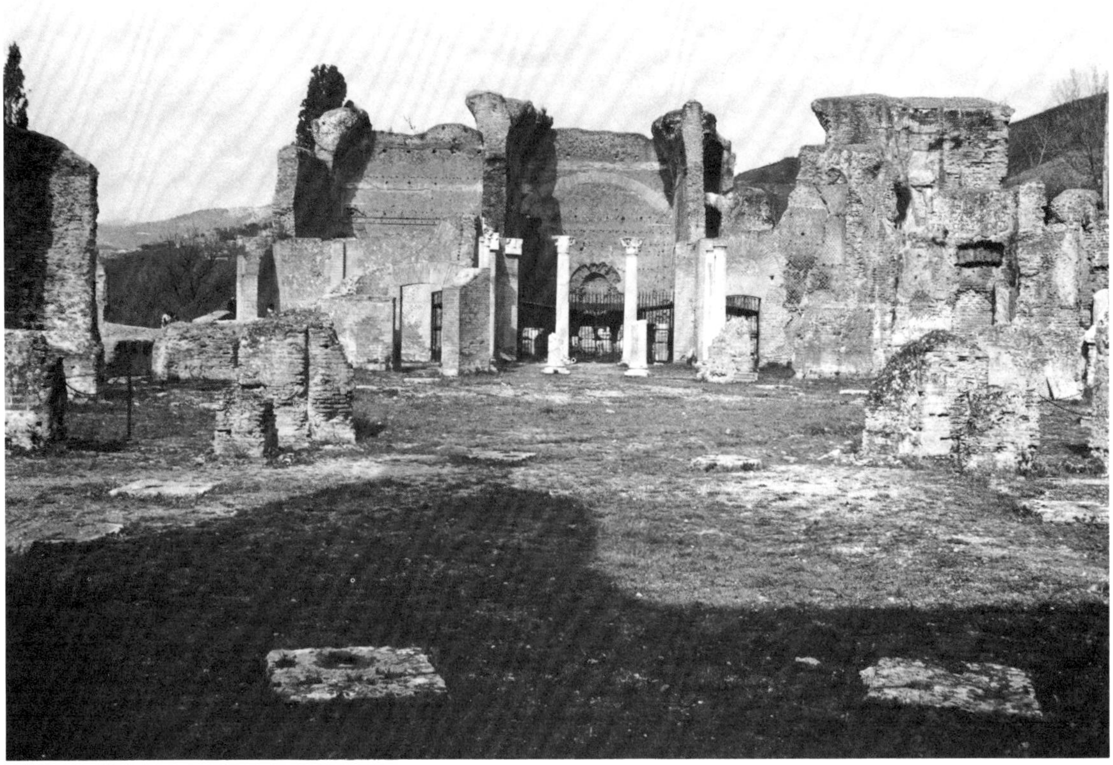

33. The east courtyard in the main pavilion of the Piazza d'Oro (photo: F. Luciolli)

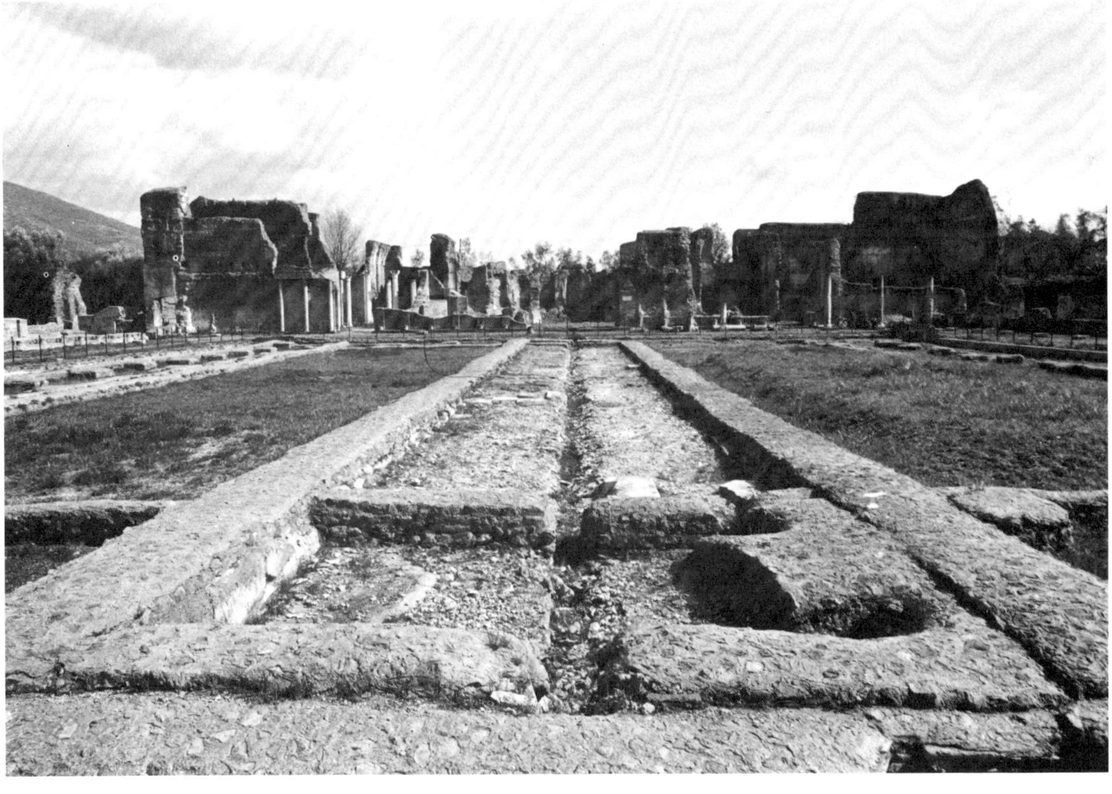

34. The garden of the Piazza d'Oro (photo: F. Luciolli)

mare tirreno
hibernaculum
triclinium
turris
sphaeristerium
bibliotheca
cavaedium
thermae
helio caminus
cryptoporticus
diaeta
culina
porticus
hortus
turris
atrium
hortus rusticus
S
O
E
N

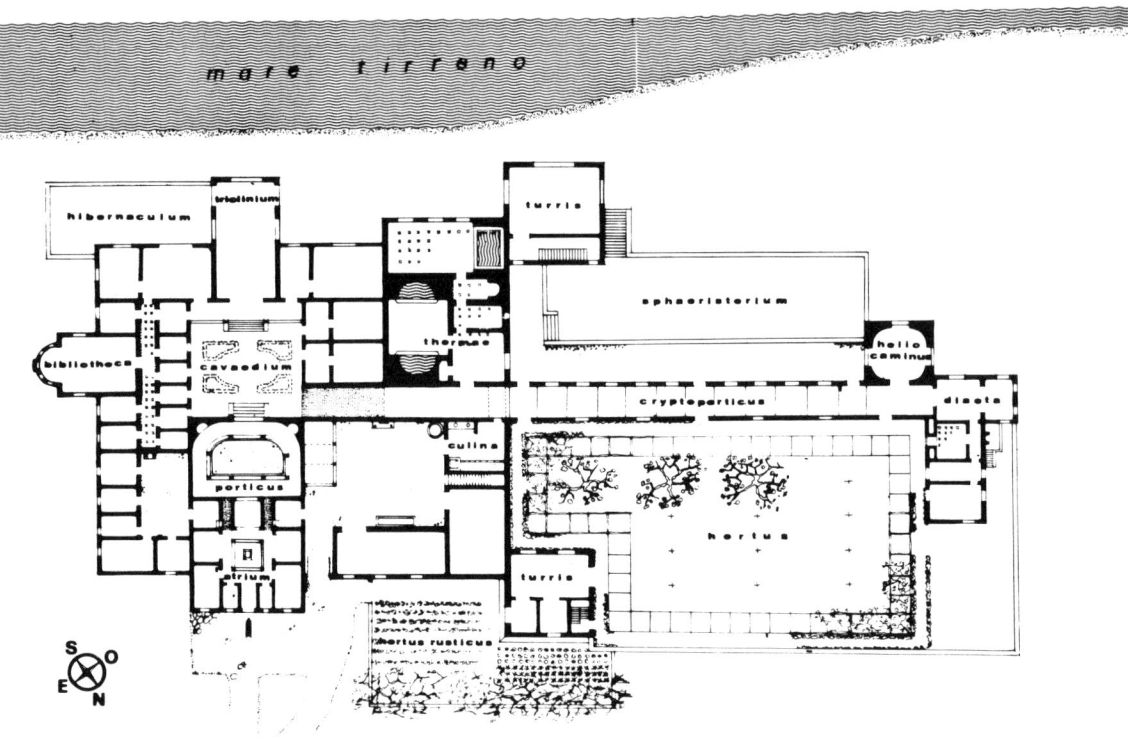

35. Reconstruction of Pliny's villa, according to his letter (author)

mare tirreno
litus plinianus
laurentum
vicus augustanus
litus plinianus
ostia
via laurentina
grotte di piastra
15 14 13 12 11 10 9 8
7 6 5 4 3 2 1
N
1 0 1 2km

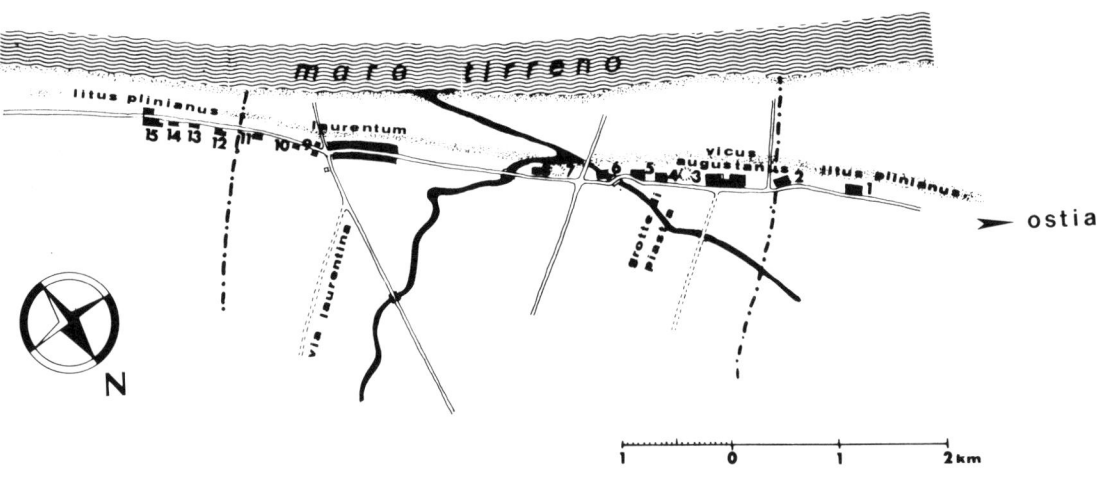

36. Map of the Laurentine area (author)

mare tirreno
T'
B
sphaeristerium
C
cryptoporch
C'
P
M
garden
T''
N
laurentum
vicus augustanus
A
hypothetical plan after the letter
mare tirreno
C
cryptoporch
C'
T'
P
A'
N
sphaeristerium
M
garden
B
laurentum
VIA SEVERIANA
vicus augustanus
A
grotte di piastra - sketch of the area

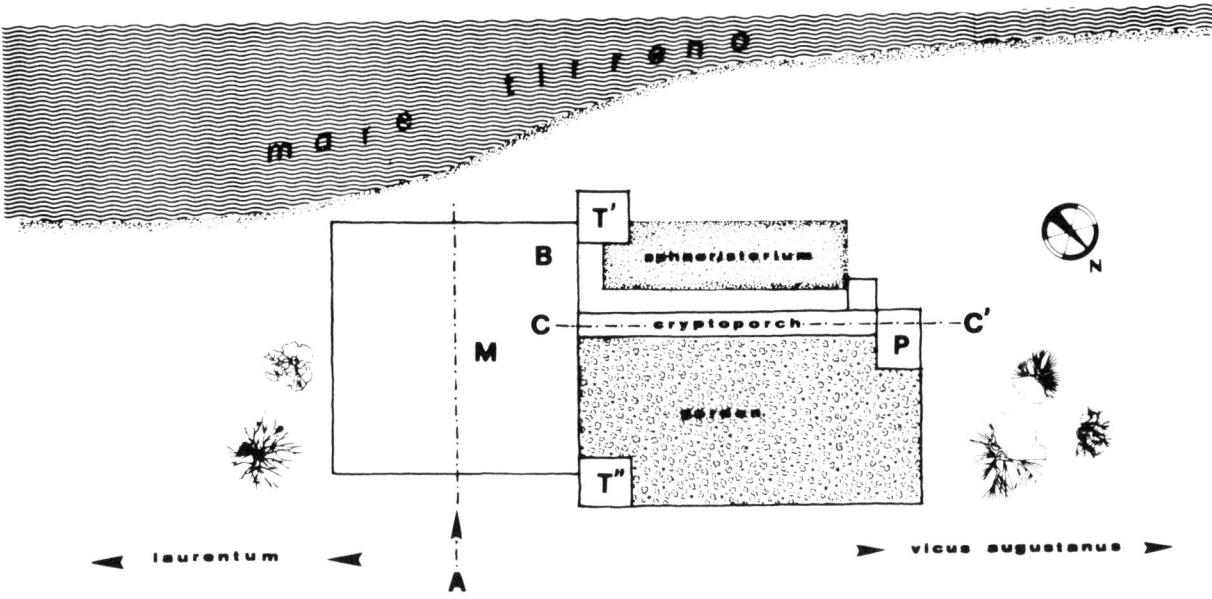

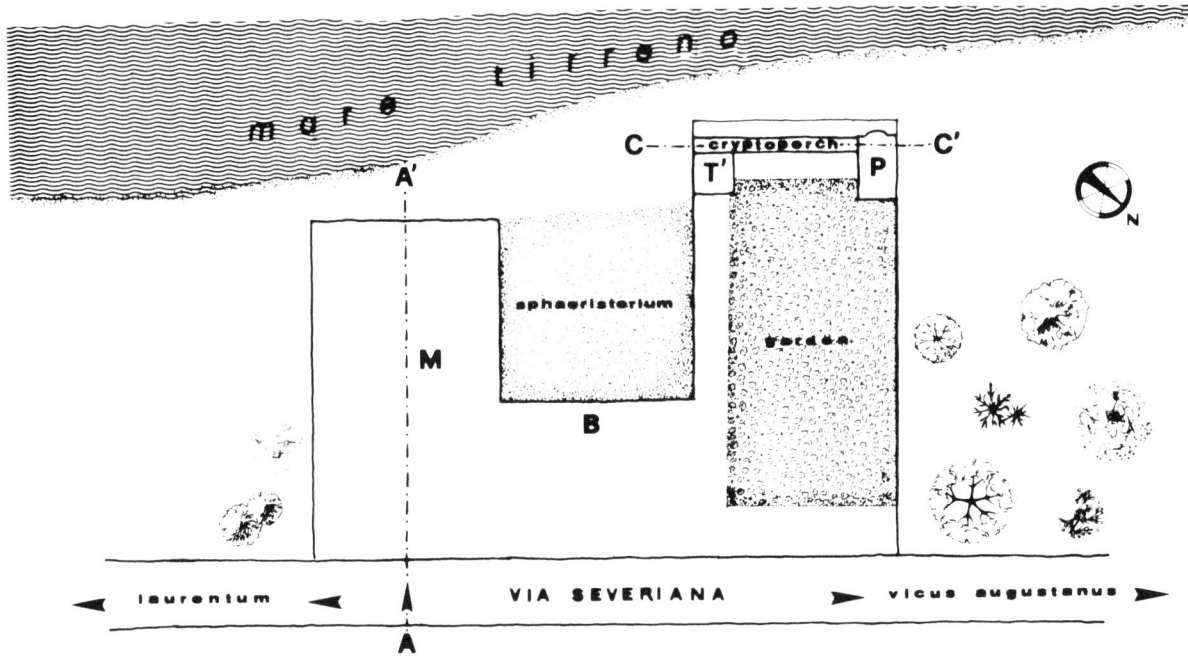

37. Comparison of the reconstruction with the actual Laurentinum (author)

grotto's mouth on the plan of the nymphaeum (Fig. 2,x and y), we find that it overhangs the servants' little footbridge. When this part caved in, the landslide killed only the servants who stood on this footbridge and the others who were bringing the food by boats and rafts to the water triclinium, for there was no connection between the island and the fishpond's bank.

In fact Tacitus, relating the accident, confirms that only slaves died in the landslide. Suetonius, on the other hand, exaggerates the number and the social position of the victims. But Suetonius always had a modern reporter's flair for depicting the facts in a sensational way: he knew very well that adding some of the guests to the list of the dead would make the story more exciting for his readers.[11]

Sperlonga's water triclinium operated in the same way as Pliny's water *stibadium*, but the setting was different. Pliny the Younger's villa was conceived at the end of the first century A.D., while Sperlonga's nymphaeum was built at least a century before and was still Hellenistic in spirit. At Sperlonga there is no Plinian garden with lawns and trees, topiary works, and the kind of geometric design that coerces nature into architectural and decorative patterns. Instead we find nature in the raw (Fig. 6). Nevertheless, it is a wonderful creation, not only from the Hellenistic point of view. The nymphaeum is part of a rocky garden of such a striking beauty that people will always find it lovely. The entrance to the grotto opens on a setting of Mediterranean shrubs such as myrtle, mastic (*Pistacia lentiscus*), and rosemary clinging to the stony slopes; in summertime, when the entire hillside is aflame with the golden mantle of flowering broom, the scenery is even more impressive. The beauty of the site is to be found in the rocks, the shrubs, the water, and the colossal nymphaeum.

There, like actors on a stage, exquisite Grecian statues enacted the tale of Ulysses and his companions blinding with a burning pole the only eye of mighty Polyphemus (Fig. 2,a) or trying to escape from the snakelike coils of the sea monster Scylla. The round pool from which Scylla's rock emerged (Fig. 2,b) was clearly a representation of Charybdis, the eddy that helped Scylla destroy ships trying to cross the strait of Messina; and the burning eye of blind, raging Polyphemus, throwing huge rocks against the little men in flight, was just as clearly a representation of the great volcano Etna.[12]

---

[11] It is unlikely that a patrician or some important personage of the emperor's retinue died in the accident. No Roman historian in his right mind would have failed to report his name and, in addition to the fact that Tacitus does not mention the death of anyone of the upper class, Suetonius gives no names.

[12] Of course no one believes any more the hypothesis that Tiberius was the creator of the splendid nymphaeum of Sperlonga. It is possible that the villa could have been left to him as a legacy, but I even doubt that, because neither Tacitus nor Suetonius says anything of the sort. They simply state that the landslide happened while Tiberius was dining there and, to the best of my knowledge, to dine in a place does not mean to own it. Sperlonga probably was built by one of the rich *piscinarii* whom Cicero criticizes so severely (Cic. *Ep.* 1.19.6; 1.20.3). It is certainly a strange coincidence that two of the principal episodes represented in the grotto are the adventures that befell Ulysses in Sicily. Moreover, Sicily itself is portrayed in the nymphaeum by two of that island's more striking features: Scylla, the sea monster, represented here in the grotto by the monumental group set on the rock that emerged from the round pool (the dangerous eddy of Charybdis in the Strait of Messina) and Etna, represented by Polyphemus, the personification of the mighty volcano with the flaming crater burning as the giant's only eye. He looms gigantic near the edge

In the middle of all this splendor stood the triclinium (Fig. 3), facing toward the inner part of the grotto where all this beauty was displayed. As Romans began their dinner early in the afternoon,[13] the declining sun would have caressed the statues, and its rays, mirrored by the ripples in the water pool, would have alighted on the marbles and given them a kind of liquid life. At sunset the spectacle must have been breathtaking. The guests could enjoy it as they dined, reclining on mattresses and pillows deftly arranged around the pool, while the servants stood on the little footbridge carving the meats and arranging the bite-sized pieces in a miniature flotilla that was sailed across the water so that the diners could help themselves.

In the meantime, on the fishpond's banks musicians, dancers, singers, and actors[14] performed and enlivened the banquet with their pranks. They probably used the lateral grotto (Fig. 2,c) as a stage (Fig. 7), but this part of the nymphaeum was certainly also meant to be a place where diners could entertain themselves before and after the party, or it could have been arranged as a triclinium in case many guests were asked for dinner. At the back of the lateral grotto a door led to a room (Fig. 2,d) with three alcoves, undoubtedly furnished with beds on which diners could relax or have a little nap, as people did in the Plinian *zoothecula*. Of course more active guests could always enjoy a brisk stroll around the piscina, a walk that took the place of the Plinian path around the Hippodrome, and, as in Pliny's Hippodrome, in the grotto at Sperlonga the strollers could find comfortable seats that gave them the opportunity to pause and admire the sculptures from various points of view.

Some years passed before I was confronted with another water triclinium. Its dining arrangement was contemporary with Pliny's *stibadium* and very similar to it. It was in Pompeii in the so-called House of Loreius Tiburtinus (II.ii.5), an elegant domus.[15] It

---

of the fishpond, just as the erupting volcano stood on the coast, overlooking the Sicilian sea and its perils. The coincidence makes one wonder if the proprietor and creator of this splendid nymphaeum might not have been someone with close ties to Sicily, an admirer of this fascinating island and maybe a rich, nostalgic patrician.

[13] Roman writers and poets give us much information about the hours of dining. We know that they used to begin their dinner just after having taken their bath in the thermae. So they entered the triclinium between 3 and 4 o'clock in the afternoon (Mart. 11.52; 4.8; 7.51). Those who were accustomed to take only a light meal had their dinner served later (Plut. *Cic.* 3). Even in those cases the meal always began before sundown and nearly all dinners ended at about the same time, just after nightfall.

[14] We find a lot of information about the custom of having actors, dancers, and musicians perform during banquets (Pliny *Ep.* 1.15; Petron. *Sat.* 53–54, 59). Sometimes the entertainment consisted simply of a recitation of poetry written by the master of the house who, as in this case, was always a rich man throwing parties just to find an audience—a captive audience, of course (Petron. 41; Mart. 11.52; 3.50). Such performances could prove very boring, and Martial criticized the practice harshly, even though there is no record of his having refused an invitation to dinner for that or for any other reason.

[15] The biclinium of Loreius Tiburtinus in Pompeii had already attracted the attention of archaeologists. Apart from all the discussion about the attribution of the property of the house to the phantom Loreius Tiburtinus (M. Della Corte, *Case ed abitanti di Pompei*, Naples, 1965, 374; P. Castren, "Ordo populusque Pompeianus," *Acta of the Finlandese Institute of Rome*, 8, Rome, 1975, 184), there were different hypotheses on the biclinium. V. Spinazzola (*Pompei alla luce dei nuovi scavi di via dell'Abbondanza*, Rome, 1952, 369) thought that it was only a decorative part of the terrace, a place where the dwellers of the house could rest or visit with friends. Della Corte (ibid., 374) rightly interpreted the biclinium as an open-air dining

is highly probable that in a later period, sometime before the Vesuvian eruption, this private mansion became a *caupona* (inn), as did many other luxurious houses all around the amphitheater.[16] The gladiatorial games lasted for days, and many people from nearby towns flocked to Pompeii to enjoy them. Of course they needed places in which to dine and celebrate the occasion with their friends. But not only people coming from the countryside patronized this kind of high-class inn.[17] Pompeians also frequented them, and not only during the amphitheater games: they had to rely on these *cauponae* because many of them lived in houses too simple and too small in which to entertain friends and were obliged to hire a triclinium whenever they wanted to give a party.

Probably the water triclinium in Loreius Tiburtinus' house (Fig. 8) existed long before this property was transformed into a deluxe *caupona*.[18] But I am quite sure that its decoration was redone, for there is a noticeable difference between the high quality of the earlier frescoes in the house and the poor quality of the paintings on the walls of

---

arrangement, but he did not understand how it worked. He suggested that perhaps a table (one of the small round tables used for triclinia, but one high enough to emerge from the water) could have been placed in the pool. In fact as the pool is 4 feet 8 inches deep, this table had to be at least 5 feet high to reach the same level as the couches. But the normal height of a dining table is 2 feet 7 inches, and even a support of this size would have been very unstable in a pool of water. It is evident that a stand for trays 5 feet high would have presented insurmountable difficulties. Moreover, the problem of serving a dinner in such conditions would have been impossible to solve.

[16] W.F. Jashemski, *The Gardens of Pompeii*, I, New Rochelle, N.Y., 1979, 172–178; T. Kleberg, *Hotels, restaurants et cabarets dans l'antiquité romaine*, Upsala, 1957, 49 ff.

[17] In A.D. 59, during some gladiatorial games in the amphitheater, a fight broke out between the Pompeians and the citizens of nearby Nuceria (Tac. *Ann*. 14.17). People became excited, and the outburst of violence was terrible. Many men were killed or maimed. As a consequence the authorities decreed that Pompeii's amphitheater had to close for ten years. But the inns that had flourished all around that area seem not to have suffered much by this fact. This shows that they had enough customers to earn a living even when the amphitheater was not operating and that travelers, merchants, and Pompeians must have patronized them quite substantially.

[18] Many facts seem to indicate that the house of Loreius Tiburtinus was transformed into a *caupona* (inn). One of these facts is something I noticed when I was doing research on kitchens: E. Salza Prina Ricotti, "Cucine e quartieri servili in epoca romana," *RendPont*, 51–52 (1978–79, 1979–80), 268–275. Going from house to house in Pompeii I realized that it was nearly impossible to find the typical Pompeian masonry stove in a *caupona* or in a *thermopolium* (a kind of bar where you could drink hot or iced wine) or in any other shop of this kind: when a kitchen was found in an inn it was never in the *caupona* itself but in the private dwelling of the *copo* (innkeeper). Moreover, when a wealthy private house was transformed into a *caupona*, the first thing that was done was to destroy the masonry stove. That happened in the Cryptoportico House, in the praedium of Iulia Felix, and also in the Loreius Tiburtinus house. The destruction was evidently connected with the imperial decree that banned the sale of cooked food in such places. These laws were first promulgated under Tiberius and lasted until Vespasian (Suet. *Tib*. 33–34; *Claud*. 38; Cass. Dio 14, 60, 62, 67), so all we can find in a *caupona* is either a barbecuelike fireplace or some small hearth near the masonry tricliniar couches. These can be easily explained by the fact that the decrees banned the sale of cooked food but not wine and did not prohibit customers cooking for themselves. Of course the fines were imposed only on innkeepers who dared to infringe the law. Yet if these merchants destroyed the kitchen just to be on the safe side, the fines must have been very heavy. These laws must have been enforced in all parts of the Roman Empire because we know that when Jesus gave instructions to his Apostles concerning the Last Supper (Matt. 26:17–19; Mark 14:12–16; Luke 22:7–13) he ordered them to go to a certain man, evidently the local *copo*, ask him for a room in which to dine, and then make all the preparations for the dinner, which they had to provide themselves.

the biclinium which are cheap and showy, even if from a certain distance they could look impressive.

Water, as ever, played an important role in this biclinium. We find the typical pool where vessels loaded with food could be floated during the banquets. This pool (Fig. 8,a) is set between two masonry couches (Fig. 8,b) that face each other and lie under a vine trellis. They are built on a terrace (Fig. 9) that overlooks a large garden or at least what must have been a large garden. Between the couches at the back of the pool there is an aedicula adorned with rocks and seashells: a kind of decoration usually employed for nymphaea.[19] In its center there is a pedestal that was probably used for the placement of some statue. One could even think that it functioned as a decorative fountain, but there is no piping to be seen. In front of the aedicula a little footbridge (Fig. 8,c), of the type we have already noticed in the other two triclinia, crosses the euripus, an artificial river that starts from the pool. Such a footbridge was the indispensable element of a water triclinium because it provided the servants a place to stand while serving the guests. Beyond the bridge the euripus ran all along the terrace. Another small footbridge cut the euripus into two parts of different lengths (Fig. 8,d). The shorter one was the farthest from the biclinium, and that created an optical illusion for the people dining there and made the artificial river seem longer than it actually was.

At one end of this second footbridge a large door led to a pleasant room decorated with frescoes (Fig. 8,e). This room could have been used as a supplementary triclinium or as a place in which to entertain friends. Opposite this room, on the other side of the footbridge, a step led to a kind of gazebo that formed the highest part of a nymphaeum (Fig. 8,f)—a very ingenious means of connecting the terrace with the garden (Fig. 10). On the terrace side of the gazebo four jets of water poured under the step and came together over a central waterspout. The water spilled onto the marble pavement and drained to the lower part of the nymphaeum in lead pipes (Fig. 8,g). From there it entered another euripus (Fig. 11) that ran the whole length of the garden, which must have been a cool, green place and a lovely example of the gardens so well depicted in many Pompeian frescoes.[20] But when the domus was sold to a *copo* (innkeeper), the garden was made into a vineyard, as the row of forty wine amphoras set along the enclosure walls and the large dolium barely emerging from the ground show. Dolia were customary features of *cauponae* vineyards; the innkeepers used them to store the must pressed from their own grapes.[21]

At the far end of the terrace, opposite the water triclinium, we find a pavilion (Fig. 8,h) with a small porch, round stucco columns, and fine frescoes on its walls. On the garden side it had a window shaded by a vine trellis. As we can easily see, this room is very similar to both the one behind the lateral grotto at Sperlonga and to Pliny's marble pavilion. Here, as in the other two *zootheculae*, people could relax and enjoy the greenish

---

[19] N. Neuerburg, "Fontane e ninfei nell'Italia antica," *Memorie dell'Accademia di Archeologia e Belle Arti di Napoli*, 5 (1965), 91, 93, 232.

[20] Jashemski, *Gardens*, I, 55–87.

[21] W.F. Jashemski, "The *Caupona* of Euxinus at Pompeii," *Archaeology*, 20 (1967), 41–42.

light filtering through the window as well as the song of the fountains. Of course more active guests could stroll around the euripus or in the garden, while others could chat under the vine trellis or sit lazily in the gazebo.

This room has often been misinterpreted, so, until I became interested in Loreius Tiburtinus' house, no one had thought of relating the biclinium to Pliny's water *stibadium*. In fact this room was believed to be a shrine dedicated to the cult of the Egyptian goddess Isis, and the euripus was even said to be a representation of the great River Nile.[22] The misunderstanding derived from the very small painting (about 7 inches high) of a man clad as a priest of Isis on a wall of this pavilion (Fig. 8,h). A name was scribbled under this figure: Loreius Tiburs. Around him gods, goddesses, nymphs, and other personages of the classical tradition, having nothing to do with Egyptian myths, danced in the fresco. Mercury dominated all of them from a high settee. For this reason it is difficult to accept the little man clad as a priest of Isis and lost in this pictorial arrangement as proof that both the room and the terrace were special places where an Isis cult was celebrated. A man called Loreius Tiburtinus could have lived there, of course, and there is little doubt that he was an Isis worshiper, but a comparison between Loreius Tiburtinus' biclinium and Pliny's *stibadium* reveals such a striking similarity that there is no doubt whatsoever that this part of the house was a water triclinium of the well-known Plinian type and not a shrine for a foreign cult.

However, water triclinia were not the only garden triclinia in which water was present. In Pompeii we find another kind of dining room in which water was employed liberally and not merely as a simple decoration. It is the one set in an exedra of the peristyle garden in Iulia Felix's praedium (Fig. 12). The property of Iulia Felix is located just a few blocks from Loreius Tiburtinus' house;[23] it is another deluxe inn with triclinia for hire.[24] The triclinium that we will examine now was one of them. The three fine marble couches had a shelf running all around the inner side—a common feature in masonry triclinia, where these shelves were used to hold glasses and food. The rear wall of this exedra was lined with irregularly cut white marble slabs. The other walls and the upper part of the rear wall were decorated with nilotic frescoes on a pale blue background. In the middle of the central wall a waterfall cascaded gently over a flight of marble steps (Fig. 12), slipped into a hole hidden behind the marble revetment, circled in a canal behind the couches, and entered, through a lead pipe, the shallow pool in the space between the couches. From here it passed into the canal in the garden. Another water triclinium? Certainly not; the couches were too high and the pool too shallow. Nobody lying on the couches could have picked up anything from a food vessel floating on the water, nor could a food vessel have floated because the water was too shallow.

So what was the function of the shallow pool? Romans were very practical-minded people: *utilitas et decor* was their motto. Nothing was made just for the beauty of it. They

---

[22] Spinazzola, *Pompei*, 369 ff; Della Corte, *Case*, 374.
[23] F. Rakob, "Ein Grottentriklinium in Pompeji," *Mitteilungen des Römischen Instituts*, 71 (1964), 182–194.
[24] *Corpus Inscriptionum Latinarum*, 1136.

always tried to make utilitarian objects decorative as well, but that was all. Of course the shallow pool was decorative enough, but at first sight it hardly seemed useful. On the contrary, it even seemed very inconvenient. Slaves must have waded through its water to serve the dinner, and guests arriving there would even have been obliged to take off their shoes and splash in the pool. Luckily the usual supports for trays, which used to be set in the middle of the couches after all the guests had taken their places,[25] would not have been there to bother them, so they could use the bench to sit on and dry their feet before dinner. That of course was the explanation of the problem: Romans always washed their feet before dinner. In the houses of rich men the slaves rendered that service to all their master's guests.[26] In a hired triclinium it is highly possible that guests had to do it themselves, and, at least in Iulia Felix's triclinium, they had running water and other comforts at their disposal. This triclinium, with its marble couches, waterfall, nilotic frescoes on a pale blue background, and even its shallow and very useful pool, is one of the finest-looking dining arrangements in Pompeii.

Water, as you see, was very important in the water triclinia—but not only in them. Water was in fact employed whenever possible in all forms of garden triclinia, the most interesting of which are the large imperial dining areas. These garden triclinia are more complex than the normal ones. Emperors on occasion felt obliged to give large parties with thousands of guests. Sometimes only a sportula[27] was offered: a basket of victuals, something like the modern box lunch. But on other occasions it was a regular dinner with tricliniar couches and all the trimmings. We know that banquets with three thousand guests or a thousand couches were not unusual. Once Crassus asked thirty thousand people to one of his banquets,[28] but Caesar surprised everybody by inviting sixty-six thousand guests to a dinner party with twenty-three thousand couches.[29] Clearly these banquets needed large areas in which to place all the couches necessary for such a crowd.

Finding a large open space in Rome or in any of the other monumental cities of the Roman Empire was simple, nor did emperors need to have special facilities in their own palaces. There were many areas in these towns suitable for large gatherings of the populace, and the mighty Caesars could always use them to entertain their subjects.[30] Of course when the emperors chose to stay in the country, as Hadrian did, and there were no towns nearby, it was necessary to create large tricliniar areas in the imperial praedia. Space was no problem, but achieving aesthetic results with these special arrangements was difficult. One had to create an enormous esplanade where the hun-

---

[25] The tables, when they were not masonry ones, were always brought after all the guests had taken their places (Ath. 1.20).

[26] *Corpus Inscriptionum Latinarum*, 7698; Petron. 31.

[27] The sportula was a basket containing cold cuts, wine, and other victuals, and it was offered not only to clients who paid respects to their patrons but also to participants at large public parties.

[28] Plut. *Crass.* 12.

[29] Plut. *Caes.* 35.31.

[30] We know from Athenaeus that when a Roman general had to offer a banquet to the people of Rome on the occasion of a triumph, they used to prepare the dinner in a square called the Square of Hercules, evidently a large drill field which I found mentioned only on this occasion (Ath. 4.153c).

dreds of couches needed for these banquets could be arranged, but it was equally important that the place should always look attractive for it had also to be used for more informal and intimate dinner parties with few guests. Obviously anyone would feel uncomfortable dining in a space that, when empty, looked like an enormous drill field.

Roman architects solved this problem by planning pleasant gardens with riverlike pools, large water basins, and fountains of all kinds and shapes. It was in fact water that helped them separate the area into many pleasing sections and quiet corners without actually dividing it. Long porches ran along the banks of water channels; marble pavilions, built on ample esplanades, were mirrored in the blue surface of large pools; vine pergolas stood near pools, protecting the couches from the fierce rays of the midafternoon sun: everywhere in these paradisiacal places fountains and waterfalls made the summer air cool and pleasant.

But this water that partitioned all the different parts of the tricliniar areas was both the backbone of their architecture and a common feature. All the elements that made up these garden triclinia were unified by it; yet at the same time they retained their own individuality. Each component could be seen as a single unit and admired for itself because all these elements were beautiful in their own right and they did not need the ephemeral decoration of a banquet to be enjoyed. An empty marble portico with its slender columns would always be admired for its design and its position among the trees and the greenery. In addition, Roman architects in solving that problem created some of the most beautiful and monumental gardens of the ancient world: the gardens of Hadrian's villa near Tivoli.

Hadrian's villa was really not a villa at all: it was a small town that had to contain everything that a great capital could offer. It was a dream translated into solid stone and marble, a miracle created by an emperor who was also an architect and an artist and who wanted to rule the Roman Empire from a congenial residence whenever he was in Italy.

Nero had already tried to build an adequate imperial residence for the masters of all the ancient world:[31] he planned his Domus Aurea to replace the heterogeneous aggregation of buildings that his forefathers had erected on the Palatine Hills. But Romans disapproved of his indiscriminate expropriations and revolted. Hadrian did not like the Palatine palaces any more than Nero did, but he was too intelligent to repeat Nero's experience. So he did the same things that Nero had done, but he did them out of the city. Nero's task was easier because he had all the conveniences and facilities of Rome at his disposal. Hadrian, instead, had to provide all the charms and luxuries that the great capital could offer, all the refinements without which none of the elegant Romans who composed his retinue would have been content. So in Hadrian's villa we find three imperial palaces; many luxurious lodgings for the emperor's guests and for his retinue; barracks for his guards; dormitories for his servants;[32] four, maybe even

---

[31] Suet. *Ner.* 31.

[32] E. Salza Prina Ricotti, "Villa Adriana nei suoi limiti e nella sua funzionalità," *Memorie della Pontificia Accademia Romana di Archeologia* (hereafter *MemPont*), ser. 3, 14 (1982), 25–45.

six,³³ thermae; two theaters; an arena; a stadium;³⁴ porches; cryptoportici; palaestrae; gymnasiums; even a temple;³⁵ and of course several triclinia which varied from the small intimate ones³⁶ in the heart of the palaces to the large areas for popular banquets just outside the imperial enclosure.

Water here was not only of the utmost importance, but was used lavishly. In Pliny's Tuscan villa, in Sperlonga, and in Pompeii we have met only calm pools, fountains with moderate jets of water, beautiful fishponds, or the small waterfall of Iulia Felix's praedium. In Hadrian's villa water was employed on a larger scale: it thundered in gigantic waterfalls, flowed in outsize water channels such as the Canopus,³⁷ or rested in large-sized pools like the rectangular one in the middle of the Poecile.³⁸ Water was everywhere: in small and large basins, in nymphaea, and in both monumental and small fountains, always singing a song that could range from a soft murmur to a mighty roar. Water was the life of Hadrian's gardens; it was their soul. A garden in fact is made not only by lawns, trees, shrubs, blossoms, blue sky, vivid colors, and perfumed breezes; it is also made by sounds: songs of birds, rustle of leaves stirred by the wind, chirring of cicadas in the summer heat, and, above all these sounds, the music of water. Hadrian's villa had all this and was a wonderful paradisiacal place that enjoyed a splendid climate. In fact even today one can still pick violets in the valley at Christmastime.

There are three tricliniar areas in Hadrian's villa. The first and most majestic of them, the Canopus, is placed near the monumental entrance hall.³⁹ It consists of a huge *stibadium* (Fig. 13,a) inserted in an enormous exedra which is covered by a very interesting dome, now partly ruined (Fig. 14). Four powerful columns sustained its weight on the euripus side and were the only frame between the exedra and the beautiful green valley crossed by the riverlike pool (Fig. 13,b). The *stibadium*, a masonry one which has been quite well restored, had the usual slope that made reclining on it very comfortable. On the floor in front of the *stibadium* circular holes, about an inch in diameter and set

---

[33] Ricotti, ibid., 36–37. There are four thermae still existing in Hadrian's villa: the bath in the Teatro Marittimo (ibid., 34, fig. 2, B and P); the bath in the so-called Palace (S. Aurigemma, *Villa Adriana*, Rome, 1961, 77 ff; Ricotti, ibid., 33, pl. IV, G and H); and the so-called Little and Great Baths (ibid., 41, 43, 49–54, pl. VIII, H and L). In addition, there were probably two other thermae, now destroyed. Pirro Ligorio saw them, or at least their heating systems. He describes *suspensurae* and *praefurnia* existing at the so-called academy where today nothing survives. It is highly probable that they were destroyed in the 17th century when Mons. Bulgarini built the gardens of his casino over them (Pirro Ligorio, Vatican Library, Barberinus lat. 4342, fol. 49r). Ligorio found other heating systems for baths in the area of the so-called lyceum. These were also noticed by Kircher (ibid., fol. 51v; A. Kircher, *Latium id est nova et parallela Latii tum veteris tum novi . . .*, Amsterdam, 1671, 149).

[34] Ricotti, "Villa Adriana," 42, pl. I, O.
[35] Ricotti, ibid., 34, pl. IX, T.
[36] Aurigemma, *Villa Adriana*, 100–126.
[37] Aurigemma, ibid., 100–133; Ricotti, "Villa Adriana," pl. VII, R.
[38] Aurigemma, ibid., 51–58; Ricotti, "Villa Adriana," pl. IX.
[39] W.L. Reichhardt, "The Vestibule Group at Hadrian's Villa," *Memoirs of the American Academy in Rome*, 11 (1933), 127–132; E. Salza Prina Ricotti, "Criptoportici e gallerie sotterranee di Villa Adriana nella loro tipologia e nelle loro funzioni," in *Les cryptoportiques dans l'architecture romaine*, Collection de l'Ecole Française de Rome, 140, Rome, 1973, 241–244, pl. X; Ricotti, "Villa Adriana," 41–42.

in groups of three, seem to suggest the presence of bronze supports for either a long shelf such as the one in Iulia Felix's triclinium or several small tables for the convenience of the diners.[40]

The wall of the exedra is decorated by a series of semicircular niches, which probably contained statues, and rectangular ones that still have flights of steps once lined with marble. The ever-present water cascaded gently down these steps. It did not have the force of a real waterfall but only made the marble shimmer and shine; it improved its quality and enhanced its colors. We can imagine the beauty of the liquid veil, ever changing in the daylight, gliding silently in a canal that circled around the back of the *stibadium,* passing under the masonry couch to flow in another canal in front of the crescent-shaped couch and, at last, through an underground pipe, reaching the large euripus that resembled a majestic and peaceful river (Fig. 15). The steep slopes overlooking the canal of the little valley were covered with green lawns and fringes of evergreen shrubs. On the riverbanks svelte marble columns and stately statues,[41] copies of famous Grecian originals, cast their reflection on the blue surface.

In the center of the exedra a deep recess very much like a miniature gorge (14 ft. 5 in. wide, 68 ft. 11 in. long, 43 ft. 11 in. deep), only partially covered by a barrel vault, ended in a foaming waterfall (Fig. 13,c) that was the focal point and dramatic terminus of the Canopus. An aqueduct coming from the hill just south of the Canopus furnished a great quantity of water which collected in a large basin just above the waterfall. Here the impurities in the water settled out. Once it had become clear and pure, it was brought by two canals, which ran at a height of 45 feet above the ground, to the various chutes. The first one of these, the one at the back end of the gorge, formed the great waterfall that attracted the attention of bystanders and was the start of the euripus. The water channel flowed from the back of the gorge, passed under the exedra, and followed its course to the end of the valley. A platform (Figs. 13,d and 16) was built over the central part of the gorge. It had marble floors and marble-lined walls, and was covered by a mosaic-encrusted vault[42]—a very luxurious decoration, which indicated that this place must have been a triclinium and one very much in evidence. Anyone dining there could not fail to attract the attention of every bystander. It was in fact a very impressive arrangement against the dramatic background of the waterfall and with the light that came on a slanted angle from the unroofed part of the deep recess. Furthermore, the platform could be reached by only one door, and water surrounded its two free sides; from the point of view of security, it was a good place for an emperor

---

[40] Petron. 34. During the banquet Trimalchio orders a table to be brought to each of his guests so that they may be freed from the constant presence of the slaves. Of course to have a little table all for oneself was considered a great refinement at the ancient dinners. Athenaeus, describing the dining arrangement in the convivial tent of Ptolemy Philadelphus, writes, "Beside the guests, as they reclined, were set three-legged tables of gold, two hundred in number, making two to each couch; they were set upon silver rests (Ath. 5.197b; tr. C.B. Gulick, Loeb ed., London, 1928).

[41] Aurigemma, *Villa Adriana,* 100–133.

[42] Garden triclinia always had some kind of roof over them. It could be a vine trellis or it could be the dome of an open pavilion.

who could be the target of any kind of treacherous attack.[43] The barrel vault that protected the place from rainfall, its elevated position, inaccessibility, and dramatic placement in respect to light were the result of careful and wise planning. These elements all show that not only was this site designed as a triclinium but also that it was the ideal setting for an imperial dining area; we can imagine Hadrian presiding there when he gave one of the huge parties mentioned earlier.

Looking more closely at the exedra we notice that this triclinium and the *stibadium* are not the only two dining arrangements there. In fact just between the *stibadium* and the valley euripus we can see a semicircular pool (Fig. 13,e) where food containers could be floated over the water (Fig. 17); it stands to reason that we have here another water triclinium, for the semicircular strip of ground between that pool and the masonry *stibadium* is large enough to allow the placing of a low semicircular couch at the pool edge and still leave a passage for the slaves who circulated the food to the guests reclining on the principal *stibadium*. The visual effect of the three triclinia set on three different levels, from the lowest one close to the ground to the highest one set on a platform,[44] must have been powerful (Fig. 18). It was also very wisely planned, because when an emperor, any emperor, was involved the scenario had to be taken into account carefully: a large part of the awe inspired by a man, who was deemed to be a god and surely would become a god on his death, depended on the way people saw him during his public appearances.[45] Certainly the emperor in all his splendor dominating the scene, with his retinue set on different levels in front of him as in a Byzantine mosaic, must have been an imposing spectacle.

In addition to the triclinia in the exedra two others were placed just at the beginning of the valley, beside the euripus. Here two charming pavilions looked on the euripus banks through delightful semicircular porches with marble columns (Figs. 13,f and 19). Two alcoves in each one of them had well-defined places, slightly elevated from the floor, for the tricliniar couches. Each one had a small sitting room overlooking the biclinia through wide openings, and in each of these *cubicula* a pedestal was placed in an apselike niche. We might well imagine that when Hadrian's villa was at its peak statues of gods or heroes associated with some well-known myth stood there facing each other through the pavilions' large openings and over the blue water of the euripus.

---

[43] All the emperors were targets of assassination plots, some planned by ambitious people who wanted to take power, some by citizens tired of the emperor's tyranny. In every imperial palace precautions were taken against these perils, and some of the emperors were so fearful that they did not even dare to stroll in their own peristyle. Domitian was one of these, and for some very good reasons. He had all the walls of his peristyle covered with a special kind of marble called *phengitis*, which was so smooth and brilliant that it was just like a mirror. When Domitian walked there he could always be sure that nobody was following him. In fact he could see everything that was happening at his back without having to turn around (Suet. *Dom.* 14).

[44] In the ancient world tricliniar couches of very important personages or gods were set higher than normal ones (Ath. 4.148, 153b).

[45] An idea of the scenario in which an emperor, at least those that followed Augustus, lived and died may be gained by reading descriptions of the apotheosis ceremony in E. Beurlier, *Culte impérial*, Paris, 1891, 28, 61–67; Dio 56.34.3; 74.4; Suet. *Aug.* 100.

The use of the pavilions' biclinia was certainly intended for high dignitaries or for members of Hadrian's retinue, as were the water triclinia and the masonry *stibadia*. People of lesser standing had to take their places on couches set on the riverbanks.[46] It should be noted that the east bank (Fig. 13,g) was shaded by a long porch, while the west bank had no protection (Fig. 20). It is interesting to speculate why there was only one porch and why, if only for the sake of symmetry, none was built on the west bank. A solution to this little problem, probably an accurate one, might be this: the Canopus tricliniar area was a summer one and it was oriented to the north (north-northeast, to be exact), so the riverbanks were set on the east and west sides of the Canopus valley. On summer afternoons the east bank would have been hit hard by the rays of the sun, so a porch was built there. But the west bank would already have been in the shade: technically it did not need any protection from the sun and, from a Roman builder's point of view, there was absolutely no reason to erect something that would have satisfied mainly an aesthetic whim, a love of symmetry and nothing else. It surely was not essential or useful. So they simply did not build a west porch.

To conclude the examination of this first imperial garden triclinium of Hadrian's villa, we must emphasize the skillful way in which all parts of this tricliniar area were arranged. We can easily see that in such a place as the Canopus it was possible to have either large parties with lots of people or small parties with only a few guests. During the great imperial banquets the place, with its well-kept gardens, festoons of fragrant leaves, flowers and fruits suspended along the colonnades, the guests wearing their most beautiful garments,[47] and the handsome slaves carrying large trays with colorful food, must have offered a gorgeous spectacle. But even when only a small party dined around the water triclinium or on the great *stibadium* the Canopus valley would have looked impressive and fascinating, and it would never give the diners enjoying their meal the feeling of being lost in a desert.

The second tricliniar area for large parties at Hadrian's villa that we will examine was composed of a series of buildings and pavilions where the covered places were harmoniously alternated with open areas, atria, peristyles, and gardens flanked by long porches (Fig. 21). Water was also present, though in a less spectacular way than in the Canopus. After passing through the present entrance of the villa and crossing the large peristyle garden of the Poecile (Fig. 22), we find what is called the Building of the Three Exedras. Its central part consists of a large space once covered by a vault, probably a carpentry one (Fig. 21,a). There are semicircular peristyle gardens on three of its sides, and on the fourth one it has a monumental fountain (Figs. 21,b and 23). It was, without

---

[46] The tricliniar couches could be arranged in many ways: they could form a horseshoe (a *triclinium*, a word that afterward was used to denote all the dining rooms), or two couches could be set like an L or facing one another (a *biclinium*). Sometimes, when there were many couches, they were placed in a row under a porch or in a large circle, like the 130 couches under the tent of King Ptolemy Philadelphus (Ath. 5.196b).

[47] In the ancient world people used to wear special dining apparel, very colorful and made of precious materials (Petron. 30).

doubt, a triclinium.[48] Between this part of the building and the so-called Stadium garden we find a great hall (Fig. 21,c) that was once decorated with two large paintings. On each side of it there are three smaller rooms (Fig. 21,d) with very large windows opening onto the surrounding gardens. These rooms were used either for entertainment or for placing in them supplementary couches, or again for offering people a corner to relax.

From this part of the building two doors led into a place now called the Stadium[49] because of its shape (Figs. 21,e–h and 24); this place was actually a garden with pools, flower beds, lawns, porches, and pavilions—a garden that evidently was also used for the great imperial banquets. From the Stadium and from the Three Exedras building, when need arose, the tricliniar arrangements could overflow into the Poecile area. For that reason this must have been the place where the larger parties were held. In the center of the Stadium there is a large, square-shaped area (Fig. 21,e) that must have been left free for actors, musicians, dancers, singers, and clowns to perform their acts. On both sides of this square two large pavilions offered a shelter for the tricliniar couches (Fig. 21,f and g). One on the southern side (Fig. 25) bordered a nymphaeum: a large pool fed by a springlike fountain that spouted in a little artificial grotto (Figs. 21,h and 26). This pool occupied nearly all the space in the semicircular area, which imitated the curved end of a real stadium. The remaining area was taken up by a flight of steps above the grotto.

On the other end of the axis a pavilion (Fig. 21,f) was placed between the central open area and a garden (Fig. 21,i). A shallow euripus flanked by two flower beds extended the length of the garden (Fig. 27). This northern pavilion was smaller than the southern one and had more space around it. Inside it we can still see the remains of the *opus sectile* that covered the floor and what is left of a shallow pool, probably a marble one. Small octagonal marble fountains and tile pedestals for garden sculptures were placed along the outside walls. An elegant portico surrounded the pavilion and garden. On the northern side of this garden, where the stables would have been placed in a real stadium, we find three luxurious rooms (Fig. 21,j) with *opus sectile* floors and frescoes on their walls. The central room, which was an exedra, contains some of the most elaborate *opus sectile* in the whole villa and has a large niche on the rear wall in which some valuable work of art was probably placed. This exedra was certainly used as a triclinium during the large imperial parties, and the two rooms on both sides were probably also arranged with tricliniar couches.

On the east side of the tricliniar area we find the palace's ground floor (Fig. 21,m and n), which was at a higher level than the Stadium and the Three Exedras building but had large openings on the square open court. The central hall (Fig. 21,n) was of the kind defined by Vitruvius as a Corinthian triclinium[50] and was probably the emperor's. We find here the same features we have already noticed in the Canopus platform: it answered the security requirements because access was easily controlled and it was ele-

---

[48] H. Kahler, *Hadrian und seine Villa bei Tivoli*, Berlin, 1950, 55–64; Aurigemma, *Villa Adriana*, 75–77.
[49] A. Hoffmann, *Das Gartenstadion in der Villa Hadriana*, Mainz, 1980.
[50] Vitr. 6.5.8.

vated. Everyone could admire the emperor in all his majesty, but at the same time this exalted personage was not obliged to come into too close contact with his guests, a practice that could prove to be very dangerous. For all these reasons this tricliniar area is well adapted to the imperial scenario that we already admired in the Canopus (Fig. 28). On both its sides minor halls were destined for the emperor's retinue. There each courtier would have been placed following the strict rules of rank at the court.

The third official reception area is called the Piazza d'Oro.[51] This name reflects the luxurious decoration and the great number of statues found in the excavations. Splendid *opus sectile* and mosaic covered its floors, elegant fluted columns with very fine Corinthian capitals and a particularly graceful frieze, in which a multitude of sea creatures and hunting Erotes played lustfully, decorated the square; porches encircled its gardens, and nymphaea made water an important architectonic element of this edifice. The Piazza d'Oro, in close proximity to the great reception buildings of the palace, was different from the other two tricliniar areas. Apart from its beauty, it offered more comfort. People, for instance, could get there with their own carriages and could dismount at the entrance hall of the Piazza d'Oro (Fig. 29) by traveling through the large underground road that linked all the principal buildings of Hadrian's villa.[52] Moreover, while in the other two tricliniar areas we find an elevated and well-protected zone that kept the emperor in absolute isolation and, at the same time, very much in view, here there was nothing of the kind. Of course the emperor would always appear in the main hall (Fig. 30,a) at the center of the building, the focal point where the principal axes of symmetry crossed each other; but apart from that there would have been no other differentiation. No walls separated one triclinium from the others; no high podium raised the emperor above the other diners, dwarfing them and keeping him aloof. The view ran the length of the building (Fig. 31), framed only by fluted columns. The emperor reclined here like a normal host among his friends and not like a god presiding over subjects.

Apart from this fundamental difference, this tricliniar area offered the same conveniences found in the other two. As in the Canopus and in the Stadium, banquets could be held with hundreds of guests or with only a few friends without altering in the least the aesthetic values of the place. The building was in fact divided into many pavilions and niches. Triclinia could be prepared in one of them, in two, or in the whole building, depending on the number of guests. For very large parties even the porches and the peristyle garden could have been set up with temporary arrangements.

Water, as always, was present here; it played in the four small nymphaea opening on the four sides of the main pavilion and dominated the central one (Fig. 30,b) which was enclosed by a massive wall gracefully curving at the back of the main hall (Fig. 32).

[51] For the Piazza d'Oro see: E. Hansen, *La Piazza d'Oro e la sua cupola*, Copenhagen, 1960, 46 ff; Kahler, *Villa*, 64 ff, pl. 15; L. Crema, "L'architettura romana," in *Enciclopedia classica*, III, 12, 1, Torino, 1959, 477, fig. 615; F.E. Brown, "Hadrianic Architecture," in *Essays in Memory of K. Lehman*, New York, 1964, 58; F. Rakob, *Die Piazza d'Oro in Villa Adriana*, Rome, 1970, passim. Everyone except Dr. Rakob is convinced that the great hall of the Piazza d'Oro was covered by a dome, and I concur.

[52] Ricotti, "Criptoportici," 231–234, pls. I, V–VII.

This arrangement recalls the plan of the octagonal hall of the Domus Aurea, Nero's great triclinium.[53] A pool followed the curve of the Piazza d'Oro's nymphaeum, and its surface reflected the series of rectangular and semicircular alternating niches that decorated the back wall (Fig. 30,b). The four smaller nymphaea (Figs. 30,c and 31) around the central hall had rectangular niches set over semicircular pools. In front of each of these pools the place for a tricliniar couch is clearly defined by a slightly elevated podium. On the other sides of the central hall two courtyards (Figs. 30,d and 33) were enclosed by straight and curved rows of columns, a beautiful example of Hadrianic baroque design. A marble basin filled with rainwater stood in the middle of each courtyard. Graceful exedras opened on three of their sides. The larger ones were placed at the extremities of the building's longitudinal axis (Fig. 30,e), and in the middle of their back walls there were semicircular niches for statues. On both sides of these two exedras there were other rooms (Fig. 30,f). We don't know exactly how they were used, but we can speculate that they had the same function as Pliny's *zoothecula*.[54]

On the cross axis, the one extending through all the garden from the principal pavilion to the entrance hall, the majestic reception room was in direct contact with the great portico of the peristyle garden and overlooked it. The portico (Fig. 30,g), with a beautiful floor covered by a fine *opus sectile*, was a double porch divided in two by a central row of columns. The walls were decorated with little tile columns that leant against brick pilaster strips. Both the long sides of the quadriportico were flanked by two monumental cryptoportici (Fig. 30,h) that made it possible to stroll leisurely even in rainy and windy weather or during the torrid summer heat. On sunny and warm days it must have been very pleasant to stroll in the quadriportico enjoying the charms of the garden.

From what we can see today this garden (Fig. 34), with its shallow euripus (Fig. 30,i), must have been a beautiful area. Along the sides of this canal the local clay soil had been replaced with fertile humus; planting beds flanked the artificial river (Fig. 30,k). We do not know if flowers were grown here. It is more likely that the principal feature of this garden consisted of boxwood hedges and that these were clipped in the most fashionable shapes that second-century topiary art could suggest—an architectonic garden well suited to the monumental character of the building.

As we have seen, it is difficult to find a Roman garden triclinium in which water was not a fundamental element of the design. But what happened when villas were built in places where there were no springs or aqueducts? Did wealthy Romans give up the enjoyment of silvery jets of fountains or the ripple that breezes created on the surface

---

[53] For the most up-to-date plan of the great octagonal hall of the Domus Aurea see L. Fabbrini, "Domus Aurea: Il piano superiore del quartiere orientale," *MemPont*, ser. 3, 14 (1982), pls. I, II.

[54] In all these tricliniar areas we have found zones undoubtedly planned for tricliniar couches. Nearly always near them there are other, more secluded rooms. This happens in the Canopus where, on the east side of the exedra, some rooms were probably used as Pliny's *zoothecula*, while on the west side there is even a large gallery, probably used to entertain people or to stroll in either during the rainy season or on hot summer days. Exactly the same kind of rooms are found in the great imperial tricliniar area of the Piazza d'Oro.

of their pools? Of course they had to, but that did not mean that they renounced the beauties of water: they had only to find other ways. It is true that Roman villas were not always placed near rivers or springs that could furnish them water to embellish their gardens, but sometimes they dominated lovely lakes or, more often, stood by the sea. They could not have fountains or waterfalls, but they could always enjoy views of the waves. We know many of these maritime villas, and many of them are splendid, but let us examine one of the best known, even if it has not yet been excavated. It is the Laurentinum of Pliny the Younger, a place where, as Pliny himself declares, the only water available was furnished by wells.

Until recently the Laurentinum was known only from the vivid description by its owner in a letter in which he asked one of his friends, Gallo, to come and visit him.[55] The description is, as always in Pliny's letters, very accurate, and many architects,[56] myself included,[57] have tried their hand at reconstructing the villa (Fig. 35). Pliny's description of the long sequence of the atrium, the D-shaped portico with glass panes between the columns, the *cavedium,* and finally the fine triclinium overlooking the sea, and built on the beach so near the shore that the waves pushed by the sirocco wind broke foaming against its buttresses, is well known.

This fascinating letter has caught the fancy of many persons, and for centuries people have not only tried to draw the plan of the building but have dreamed of finding it again. In 1935–36 a villa that was said to be the Laurentinum of Pliny was excavated by Professor Antonio Maria Colini. The location of this villa was established on the basis of Pliny's statement that the Laurentinum was very near a village and that there was only one other building between his villa and the hamlet. When the village was found (it was a *vicus* called Vicus Augustanus)[58] Prince Chigi, who owned the adjoining estate, affirmed that the remains of a Roman villa found on his property had to be the Laurentinum. It was in fact the second building from the Vicus Augustanus in the direction of Ostia.

When the villa was excavated it had nothing in common with Pliny's description. However, many archaeologists, R. Lanciani among them, accepted the identification. Lanciani dismissed doubt about the identity of the villa stating that since the building had lasted until the fifth century A.D. it had surely suffered some alterations.[59] As an

---

[55] Pliny *Ep.* 2.17.

[56] Tanzer's book (above, n. 2) was published in 1924. Other reconstructions have been made since then. One of the most recent is by L. Krier (*La Laurentine et l'invention de la villa romaine,* Paris, 1982). Dr. Krier does not seem to be acquainted with the Laurentinum's flat and sandy topography, for he solved the problem by imagining a rocky promontory, the kind of landscape one can find only on the island of Capri or around Positano. The reconstruction, because it is not based on the actual physical condition of the site, has no validity.

[57] E. Salza Prina Ricotti, "La Villa Laurentina di Plinio il Giovane: Un'ennesima ricostruzione," *Lunario romano* (1983), 229–251.

[58] The Vicus Augustanus was studied and published by G. Simonazzi Masarich, "Vicus Augustanus Laurentinum," *Monumenti dei Lincei—Miscellanea,* I, 5 (1973), 289–306.

[59] R. Lanciani, "Le antichità del territorio Laurentino nella Reale Tenuta di Castel Porziano," *Monumenti antichi dei Lincei,* 13 (1903), 193.

architect I could not agree, because even if one can greatly alter a house, it is impossible to change its fundamental structure. So when Professor Colini[60] asked me to do research on it, I declared that to the best of my knowledge the so-called "Pliny's villa of Castel Fusano" was not the Laurentinum. To turn the Laurentinum into the Castel Fusano villa all its walls would have had to be destroyed and its foundations uprooted. Then one would have to rebuild it *ex novo* and make an entirely new edifice bearing no relationship to the old one. If this had been the case, all the masonry of its walls would have been later than the second century A.D., while the Castel Fusano villa is mostly built with *opus reticulatum* of the first century B.C. and it certainly does not seem to have suffered any kind of radical alteration since then.

After having established this fact, I decided to have a look around because the real Laurentinum could not have been very far away. As I have already pointed out, in his letter Pliny says that the Laurentinum was near a village (*vicus*) and he also says that to reach the Laurentinum one could use the Ostiense road as well as the Laurentina. It stands to reason that they were equivalent and that both the *vicus* and the villa had to be on the stretch of coast that extends between the end of the two roads. But on this shore there is only the village of the Vicus Augustanus: so it had to be the one Pliny was speaking about. Moreover, we already know from Pliny's letter that there was only one other building between his villa and the *vicus*. Since the villa in this location on the Ostia side had already been excavated and had proved *not* to be the Laurentinum, then Pliny's villa had to be on the other side. In fact the only thing that Pliny does not say in his letter is on which side of the *vicus* the Laurentinum was located.

Of course all these indications helped me greatly in my research and made my work easier: Pliny had told his friend how to reach the Laurentinum coming from Rome, the *vicus* had been found, and the villa on the other side had already been excavated, making it possible to eliminate it as the Laurentinum. So the only thing I had to do was to sit down at my drawing board, look at the plans and maps, and pinpoint the location of Pliny's villa (Fig. 36).

Knowing what to look for, I went to explore the actual spot. Deep in the woods I found the ruins of a large building, the second one starting from the Vicus Augustanus and going toward Laurentum. Finding the place where the Laurentinum stood was easy, certainly much easier than making a survey of it. That was indeed very hard work. But thanks to my innate stubbornness, I succeeded in drawing a plan of the surface remains and of the heap of rubble formed by tiles, broken marbles, ruins of walls, and large chunks of concrete and plaster.[61] The plan at this time is very sketchy, but it has many points of contact with my previous reconstruction (Fig. 37). There is a striking correspondence between the disposition of the different parts of the building on the

---

[60] I wish to acknowledge the kindness of Prof. Antonio Maria Colini who gave me the plan, surveyed and drawn by himself, of the Castel Fusano villa; moreover, he persuaded me to do that interesting research and offered me all the help, support, and encouragement needed for my work.

[61] On 10 December 1983 I gave the news of my discovery to the Accademia dei Lincei; the result of my research, along with the map, will appear in the *Rendiconti dell'Accademia dei Lincei*.

ground and the villa described in Pliny's letter. Notably, the position of the garden, the tower near the sea, the cryptoportico, and the private pavilion, so enjoyed by Pliny, correspond to his description, as does the position of the principal parts of the villa with respect to the garden and its buildings.

The excavations will give the final word. If my thesis should prove to be correct, we might be able to see the fine triclinium on the shore, but only if the sea, too near to its walls, has not washed it away, as I greatly fear. Perhaps at least something will be left and we will understand how it was. At that moment and only at that moment will we be able to fully savor the importance that water, any form of water, played in the decoration of Roman triclinia and how much a charming essential it was considered at Roman banquets. There was no running water in the Laurentinum, it is true, but, as you can see, Pliny solved the problem all the same and, while dining, he could enjoy the ever-moving view of the rolling waves and the beauty of the sun sinking into them in a triumph of gold and purple.[62]

---

[62] I must now acknowledge the help that has been given to me by Dr. Elisabeth Blair MacDougall who very kindly revised this text. I must also thank for their help the Superintendent of Latium, Dr. Maria Luisa Veloccia; the then Superintendent of Pompeii, Dr. Giuseppina Cerulli Irelli; the Superintendent of Ostia, Dr. Valnea Scrinari Santamaria; the Directors of the Park of Castel Porziano: first, the late Dr. Gian Lauro Costantini and now the new director, Dr. Giovanni Emiliani. I also extend my thanks to Dr. Betty Jo Majeska and Edward Lynch who had the patience to read my paper and give me some suggestions, and to Fabrizio Luciolli who took many of the photographs needed to illustrate it. A very special acknowledgment goes to Prof. Wilhelmina Jashemski and to Dumbarton Oaks.

Town in Country and Country in Town

NICHOLAS PURCELL

Gardens mean something quite different in every culture, and garden art has very different associations for different societies. Landscape is a fundamental ingredient of Roman gardens, but they were not, in any sense of the term that is familiar to us, landscape gardens. This paper is a historian's attempt to explore some of the attitudes and traditions which lay behind the complex relationships between gardens, architecture, and the landscape in Italy in the first century A.D. It is written in the belief that it is only by attempting to dissect these associations that it is possible to appreciate the choice of particular patterns and elements in the domestic architecture and design of antiquity; and that the exercise is important because that choice tells us important things about the perceptions and preferences of the Romans, a fascinatingly alien society. In the case of the theme of this paper to attempt this is not to be excessively subtle, because domestic and garden architecture was an intellectually rarefied, highly allusive creation, dominated by complex traditions and consciously linked with important philosophical questions of how man should behave and what is his relationship with the natural setting in which he finds himself. I hope that this aim of investigating a little of the ancient view of the place of humanity in nature through the study of garden art would have appealed to Mildred Bliss, one of the founders of Dumbarton Oaks, who clearly understood how fruitful this kind of research could be.[1]

A mental picture of the reality of town and country in the Roman period, and of the zone of transition between them, is a basic prerequisite for understanding how wealthy proprietors reacted to each in commissioning designs for villas, houses, and their settings. I therefore preface this paper with a description of the changing view as it would have been seen by a traveler leaving Rome in about A.D. 55, with Nero as emperor. The exercise is necessarily imaginative, but constructed with the belief that what was possible can be as important to scholarship as what can be proven to have been so.

We leave the Roman Forum beside the luxury food market and head northeast. Our ancient street, the Argiletum (near the present Vie Leonina and Urbana) is at first lined with quite expensive shops in the ground floors of very high tenement buildings. Up side streets, very narrow alleys, we can see the ground rising very steeply, especially on the right. Behind the serried ranks of apartment blocks up there every now and then one can see at the top of the hill the foliage of plane trees or cypresses projecting above the low roofs of the wealthy peristyle houses of the Carinae district. We start to climb, the shops become rather more ordinary; we pass a square dominated by the grand

---

[1] I should like to thank Professors E. MacDougall and W. Jashemski and Dumbarton Oaks for their kind invitation to give this paper and for their hospitality, and also the audience at the Symposium for their helpful reactions. All abbreviations below for ancient authors and their works are those found in N.G.L. Hammond and H.H. Scullard, eds., *The Oxford Classical Dictionary*, 2nd ed., Oxford, 1970, ix–xxii. All translations are my own.

facade of the portico of Livia and containing a public reservoir and fountain decorated with a statue of Orpheus. The road (the ancient Via Tiburtina) climbs steeply and takes us through a monumental marble arch out of the ancient city at the Esquiline Gate. The view is now rather different; the road ahead is dead straight for one thing, and there is much less building. We still see occasional, rather lower blocks of apartments, but in between are tombs, and long stuccoed rubble walls along the road and its branches.[2] They are just too high to peer over, but the trees planted behind them are much taller and form thick shady groves. Through the shade, groups of buildings can be seen, porticoes opening onto the trees, isolated pavilions or towers amid the woodland, and quite extensive houses near which much more exotic foliage than bay or oak is to be seen. Water is running everywhere—an aqueduct runs beside our route, and the noise of fountains is clearly to be heard from these properties from which we are excluded. On our right, just opposite the ill-omened sacred wood of Libitina, the goddess of funerals, is a particularly fine cluster of buildings and gardens, which seems to have taken over the old city wall entirely; this we know to be the emperor's property, the Gardens of Maecenas, and it is crowned by a fine tower which is a well-known feature of the Roman skyline.[3] As we proceed beside the boundary walls of the various gardens the style becomes less opulent. The tombs are now often set in little plots of land which have been planted with a vine or a couple of apple trees.[4] In some it is clear that even cabbages and leeks are being grown beside the podium of the tomb, within the enclosure of its outer wall. We cross rather dirty ditches on whose banks the reeds are being cut for vine props.[5] Now some of the properties are clearly agricultural, designed, in many cases, for the production of flowers for ceremonial garlands.[6] There are still quite a lot of dwelling houses, now very modest and each clearly dependent on an obsessively cultivated market garden.

Quite suddenly, as we approach the edge of a larger stream valley the view opens out, right across the rolling Campagna to the slopes of the Appennines eighteen miles ahead; they are spotted with the white stucco of rich houses, and we can just see the

---

[2] For sand pits and small estates outside the Porta Esquilina see Cic., *Clu.* 37 (shortly before the tidying up of the area, on which see n. 27 below).

[3] For the tower see Hor. *Carm.* 3.29; Suet. *Ner.* 38; cf. below, 194 f and n. 34.

[4] Inscriptions from thse *cepotaphia* (garden tombs) describe many such plots in detail. See *Corpus Inscriptionum Latinarum*, VI, 13823: "to this tomb belong the vegetable garden which is enclosed within the wall, and the summer house built beside the door to serve as a porter's lodge"; ibid., 31852: "shops, three in number, to left and right of the tomb . . . and the enclosed market garden within, and including the lodgings on the upper stories of the shops"; ibid., 15993: "the garden in which are the dining rooms, the vine pergola, the well and the shrine . . . ." See W.F. Jashemski, *The Gardens of Pompeii*, New Rochelle, N.Y., 1979, chap. 6.

[5] Note, for example, the *fossa* (ditch) and reed bed (*harundinetum*) marked on the plan of a *cepotaphium* (*Corpus Inscriptionum Latinarum*, VI, 8692; cf. the reed cutter, *harundinarius*, ibid., 9456); see C. Huelsen, "Piante iconografiche incise in marmo," *Deutsches archäologisches Institut. Römische Mitteilungen*, 5 (1890), 46 ff.

[6] On garland making see P. Grimal, *Les jardins romains*, 2nd ed., Paris, 1969, 60; cf. Cato *Agr.* 8; Varro *Rust.* 1.16.3: "and in the vicinity of the city it is a good thing to have extensive market gardens, and violet and rose beds and so on, for the various things which the city consumes."

gold of the roof of the Temple of Hercules at Tivoli glinting in the sun. Here, along the valley edge on both sides of the road, massive foundations have leveled the slope and opulent houses are arranged on them to exploit the view that we too are enjoying. They too have greenery in their courtyards and in enclosures beside them on the terraces; they are an impressive sight, raised above road and countryside, and round them are quite extensive outbuildings which show that they house numerous dependents. At a road junction further on there are some bars and quite a village has grown up on the strength of the main road; around it the fields are like those we have passed, but beyond it instead of cucumbers, lettuce, artichokes, violets, and lilies, the view is of fields of wheat and barley and quite a number of vineyards.[7] The big houses by the road, though still impressive, have farmyards attached now, and only where the view is particularly good are they as grand as the ones we saw earlier. There is still a feeling of bustle, and the countryside is clearly well populated and prosperous; but the hills ahead and to our right, more clearly visible as the sun begins to wester after our ten-mile walk, are clearly all forested and wild; it is only sharp to our right on the ridge of Tusculum that the hand of man is apparent in another handsome collection of villas and country houses. It is appropriate to end our imaginative tour at this point, in the depths of the Roman Campagna.[8]

If we took a walk similar to this through the outskirts of a modern city—naturally something more than an afternoon stroll—I have little doubt that we could agree about the point at which the city stopped and the countryside began. "Countryside" is a crucial, and very distinctive, term. It is one that is very rich in associations which we should be extremely wary of linking to the various translations of the word which are possible in the languages of other cultures. This is a caution which is oddly rare, or I should not emphasize it so. It is for us, to begin with, a landscape term, and I am far from certain that in Latin *rus* is also a landscape term. We would, I think, have taken the built-up area as a basic guide to our decision as to where the countryside around a modern city began. The Romans too had a sophisticated notion of "built-up area," the *continentia aedificia*, "buildings with no space in between," by which their jurists were accustomed to define a city which like Rome had sprawled beyond the girdle of its walls.[9] But it would not, I feel, have occurred to people to say, "Here is the edge of the *continentia aedificia*, the *rus* starts here." That is not an opposition which was made. The conse-

---

[7] For intensive horticulture in the neighborhood of Rome, see Cic. *Fam.* 16.18.2; Pliny *HN* 19.110 (leeks and cabbages of Aricia); also Aethicus, *Geographi Latini Minores*, ed. A. Riese, Heilbronn, 1878, 83, quoted by R. Meiggs, *Roman Ostia*, 2nd ed., Oxford, 1973, 265. See also Jashemski, *Gardens of Pompeii*, chap. 15.

[8] In general on the density of habitation in the imperial period in this part of the Campagna see L. Quilici, *Collatia* (= *Forma Italiae*, reg. 1, vol. 10), Rome, 1974, 45 ff; on the built-up *suburbium* G. Lugli, "Il suburbio di Roma," *Bullettino della Commissione Archeologica Comunale di Roma*, 51 (1923), 3 ff; L. Quilici, "La Campagna romana come suburbio di Roma antica," *Parola del passato*, 158–159 (1974), 410 ff; E. Champlin, "The *Suburbium* of Rome," *Classical Quarterly* (forthcoming); and the monograph of the present author, *The Gardens of Rome* (forthcoming).

[9] *Dig.* 33.9.4.4–5; 50.16.2 Compare Dionysius of Halicarnassus 4.13 on Rome's "endless urban sprawl" in the reign of Augustus.

quence is that we must not look only for scenic reconstructions of the rural environment in our search for *rus in urbe*. They may be present, but we must be very careful about assuming that they are the important feature.

It is, of course, the case that ancient writers talk about the imitation of nature. Probably the most famous passage is to be found in a quotation of the Augustan moralist Papirius Fabianus in the *Controversiae* of Seneca the Elder, which needs to be quoted in full. "They copy," he says of the luxurious proprietors of the time, "even mountains and forests in their damp houses, and in the sunless smog green places, coastlines, and streams. For my part I find it incredible that they have ever seen a wood or a meadow fresh with grass [if they think that their puny creations rival nature]."[10] What is happening here? Fabianus is attacking the callous inversion of the natural order—a concern which we shall meet again repeatedly—and the self-deceit of those who flatter themselves that they are able to create like nature. Now, if I sow some wild flower seeds in my shrubbery at home, I do not expect my attempt at evoking the wild places of the English hedgerows to attract this sort of unfavorable attention. To understand the objection of Fabianus and his Stoic friends we will need a larger concept than *rus in urbe*. The fact is that imitating the natural world did not, for a moneyed Roman, stop at an arbor and a grotto with a spring.

The Romans knew a fable—it had become almost a proverb by the age of Cicero—that a man had once approached Alexander the Great, that grandest of rulers, with a proposal for a statue of the king which alone, he claimed, would do justice to his royal stature and standing. His modest plan was to fashion Mount Athos (which is thirty miles long and rises to nearly six and a half thousand feet in a great cliff above the Aegean) into a colossal likeness of Alexander. In the monarch's left hand a city of thousands of inhabitants would rise, while the right hand would bear a huge sculpted sacrificial dish into which all the waters of the mountain would collect and be poured out in a great perpetual stream into the sea.[11] Not even the monument of Mount Rushmore was devised on quite so lavish a scale. As is worthy of the most superlative of ancient rulers, we have here the most ludicrously extreme example of a tendency which was widely recognized in antiquity for absolute kings to wish to express their power by altering the face of nature—and one source remarks that Alexander was occupied in making many much more bizarre and expensive plans![12] This is not the place to explore the back-

---

[10] Sen. *Controv.* 2.1.3. Another locus classicus is Sen. *Ep.* 122, where he attacks various unnatural practices, like drinking before meals and transvestism: "Do they not seem to you to live against nature who long for roses in winter and force spring flowers with hot water treatments and careful adjustment of sites in cold weather? Or those who sow orchards on top of towers—their woods toss on the summits and pinnacles of buildings, with their roots where the roofs should be? Or those who lay the foundations of their baths out to sea and don't think they are bathing comfortably unless tide and storm agitate their hot pools?" See also [Quint.], *Declamationes* (ed. M. Winterbottom, *The Minor Declamations Ascribed to Quintilian*, Berlin, 1984) 298: "compare the perennial flow of rivers with the waters which your walls confine. What is so good about your groves? What is remarkable about all this except that it counterfeits the countryside?"

[11] Vitr. *De Arch.* 2, *pr.* (calling the designer, probably correctly, Deinocrates), cf. Cic. *Rep.* 3, fr. 5; Plut. *Mor.* 335c, cf. *Alex.* 72.3–4 (calling him Stasicrates); Strab. 14.641 (Cheirocrates); Scholia to *Il.* 14.229 (Diocles); Lucian, *Hist. conscr.* 12; cf. *pro imag.* 9.

[12] Plut. *Alex.* loc. cit. (n. 11): πολλῷ δ' ἀτοπώτερα καὶ δαπανηρότερα τούτων σοφιζόμενος.

ground of this, in the great reliefs of the Persian kings, the harbors and drainage projects of the archaic Greek tyrants, and the universal awe which was felt for works of the Egyptian New Kingdom such as the monuments of Abu Simbel. But that is undoubtedly the background to the much more modest perversions of nature which entertained the Hellenistic monarchs who succeeded Alexander, and the copycat nobility of the Roman Republic which conquered them.

Before we have a look at some of the expressions of this tradition, I want to display briefly two slightly different lines of development which one can associate with the Mount Athos story, as they will be relevant to our discussion later on. First I should like you to observe the left hand of the Athos Alexander, and consider the many great cities of the succeeding centuries which were developed to mold—or better, to sculpt—the landscape on which they stood. Pergamum, Rhodes, Alexandria, if they did not force their settings into the image of a regal hand, did at least win great fame by the extent to which they imposed their ordered beauty onto the natural relief and hydrography where they found themselves, in a way which would have been congenial, if rather gimcrack, to our megalomaniac designer of Mount Athos.[13] Second, think of the possible intentions of the people of Rhodes who commissioned for their harbor, the focal point of their astonishing city, a colossal statue of their tutelary god, the Sun. The impact on the cityscape of superhuman—if not quite geological—proportions was not, in that case, only a matter of the realm of fable.[14] In one version, moreover, the Athos visionary may have been a Rhodian; we may also compare the example of the Cnidian architect Sostratus, who built the lighthouse of the harbor at Alexandria, another wonder of the world and impressive innovatory cityscape ingredient, and who was also hailed as the inventor of terraced public promenades. The cross-connections and associations of the world I am describing are extremely complex, but all form part of the conceptual inheritance of the Roman proprietor of the early imperial period.[15]

Since changing the landscape was actually rather hard to do, even for the extensive resources of the very powerful, there naturally developed certain rather stereotyped ways of doing it. I shall mention three, with some of their associations. Tampering with the sea is the first here, and the model is King Xerxes, always a proverbial figure in these contexts, with his pontoon boat-bridge across the Hellespont.[16] Building the jetties of a great harbor where there were no natural promontories, or making causeways across the shallow sea as Alexander had done to conquer the island city of Tyre was the

---

[13] The best discussion of Hellenistic city planning is R. Martin, *L'urbanisme dans la Grèce antique*, 4th. ed., Paris, 1969, sec. 2, chap. 3.

[14] On the colossus of Rhodes see *Paulys Real-Encyclopädie der classischen Altertumswissenschaft*, III (1899), 2130–2131.

[15] Rhodes: Scholia to *Il.* 14.229; but the text is corrupt. For the architect of the *pharos*, Sostratus of Cnidus, see Pliny *HN* 36.83 (cf. [Lucian], *Amores* 11) with P.M. Fraser, *Ptolemaic Alexandria*, Oxford, 1972, I, 19–20 and II, 50, n. 111, rather skeptical. For an example of a grand temple as focal point of the city's landscape see Philostr. *VS* 1.25 (Smyrna).

[16] Xerxes' bridge: Herodotus 7.33–37. For commonplaces about Xerxes, which are very numerous, see J.E.B. Mayor, *Thirteen Satires of Juvenal with a Commentary*, 3rd ed., London, 1881, II, 127–128. For Roman luxury as Persian see Strab. 5.223.

grand style of doing this, and latter-day tyrants like Caligula who built a pontoon bridge across part of the Bay of Naples had learned their lesson well.[17] On a domestic scale you could have a dining room like the Younger Pliny's where the salt spray sometimes came in, but better still to extend your promenades, peristyles, and gardens on concrete platforms actually out over the waves.[18] This was turning sea into land, and you could not expect your philosopher friend to approve. The use of these extensions to house elaborate fishponds was no better, and of course the fishpond owners were a byword for effeteness to Cicero and his circle.[19]

The second of my types also concerns rivers, creating canals, waterways, culverts, waterfalls, and so on where there were none before. This too was tyrannical; Xerxes again had built a canal, by an odd coincidence, to cut Mount Athos off from the mainland; Nero was canal-mad and not only tried to sever the isthmus of Corinth (a dismal failure) but planned a ship canal a hundred and twenty miles long to make Rome a safer port.[20] Another case on a smaller scale is the long ornamental culvert with which Agrippa decorated the recreational part of Rome. It was a mile long, about ten feet wide, and crossed by miniature marble bridges; he called it Euripus after the straits between Euboea and the mainland in Greece, where the tide changes direction four times a day.[21] Anybody who has been there will at once echo Papirius Fabianus' perplexity at how anybody can call this seriously imitating nature! And so too with the thousand types of channels, waterways, lily ponds, riverbank walks, and ornamental bridges in the gardens of the Romans. Varro's description of the riverbank décor of his villa at Monte Cassino is a fine example: "I own," says Varro, "a river which runs through my estate in the plain below Casinum. It is clear and deep, and its sides are of built stone; it's fifty-seven feet across and crossed by bridges which join one part of the villa to the other. The whole thing is nine hundred and fifty feet long, from an island downstream

---

[17] Joseph. *BJ* 1.409 (Herod's great harbor in his new city of Caesarea) is a good example. Alexander at Tyre: Quintus Curtius 4.2 ff; Diod. Sic. 42.5 ff. Caligula at Baiae: Suet. *Calig.* 32; Cass. Dio 59.17–18. For the Puteoli region as the stage for imperial display see N. Purcell in M.W. Frederiksen, *Campania*, London, 1984, chap. 14; Agrippa's harbor works are a classic instance.

[18] Pliny *Ep.* 2.17.5 for the dining room. For the platforms of seashore villas Verg. *Aen.* 9.710–718 and Hor. *Carm.* 2.18.17–22 are the standard passages: other allusions collected by M. Hubbard and R.G.M. Nisbet, *A Commentary on Horace, Odes Book II*, Oxford, 1978, 301 ff (add Sen. *Thyestes* 459–460; Suet. *Gaius* 37, with nn. 24 and 56 below). And see in particular Rut. Namat. 1.527 ff on the island villa of Triturrita in Etruria. Philostr. *VS* 2.23 describes the seaside properties of the very wealthy sophist Damian as having "man-made islands and harbor moles securing the anchorages for the coming and going of merchant ships."

[19] Cic. *Att.* 2.1 (= Shackleton-Bailey 21), 7; cf. 1.18 (Shackleton-Bailey 18); 1.19 (Shackleton-Bailey 19), 6; 2.9 (= Shackleton-Bailey 29), 1 etc.; Macrob. *Sat.* 3.15.

[20] Xerxes' canal, Herodotus 7.23 ff. (cf. n. 16 above). Nero's ship canal: Tac. *Ann.* 15.42. His efforts at Corinth became proverbial folly: see Lucian's comic dialogue *Nero, or Digging through the Isthmus*. For Alexander and a canal at Erythrae see Pliny *HN* 5.116; Paus. 2.1.5. A similar scheme was attributed to that most flamboyant figure Herodes Atticus (on whom cf. n. 67 below); Philostr. *VS* 2.1.

[21] E. Nash, *Pictorial Dictionary of Ancient Rome*, rev. ed., London, 1968, s.v. Euripus; F. Coarelli, "Il Campo Marzio occidentale, storia e topografia," *Mélanges de l'Ecole Française de Rome, Antiquité*, 89 (1977), 807 ff.

at the confluence of a tributary up to my Museum. Both banks have a ten-foot-wide open-air promenade, and it is on the countryside edge of this that I have built my Aviary"—which he then proceeds to describe at great length.[22] Finally, the preservation of moisture on even a tiny scale could be blamed; Pliny attacks those who build porticoes just to keep the sun off their moss![23]

The third easy landscape modification was artificial altitude, the illusion that you could make or move mountains yourself. Here the tumulus, pyramid, and ziggurat traditions converge. Great excavations, cuttings, or tunnels belong in this category, but remained on the larger-than-domestic scale, so that here we should only note them in passing.[24] But the piling up of loose material to make artificial banks, ridges, and mounds, the sculpting and tailoring of existing hillslopes to suit the purpose of the local proprietors, and above all the creation of new level surfaces or terraces through the construction of masonry substructures, all these were practiced by many a wealthy owner in his own property. The technical term for the last of these types in Latin is *opus pensile,* literally "work that hangs," because of the possibility of seeing the top of these buildings as suspended. It is impossible for us to appreciate fully the note of wonder and precariousness that is struck in ancient descriptions of these works, so accustomed are we to reliable, permanent, universal reinforced concrete construction. But to Pliny the Elder ancient Rome, built out on terraces from the steep slopes of the Seven Hills and comprising so many monuments built on great foundations and many levels, with warrens of ten-story apartment buildings up between them, seemed a hanging city, miraculously held up like some crystalline fabric, and the description became a commonplace of praises of Rome.[25] On a local scale this type of construction became enormously common. The vast substructions of the seats of theaters and amphitheaters were designed with this in mind; they are artificial recreations of natural slopes. Aqueducts too, rivers running on high arches, can be seen in this context of creating a man-made landscape. There can be no doubt now that it was in this way that the famous Hanging Gardens of Babylon were imagined by the Greeks and Romans who read about them.[26]

---

[22] Varro *Rust.* 2.5.9–10; cf. Pliny *HN* 9.170: the canal and waterworks at Lucullus' estate near Naples (cf. n. 28 below) cost more than the rest of the villa.

[23] Pliny *HN* 19.24. For hostility to shade see also the passage of Pliny quoted below, n. 60, and Sen. *Dial.* 7.17.2: "why sow trees that give nothing but shade," which picks up in addition the sterility theme; cf. n. 66 below.

[24] The tunnels connected with Agrippa's harbor works between Naples and Cumae (see n. 17 above) are a good example; or the excision of a cliff at Terracina for a new line of the Via Appia by Trajan (S. Aurigemma, *Circeo, Terracina, Fondi,* 2nd ed., Rome, 1966); or the same emperor's removal of a saddle of high ground in Rome to level the site for his new Forum: S.B. Platner and T. Ashby, *A Topographical Dictionary of Ancient Rome,* London, 1929, s.v. Forum Traiani. Note also Suet. *Gaius* 37; the emperor's grandiose building projects involved "the cutting away of cliffs of the hardest rock, and the leveling of ridges by excavations."

[25] Pliny *HN* 3.67; but cf. Aelius Aristides *Oration* 26.6–9 and Strab. 5.3.8. Mary Beagon points out to me the good example in Pliny *HN* 4.29 of Nature imitating art in this context, the description of Mount Nymphaeus: "topiario naturae opere spectabilis," "remarkable for the landscape gardening of Nature."

[26] The most famous *horti pensiles* were of course those of Babylon: Diod. Sic. 2.10; Strab. 16.738; Berossus fr. 14; Abydenus fr. 8. Cf. also the *pensilis ambulatio* of p. 191 above.

Horace alludes to the elevated walk which his patron Maecenas constructed in his suburban estate on the embankment of the now obsolete city wall.[27] At Naples the estate of Lucullus is said to have comprised hills suspended over vast grottoes and caverns.[28] The extant remains of the palaces on the Palatine, of Hadrian's villa, and of the suburban estates beneath the Spanish Steps make it clear that the literary sources were not exaggerated.[29] And as before, the philosophers weigh in: "no forest reared upon my roof shakes in the breeze."[30] "Do they not live at odds with nature who sow orchards at the top of towers?"[31] "Making on the highest roofs false copses and harbor-sized swimming pools."[32]

A part of the intention of all this was to provide a vantage point. The landscape around on the larger scale was part of the design of the building. It is only necessary to look at the set-piece descriptions of Horace's and Pliny's villas to see how conscious a Roman villa owner was of the landscape on which he was making his mark by the construction of his new home.[33] Through the capturing of the view, indeed, the whole wider landscape was made subservient to the one villa and could be thought of as serving the purposes of its owner. To emphasize this the villas were often equipped with high towers. The most famous is that one, again in the suburban estate of Maecenas, on which Nero is said to have stood to watch the burning of Rome and recall the burning

---

[27] Hor. *Sat.* 1. 8: "now we may dwell in health on the Esquiline and stroll in the warm sun on the city rampart." The Romans were conscious that open spaces conduced to health (*salubritas*); see Grimal, *Jardins*, 9 ff, perhaps making this knowledge too systematic and reminiscent of the 19th-century parks movement. Certainly the area of the Porta Esquilina (cf. n. 2 above) had been extremely unpleasant.

[28] Plut. *Luc.* 39.3; cf. J. d'Arms, *The Romans on the Bay of Naples*, Cambridge, Mass., 1970, 184–186. Pompey (Vell. Pat. 2.33.4) called Lucullus Xerxes in a toga (cf. n. 16 above) "because of the masses of material he had thrown into the sea and the entrances made for the sea through the undermining of mountains." Cf. Pliny *HN* 9.170; Varro *Rust.* 3.17; Sall. *Cat.* 13.2.

[29] The so-called *inferi* of Hadrian's villa (see E. Salza Prina Ricotti in *Les cryptoportiques dans l'architecture romaine*, Rome, 1973, 219 ff) comprise many hundreds of yards of underground roads and passages, quite apart from the enormous terraces which attend the villa platform in the manner of the substructions built by the Palatine palaces under Septimius Severus. On the latter see Nash, *Dictionary*, s.v. Domus Augustiana. For the extensive terraced remains beneath the Spanish Steps, which are very likely a 1st-century A.D. rebuilding of Lucullus' famous *horti* in Rome (for the term see below, 203), see Nash, op. cit., s.v. Horti Aciliorum; G.M. Andres, *The Villa Medici in Rome*, New York, 1976 (= diss., Princeton, 1970), chap. 1. For the elaborately terraced villa of Domitian at Alba Longa see n. 35 below.

[30] Sen. *Thyestes* 464–465.

[31] Sen. *Ep.* 122.8, also inveighing against hot baths, extending buildings over the sea, and forcing flowers out of season.

[32] Sen. *Controv.* 2.2.

[33] Hor. *Epist.* 1.16.1–16, emphasizing the circuit of enclosing hills. Pliny *Ep.* 5.6.7–8: "the form of the setting is lovely. Picture an enormous amphitheater, of the sort only nature can create. A wide and rambling plain is surrounded by hills and these are crowned with luxuriant ancient woodland. There is an abundance of all kinds of game there. . . ." For the comparison of building and natural setting see the discussion below, 199 f; for hunting, 200 f. I owe to Mary Beagon the spectacular example of the building metaphor in landscape description in Pliny *HN* 4.30: "the mountains are all arranged in a curve like a theater, with seventy-five cities in the *cavea* before them."

of Troy.³⁴ From this place, which is, in fact, the highest summit in Rome, the whole city could be seen, and readily, in those days before air pollution reached its present disastrous level, and also the wonderful basin of hills in which Rome sits, the wall of the Appennines, the sharp crag of Soracte, the spreading comfortable bulk of the Alban Hills and their sacred summit. This is an important case. I want to emphasize that in the area of associations which I have been discussing now for some time, *both* town and country and their mutual connections were part of the total landscape into which the house of the wealthy man was inserted. When the smog disperses, the view from Castel Gandolfo down to distant Rome is still an overwhelming sight; it is that view which dominates the siting of the sei- and settecento villas of the area, and beneath each of them, for the same reason, is a great Roman villa; beside the Villa Aldobrandini at Frascati (hanging on terraces which are now the wine cellars of the town), the enormous Tusculan villa of Pompey the Great; and under the Villa Barberini of Castel Gandolfo, the Alban palace of Emperor Domitian.³⁵ Not often visited in the vast complex of Hadrian's villa is the footing of a huge tower, now called Roccabruna, whose sweeping view down across the foothills of the Appennine scarp is unimagined from the sequestered cypress and olive groves of the rest of the site.³⁶

The Romans also enjoyed the framing of a view by natural features, the view up a narrow valley, or, best of all, out of a cave. Part of Domitian's villa at Alba is down hundreds of feet below the great vista I have just mentioned, on the lake edge, in the Alban crater; and here there is a sumptuous nymphaeum cut into the rock in whose entrance is framed exactly the view of the Alban mount itself across the dead still lake and its wooded sides.³⁷ Wild enough, even when a gleaming villa occupied every site with a fine view round the crater edge, and when the marble of the Temple of Jupiter Latiaris shone instead of the microwave transmitters on the top of the mountain. To reiterate the point made above, however, if we look at the other well-known imperial cave-villa at Sperlonga, on the coast of Latium, the appeal of the cave is clearly that its opening exactly frames the promontory on the other side of the bay where the white-

---

³⁴ Cf. n. 3 above; on towers in Roman villas see P. Grimal, "Les maisons à tour hellénistiques et romaines," *Ecole Française de Rome. Mélanges d'archéologie et d'histoire*, 56 (1939), 28 ff. For disapproval of this fashion cf. below, n. 45.

³⁵ For the Tusculan villas under Frascati see F. Grossi-Gondi, *Il Tusculano nell'età classica*, Rome, 1908; T. Ashby, "The Classical Topography of the Roman Campagna, III (the Via Latina)," *Papers of the British School at Rome*, 5 (1910), 327 ff. Notice Strabo's recognition that these villas were sited for their view of Rome (5.3.12). For Domitian's Alban villa see G. Lugli, "La villa di Domiziano sui colli albani," I, *Bullettino della Commissione Archeologica Comunale di Roma*, 45 (1917), 29 ff; II, ibid., 46 (1918), 3 ff; III, ibid., 47 (1919), 153 ff; IV, ibid., 48 (1920), 3 ff.

³⁶ G. Lugli (ill. R. Bonelli), "La torre di Roccabruna," *Palladio*, 4 (1940), 257 ff.

³⁷ On this cave, the "Antro Bergantino," see K. De Fine Licht, "*Antrum Albanum*," *Analecta romana*, 7 (1976), 37 ff; cf. A. Balland, "Une transposition de la grotte de Tibère à Sperlonga: Le Ninfeo Bergantino de Castelgandolfo, *Ecole Française de Rome. Mélanges d'archéologie et d'histoire*, 79 (1967), 421 ff. Cf. also Pomponius Mela on the Corycian Cave (cf. n. 57 below), 1.71–76; and Sen. *Ep.* 55 on the two caves built into a villa at Cumae, one always in shade, the other sunny all afternoon. For caves cf. also the passage from Philostratus cited in n. 63 below.

painted town projects—as its predecessor projected—on its high rocks into the blue sea: a thoroughly picturesque scene, but one which is not wholly rural, indeed one which depends on the presence of a town.³⁸

Pliny's villa on the shore at Laurentum did not have the benefit of a cave, but he is very enthusiastic about the fact that on either side he can see the palatial residences of his neighbors, like so many towns along the coastline.³⁹ The cities of the Hellenistic Mediterranean arranged their plans, which we touched on a while ago, to be visible from the sea over which most of their visitors came. So along the harbor ran esplanades with porticoes behind, and the city rose in fine terraces to great sanctuaries crowning conspicuous hills. Lighthouses or colossal statues or other monuments caught the eye. This ideal lay behind the Roman coastal villa too, and the image which the Bay of Naples came to acquire by the first century A.D. was one in which the real cities and the private buildings of the Roman élite merged into each other along the whole coastline: again not only the remains and descriptions but the beautiful frescoes of coastal scenes from Pompeii give us a very vivid idea of this extraordinary development. On the modern Mediterranean Riviera sites which cannot see or be seen by other villas today fetch the highest prices, and there can be few of us who would not heartily condemn the tendency for the shore of modern Campania, like so many others, to bear city without break from Pozzuoli through Naples to Torre del Greco, Torre Annunziata, and Pompeii. Our taste is for the desolate, unurbanized landscape; the Romans, for all their penchant for *rus in urbe,* as I hope to have shown you, did not have this view.⁴⁰ Their landscape consciousness definitely included—if it did not indeed center on—the *city*.

A corollary of what I have just said is that the villa owner and his architect were very concerned about the view had by others of their villa and of the vantage points from which it could be seen. Nothing could be further removed from the inward-looking concept of the old Italian domus, as we know it from the older houses of Pompeii and the descriptions of Vitruvius. In fact it is likely that in Rome itself even the town houses of the richest senators had abandoned this; anecdotes of Republican history told in contemporary terms and other snippets of information suggest that houses of politicians on the hillcrests overlooking the central business district of Rome in the Forum valley were desirable for the opportunity for outward display which they gave. Where conditions were less crowded than in Rome, this consideration was naturally even more important. We naturally forget as we poke about in the foundations of Ro-

---

³⁸ G. Jacopi, *L'antro di Tiberio e il Museo archeologico nazionale di Sperlonga,* Rome, 1965; cf. Strab. 5.3.6: "huge caves open there holding large and expensive residences." The high cape of Terracina crowned by the temple of Jupiter Anxuranus is also framed in the opening. For the whole coast see X. Lafon, "A propos des villas de la zone de Sperlonga: Les origines de la ‹villa maritima› sur le littoral tyrrhénienne à l'époque républicaine," *Mélanges de l'Ecole Française de Rome, Antiquité,* 93 (1981), 297 ff, good on the idea of *villa maritima*.

³⁹ Pliny *Ep.* 2.17.27: "the roofs of the villas decorate the shore, now clustered, now scattered, just like so many cities, whether you are at sea or on the beach."

⁴⁰ The choice of some seaside villas was influenced by isolation, especially on islands: Lafon, op. cit. (n. 38), 340 ff. Cf., in this context, the so-called *Teatro marittimo* of Hadrian's villa, a series of pavilions on an artificial island. For the city as an improvement to a wild landscape see also n. 58 below.

man villas how vital a part in their design the elevation played. This is best seen from the rather later examples which survive, the mysterious Torre di Sto. Stefano near Anguillara Sabazia and above all the huge villa complexes of the Villa of the Quintilii on the Appian and the Villa of Sette Bassi on the Latin Ways. Here the central buildings of the villa are in a nearly imperishable brick-faced concrete and remain to a height of seventy feet and more; when surrounded with their outbuildings, whose remains stretch for acres around, these must truly have given the impression of cities. But it was principally in being built in less permanent materials that the villas of the Late Republic and Early Empire differed from these Antonine constructions.[41]

Villa urbana is a complicated phrase. It means at least three things: a villa built in the unrestricted manner appropriate to the country actually in a town; a country villa with all the advantages of a great town house; and, I maintain, a villa which is urban in its scale, large enough to suggest, at least to the imaginative designer of artificial woods and mountains and seas, whole cities. And this is reflected in various aspects of the design of Roman villas. In the first place they are a mass of buildings crowned by monumental structures and towers and rising high above the ground around by means of a great artificial base, or fronting a river or the sea in the manner of a Hellenistic harbor town (some even had their own harbors). Some had imitation town walls; in the area of Cosa in Tuscany (originally Etruria) walls surrounding the ornamental gardens of country houses were decorated with miniature turrets with battlements and blank window apertures.[42] The principal approach sometimes, as with the late villa at Piazza Armerina in Sicily, has a monumental gateway which would be worthy of a town.[43] Within the larger complexes could be found temples which retained a semipublic role and of course the dwellings of huge numbers of domestic staff whose comings and goings provided an urban bustle.[44] A great man conducted much of his business, even if it was public, in the reception rooms of his own house; as Vitruvius says, "for the *nobiles*, who undertake duties for their fellow citizens in holding state posts and magistracies, it is necessary to build tall, palatial entrance halls, very capacious atria and peristyles, and groves and promenades designed on the more ample scale which is suitable for their grand public image."[45] It is worth noticing that here the garden section of the house is

---

[41] Villa of the Quintilii: T. Ashby, "La villa dei Quintilii," *Ausonia*, 4 (1909), 48 ff. Sette Bassi (now rapidly decaying but, not before time, the object of serious investigation): N. Lupu, "La villa dei Sette Bassi sulla Via Latina," *Ephemeris Daco-romana*, 7 (1937), 117 ff.

[42] See A. Carandini and S. Settis, *Schiavi e padroni nell'Etruria romana*, Bari, 1979, or, in English, A. Carandini and T. Tatton-Brown, "Excavations at the Roman Villa of 'Settefinestre,'" in *Roman Villas in Italy*, ed. K. Painter, London, 1980, 9 ff.

[43] R. Wilson, *Piazza Armerina*, Austin, 1983, 16, 86, 91.

[44] Platner and Ashby, *Dictionary*, s.v. Fortuna Seiani, Aedes; Tres Fortunae, Aedes; Venus Erucina, Aedes: three Roman examples.

[45] Vitr. *De Arch.* 6.5.2. It is a commonplace, derived from the domestic architecture of Pompeii, that Roman houses were introverted and presented an unexciting facade to the world outside. Not so with the patrician houses of Rome, as this passage implies and as the passions raised by the dispute on Cicero's Palatine house (*de domo sua*, passim) confirm. Note too the contentions about over-grand houses which feature in the early history of Rome as composed in the Late Republic. And cf. Sen. *Thyestes* 455–456: "nor

included in the parts with a public function. It was this ambiguity between public and private which so inhibited the development of purpose-built governmental buildings in the ancient world, and this also made it easier for the conceit that blurs the distinction between the house and the town to gain ground.[46]

As modern excavations explore the sites of the little hill towns of the Latial culture, which in the eighth and seventh centuries were rivals as well as neighbors of Rome, in place after place it is found that the only occupation in the Late Republic and Early Empire was a single large villa.[47] This is an interesting coincidence, as the Romans themselves were aware of this development. Strabo says that what were once separate communities are now "the possessions of private proprietors," and in the case of Antium that "at the present Antium is given up to the Roman ruling class for their leisure activities and repose from political life when they have an opportunity, and is for that reason built up throughout with many extremely expensive houses for this *villegiatura*."[48] The same thought is expressed in a vital passage of the Elder Seneca, attacking the rich: "you own estates as large as the territories of cities and fill whole cities with your homes; inside your buildings you have penned up the forests and the ocean waves";[49] and in the poetry of the Later Empire: "small towns they had been before, but now they were enormous estates"[50] and "one house is the size of a city, so that the city itself is composed of a myriad towns."[51] Behind the glib commonplace lies a sober social development, by which the rural population of Italy came to occupy villages whose raison d'être was a great estate, rather than nucleated rural centers of greater independence, as had earlier been the case; but it is not that which concerns us now. We must turn, at least briefly, to the most spectacular case of the supposed ambiguity between house and town—the Golden House of Nero.

The Romans hated the Golden House because it was too big and right in the heart of the city. Their pasquinade ran: "Rome has become a house; citizens, emigrate to Veii; but watch out that the House does not extend that far too" (about twelve miles).[52] For

is my house perched on the summit of a high hill, a source of terror in its lofty situation for the humble city below."

[46] See N. Purcell, "The Arts of Government," in *Oxford History of the Classical World*, ed. J. Boardman, J. Griffin, O. Murray, Oxford, 1986, chap. 23.

[47] Some examples: Collatia, Quilici, *Collatia* (n. 8 above); Antemnae, L. Quilici and S. Quilici Gigli, *Antemnae*, Rome, 1978, 116; Cures, *Archeologia laziale*, III, Rome, 1979, 198; Ficana, Meiggs, *Ostia* (n. 7 above), 264.

[48] Strab. 5.3.2; cf. Pliny *HN* 3.70, Stabiae "which has turned into a villa" (*quod nunc in villam abiit*).

[49] Sen. *Controv.* 5.5.1. Cf. Sall. *Cat.* 12: "houses and villas built up like cities"; Ov. *Fast.* 6.639: "one house was on the scale of a city, and occupied a space larger than many towns." This is the house of the notoriously luxurious Vedius Pollio, demolished for the construction of the Porticus of Livia.

[50] Rut. Namat. 1.224: "big villas at that time, but earlier little towns."

[51] Olympiodorus fr. 43 (cf. J. Rougé, "Une émeute à Rome au IVe siècle," *Revue des études anciennes*, 63 [1961], 59 ff, at 66, n.2): "report has it that each of the great houses of Rome has more facilities than a decent-sized city, a racetrack and marketplaces and temples (cf. n. 44 above) and fountains and various baths: which is why the author [i.e., Olympiodorus] has said 'one house . . . etc.'" Cf. also the play on city and palace at Joseph. *BJ* 1.421.

[52] Suet. *Ner.* 39. Cf. Pliny *HN* 18.7 of the days of Romulus: "two acres apiece was enough for Romans then and to none did he give more. In our times what slave of Nero's would have been content with a flower garden (*viridiarium*) of that size—or swimming pool—or even [taking the *topos* a little *too* far] a kitchen?"!

Pliny's generation the accumulation of suburban property by the emperors had, he says, twice threatened to engulf Rome, under Nero and earlier under Caligula.[53] But for the fortunate owners of these estates, as I think we may now be in a position to see, the urban location of their villas was in itself a piquant paradox which made the estate more special. For Nero this *frisson* may have been an important ingredient of his extraordinary boast that only in the Golden House could he at last begin to exist as a human being.[54] This is the other side of the coin from the warnings of the moralists, and when we look a little more closely at the details of Nero's project we can, I think, see the sort of thing that we have been discussing in its most spectacular exemplification.

"Its vestibule was of sufficient size to accommodate a colossus one hundred and twenty feet high with Nero's features; it was spacious enough to have a threefold *porticus miliaria* [a colonnade deliberately constructed to measure a Roman mile in length], a pond like the sea enclosed with *buildings like cities;* countryside there was too, the variety of which included ploughland, vineyard, pasture, and forest, all teeming with every kind of domestic and wild animal."[55] Thus Suetonius; Tacitus' summary is even more to our point: "Nero took full advantage of the devastation of his native city [by the Great Fire]; he built himself a house in which the novelties were not the precious stones and gold, now old hat and debased by the long practice of luxury, but the arable fields and lakes and artificial wild country (*in modum solitudinum*) with woodland and open spaces or vistas mixed in. The architects and engineers of all this were called Severus and Celer, whose daring genius lay in skillfully attempting to use the resources of an emperor to create a *semblance of what Nature had refused.*"[56] These two descriptions contain many familiar themes; the colossus, for example, standing dominating the view of the villa from its principal approach up the Sacred Way from the Forum Romanum, and also presiding over the clustered buildings, on the edge of the lake like a sea, which resembled cities, in just the way that we have seen on the Campanian coast. Clear too is the paradoxical juxtaposition of this civilized scene with the open emptiness of both the cultivated and the wild countryside. The importance of the view (*conspectus*) in the whole is emphasized—one of the great advantages of the site was that it comprised hilltops and relatively steep slopes as well as the declivities between them. Finally the description of Tacitus, and to a lesser extent that of Suetonius, markedly echoes the stern hostility to the extravagant, the modish, the self-indulgent, and the unnatural which has informed so many of the allusions to Roman landscape architecture that we have been discussing.

So the Roman idea of countryside did not have the same associations with land-

[53] Pliny *HN* 36.111.

[54] Suet. *Ner.* 31.2. Only here were the full range of human pursuits and their settings in nature all available together. Note that Vitellius, who had to spend fifty million sesterces on the Domus Aurea to make it habitable, praised its ἐπιτηδεύματα, its "pursuits," "lifestyles." Nero had been trying to sum up human experience (Cass. Dio 65.4.1). Compare now the account of Nero's tastes and their significance in M.T. Griffin, *Nero, the End of a Dynasty,* London, 1985, chaps. 8–9.

[55] Suet. *Ner.* 31.1. The parallel with the Rhodian colossus is made explicitly by Mart. 1.71.

[56] Tac. *Ann.* 15.42. A very close parallel in Suet. *Gaius* 37: "there was nothing he was so keen to achieve as what was said to be impossible." It is also claimed that amazing speed in completing projects was part of his plan.

scape as our own. The natural landscape for the Romans included the works of man and above all the city. As we have investigated these propositions we have acquired considerable information about the connotations that *rus* did possess. It is interesting first to see the distinction between wild and tame countryside made by Tacitus in the description of the Golden House; woods and empty spaces—*solitudines*—are to be set against the scenes of agricultural activity. The *nemora*, groves, and *silvae*, coppices, although no more natural, no doubt, in their literal appearance than the thickets of bay in the *bosco* of an Italian Renaissance garden, had this association for the Romans, powerfully reinforced by the link with the proverbially dark and still sacred grove, the dwelling place of certainly wild divinities.[57] In Roman paintings the mountains and *maquis* which form the background to mythological or genre scenes are the *solitudines*. These were naturally more difficult to create on the domestic scale, though I mentioned the possibility of constructing *montes* on a small scale as an illusionistic background to plantings and architectural decoration. There is little enough evidence that the Romans enjoyed the real thing. In the mountains villas are not common. The grand scenery of the Sabine and Umbrian hills was an incentive in the case of the villas of Horace and Pliny the Younger, but here the landscape of the valley itself was populous and smiling, not bleak or bare. Interestingly, the only example known to me of a luxury villa in a really remote and tremendous location of the kind that would appeal to a modern romantic belonged to, and was probably first built for, Emperor Nero. This is the villa of Sublaqueum, whose remains lie below the great Benedictine abbey of Subiaco at the mouth of a grim gorge with beetling sides and distant glimpses of uncompromising crags. Even in the outer valley below there is little agriculture at this altitude. The villa's architect dammed the mouth of the gorge and created a deep narrow lake winding back picturesquely into the mountains, onto which the villa's rooms looked.[58]

One of the comforts and attractions of a villa in a place like this, apart from the summer cool, was the hunting. This is a greatly underestimated aspect of the ancient view of the natural landscape. Some modern scholars of Greek religion have explored the ways in which in connection with certain cults the practice of hunting is conceived

---

[57] On woods note the distinction quoted in n. 33 between the wild forests where the hunting was good and cultivated woodland (*silvae caeduae*); cf. [Tib.] 3.3.15: "woods in houses after the model of sacred groves"; and Pomponius Mela 1.73: "a narrow descent through pleasant woods (*amoenus*) and shadowy glades whose murmur has something rural (*agreste*) about it"; all this in sharp contrast to the vividly described horrors of the cave at the bottom. The *amoenitas* of Atticus' modest home on the Quirinal derived from the *silva*, not from the building (Cornelius Nepos *Atticus* 13.2); such woods and plantations were the principal ingredient of Roman gardens. Their landscape significance is clear.

[58] Sublaqueum: Tac. *Ann.* 15.22; G.M. De Rossi, *Lazio ieri e oggi*, 9, 1973, 286 ff; F. Coarelli, *Lazio*, Bari, 1982, 115. Cf. Pliny *HN* 3.109 describing "three lakes outstanding in *amoenitas*." The Anio, further down famous for its waterfalls (now ruined), is revealingly called "groved," καταλσῆ, by Strab. 5.3.11. For ancient attitudes to mountains see W.W. Hyde, "The Ancient Attitude to Mountain Scenery," *Classical Journal*, 11 (1915), 70 ff; L. Friedländer, *Sittengeschichte*, I, 4th ed., Leipzig, 1919, 478 ff. The locus classicus for the view that man's works improve on otherwise wild, ferocious Nature is Cic. *Nat. D.* 2.99; cf. Apul. *De mundo* 4: "hollow with embayed shores, picked out with islands, small villas, and gleaming with the cities which the knowing race, humanity, has constructed for the common good."

of as taking place beyond society in the debatable outer wilderness, across the boundaries which mark the edges of the world of the city.[59] This conception survived, and the inclusion within a property, within human control, of a place to hunt, is one of the earliest piquant inversions associated with ancient landscape architecture. The paradises of the eastern civilizations and their Greek and Hellenistic successors are the background here. Varro's aviary, the exotic fishponds of the Campanian villas, and the elephant park of the Roman emperors in the woods of the Latin coastland are the heirs of this tradition, all enjoying the paradox of domesticating the wild, the extraordinary. Nero is taking this one step further, as it is to the town that he has introduced not only the world of the farms which depend on the town but even the outer wild to which the town is wholly alien.[60]

I should like to emphasize that the Roman view of nature and landscape is a very literary and traditional one. The paintings which provided stage scenery for mythological drama, the tableaux which illustrated the narrative of a general's wars in the spectacle of his triumphal procession, and the creation of appropriate scenery for exotic fighters or animals in the amphitheater are very important strands in the Roman creation of landscape.[61] Before we dismiss Nero's fantasy park as hopelessly exotic, perhaps we should recall how it was on the very spot where his lake had lain that the Flavian emperors constructed the Colosseum, a building designed to enable the Roman populace who had been excluded from Nero's cultural menagerie to share at least as spectators in the excitement of hunting at the *venationes*. The recreation of flooded Nile or northern mountains as the setting for those murderous games is in the direct tradition of landscape architecture, on some of the domestic aspects of which we have been concentrating, and a deliberate response to the Golden House.[62]

To conclude, since the discussion has now deposited us in the uninhabited forests and open mountainsides beyond civilization, I should like to conduct you back to the city by rather broader and more theoretical stages than the imaginative journey which brought us out of Rome at the beginning. Something like the progression made by our return journey is presented by the Younger Seneca in another revealing examination of the bizarre range of incompatible tastes characteristic of his age. "So they undertake protracted tours and explore pathless shores; now by land, now by sea we find the working out of the kind of frivolity which can't stand the same thing for long. 'Now let's

---

[59] E.g., P. Vidal-Naquet, "The Black Hunter and the Origins of the Athenian *Ephebeia*," in *Myth, Religion and Society*, ed. R.L. Gordon, Cambridge, 1981, 147 ff. Also J. Aymard, *Les chasses romaines*, Paris, 1951, passim.

[60] *Paradeisoi*: Aymard, *Chasses*, 68 ff. On exotica note Pliny *HN* 12.6 on the plane: "but who will not be astonished at the fact that a tree useful for its shade alone should have been brought from an alien world (*ex alieno orbe*)?"

[61] For these landscape tableaux see Aymard, *Chasses*, 189 ff. S.H.A. *V. Probi* 19.3–4 is a good example: "the spectacle was like this: large trees torn up by their roots by soldiers and linked on every side with planks were set up and soil piled up so that the whole circus burst into leaf with the new greenery and looked just like a forest. Then through every opening they let in a thousand ostriches, a thousand deer, a thousand boars. . . ."

[62] See Aymard, *Chasses*, chap. 10.

go to Campania'—but then the exquisite becomes a bore, it's the turn of the wilderness—'let's make for Calabria and the forests of Lucania.' But in the wilds they miss that little bit of the comfortable and pleasant (*amoeni* [note that it is incompatible with serious wildness]) with which their over-refined perception might refresh itself after the endlessly uncouth views. So Tarentum next, famous harbor, mild winters, and, even by ancient standards, proverbial wealth. But where is the clapping and shouting? And it's been a long time since they've seen a good bit of bloodshed. 'It has to be back to the Metropolis.'" Here the contrasts which we have been examining are quite clear. Some do like the outer wild, but it is a very perverted taste. The *amoenum* is a more normal and quite distinct taste. Not even that can really rival the standard excitements of the City, with its turbulent crowds and packed spectacles. The variation of the scenery is the secret of luxury, and the only thing the different locales have in common is the disdain of the philosopher![63]

Our case studies have shown now what we are to expect of *rus*. It is much more cheery at least in its idealized form than the woods, stones, and swamps of the real wild. And it is conveyed to the Romans not so much by what it looked like but by what went on there. The country is the scene of the vintage, the harvest festival, the ploughman returning home, the simple rustic celebration. Hence Nero's vineyards and the domesticated animals of the Golden House (which, one hopes, he kept in a different part of the *tout ensemble* from the wild ones). Cassiodorus' description of his villa on the outskirts of Scylacium (modern Squillace) in Lucania makes the point well: "the sight of men toiling honestly (*pulchre laborantium*) is not denied to those who stay in town. The rich vintages are on display, and the heavy yield of the threshing floor, and the green olive trees—a person who can see it all from the town lacks none of the charms (*amoenitate*) of the fields. Scylacium has no walls, so you might think it a mere country town; but the villa you would call urban. It is between two worlds, and so receives the most lavish praise." Here the rich senator owns a *villa rustica*.[64]

Much more civilized is the *suburbanum*. Far enough from the city to be secluded, but accessible from it in a day, and yet in an area distinguished by sophisticated and hospitable neighbors, these houses are the focus of much of their owners' attention. On the slopes of the Alban Hills, along the Latin coast, at the watering places of the Tuscan lakes, even in Campania, the juxtaposition of dozens of these premises creates a social, economic, and political milieu in west central Italy which on this scale has no parallel in the ancient world. The architecture and décor of these establishments are lavish, but the villas here are more likely to play with the image of the town than they are to

---

[63] Sen. *Tranq.* 2.13. The same tripartite scheme is reflected in Philostr. *VS* 2.23: "his suburban dwellings were in some cases built in the urban style, while others took the form of caves"; some of Damian's conceits, in other words, were town houses in the country, others really wild habitations juxtaposed with the city.

[64] Cassiod. *Var.* 12.15. Examples of the "Marie Antoinette's dairy" theme in Roman design include Varro's fruit store dining room, *oporotheca*, *Rust.* 59.2. Compare the purpose of Herodes Atticus' wild rustic companion Heracles-Agathion (Philostr. *VS* 2.1), reminiscent as it is of the picturesque hermits of the 18th century.

attempt the parody of nature, as are the *villae rusticae* too. In the country there is no point in imitating nature. It is out in the countryside that these buildings rise on their craglike foundation terraces, like citadels over the consular roads, topped by the towers which use the view, making use of springs and woods in their gardens and perhaps surrounded by pretend city fortifications.

Further in the plutocrat had *horti*.[65] *Horti* are not really *Gardens*. On maps of ancient Rome green areas labeled Gardens of Maecenas or Gardens of Lucullus cover huge tracts of the outer edge of the town, as if they were a Bois de Boulogne or a Villa Borghese. The *horti* of Rome were very select *suburbana*, distinguished by being right beside the city and so very expensive, by the fact of their urban setting which enabled their gardens to play with the paradoxes at which we have been looking. The importance of landscape gardening in their design and the fact that suburban property inherited the associations of its earlier use, in more restrained and moral days, for truck farming is what brings it about that these palatial properties are called *horti*.[66] But that they are lavish residences first, and landscape fantasies next and subordinately, there is no doubt. These are the estates which most evoke the wrath of the moralist. From their origins in the middle of the first century B.C. they developed a style of domestic luxury and an architectural sophistication which is unique in antiquity. Their great heyday was the Julio-Claudian period, after which they almost all passed to the emperor, a story which is well known. In the second century great senators like Herodes Atticus or the Quintilii had *suburbana* on an enormous scale, but the private *horti* in their most elaborate form were a thing of the past.[67] The most spectacular set of *horti* of all time was the Golden House, which took the paradox of the juxtaposition of town and country further than ever before; it transposed to the very center of Rome what had previously been daring and provocative on the periphery. Domitian and Hadrian chose Alba and Tivoli as the sites for *their* ambitious plans; the Neronian experiment was never tried again.[68]

---

[65] The standard treatment of the Roman *horti* is Grimal, *Jardins* (n. 6 above); I hope to deal fully with them in the book mentioned in n. 8 above.

[66] The contrast between the sterility of the ornamental plants of these *horti* and the fruitfulness of serious agriculture was a commonplace: Hor. *Carm.* 2.15 and Quint. *Inst.* 8.3.8: "am I likely to think a farmstead better organized (*cultiorem*) in which a person shows me lilies, violets, and anemones growing untilled than one where there are cereal crops and vines heavy with fruit? Should I prefer the fruitless plane and clipped myrtle bushes to the wedded elm [*sc.* to the vine] and rich olive trees?"

[67] The Quintilii et al., above, n. 41. For Herodes Atticus' estate, L. Moretti, *Inscriptiones Graecae Urbis Romae*, Rome, 1968–79, nos. 339–341 and 1155; G. Pisani Sartorio and R. Calza, *La Villa di Massenzio sulla via Appia*, Rome, 1976.

[68] Though note the setting, dominating both city and the entrance to Bosphorus and Golden Horn, of the Great Palace of Constantinople: R. Krautheimer, *Three Christian Capitals*, Berkeley, 1982, 49 ff; W. Müller-Wiener, *Bildlexicon zur Topographie Istanbuls*, Tübingen, 1977, 229. It is of some interest that Constantine not only planned his city round a vast central palace complex, but also set up a colossal statue of himself as sun god in the central forum (Krautheimer, op. cit., 55–56, cf. 62). It remains possible that the Golden House too was intended to be an integral part of the Neronian New Rome; the original model would have been the Palace Quarter of Alexandria (Fraser, *Alexandria* [n. 15 above], 22–24). But about this, although the parallels are suggestive, we know all too little.

Montmaurin: A Garden Villa

JEAN-MARIE PAILLER

To deal with Montmaurin's villa gardens requires two preliminary remarks. First, the Montmaurin Roman villa is both typical and exceptional. Typical, in the sense that several other great *villae urbanae*, dating back to the end of the Roman Empire, are known in the same region of France. One may cite Chiragan, Lalonquette, Séviac, among several others. But Montmaurin is also exceptional, because it is the largest and richest one, especially from the point of view that interests us—the gardens; in this respect it has been spoken of as a villa in the "Italian" style. Perhaps it would be better to say the "princely" Greco-Roman style, a kind of palatial residence. One last peculiarity of Montmaurin is that it is by far the best known of all.

Here the second remark comes in. Mr. Georges Fouet, the local resident and scientist who for years devoted his attention to the excavation and study of the villa, has most recently published a second and somewhat enlarged edition of his fundamental book, *La villa gallo-romaine de Montmaurin,* first issued in 1969 as a supplement to the French archaeological review *Gallia.*[1] The book remains the indispensable basis for any further study. It is a cautious, detailed, and fairly exhaustive work: an exceptional document, as is the villa itself—now preserved as a *monument historique* and open to visitors every day. Nevertheless, it must be said that, while coping with their immense task, the excavators lacked the time and means to reconstitute the gardens, as has been done at Pompeii and elsewhere. Finally, I must confess that, since I did not participate in the excavations, the present study is essentially based on Fouet's work, frequent visits to the site, and some personal reflections on the problem of the villa gardens.

Although the general layout of the Roman villa at Montmaurin in southwestern France, near the Pyrenees and a short distance from the Garonne valley (Fig. 1) may be familiar, some characteristic features of this settlement, one of the most considerable private Roman achievements in Gaul, should be emphasized.

First of all, a few words about the site and natural conditions. Fouet summed up very well these mostly favorable conditions:[2] plenty of timber from the wooded neighborhood, plenty of good building stone, water galore from the nearby river and the rainfall characteristic of the mild Atlantic climate, with the gently sloping ground of the left bank of the river Save, tributary of the Garonne, providing the right conditions for crops, pasturing, vineyards, and of course garden plants and shrubs. The only natural risk is that of floods of the Save, which in actual fact overflowed the site in modern and at least on one occasion in ancient times.[3]

Then, the chronology. I would like to stress that the excavations of the '60s have proved the existence of a first phase of the villa, which may date to the middle of the

---

[1] G. Fouet, *La villa gallo-romaine de Montmaurin,* XXe Supplément à *Gallia,* Editions du CNRS, Paris, 1969 (392 pp.; 2nd ed., 1984).
[2] Ibid., 13–19.
[3] Ibid., 18, 45.

first century A.D. and was ended by a flood of the Save, possibly by the end of the second century.[4] This first stage was predominantly a rural settlement in a rectangular area of about 800 × 225 meters, ca. 20 hectares (50 acres), bounded by the Save on the east side and enclosed by walls on the other three sides. The *pars rustica* consisted of parallel lines of carefully organized rural outbuildings extending from a central construction, about 180 × 130 meters. The site and orientation of this *pars urbana* were naturally imposed by the general situation of the rural settlement, roughly at equal distance from the Save and the ditch draining the dampness at the bottom of the slopes away to the natural pool farther below.

We know few details of the first *villa urbana* (Fig. 2), but we may infer that its plan was axial, with two successive porticoed courtyards (102 and 75), the second of which (75), an inner peristyle which certainly had ornamental planting, opened directly to the northwest onto a large outer garden. It is worth noting that a room (38), most probably a summer triclinium situated at the north angle of the first courtyard, opened onto this garden as well, and that at the far end of the villa the left wing terminated in a circular tower (100) which projected into the same garden.

We may be brief on this first *villa urbana*, especially as most of its floors and inner spaces are situated underneath the Late Empire buildings and pavements and could not therefore be unearthed. Let me make only a few remarks.

Fouet compares the design of this first-century building to that of contemporary Pompeian houses like the Casa di Pansa or the Casa del Chirurgo, with the so-called canonical plan: atrium—peristyle—hortus.[5] One must admit there is obvious Italian influence at Montmaurin, but there is no atrium at this phase: the first central courtyard (102) is a porticoed one, as Vitruvius prescribes for a rural villa, and the comparison would seem more appropriate with suburban Campanian villas, with their two successive peristyles and their gardens at the center or at the end of the second one. Let us think, for example, of the Villa di Diomede or of the sumptuous Villa dei Papiri at Herculaneum.

Before discussing the second phase, let us note that the narrowing perspective from the facade to the rear of the villa, which may evoke that of the Villa dei Misteri, will remain that of the Late Empire construction at Montmaurin. The main difference is that the first-century villa did not yet have gardens or plantings either in the entrance area, inside the room at the end of the axis (97), or around the second peristyle (75). There was a kind of specialized garden corner, especially designed for summer enjoyment and surrounded on three sides respectively by the triclinium (38), the peristyle (75), and the circular tower (100). One may recall the frequency of this kind of garden rotunda in first-century villa gardens, as P. Grimal demonstrated in his pioneer work *Les jardins romains* and, even before that, in a paper published in 1939.[6]

[4] Ibid., chap. 2, 31 ff.

[5] Ibid., 47 ff.

[6] P. Grimal, *Les jardins romains*, Paris, 1943 (2nd ed., 1969); idem, "Les maisons à tour hellénistiques et romaines," *Mélanges d'archéologie et d'histoire*, Ecole Française de Rome (1939), 28–59.

OCÉAN ATLANTIQUE
BORDEAUX
ISLE
PERIGUEUX
DORDOGNE
VÉZERE
CORREZE
TULLE
LOT
CAHORS
AVEYRON
RODEZ
AGEN
TARN
MONTAUBAN
ALBI
BAISE
GERS
GIMONNE
SAVE
MONT-DE-MARSAN
ADOUR
DAX
GAVE
AUCH
TOULOUSE
GARONNE
ARIÈGE
PAU
TARBES
BOULOGNE
MONTMAURIN
ST. GAUDENS
VALENTINE
ST.-BERTRAND
CARCASSONNE
AUDE
FOIX
PERPIGNAN
TET
MEDITERRANÉE
ESPAGNE

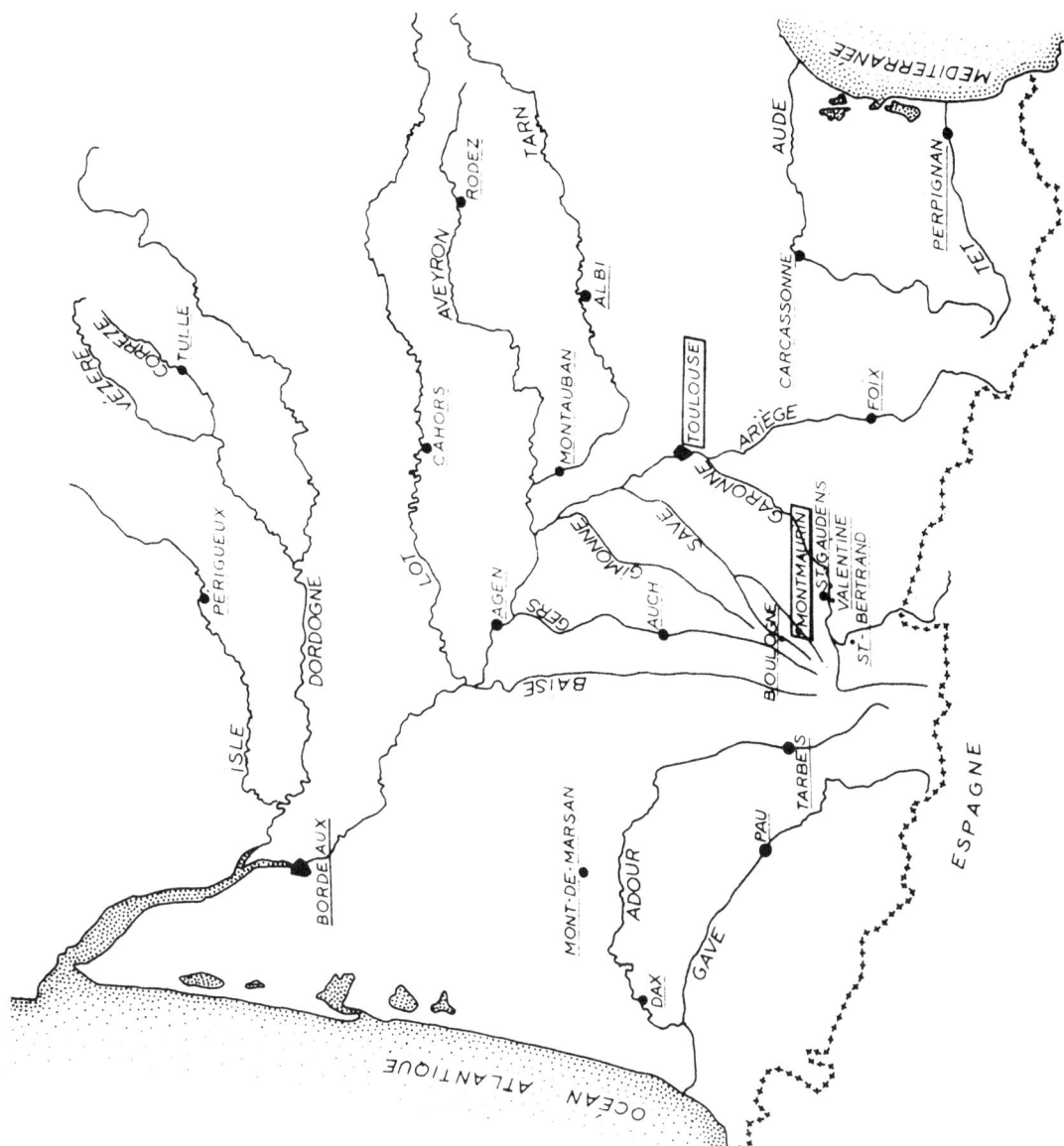

1. The location of the Montmaurin villa (after G. Fouet, *La villa gallo-romaine de Montmaurin*, Paris, 1969, fig. 1)

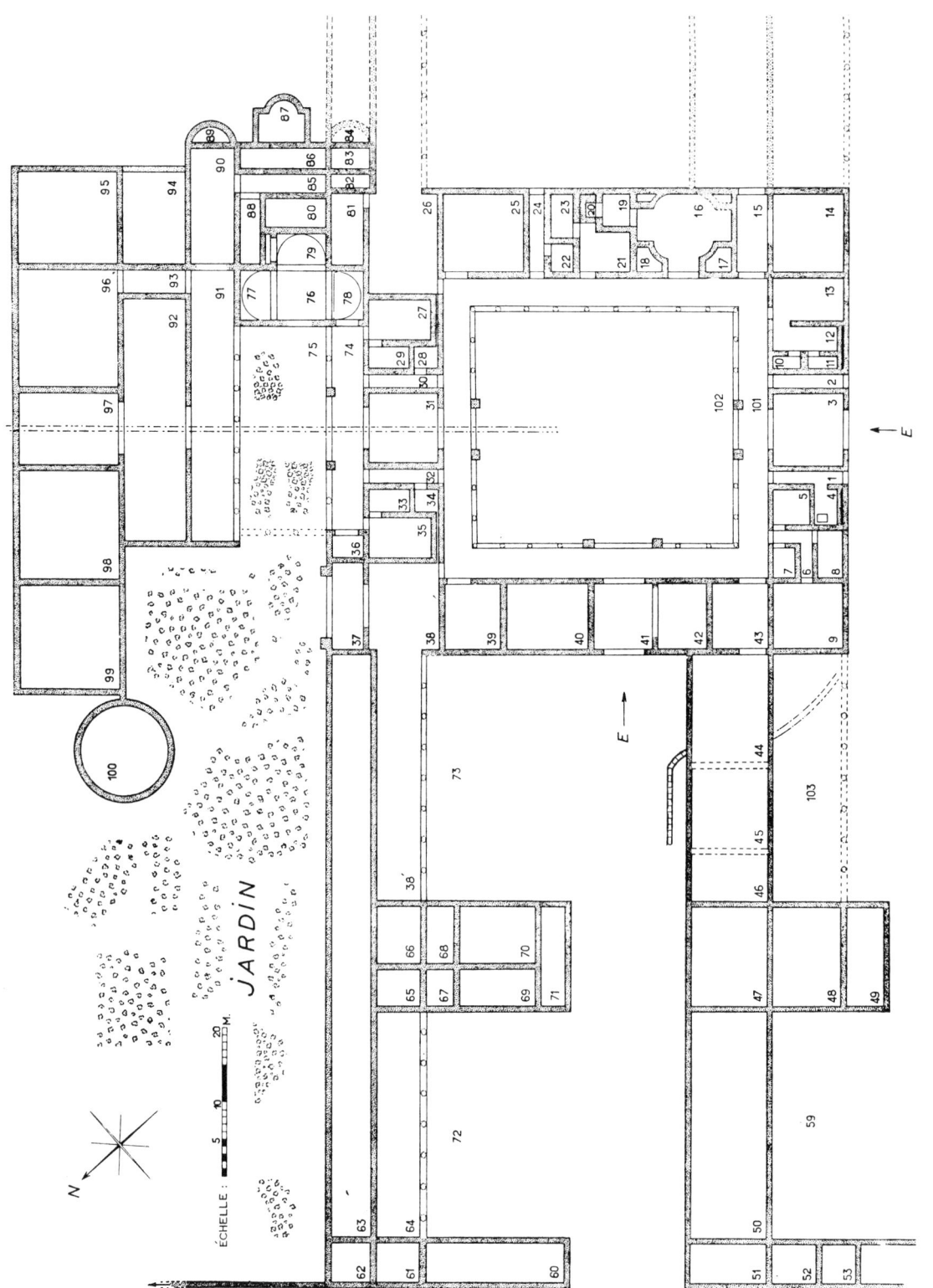

2. Plan of the first *villa urbana*: detail of the "garden corner" (after Fouet, *Montmaurin*, fig. 18)

MONTMAURIN
VILLA URBANA
VERS 350
N
JARDINS EXTERIEURS
COUR DE COMMUNS
FORGE
_G.F_1961_

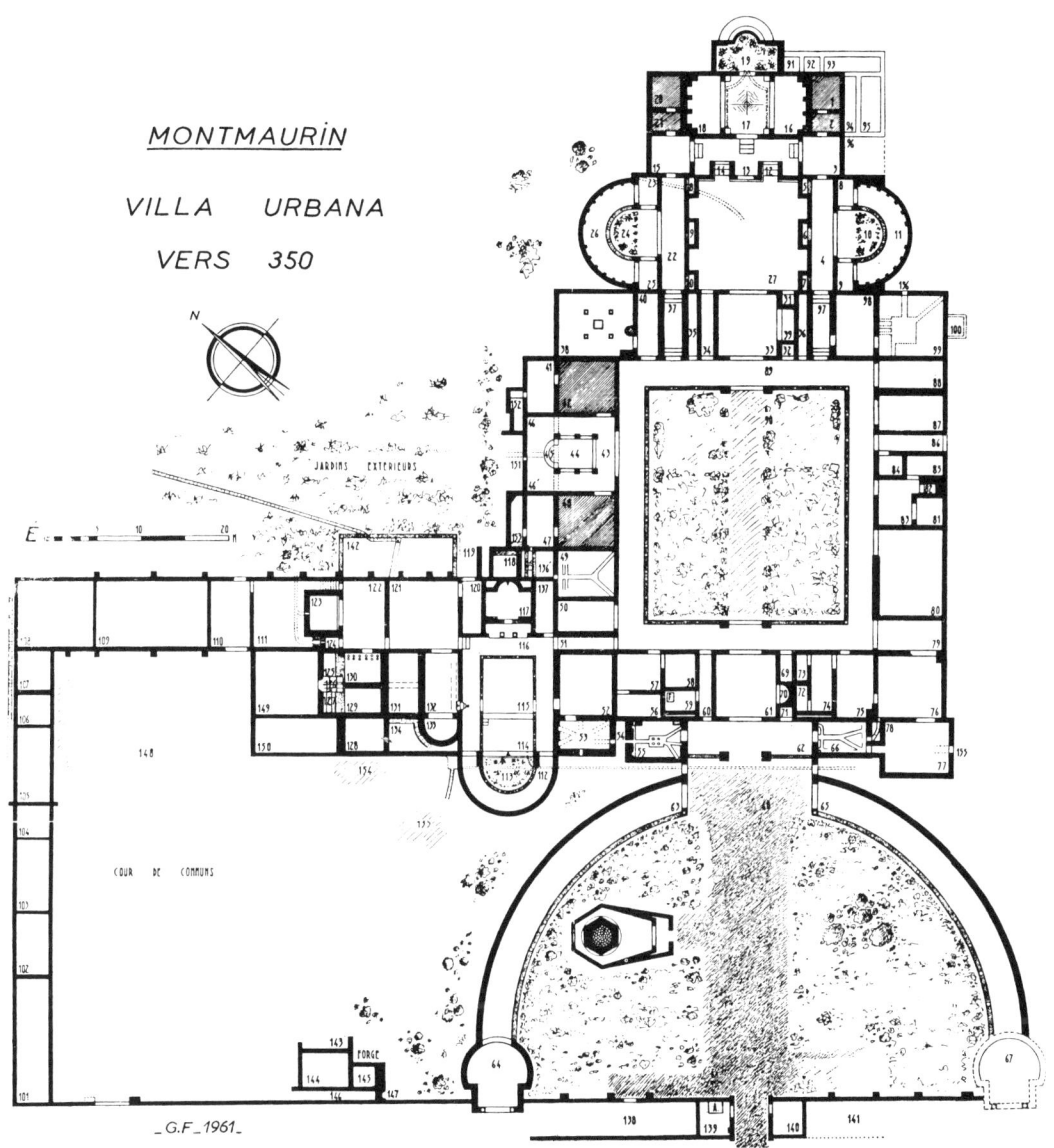

3. The Late Empire villa: general plan (after Fouet, *Montmaurin,* fig. 23)

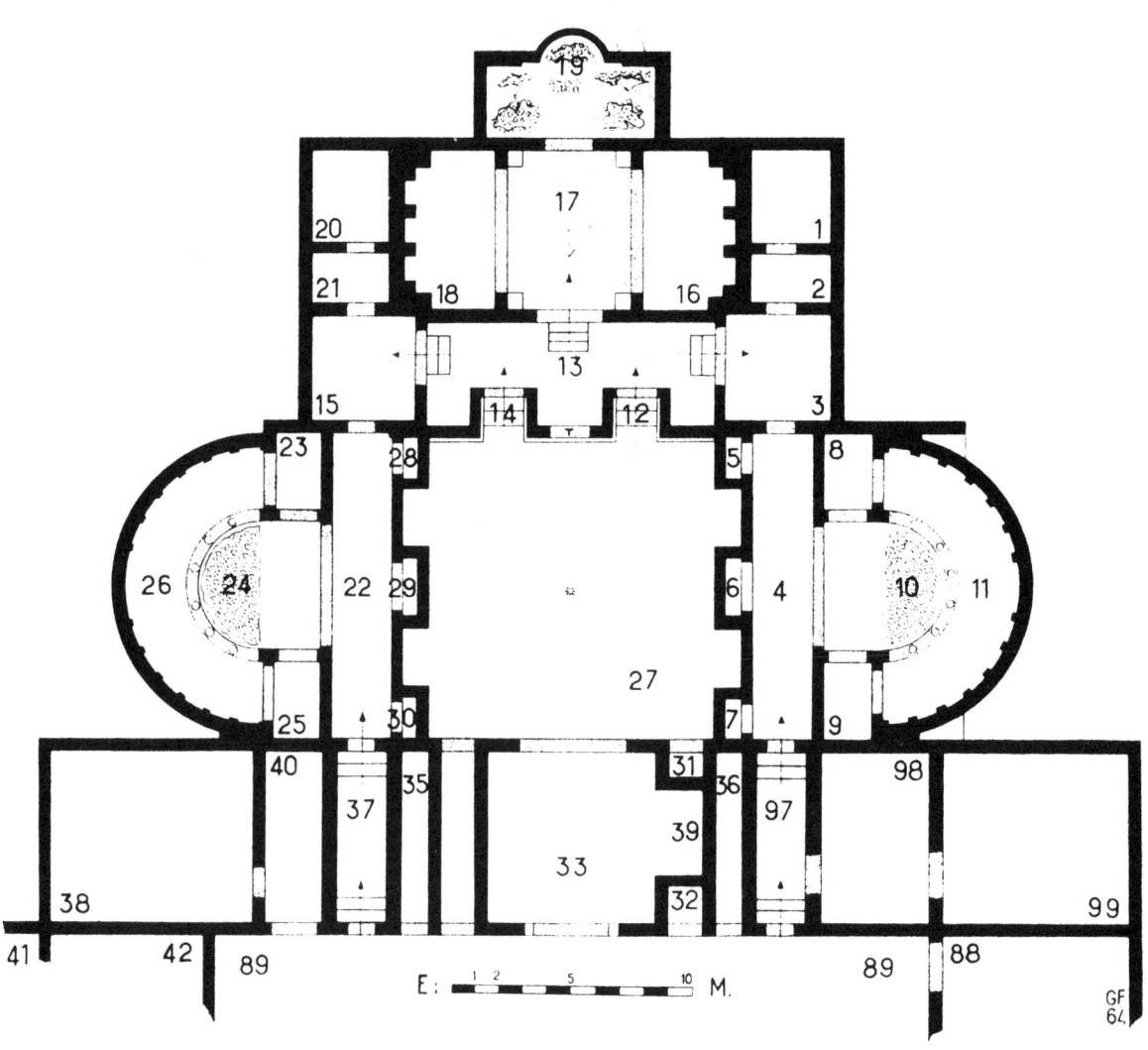

4. The Late Empire villa: the second peristyle (after Fouet, *Montmaurin*, fig. 38)

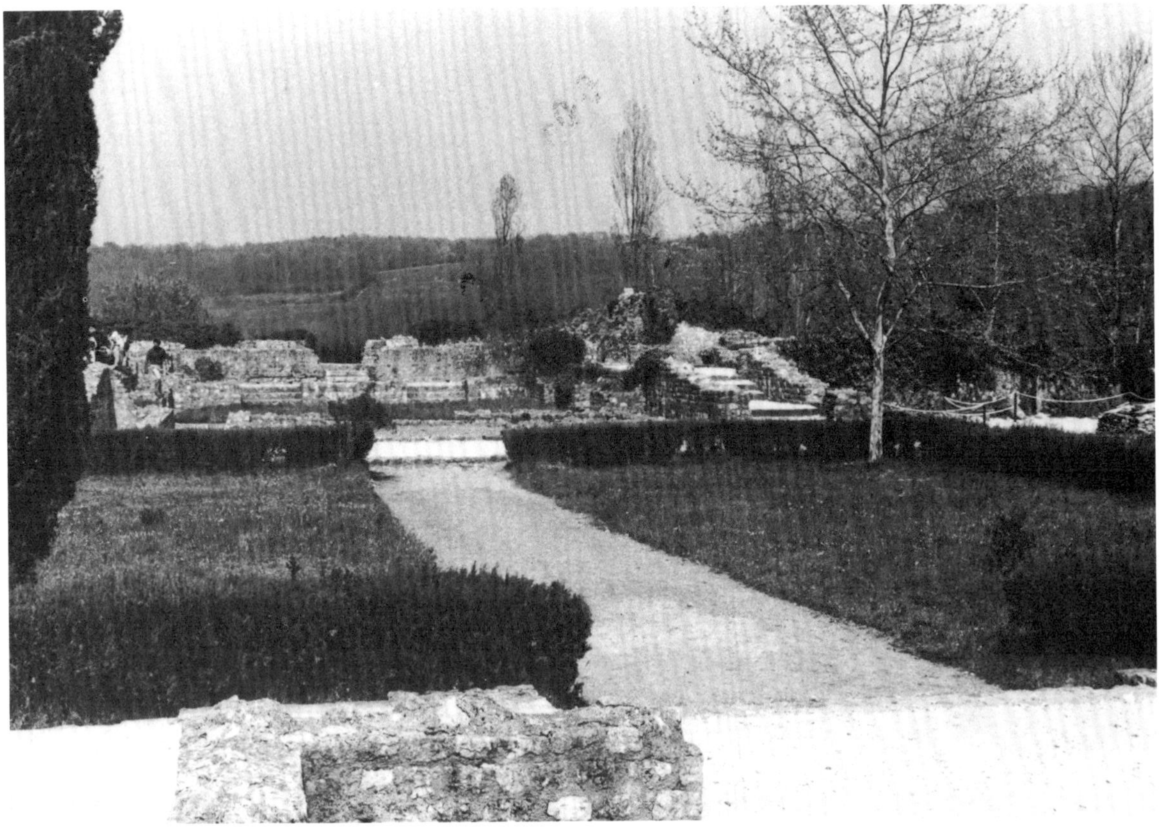
5. The central axis, toward the back part (photo: author)

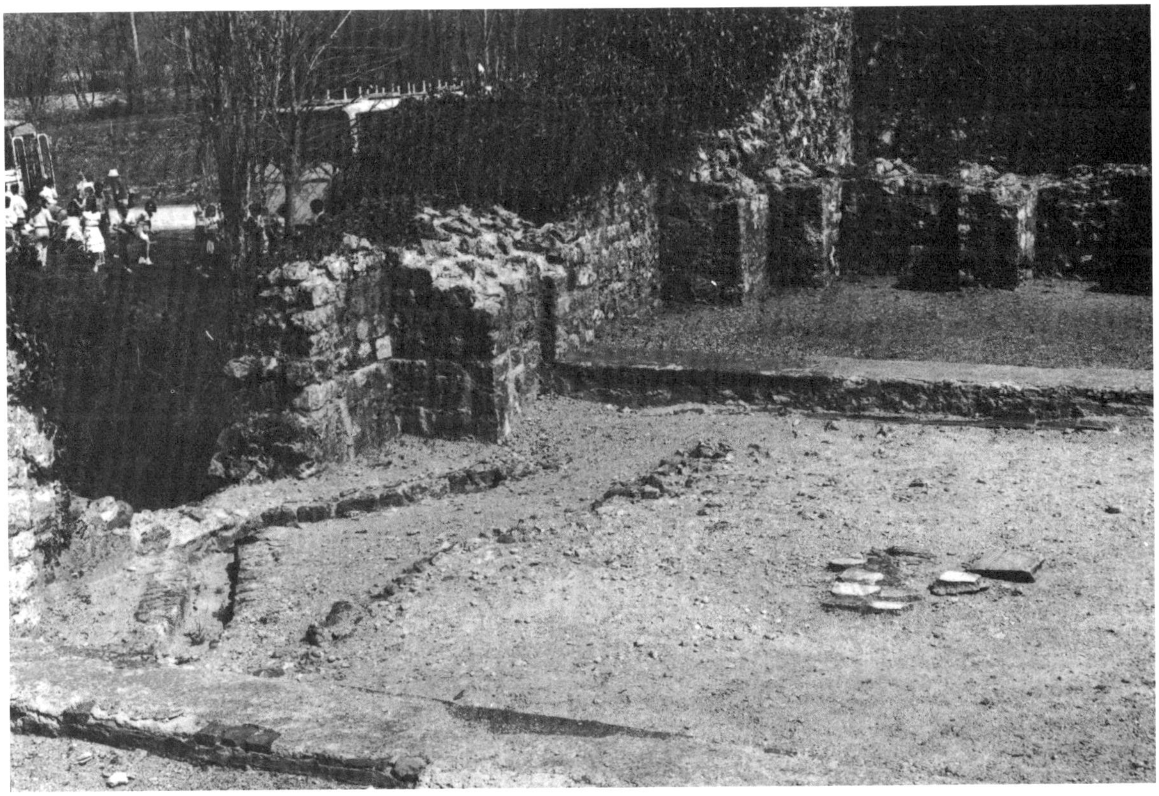
6. Rooms 17 and 16, from room 18; on the left, suspended garden 19 (destroyed) (photo: author)

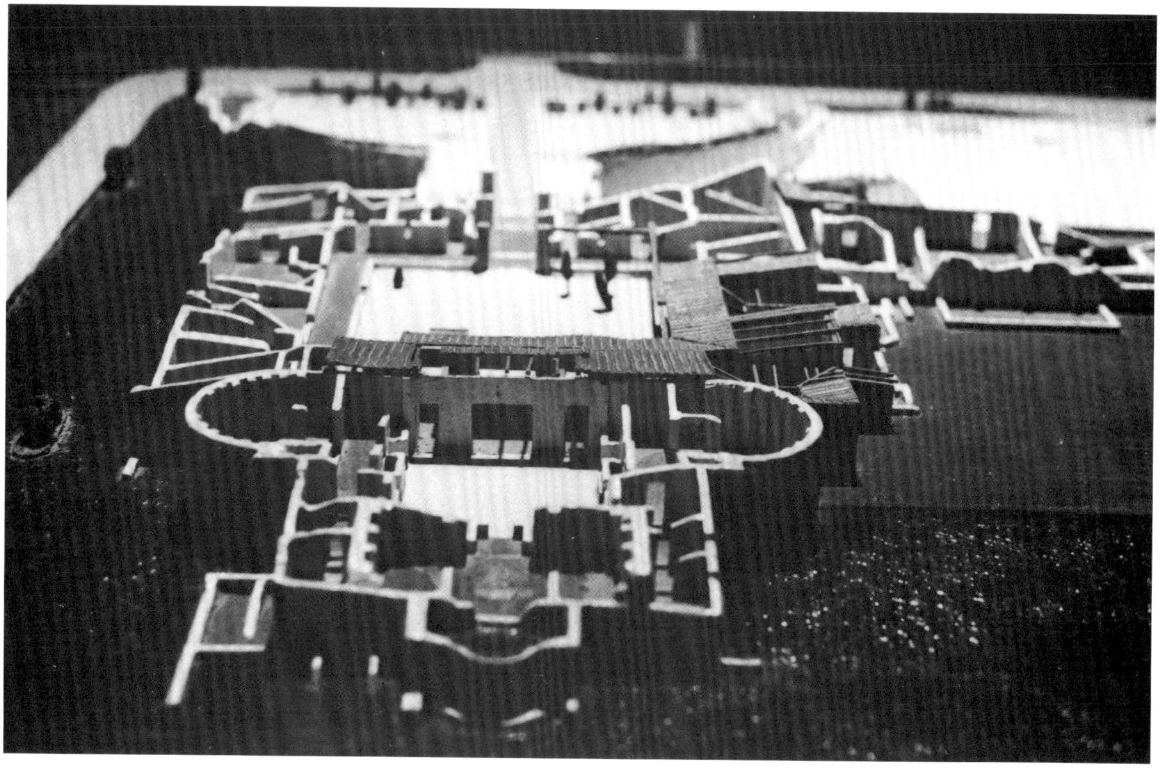

7. Model of the Late Empire villa (Museum of Montmaurin) from behind the suspended garden 19 (photo: author)

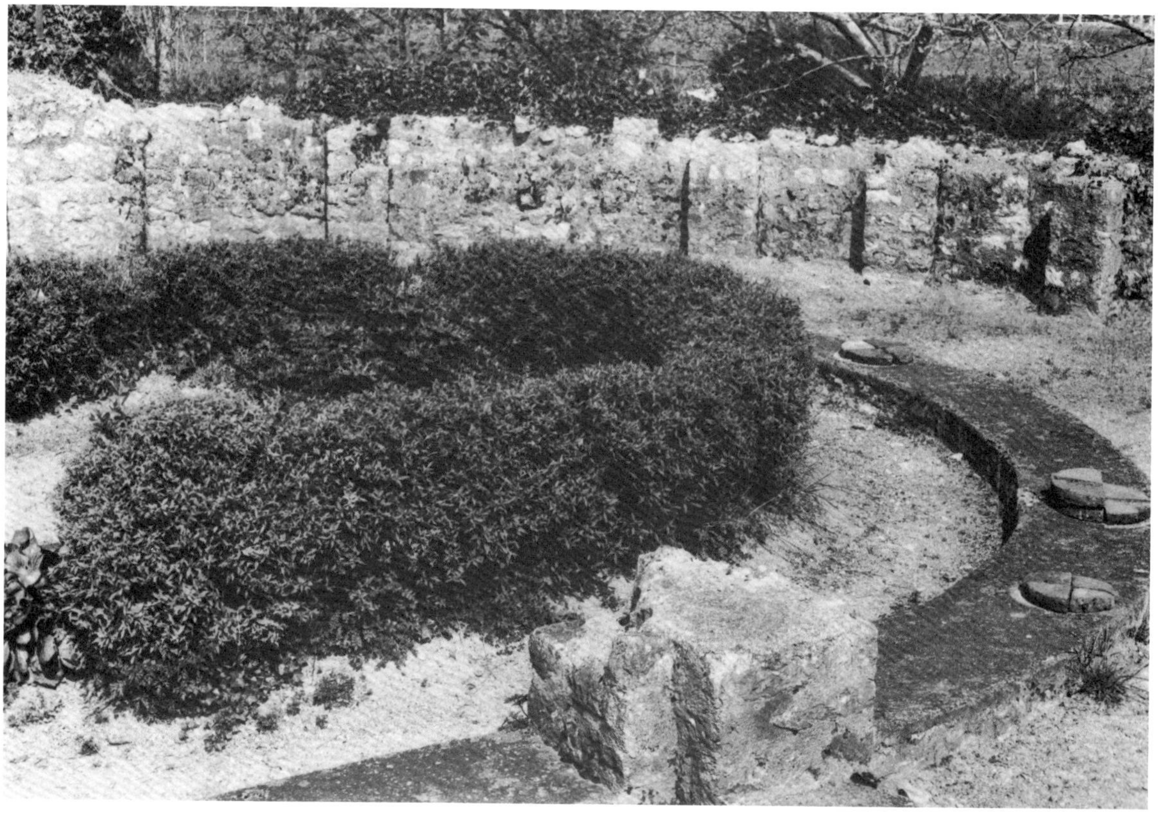

8. Garden 10, portico 11 (photo: author)

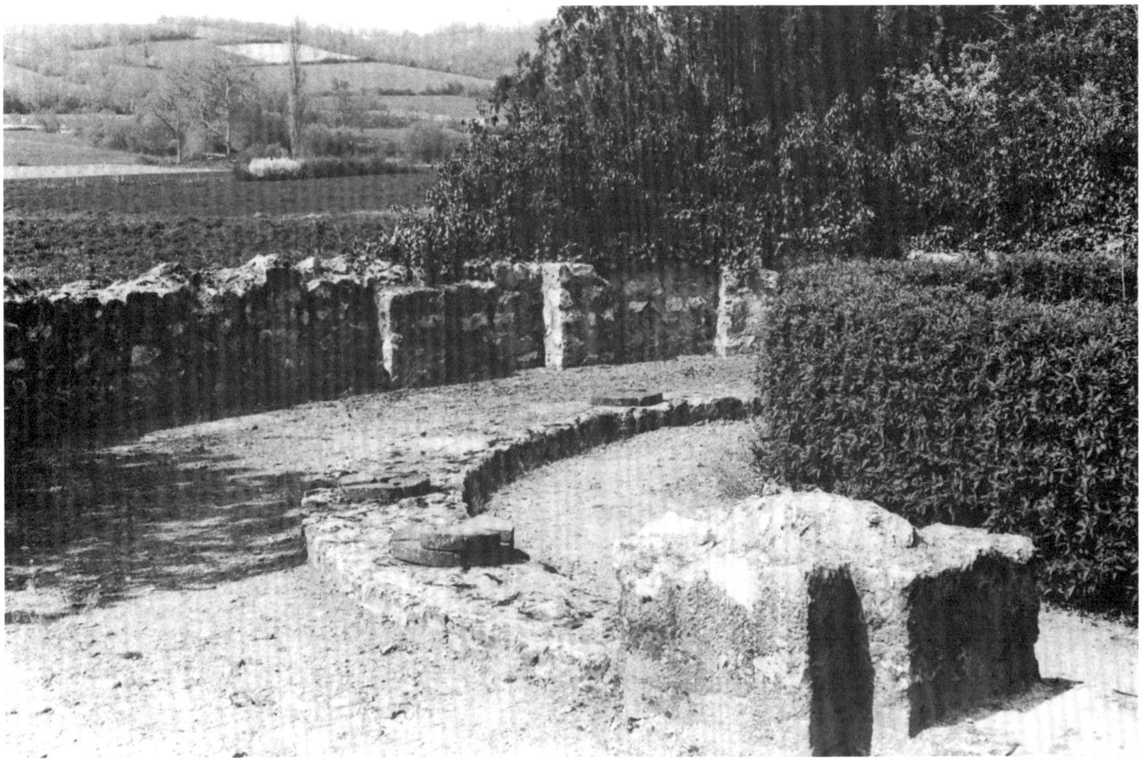

9. Garden 24, portico 26 (photo: author)

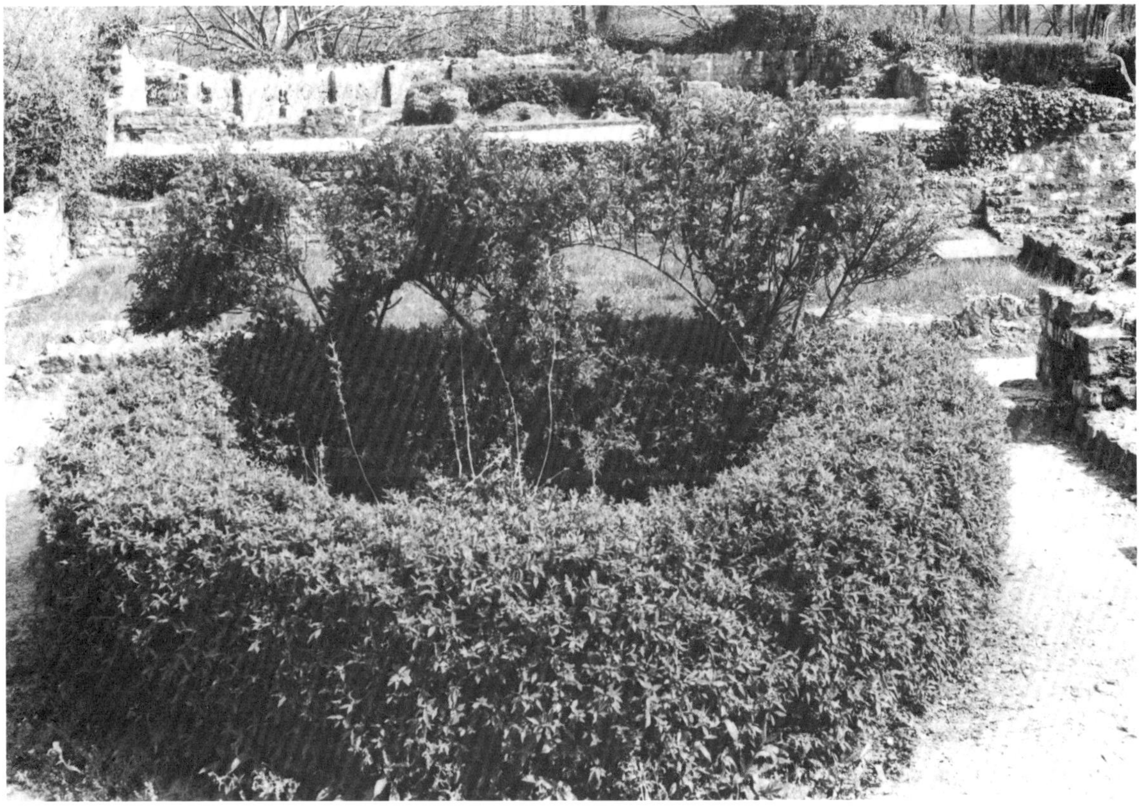

10. Garden 10 from behind garden 24 (photo: author)

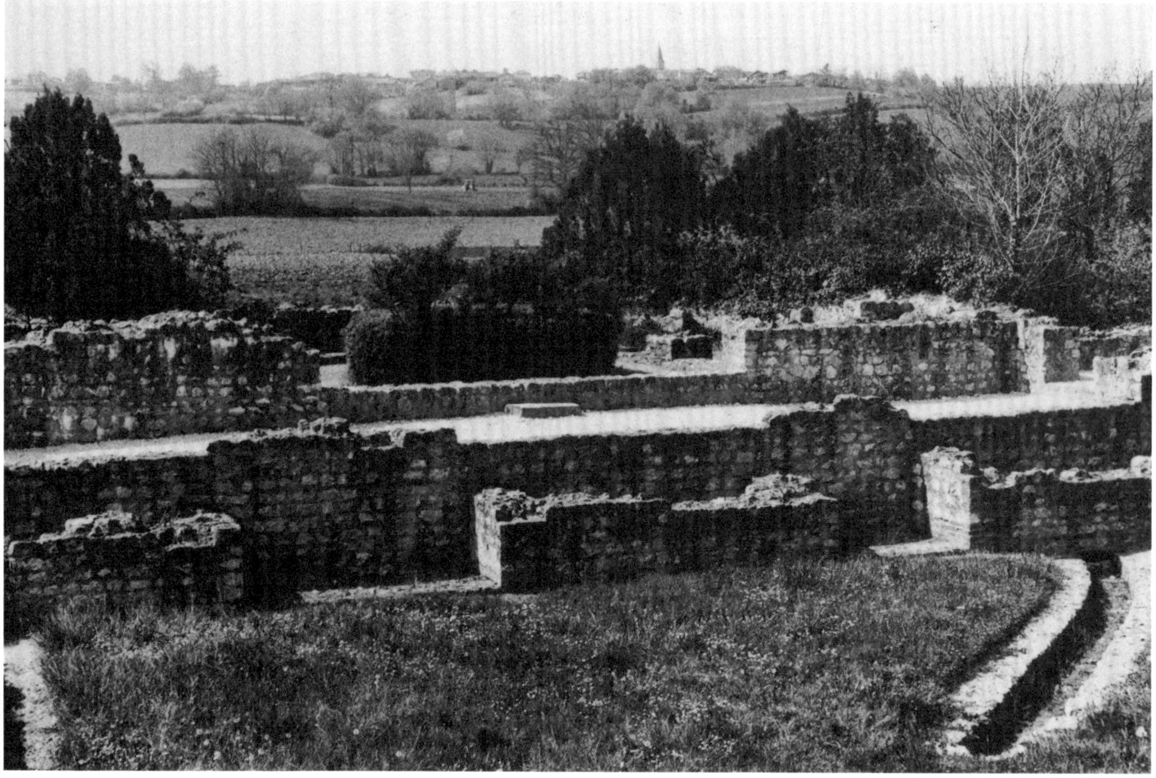

11. Courtyard 27, basins 28–30, garden 24 from walk 4 (in the background, the modern village of Montmaurin) (photo: author)

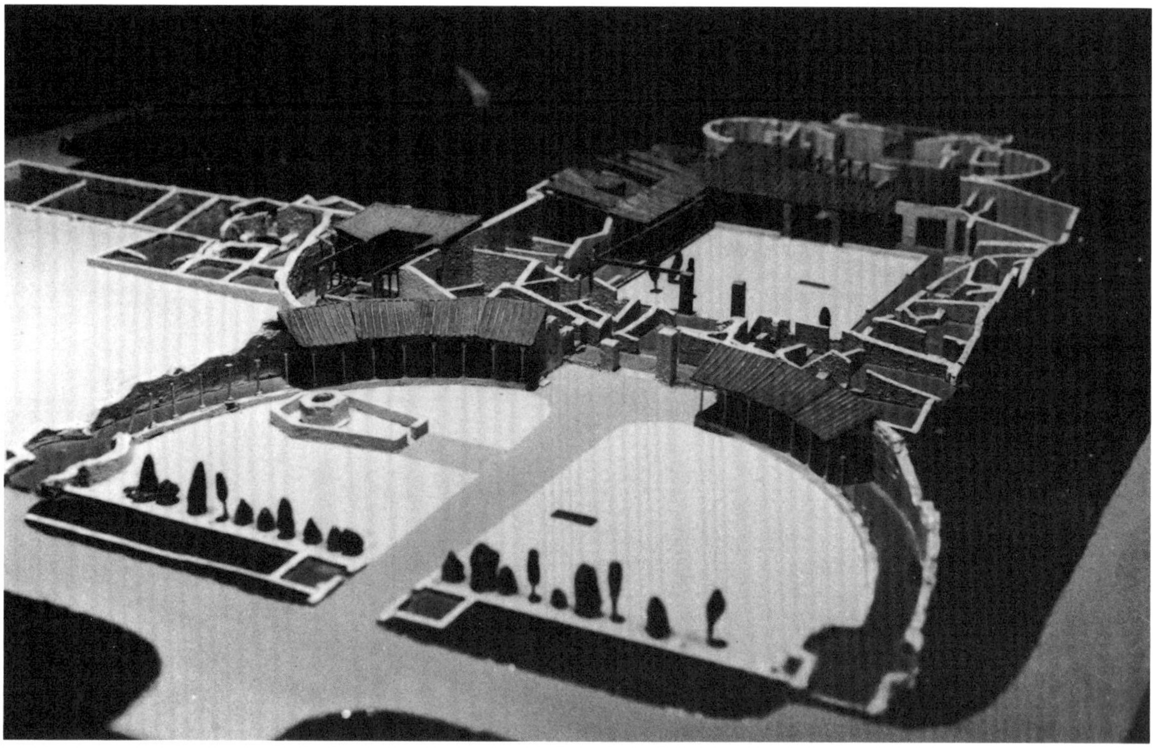

12. General view of the model, from the entrance gate (photo: author)

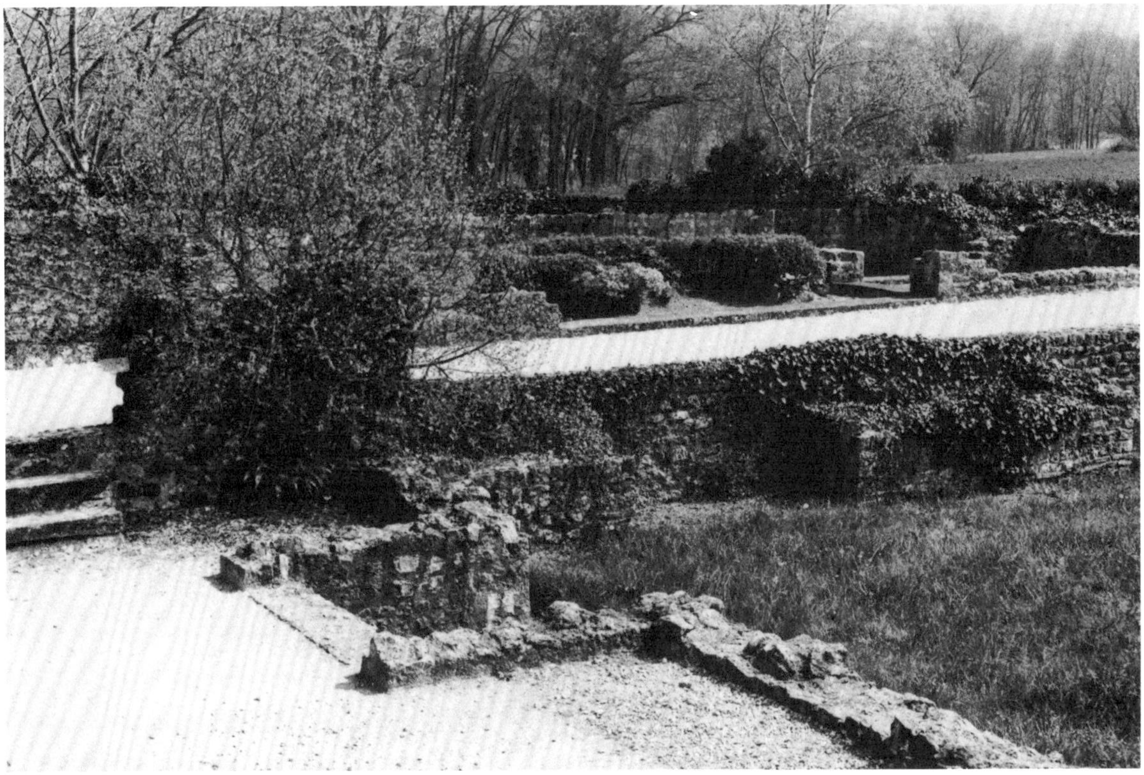

13. Courtyard 27, basins 5 and 6, garden 10, from the back part of the villa (flower boxes after A.D. 350) (photo: author)

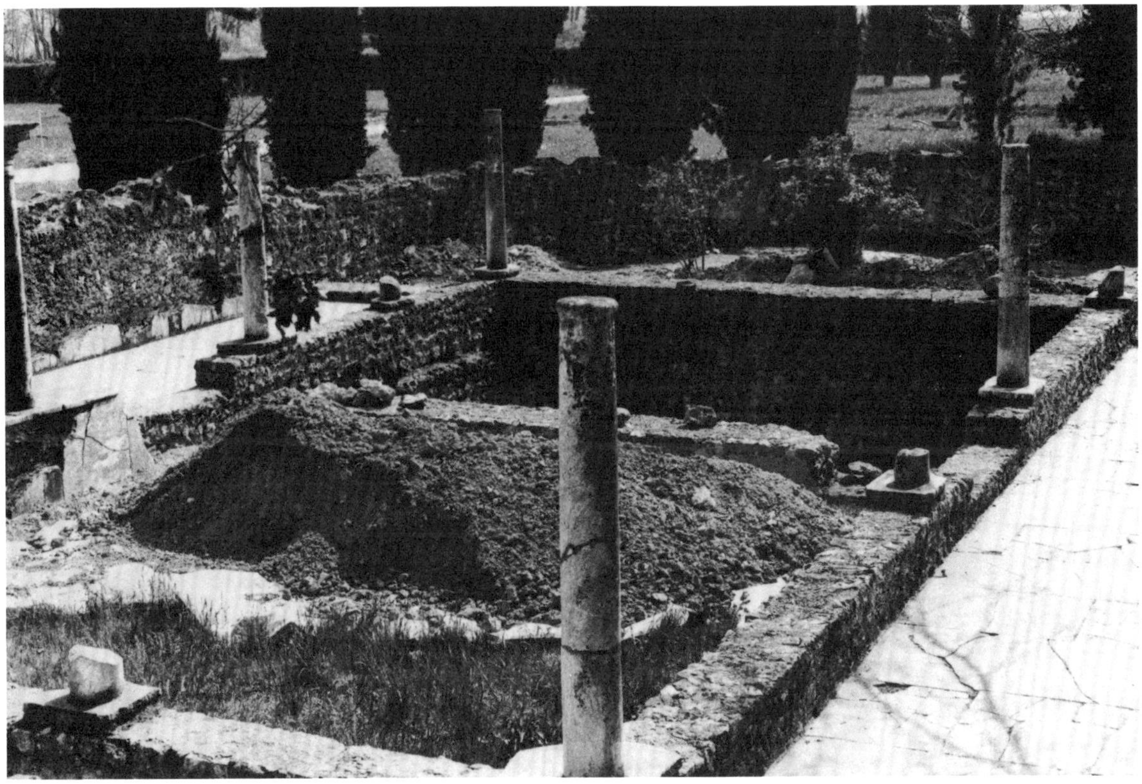

14. Modern restoration (1984) in the nymphaeum: courtyard 115 and piscina 114, added to garden 113 after A.D. 350 (photo: author)

A flood, mentioned above, wrecked the villa ca. A.D. 200. After a first restoration at the time of Constantine, it was partly burned and then rebuilt around the middle of the fourth century, following the same general orientation but with an entirely new design and on a slightly smaller scale.

The main feature of the new construction is that it was almost entirely walled in, with every part of it opening onto the inner courtyards. As compensation, the other innovation is that many of those central or peripheral, but always axially laid-out, elements became gardens.

The general plan of the Montmaurin Palace during the Late Empire is sufficiently known and clear (Fig. 3) for us to say but a few words about it: a vast semicircular porticoed vestibule, planted with trees and flowers precedes the dwelling quarters which surround a central square porticoed and planted over (90). Behind this second part a third one consists of terraces with rooms and apse-shaped gardens rising in tiers around and behind a second peristyle (27, Fig. 4): two lateral porticoed gardens (10 and 24) face each other, and the one at the far end (19) towers above everything else. One of the striking features of the overall design is the central allée (Fig. 5) leading straight through from the entrance gate to the terminal exedra garden. Northwest of the main dwelling quarters a thermal wing with a splendid nymphaeum separates the palace from the rustic outbuildings at the western corner, with a great courtyard (148) hidden behind the vestibule and the great facade wall. At the north angle one notes again the presence of the vast rectangular outer gardens beyond pergola 142, enclosed by a long perimetrical wall.

What about the gardens themselves? As mentioned above, we do not know the exact nature of the plantings inside, but for two exceptions: in front of the hanging garden (19) the four angular pillars of the preceding room (17, Figs. 6, 7) must have supported wooden beams over which ran the branches of the vines from the garden above, forming a kind of arbor roof for the space below. This space itself was otherwise hypaethral, with a sumptuous marble floor and a system of lateral gutters leading away to the gardens the rainwater from the surrounding roofs of the symmetrical rooms (16 and 18) that flanked it.

This terminal building of the palace has now disappeared (Fig. 6), so that we can say nothing more about it. The same must be said of another pergola (142, Fig. 3): it rested on four limestone columns of the Tuscan order, probably supported vine arbors and sheltered a fountain, and opened onto the vast outer gardens, which could be entered through the passage (119–120) that faced the western wing of the nymphaeum portico.

As for the planting in the main courtyards, all one may say is that the soil of the vestibule consisted of a layer of dark, rich compost, which testifies to the presence of clumps of shrubs and various plants separated by paths. Shrubs must have been especially numerous along the semicircular porticoes where the earth is thicker and the water could fall abundantly from the roofs. Trees and shrubs must also have surrounded the temple in the forecourt, except in front of it. One must imagine narrow paths between the plants, except in the case of the large, axial allée and the short one that leads to the temple on the left.[7]

The central courtyard (90) was covered, on each side of the central walk, with the same kind of compost. There were identifiable traces of vegetation along the central path and the porticoes. Grass and flowers must have grown in the beds, except in the back part of the courtyard. The following courtyard (27, Fig. 4), in the middle of the second peristyle, was at first paved with marble slabs, where a system of water supply could feed the lateral basins (5, 6, 7 and 8, 9, 10) used as ponds for oysters and shellfish. After A.D. 350 the marble slabs and their mortar base were taken away and replaced by a thick layer of earth, while the basins were transformed into flower boxes. The same evolution is recognizable in the piscina (114) and the courtyard (115) of the nymphaeum, so that the whole interior part of the nymphaeum became a garden.

As for the lateral porticoed gardens (10 and 24, Fig. 4) and the one in the nymphaeum (113, Fig. 3), the first thing to note is that they are similar in form and size (Figs. 8, 9): the diameter of their semicircle is 5.50 meters long. Fouet writes, "Enclosed in a splendid marble colonnade, each of these areas, the surface of which was about a dozen square meters, must have displayed a number of exquisite adornments, with colorful plantings no doubt surrounding works of sculpture."[8] Unfortunately we do not have the slightest idea which plants and ornaments embellished these lovely places, except for the rear of the nymphaeum, adorned with the Adonis sculpture which I shall return to later. There remains to note a significant architectural feature: in front of the lateral gardens (10 and 24), the walks (4 and 22) were bordered, on each side of the central courtyard, by walls in which symmetrical openings allowed, just above the lateral basins, visual communication between the gardens through the courtyard (Figs. 10, 11).

It is now clear how numerous, important, and various the gardens are in the plan of the Late Empire Roman villa at Montmaurin. But a no less striking feature is the extraordinarily coherent organization of these gardens and the fine interrelationship between them and the architecture. Finally, I would like to make a few last remarks about the significance of the gardens in the Montmaurin Palace.

First, *the permanent role of the outer gardens*. These gardens, at the northern corner of the settlement, were a constant pivotal feature, from the first to the last phase of its history. One might speak of a "corner garden," as one does of a "cornerstone," not only in the architectural but in the functional sense of the word. In fact, even after the summer triclinium of the first century had disappeared, these gardens went on playing the same double role of ornamental perspective (from the portico of the nymphaeum, 116, and the pergola, 142) and kitchen garden (behind the kitchens, 151–153). The permanence of gardens in the same area with the same function, while everything else in the architecture around them was to change, seems highly significant for our purpose.

[7] Fouet, *Montmaurin*, 62–63, 129–130.
[8] Ibid., 129.

Second point: the organization of the gardens and the architecture is in itself significant, in the sense that it is *at once axial, transparent, and hierarchical*. We already noticed the narrowing perspective of the whole, from the facade wall up to the terminal, upper room with its apse-shaped garden, a typical private lodging certainly reserved for the master of the palace and his relatives. Let us have a look at the model displayed in the Museum of Montmaurin (Figs. 7, 12): from the upper tier one can look down the central axis and supervise the life of the entire villa. It is especially worth noting that only the Montmaurin gardens present both these features—the apse-shaped structure and the elevated position. The apse-shaped structure causes the inner part of the villa to be shut out by the gardens from all exterior influence, while its rooms look down onto the central area (Fig. 4).

The second feature is no less symbolic. Let us compare, for instance, the Montmaurin villa's layout with that of the Piazza Armerina Palace;[9] it is striking to notice there a more or less similar sequence of rooms, with the exception that at the rear of the Piazza Armerina villa we find a vast basilican hall with an exedral niche in the middle of the back wall in lieu of the Montmaurin garden quarters. The parallel corroborates the kind of supervisory character assigned to the Montmaurin Late Empire garden.

No less symbolic—and this is my third point—is *the presence of the religious element* everywhere in the garden quarters of the Montmaurin villa. We do not know the exact nature of the probably mythological sculptures that adorned the three lateral gardens along the second peristyle. Fouet assumes, with good reasons, that at least some of them might have evoked Venus' protection over the growth of flowers and vegetation, a type of Venus presumably confused with the local goddess Tutela wearing the cornucopia.[10] Again, a marble statue of Venus was surely placed in the middle of the nymphaeum garden (113), among other figures (a young man, a tree, and a wild boar) that represent the Adonis myth—the typical garden myth. In actual fact, the life of Adonis symbolized the vegetation cycle, from the growth of plants in springtime to their fading away in the fall. To quote Fouet again: "This group was all for the glory of the great female deity Venus, who, reigning over the waters from which she issued, awakening in the spring the generative forces of the earth, appeared as the goddess of growing things, an embodiment of earthly fertility. In all probability, in springtime this scene presided over a ritual of the Adonis Gardens in the nymphaeum. The custom was to plant all sorts of seeds to germinate and grow rapidly in little cups, ceramic potsherds, and other small receptacles. Quickly withered, were these little artificial gardens evoking Adonis' brief life finally thrown into the waters?"[11]

As for the polygonal temple in the semicircular courtyard at the entrance, we can note that it is a Celtic shape and type, with a peripheral gallery surrounding the big hexagonal altar and the central, circular well, filled in and used as the base of a ritual

---

[9] Cf. G.V. Gentili, *La villa imperiale di Piazza Armerina*, Rome, 1956.
[10] Fouet, *Montmaurin*, 169, 176.
[11] Ibid., 170; pls. LIII–LIV.

hearthstone (Fig. 12). What we must here add to Fouet's careful commentary may be summed up briefly; the entrance area of the villa was the meeting point of the Roman villa and its inhabitants with their rural surroundings and of the Italian princely architecture with the traditional, religious, Celtic one. This meeting point, as we noted, is set in a garden, and the whole semicircular courtyard can therefore be viewed as an immense apse-shaped porticoed garden. Thus the area is very likely to have been dedicated not only to chthonian (remember the ritual pit) but to garden deities such as Venus-Tutela. Considering that this kind of devotion must have been shared equally by the Gallic peasants and their Roman master, is it not tempting to see in such a community of ritual, if not of feelings, one of the reasons for pagan resistance to Christianity during the Late Empire?[12]

Finally, the importance of the gardens in Montmaurin's ancient life will be further enhanced if we consider the last transformations undergone by the villa after A.D. 350, when the oyster ponds below the lateral gardens were replaced by flower boxes and the piscina of the nymphaeum was filled in so that the entire nymphaeum area became a garden (Figs. 13, 14). Whatever may have been the reason for it, this ultimate alteration and definitive victory of the gardens confirm us in the idea that we can speak not only of Montmaurin's villa gardens but of Montmaurin as a "garden villa."

---

[12] Cf. J.-M. Pailler, "L'énigme Nymfius," *Gallia*, 1986 (forthcoming).

Land Use at the Via Gabina Villas

WALTER M. WIDRIG

Philip Oliver-Smith and I began our study of the Via Gabina villas in 1976.[1] From the start the study was conceived as a long-term project of excavation and research, and no end is yet in sight. Therefore, the conclusions presented here must be regarded as tentative until all the evidence is collected. However, the facts from excavation stand on their own.

As is the case with all long-term projects, it is hard to set limits on the work. Each year brings new insights which require further digging for verification and, in turn, more material from the field for analysis. Even initially our goals were ambitious: (1) to test the data and assumptions drawn from several surface surveys of ancient sites in the general region of the Via Gabina;[2] (2) to trace the development of villa types from the Late Republic to the Late Empire in this rural area about 14 kilometers from the center of Rome;[3] (3) to shed light on the broader economic and social context of these villas.[4]

---

[1] Our work is sponsored by Rice University and funded through gifts and contributions from individuals and small local foundations. These individuals and foundations are too numerous to list separately, but we are indeed grateful for their loyal support. All seasons of excavation have been in association with the Soprintendenza alle Antichità di Roma. In this regard we give special thanks to Prof. Adriano La Regina, Superintendent, and to Dr. Anna Maria Bietti Sestieri and Dr. Matilde de Angelis d'Ossat, Inspectors, for their generous help and patience. We also acknowledge the invaluable assistance of Dr. M. Aylwin Cotton at every stage of the project and the gracious cooperation of the American Academy in Rome and the British School at Rome.

In May 1984, shortly after this paper was written, Molly Cotton died in Rome. I dedicate this paper to the memory of a dear friend.

[2] See esp. L. Quilici, "La Via Prenestina," *Passeggiate nel Lazio*, II, Rome, 1977; *Collatia* (=*Forma Italiae*, reg. 1, vol. 10), Rome, 1974; and *Urbanistica*, 54–55 (1969), i–xx; J.B. Ward-Perkins and A. Kahane, "The Via Gabina," *Papers of the British School at Rome*, 40 (1972), 91–126; P. Schutzmann-Bolzon, "Archeologia in Borgata: Il gruppo di Tor Angela," *Archeologia*, n.s. 1 (1972), 33–36; Jean Coste, S.M., "Ricerca dei bolli laterizi in una zona dell'agro romano Torre Angela," *Rendiconti della Pontificia Accademia Romana di Archeologia*, 43 (1971), 71–108; G.M. De Rossi, *Torre e castelli medievali della Campagna Romana*, Rome, 1969; G. Tomassetti, "Vie Labicana e Prenestina," *La Campagna Romana*, III, Rome, 1913, 377–599; T. Ashby, "Classical Topography of the Campagna Romana, I," *Papers of the British School at Rome*, 1 (1902), 125–281; and, most recently, the exhibition catalogue *Roma, Archeologia e Progetto*, Rome, 1983, 28–30.

[3] With the exception of the area around Vesuvius, surprisingly few villa sites have been excavated in Italy. The work at these few sites has often been incomplete and the stratigraphy virtually ignored. Fragments of villa plans and inaccurate dating are of little use in tracing the development of types, even in establishing types. In recent years the situation has improved considerably. See *Roman Villas in Italy, British Museum Occasional Paper 24*, ed. K. Painter, London, 1980. Two commendable reports are M. Aylwin Cotton, *The Late Republican Villa at Posto, Francolise*, London, 1979; and A. Carandini, *Settefinestre*, 3 vols., Modena, 1985. However, Lazio in particular has not received the attention it rightfully deserves.

M. Aylwin Cotton briefly discusses the dramatic change taking place in Italy in regard to the investigation of villas: "Some Research Work on Roman Villas in Italy, 1960–1980," *Rome and Her Northern Provinces*, ed. B.R. Hartley and J.S. Wacher, Oxford, 1983, 56–66. Dr. Cotton's cited bibliography is particularly valuable, although some American work of these years has been missed.

[4] Little of what we know of rural life from writers such as Cato, Varro, and Columella has ever been verified by material remains. A bucolic existence may be simple in some ways, but not in its patterns of organization.

We have made considerable progress in achieving all of these goals, but perhaps our most surprising results apply to the third. We are increasingly aware how shifts in the economic and social organization of these villas reflect the fluctuating fortunes of Rome, both city and state. Changes in land use and degree of economic cooperation are key factors in understanding the complex pattern of interrelationships for this agricultural yet suburban region which, we presume, always helped to stock the table of metropolitan Rome.

It is now our intention to carry our study up to the present day rather than restrict it to antiquity. Our sites and others close by from the medieval period are still unencumbered by modern structures, and the land continues to be farmed, having its own complex history over the past century and a half. The rapid urbanization of the periphery of Rome means that a similar opportunity may never again exist. For that matter, the actual area where we dig could also, in a few years' time, fall prey to the developer.[5] Our chief concern is not so much the ravages of the plough as Rome's expansion into the *campagna*.

Surface surveys provide only cursory data, but they do offer the excavator a frame of reference and working hypotheses for actual digging. In this regard we acknowledge our enormous debt to the Via Gabina survey conducted by John Ward-Perkins and Anne Kahane in 1964 (Fig. 1).[6] From their catalogue of thirty-five sites we selected three for excavation by means of the following criteria: (1) likelihood that the architectural remains would prove to be villas with both residential and agricultural facilities; (2) assurance of long occupation; (3) proximity of the three sites to one another for maximum interaction in antiquity and of each to the Via Gabina for easy access to Rome. In order to avoid repeated and lengthy negotiations we knew that equally important would be the single ownership today of the property on which these three sites might lie. The three sites we chose—Sites 10, 11, and 13—we felt best met our criteria, and we have found it useful to keep the same number designations. All three lie within the property of the Vaselli family known as the Tenuta di Tor Bella Monaca (sometimes also referred to as the Tenuta di Tor Angela).[7] Eight six-week seasons of fieldwork have enabled us to explore Sites 10 and 11 by extensive excavation and to locate the architectural remains of Site 13 by trial trenches.[8] The sequence of exploration of the three was deter-

---

[5] The *tenuta* where we work is included in a "master plan" for urban development by the Comune di Roma. Already we have witnessed the creation of a new town for twenty thousand persons just outside the gates and along the southern boundary of this farm. In fact, a few small parcels of its land were sold to make such urban expansion possible. Each year more and more houses are built, many illegally, on the periphery, so that now most of the farm is encircled. Site 10 backs up to a solid row of new multistoried suburban residences. The Soprintendenza has kept pace with this building boom, but it can do little more than rescue archaeology. See the exhibition catalogue *Roma, Archeologia e Progetto*, esp. 28–30.

[6] Ward-Perkins and Kahane, "The Via Gabina." The site numbers we are using are taken from their survey enumeration.

[7] The designations Tor Bella Monaca and Tor Angela are medieval in origin. The documentation for these towers goes back to the 12th century, and the physical remains of the Tor Angela exist today as part of a recently abandoned farmhouse on the *tenuta*.

[8] Since the writing of this paper there have been two more full seasons of excavation at Site 10. The

mined by schedules of crop rotation on the *tenuta* and the assessment of further plough damage if digging should be delayed for some years at any of the sites (the case at Site 13). The number of persons we could accommodate as our labor crew, all volunteers, also played a part.[9]

Because of the topic of this Symposium, "Villa Gardens of the Roman Empire," and the title of this paper, "Land Use at the Via Gabina Villas," I shall try to focus on these matters in the rest of what I have to say. It must be kept in mind that I shall be dealing with a twelve-hundred-year span of time, from the beginning of the third century B.C. to perhaps the end of the ninth century A.D.

SITE 11

Two seasons of excavation were sufficient to determine the full extent of the villa at Site 11. It was found to have two major periods of construction, each with three phases.[10] Subsequent work has allowed us to reconstruct the villa's appearance over the centuries and to refine our interpretation of its economic role in the region.[11]

Period 1

We have only a fragment of the initial plan of the villa (Phase 1A; Fig. 2) and are therefore in doubt as to its orientation. We are fairly secure, however, in dating this phase to the beginning of the third century B.C. By the middle of the century new rooms firmly established a U-shaped form (Phase 1B; Fig. 3) with the base of the U on the north. This base contained the residential quarters of the villa, while the arms of the U

---

new information gathered is startling, but it does not invalidate what is presented here. Rather than rewrite the paper, which, after all, is meant to be a document of what was said and discussed at the symposium, I have chosen to do necessary updating in the footnotes. As I said in my first paragraph, conclusions must be regarded as tentative until all the data is collected and processed. Bibliography from the past two years has been inserted into the footnotes when I have thought it useful.

[9] Since we cannot afford paid workmen, we use student volunteers whom we both house and feed. The availability of lodging near our sites as well as our small budget for excavation have set limits on the size of the operation each year.

[10] Our first interim report, written after the 1977 season, gives what was then known of the plans and phases for the villa: P. Oliver-Smith and W. Widrig, "Villa rustica romana. Relazione preliminare sulle campagne di scavo 1976 e 1977 nell'agro romano," *Notizie degli scavi di antichità* (hereafter *NS*), ser. 8, 35, 1981 (Lincei, 1982), 99–114; see also M.A. Cotton, "Una villa ed un grande edificio romani lungo la via Gabina," *Archeologia laziale*, 2 (1979), 82–85. No major revision of these two reports has become necessary because of newly excavated material. More precise dating of the phases, especially those of Period 2, is found in W. Widrig, "Excavations on the Via Gabina: Second Preliminary Report," *NS* (forthcoming), a report written after a careful stratigraphic analysis by Joann Freed of the pottery from the site.

[11] See W. Widrig, "Two Sites on the Ancient Via Gabina," *British Museum Occasional Paper* 24 (1980), 119–141; "Excavations on the Ancient Via Gabina: Second Preliminary Report," *NS* (forthcoming), written after the 1980 season; "Two Villas and a Late Antique Horreum" (summary), *American Journal of Archaeology* (hereafter *AJA*), 85 (April 1981), 224; and "Twelve Centuries of Occupation along the Via Gabina" (summary), *AJA*, 87 (April 1983), 269. See also P. Oliver-Smith and W. Widrig, "Excavations on the Via Gabina," *Archaeology*, 33 (May–June 1980), 56–59; and "Nine Centuries of Social and Economic Change along the Via Gabina," a forthcoming article to be published by the Soprintendenza alle Antichità di Roma and the Comune di Roma.

1000
500
0
1km
VIA COLLATINA
VIA PONTE DI NONA
VIA FOSSO DELL'OSA
OST. DELL'OSA
Gabii
VIA PRENESTINA
TOR ANGELA VECCHIA
MURACCIO DI RISCHIARO
STRADA DI TORRE NOVA
TOR BELLA MONACA
LA BORGHESIANA
FATTORIA PRATOLUNGO
STRADA DELLA BORGHESIANA
VIA DI ROCCA CENCIA
VIA CASILINA
TORRE NOVA
TORRE GAIA
1000
500
0
1km
COLLATIA
VIA COLLATINA
GABII
AD NONUM
VIA PRAENESTINA
VIA GABINA
AQUA ALEXANDRIANA
VIA LABICANA

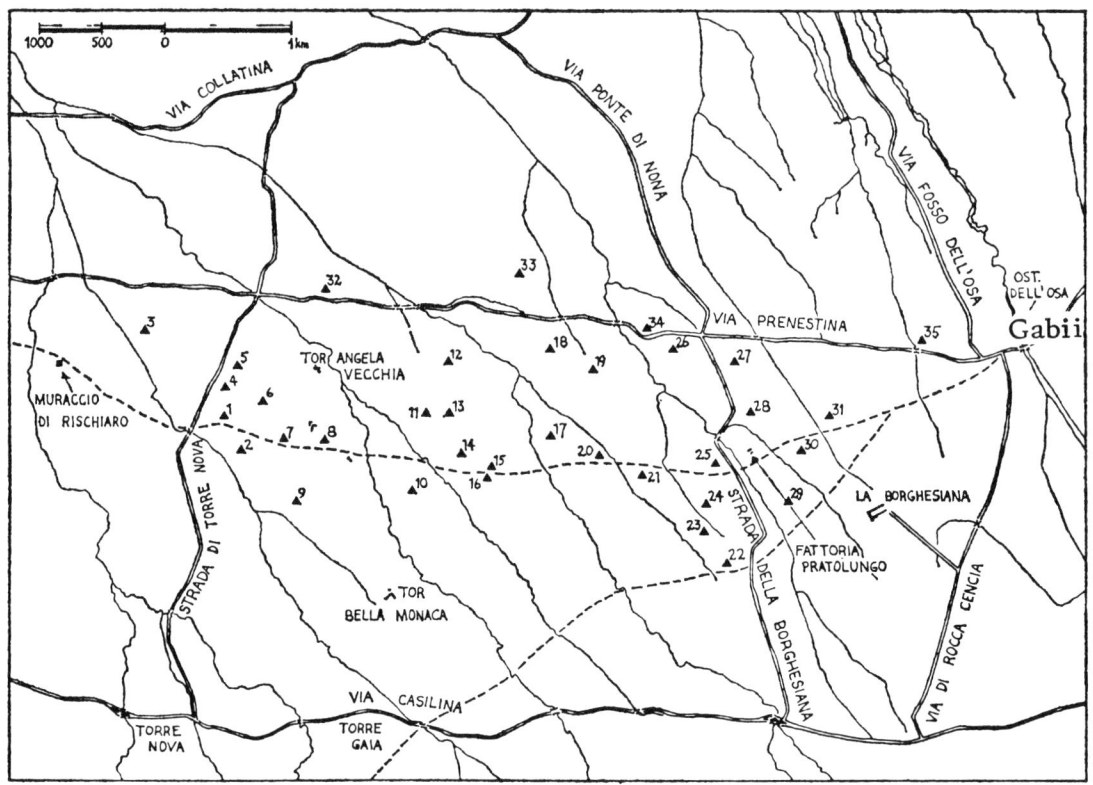

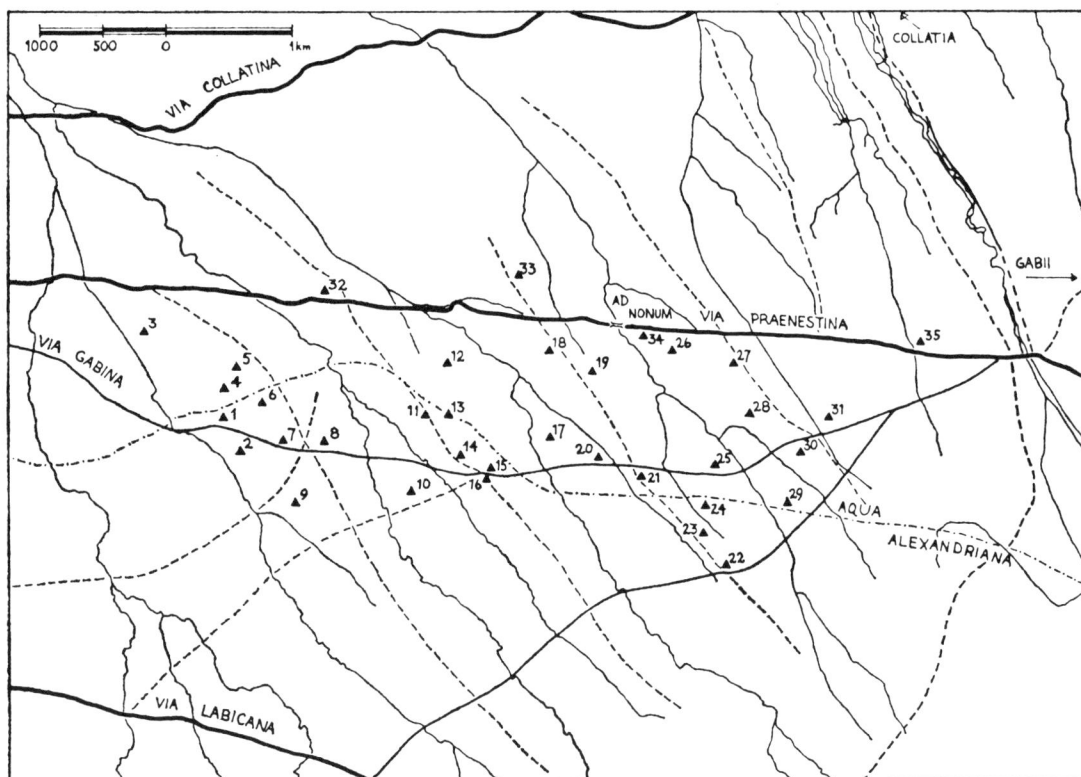

1. Maps of the Via Gabina region (modern and ancient) from the Ward-Perkins and Kahane survey (*Papers of the British School at Rome,* 40 [1972], 92)

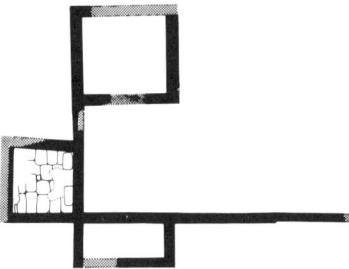

2. Via Gabina Site 11, plan of the villa, Phase 1A (author)

DOMUS
HORTUS
well
work platform
COURTYARD
Via Gabina 11
Phase 1b
0 1 2 3
N

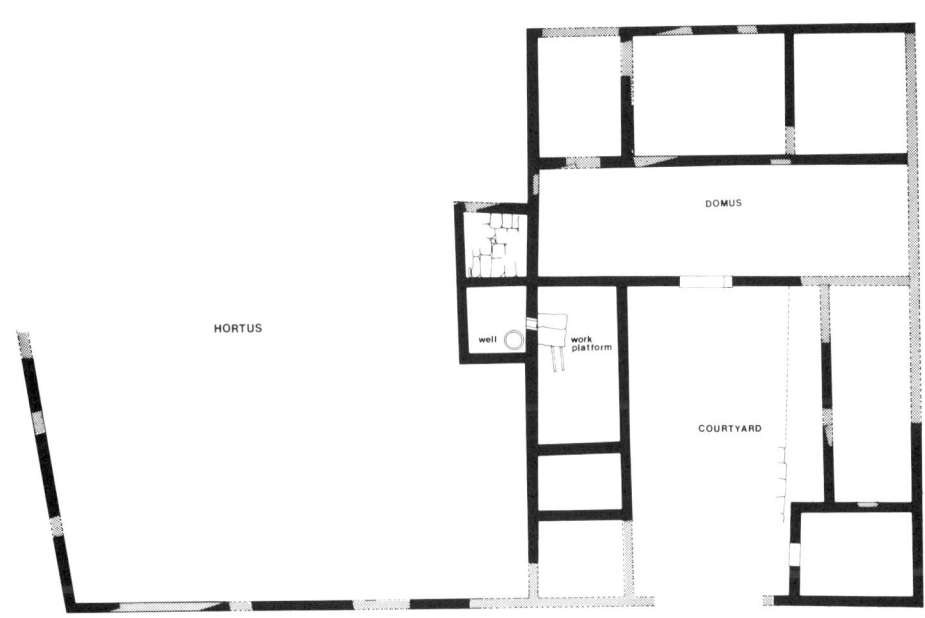

3. Via Gabina Site 11, plan of the villa, Phase 1B (author)

DOMUS
HORTUS
well
work platform
COURTYARD
Via Gabina 11
Phase 1c
0 1 2 3
N

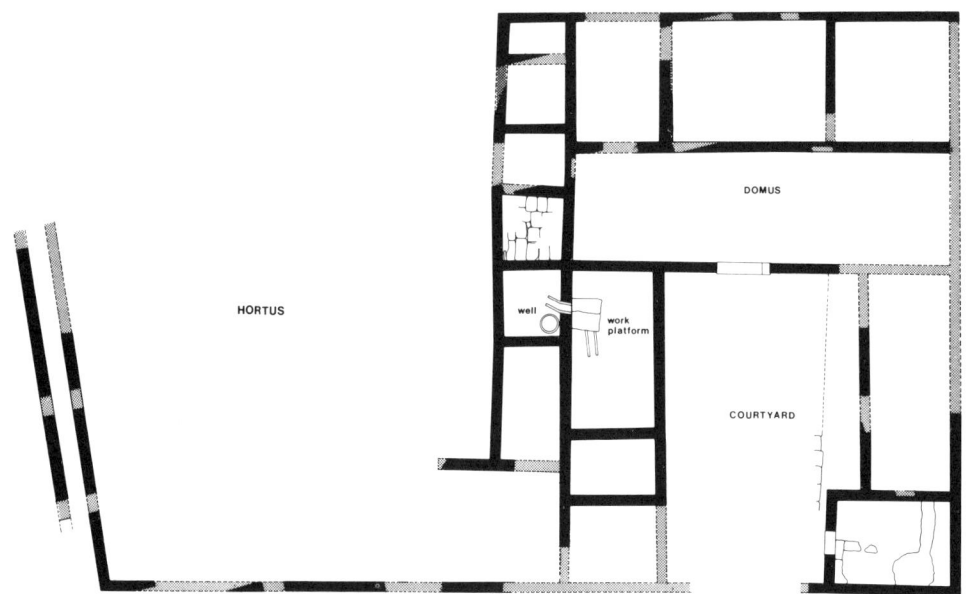

4. Via Gabina Site 11, plan of the villa, Phase 1C (author)

Via Gabina 11
Axonometric Reconstruction
Phase 1c
0 1 2 3 4 5m

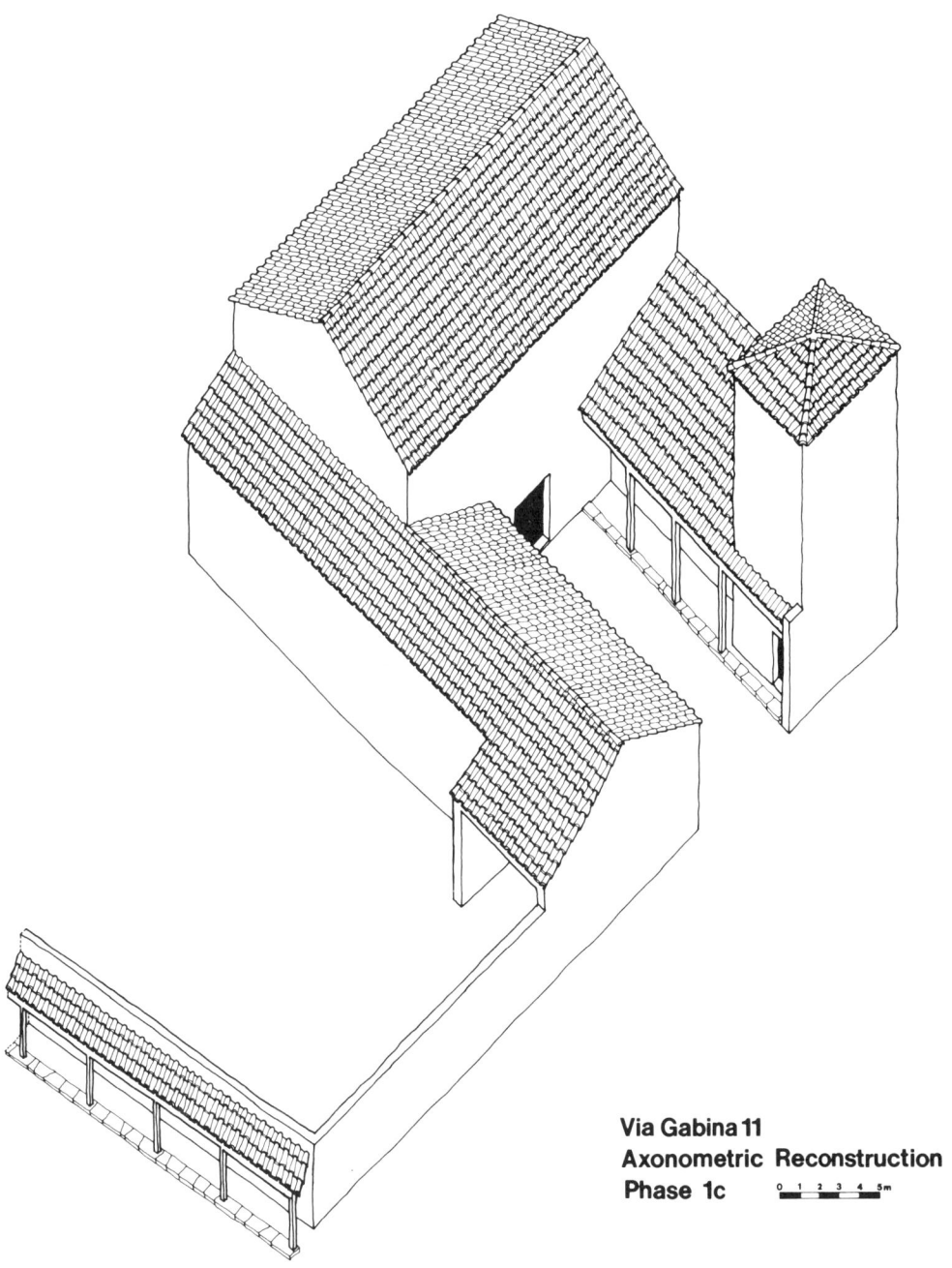

5. Via Gabina Site 11, axonometric reconstruction of the villa, Phase 1C (R. Lewis)

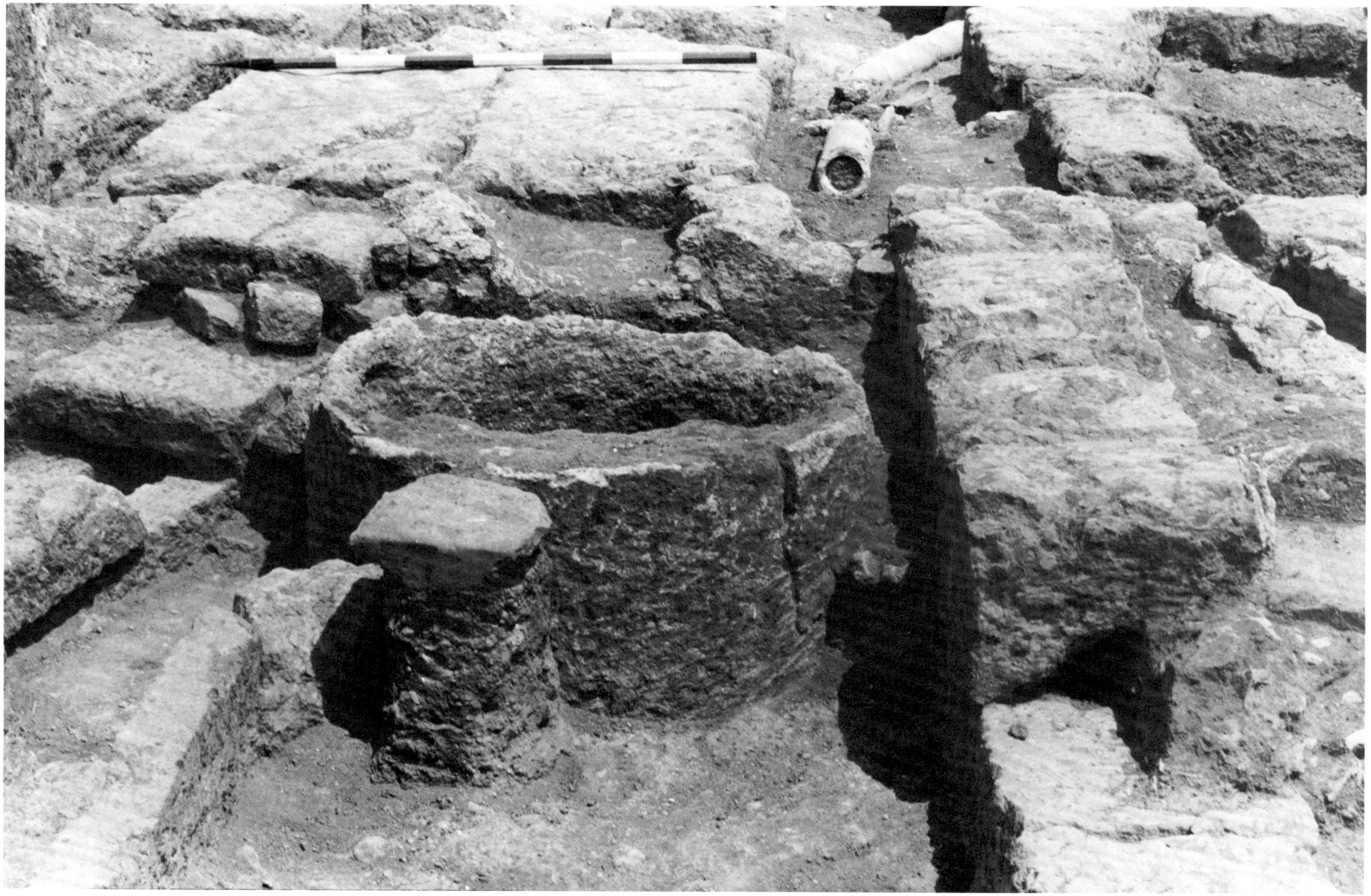

6. Via Gabina Site 11, channeled platform (background, left) in the western arm of the villa, Phase 1B/C (photo: P. Oliver-Smith)

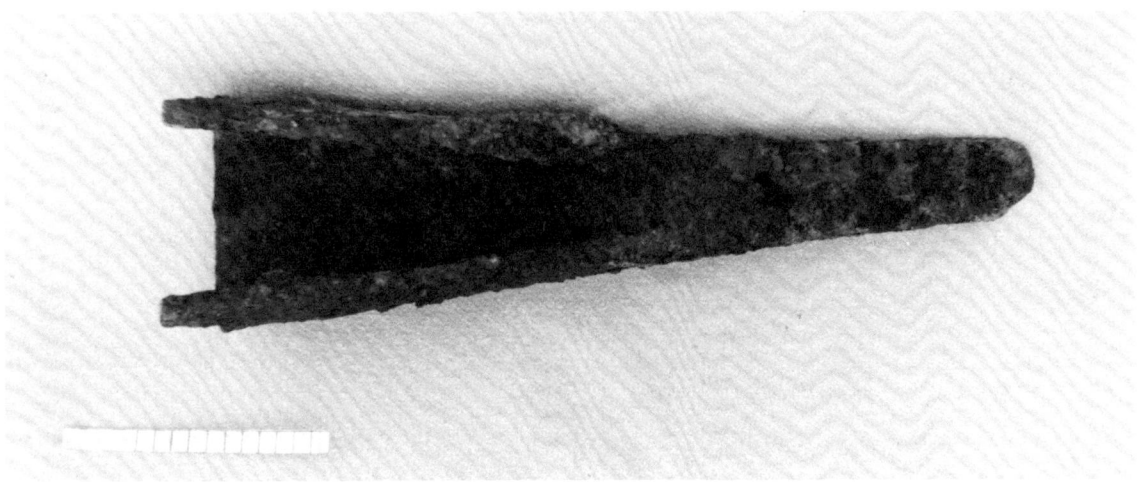

7. Via Gabina Site 11, iron ploughshare from Phase 1C (photo: P. Oliver-Smith)

8. Via Gabina Site 11, billhook or pruning blade from Phase 1C (photo: P. Oliver-Smith)

triclinium
HORTUS
well
DOMUS
impluvium
atrium
basin
Via Gabina 11
Phase 2a
0 1 2 3
N

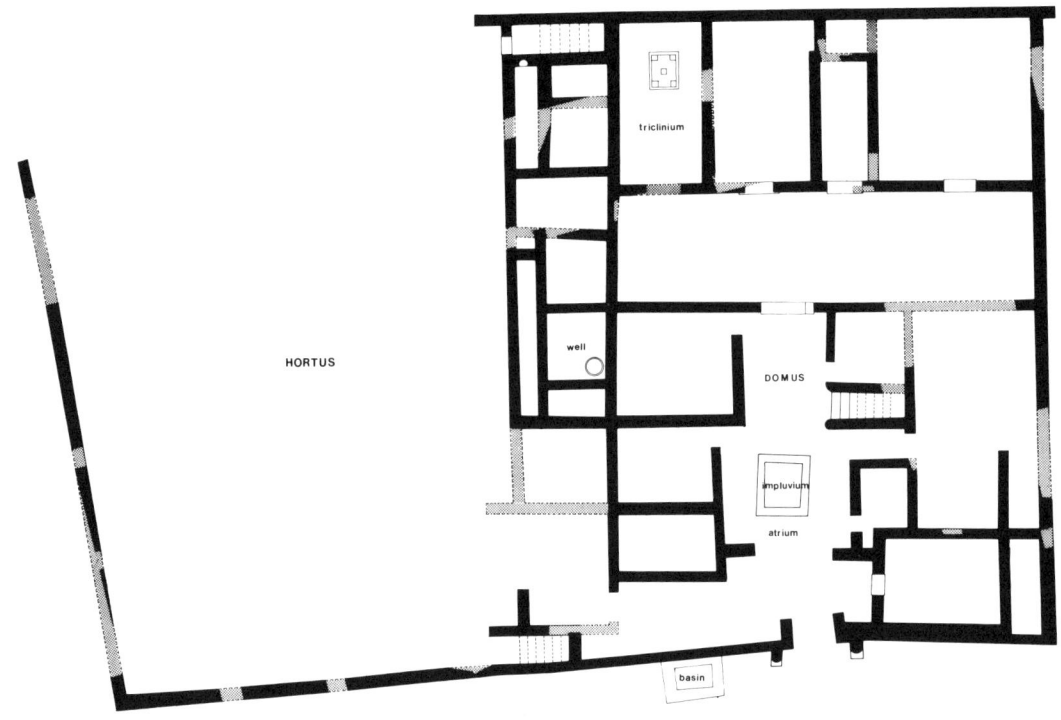

9. Via Gabina Site 11, plan of the villa, Phase 2A (author)

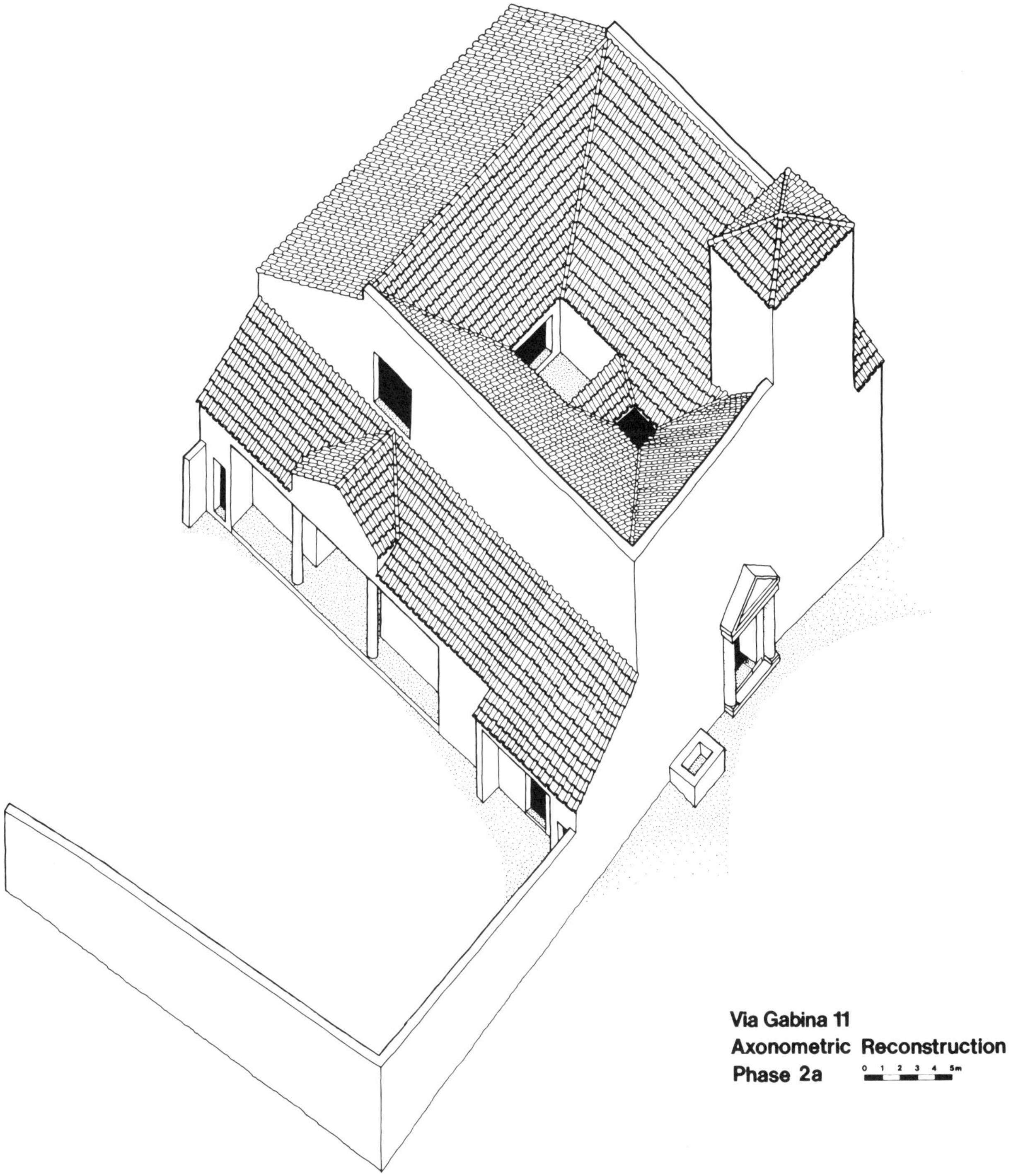
Via Gabina 11
Axonometric Reconstruction
Phase 2a
0 1 2 3 4 5m

10. Via Gabina Site 11, axonometric reconstruction of the villa, Phase 2A (R. Lewis)

basin
basin
basin
basin
tank
press
tank
triclinium
overflow
pool
well
DOMUS
hot
plunge
tepidarium
impluvium
basin
caldarium
HORTUS
atrium
basin
Via Gabina 11
Phase 2b/c
0 1 2 3

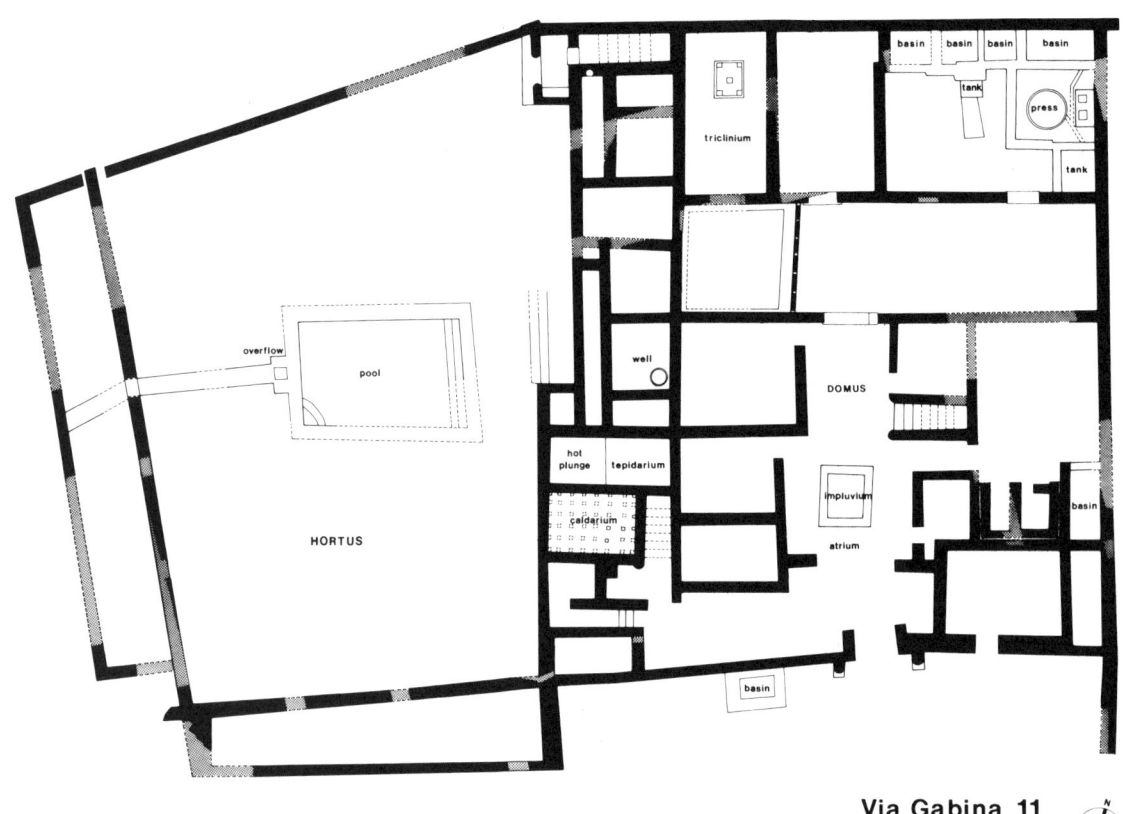

11. Via Gabina Site 11, plan of the villa, Phase 2B/C (author)

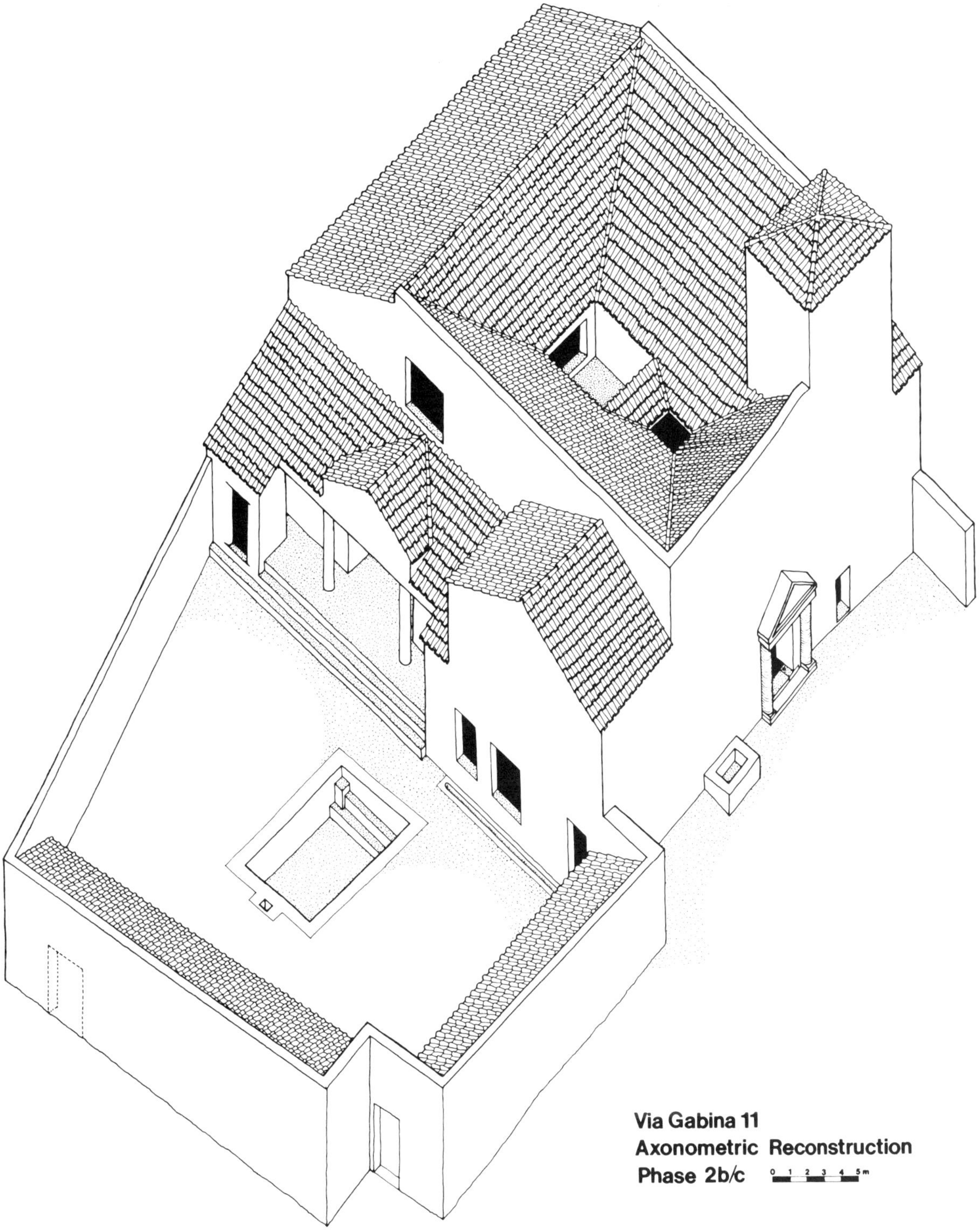
Via Gabina 11
Axonometric Reconstruction
Phase 2b/c
0 1 2 3 4 5m

12. Via Gabina Site 11, axonometric reconstruction of the villa, Phase 2B/C (R. Lewis)

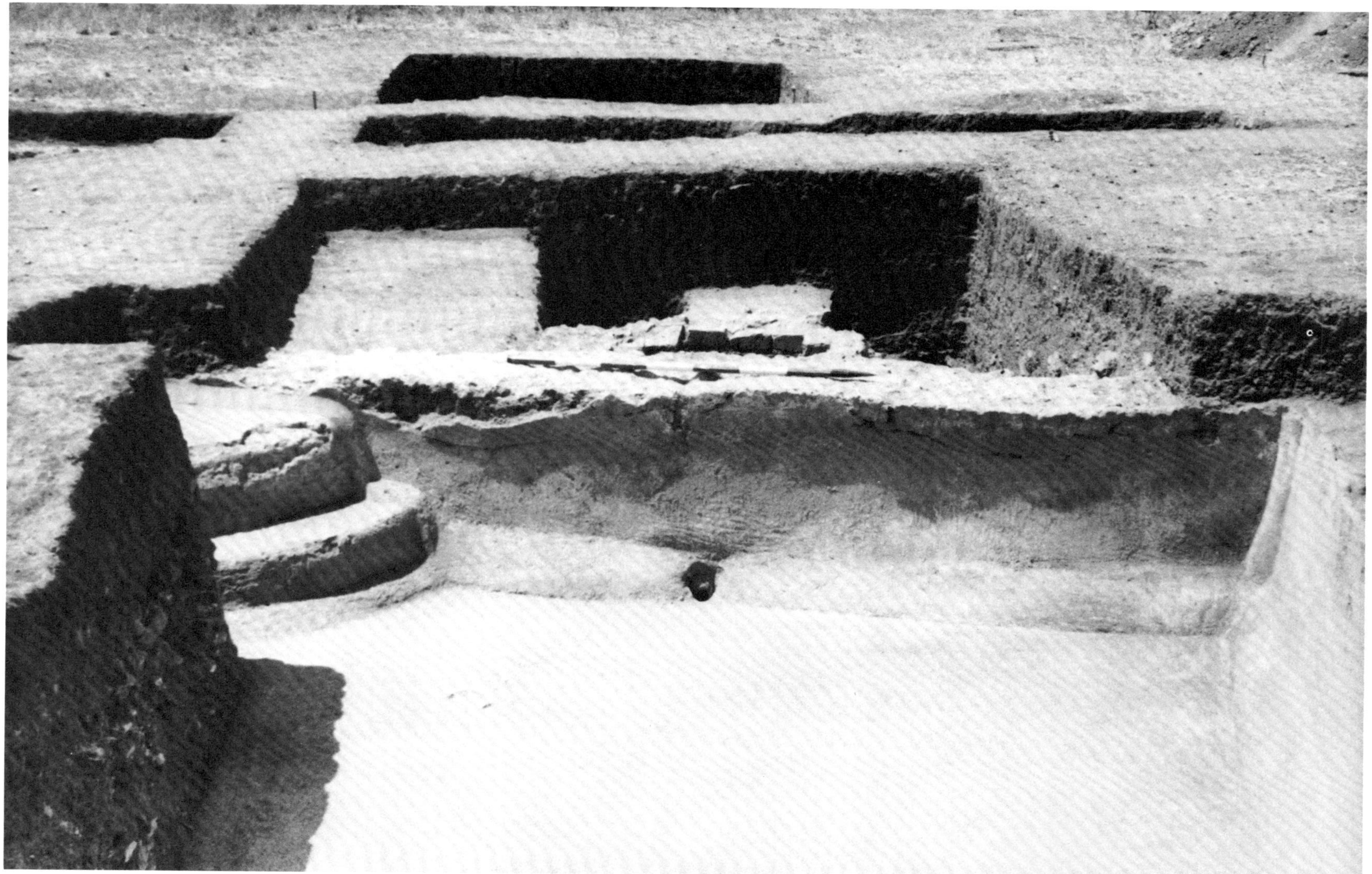

13. Via Gabina Site 11, garden pool of the villa, Phase 2B/C (photo: P. Oliver-Smith)

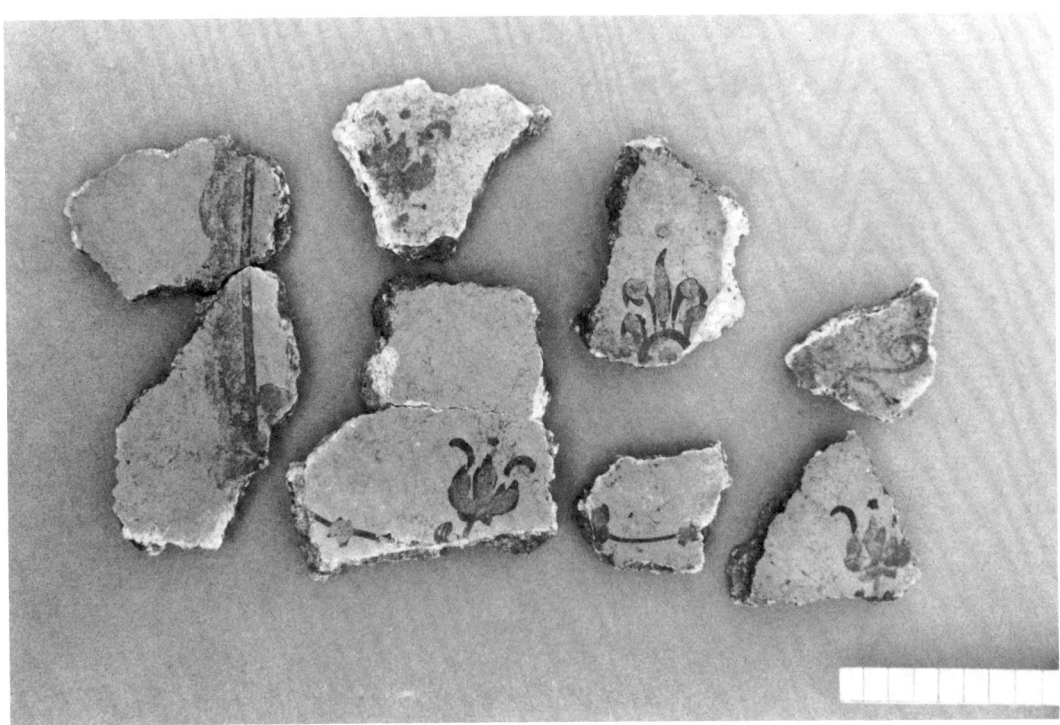

14. Via Gabina Site 11, plaster fragments with floral motif retrieved from the garden pool (photo: P. Oliver-Smith)

15. Via Gabina Site 11, plaster fragment with trellis pattern retrieved from the garden pool (photo: P. Oliver-Smith)

TORCULARIUM
0
1
2
3
VIA GABINA 11

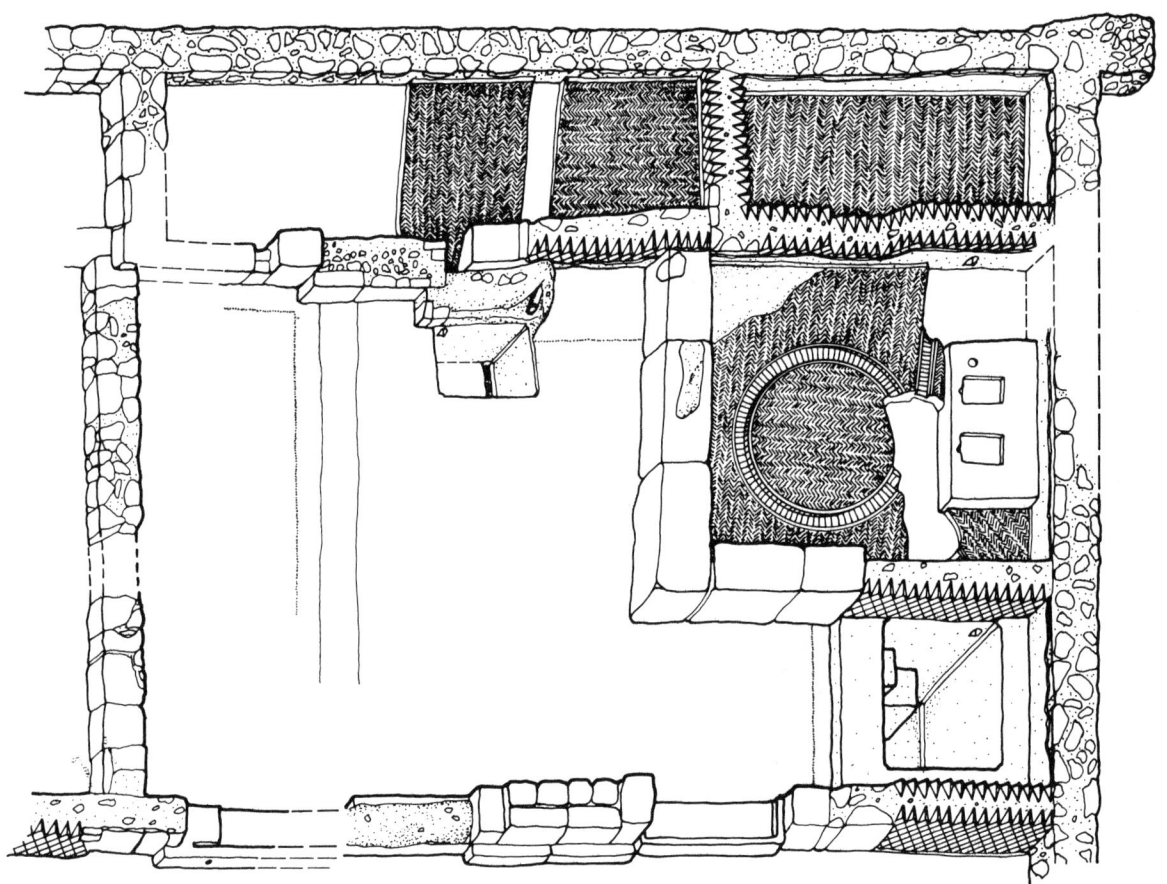

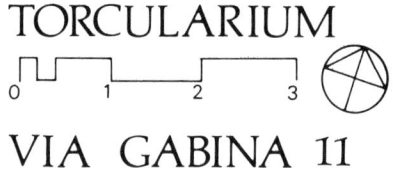

16. Via Gabina Site 11, axonometric drawing of the preserved oil-processing facilities of the villa, Phase 2B/C (D. Berg)

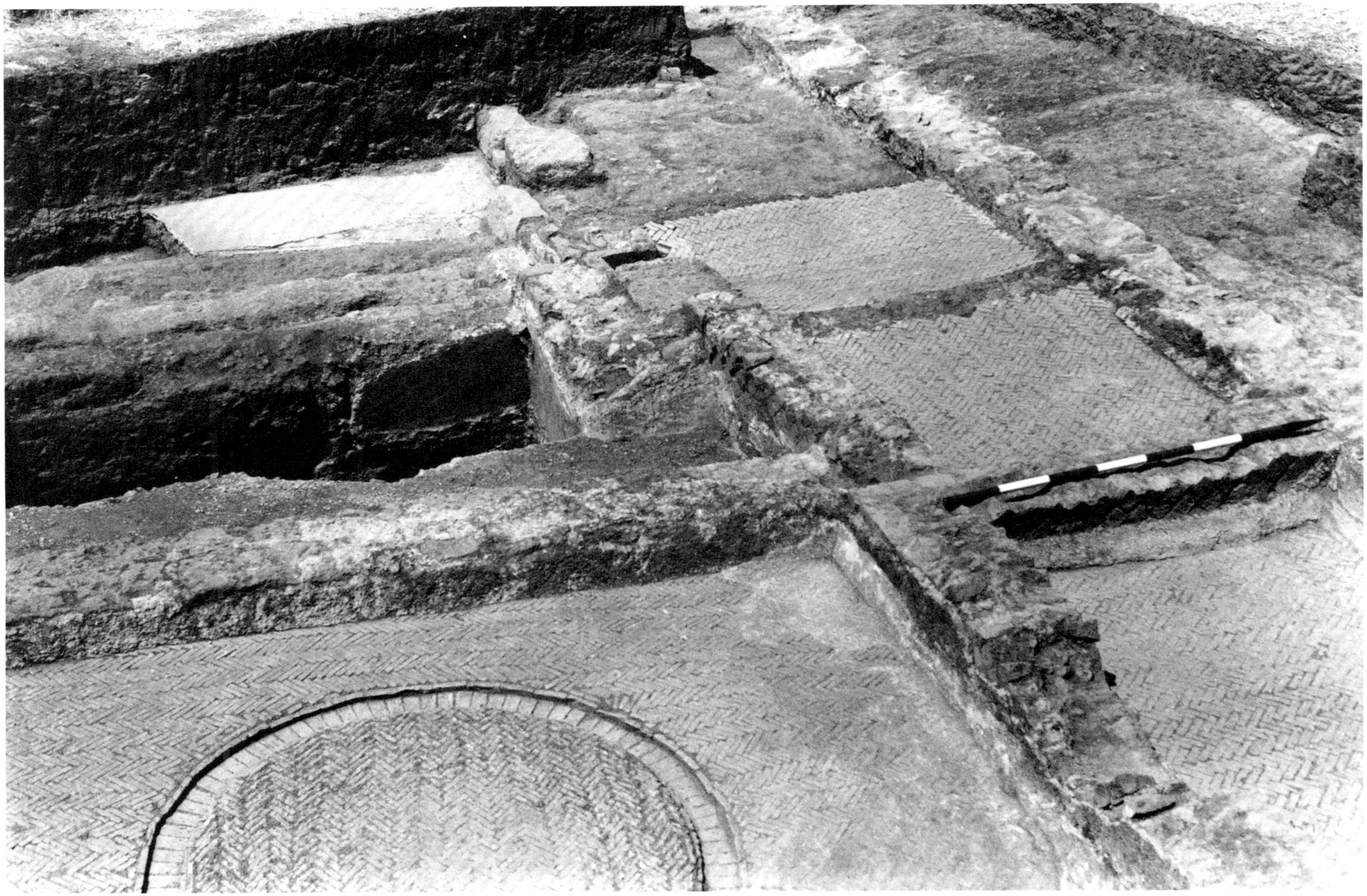

17. Via Gabina Site 11, view of the oil-processing facilities of the villa, Phase 2B/C (from the east) (photo: P. Oliver-Smith)

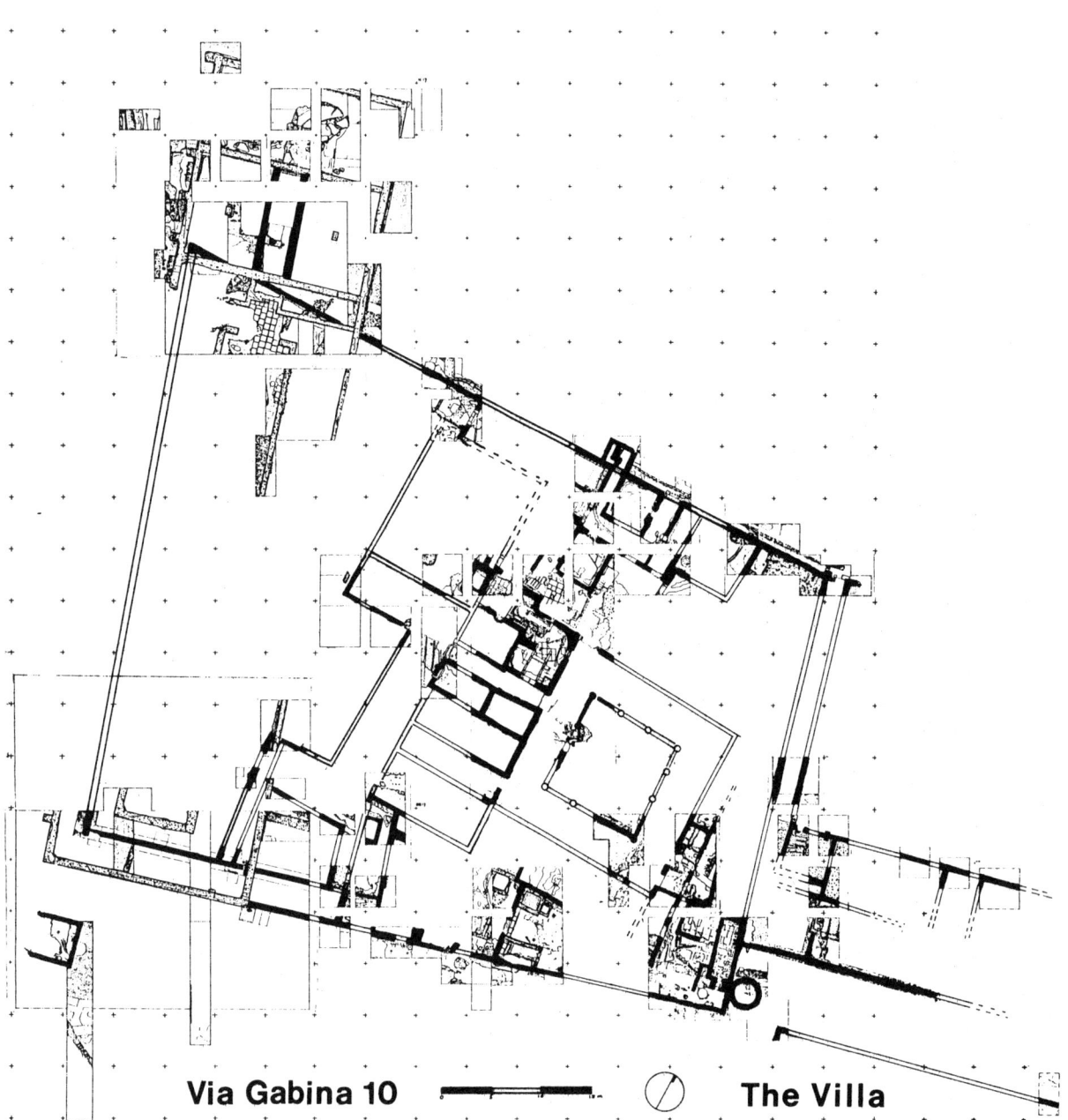

18. Via Gabina Site 10, plan of the Augustan villa as revealed in 1983 (author)

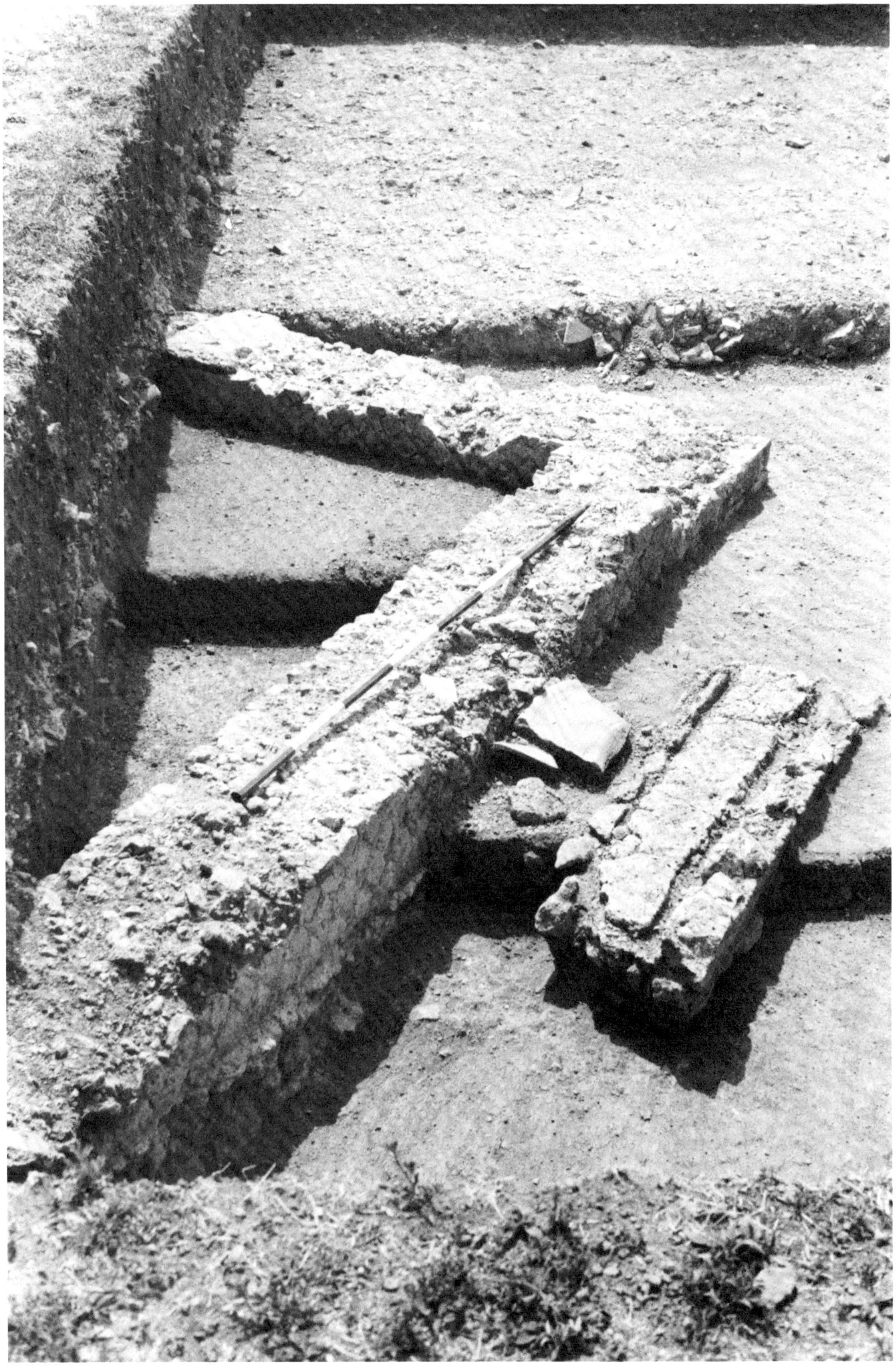

19. Via Gabina Site 10, foundations of the U-shaped portico overlooking the western garden of the Augustan villa (photo: P. Oliver-Smith)

20. Via Gabina Site 10, marble pilaster capital from the Augustan villa (photo: P. Oliver-Smith)

21. Via Gabina Site 10, fragment of painted plaster with naturalistic floral motif from the Augustan villa (photo: P. Oliver-Smith)

22. Via Gabina Site 10, fragment of painted plaster with delicately modeled woman's head from the Augustan villa (photo: P. Oliver-Smith)

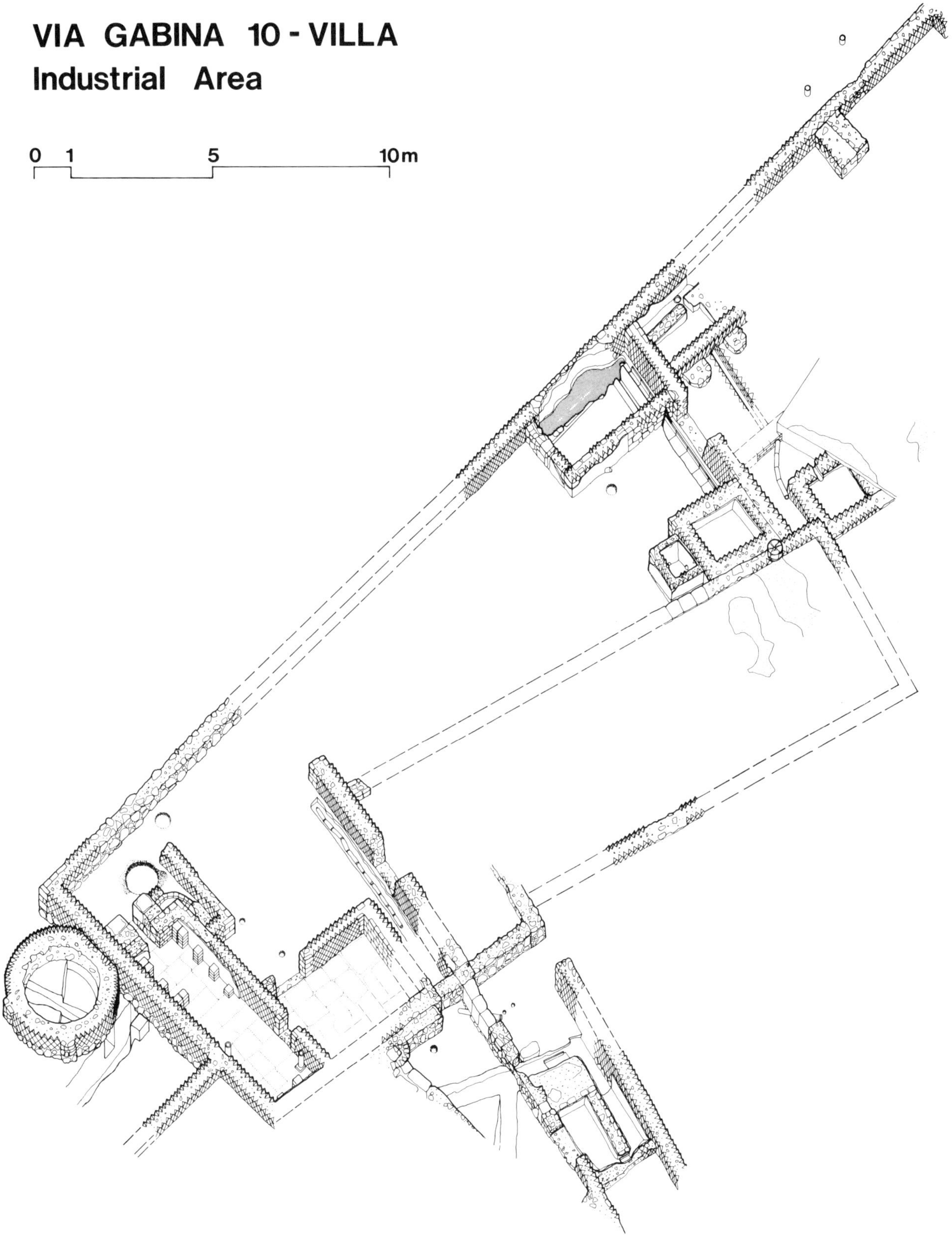
VIA GABINA 10 - VILLA
Industrial Area
0 1 5 10m

23. Via Gabina Site 10, axonometric drawing of the agricultural facilities of the southern end of the Augustan villa as revealed in 1983 (D. Berg)

24. Via Gabina Site 10, view of the several treading floors (foreground and background) and a collecting basin (background, right) for wine-making(?) from the Augustan villa (view from the south) (photo: P. Oliver-Smith)

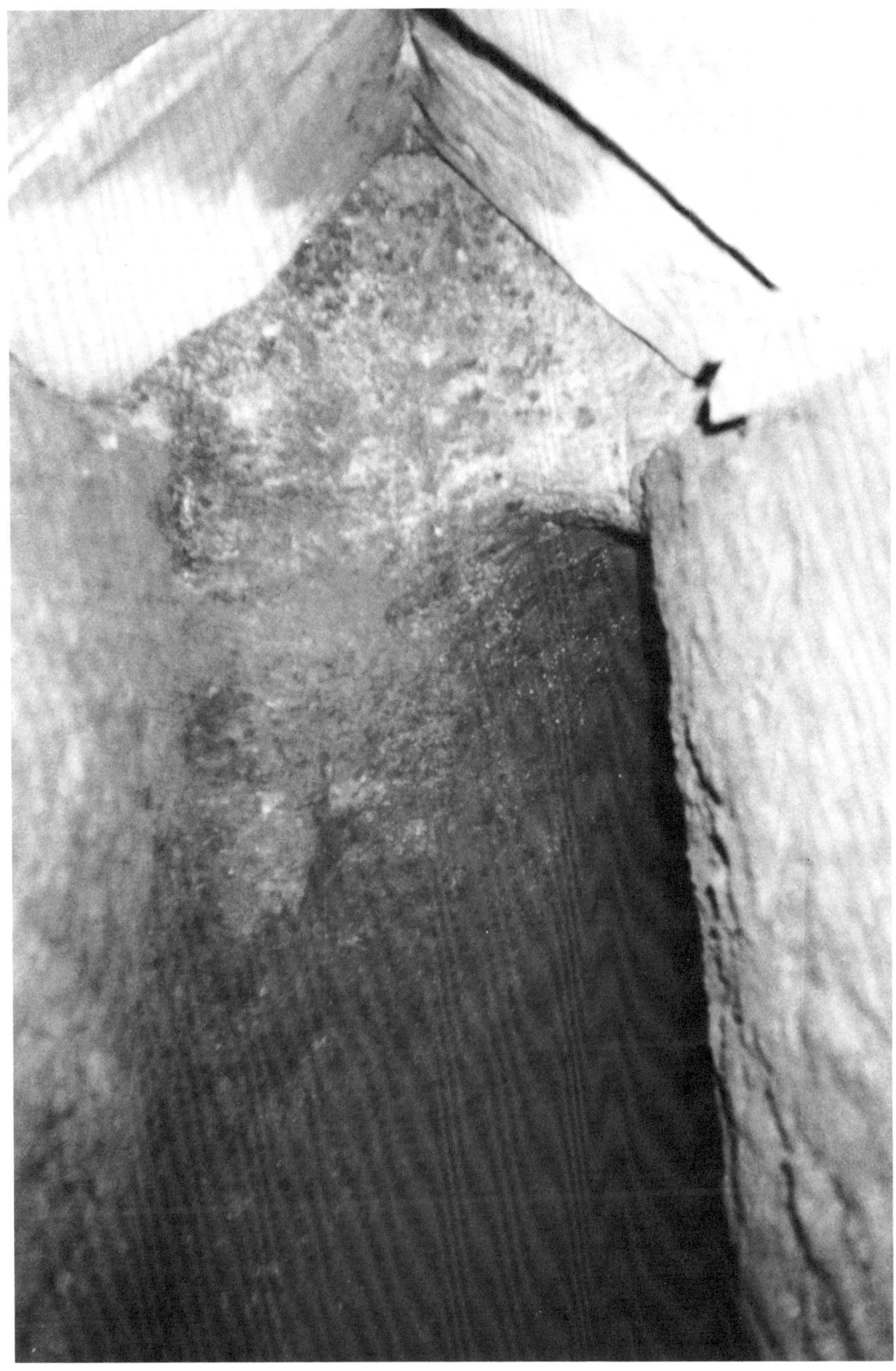

25. Via Gabina Site 10, one of the underground passageways forming the cuniculus system beneath the industrial area of the Augustan villa (photo: M. La Gess)

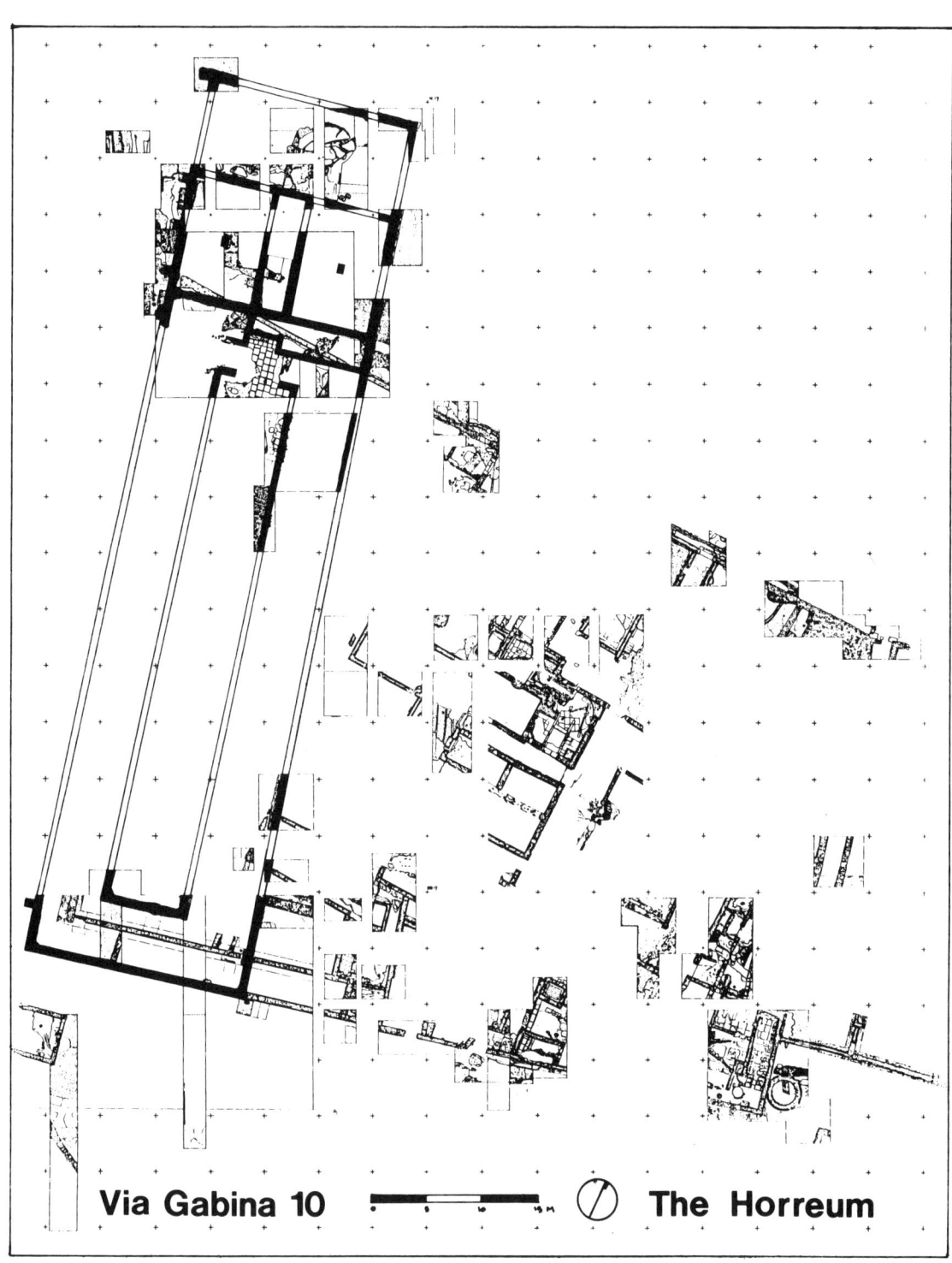

26. Via Gabina Site 10, plan of the *horreum* or granary (author)

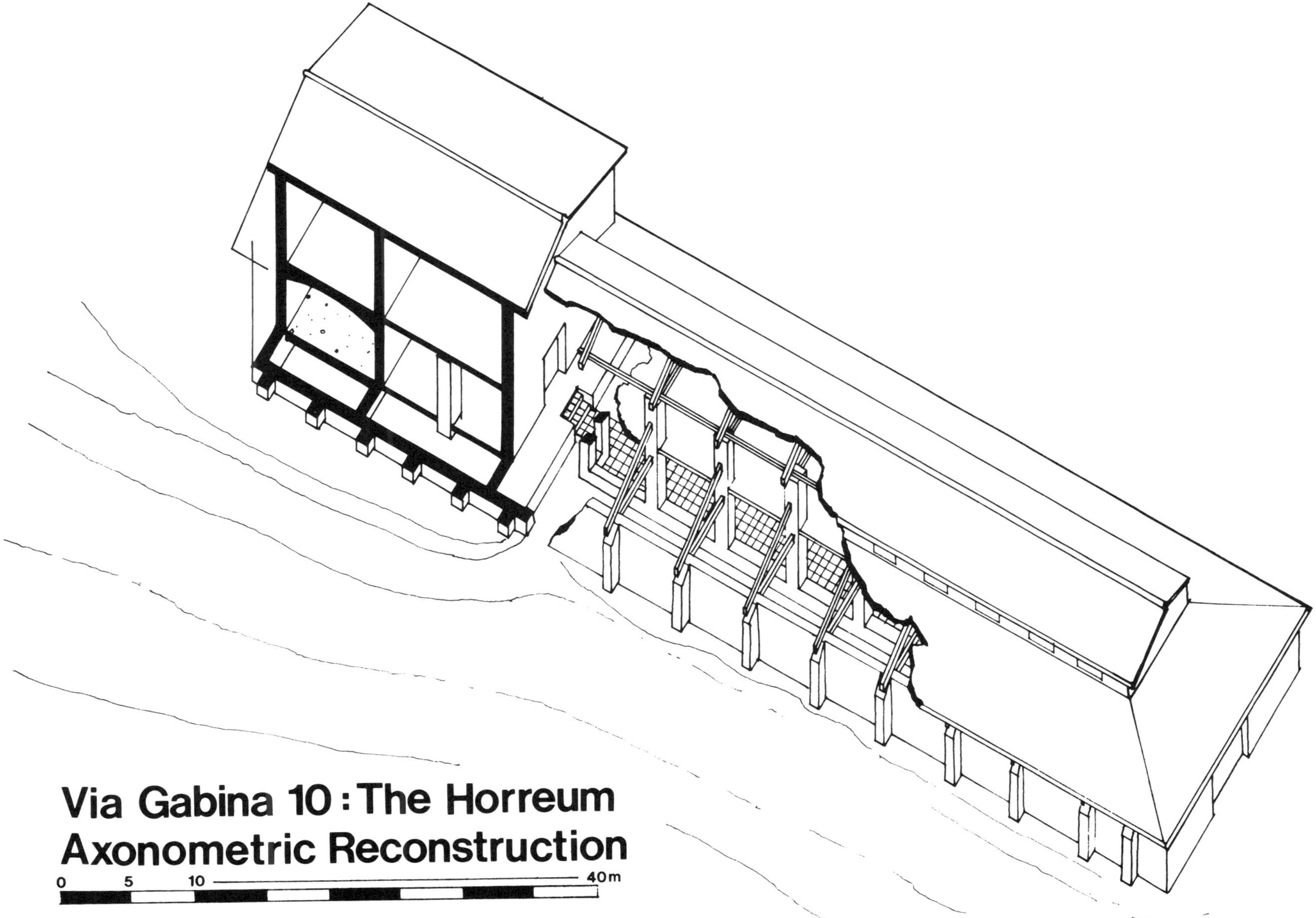
Via Gabina 10 : The Horreum
Axonometric Reconstruction
0 5 10 40m

27. Via Gabina Site 10, axonometric reconstruction of the *horreum* or granary (R. Heymann)

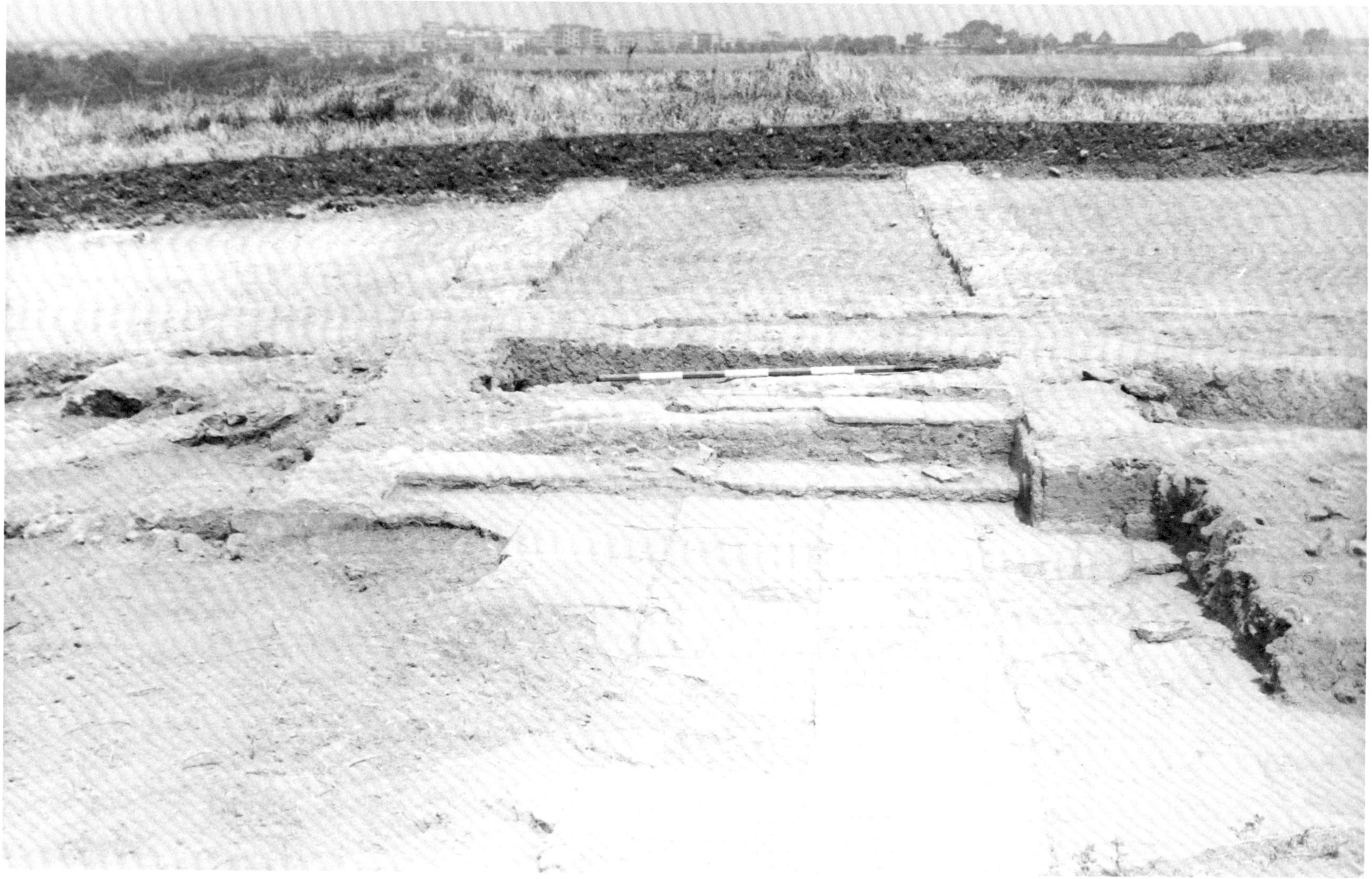

28. Via Gabina Site 10, view of the northern storage unit of the *horreum* or granary (from the south) (photo: P. Oliver-Smith)

had facilities for storage and processing of crops. At about this time a channeled platform, probably a pressing floor for olives or grapes, perhaps both, was built in one of the rooms of the western arm (Fig. 6). Even before the end of the third century B.C., when rooms were added along the western flank of the villa (Phase 1C; Figs. 4, 5), the garden immediately to the west was walled on two, if not three, sides. Since the space between the arms of the U must always have been a service court as well as the principal entrance into the residential quarters, we believe the newly delineated area on the west was primarily a kitchen garden rather than a place for the loading and unloading of farm carts. We are still uncertain what purpose was served by the lean-to built against the outer face of the western garden wall at some later time during Period 1 (see Fig. 5).

The landholding represented by the Period 1 villa must have been small throughout its three centuries of cultivation. In all directions from the villa building are other sites, at most no more than 400 meters away. The occupation material from these other sites also goes back to the Late Republic and seems to indicate they too were villas. The topographical configuration of the land today, surely not much changed from antiquity, reinforces the argument that the total holding for the villa at Site 11 might have been only about four hectares (10 acres). As for what crops would have been grown on this small farm, the tools found abandoned in one of the western rooms of the Period 1 villa are significant. These include an iron ploughshare and a billhook or pruning blade (Figs. 7, 8). Mindful of the pressing platform, mentioned above, and the character of the storage rooms, we suggest that what was cultivated was grain, a few olive trees, and a small vineyard, as well as vegetables and perhaps fruit trees in the kitchen garden. Some livestock, even pigs, should not be ruled out. The farm would seem to be a totally independent entity which could provide nicely for most of the needs of its owner and his family. Numerous slaves would not have been required by this kind of economic unit. A resident manager or overseer would have been necessary only if this were a secondary house, a country retreat, for its owner.

Period 2

In the Augustan Age the villa of Period 1 was drastically altered in form. It was rebuilt as a two-storied, standard type of atrium house (Phase 2A; Figs. 9, 10). This conversion was accomplished in such a way that there was no need to interrupt the residential occupation of the villa. New walls were constructed around the perimeter of the old building without destroying any supporting elements. The new walls enlarged the villa on three sides by about one and a half meters and on the fourth side closed off the courtyard space between the arms of the U. The former courtyard thus became an atrium with a small impluvium at its center and a compluvium above. The facilities for storage and processing of crops, with the possible exception of the channeled work platform, were eliminated in order that the entire villa might serve as a residence.

I want to note at this point how the sequence of building operations at Site 11 corresponds to Giovanni Patroni's theory for the evolution of the atrium house. In 1902 Patroni hypothesized that the atrium house descended from a prototypical U-plan Italic farmhouse in exactly the manner in which our Via Gabina Period 1 villa was transformed in Period 2.[12] No one has taken Patroni very seriously since, to my knowledge, not a single U-plan farmhouse has been identified until now in all of Italy. Most scholars have preferred to derive the atrium house from the Hellenistic courtyard type villa or house. J.W. Graham even reconstructs Patroni's prototypical U-plan as a kind of megaron with arms.[13] Clearly we need to withhold judgment until more early Italic farmhouses have been excavated and more is known about the first atrium forms.[14]

At the same time that the villa itself was undergoing alteration, the garden to the west was enlarged to conform with the villa's new dimensions. In this phase of Period 2 the garden was still defined by simple walls and not enclosed by low buildings or a peristyle (see Fig. 10). However, the western facade of the villa had a columned portico overlooking the garden to which one descended by means of a few steps. The portico demonstrates that in Period 2 the garden became a more important element of the total plan. Whether or not vegetables or other edible produce continued to be grown here is hard to say, but certainly the garden would have been planted in a more formal manner. Its appearance would have been of as much concern as its utility for the kitchen.

In the time of Trajan the villa again underwent significant changes although these were achieved through relatively minor physical alterations (Phase 2B; Figs. 11, 12).[15] The most obvious change in plan and elevation occurred with the creation of a small bath suite, which had heated sleeping rooms above,[16] in the southwestern corner of the villa. The new suite entailed a reworking of the western facade overlooking the garden (cf. Figs. 10 and 12) and the sinking of a concrete-lined pool in the center of the garden to serve as a cold plunge, a final indulgence in the bathing sequence (Fig. 13). This piscina was even more utilitarian than just stated since its overflow irrigated the field below the garden terrace. It was filled from a cistern for collecting roof water located above the tablinum of the house.[17] The garden was further enhanced by the construction of what were probably porticoes framing the space on the south and west (see Fig. 12). At the intersection of these porticoes a fine new entrance into the garden was constructed. This might have been necessary because of the addition (or rebuilding?) of a wall on the north which would then have closed off the garden and prevented access

---

[12] G. Patroni, "L'origine della domus," *Rendiconti dell'Accademia dei Lincei*, 5, 11 (1902), 467–507.

[13] J.W. Graham, "The Greek and the Roman House," *Phoenix*, 20 (1966), 3–31.

[14] Two general books on Roman villas should be noted: J. Percival, *The Roman Villa*, Berkeley, 1976, and A.G. McKay, *Houses, Villas and Palaces in the Roman World*, Ithaca, N.Y., 1975. Both works cite extensive bibliography.

[15] Both Phase 2B and Phase 2C were characterized by Oliver-Smith and me as construction phases in *NS* in 1981. We want here to correct this interpretation. Only Phase 2B involves physical alteration. Phase 2C represents the giving up of all residential function without any change to the structure of the villa. The correction is first made in Widrig, *NS* (forthcoming).

[16] We have been challenged on this point, but offer Palladius (I.41.V) to bolster the physical evidence. See Widrig, "Two Sites," 124–126, for a brief presentation of some of the evidence and arguments about communication on the upper floor.

[17] For a fuller description of the cistern above the tablinum see Widrig, "Two Sites," 125.

from that side.¹⁸ This new entrance very possibly became the principal entrance into the residential quarters of the villa (see below).

Tidy squatters who occupied the villa during its slow decay in the third century A.D. filled the piscina with thousands of fragments of painted plaster, many with naturalistic floral motifs and some with trellis patterns (Figs. 14, 15). There can be no doubt that the rooms on both levels facing the garden were thus handsomely decorated by means of their own garden imitations. The plaster "dump" is fortunate in preserving many fragments that might otherwise have been carried by the plough far down the slope to the west; but, at the same time, these fragments have been removed from their original locations and context.¹⁹

Still in Phase 2B other changes took place which ultimately were more important than the bathing and garden enhancements. The eastern two-thirds of the ground floor, including the villa's atrium, was turned over to the commercial production of olive oil. Elaborate facilities consisting of a press room and basins for the storage, washing, and bruising of the olives were built into the former living quarters of the villa at its northeastern corner (Figs. 16, 17). A deep tank, concrete-lined, for the collection of the oil was created to the south of the press. Farther south other rooms were assigned to final steps in the processing of the oil and to its storage before shipment to market. The raised basin or treading floor(?) in one of these southern rooms perhaps accommodated the making of wine in small quantities.²⁰ It may have replaced the channeled platform in the former western arm floored over only now with the construction of the bath suite.

Few sherds of domestic pottery from the site can be dated after A.D. 180.²¹ Other types of pottery, particularly amphoras, carry on until the first or second decade of the third century. We believe, therefore, that the residential function of the villa was given up at this time and that it became primarily an oil factory. We have no explanation for why this should have occurred. Nonetheless, we think this shift in function sufficiently important to maintain the phase designation C. Originally we applied C to the construction phase that created the oil processing facilities (see note 15). The squatters, about whom I have already spoken, probably occupied the villa-factory soon after it was abandoned in the early third century A.D. Their stay was not of much consequence, however tidy they may have been in their habits.

There is no evidence to suggest that the landholding at Site 11 was expanded in Phase 2A. On the contrary, the Early Empire saw increased activity in the region of the Via Gabina and intensification of occupation. Nothing close to a system of latifundia

---

¹⁸ One good reason for closing the garden to the north would have been to retain the earth of the northern slope and prevent it from eroding into the pool. All the garden walls should be considered retaining walls for the garden terrace.

¹⁹ Even where the wall plaster was found in room spaces, the two-story character of the building in Period 2 means that plaster from both floors is mixed together. All colored pieces have been carefully quantified in the hope that at least the color of the backgrounds for what is often 3rd style painting can be established.

²⁰ See Widrig, "Two Sites," 127–128, for more discussion.

²¹ See app. 1 by Joann Freed in the forthcoming "Second Preliminary Report" (Widrig, NS).

can be claimed. The new house is not elaborate enough for a very rich man to live in permanently; yet, as rebuilt, it is not appropriate for a resident manager either, unless the owner came out on frequent visits. A few slaves could have been lodged in any of several upper-story areas of the villa,[22] and these few would have been sufficient to maintain the house and fields. Just as there is no reason to suppose the landholding was expanded, there is no need to assume a change of ownership for the A phase of Period 2. As before, the owner and his family could have lived here all the time or used it simply as a secondary residence away from the congestion of the city. It would have been considerably more attractive and more up-to-date than the earlier villa. The forfeited agricultural facilities within the villa itself might have been replaced by a small compound of outbuildings.[23] On the other hand, any surplus crops could have been transported directly into town, thus avoiding the necessity of long-term storage.

Changes in the size of the estate or ownership would be best reflected in Phase 2B when processing facilities for olive oil were created on a commercial scale. A neighbor's *olivetum* could have been acquired at this time. More likely, however, would be the initiation of collective action between neighbors in the form of "cooperatives" for processing agricultural foodstuffs, even for marketing the final product. Our present assumption of wine-making facilities at Site 10, especially should these prove to be commercial in scale, gives considerable strength to this view. The expectation of handsome profits from oil production could have provided the incentive to embellish the villa with a bath and outdoor pool. Certainly the existence of the garden on the west figured in the decision to place the bath on that side and to assign the eastern rooms to processing. Phase C of Period 2 could indicate nothing more than lost interest in using the villa as a country retreat and a desire to realize its full economic potential as a factory.

The abandonment of the villa in the first decades of the third century may be the result of local disruptions rather than more general economic conditions. Chief among the local factors was the construction less than 200 meters away of the Aqua Alexandriana (Fig. 1). Could the state have confiscated the property and buildings of Site 11 in order to protect the graded flow of its new aqueduct?[24] Exactly when the land would have again been cultivated is equally speculative. We know only that there was a brief period of squatter occupations while the villa itself was physically decaying.

---

[22] Widrig, "Two Sites," 124, 125, and 126.

[23] Remains of outbuildings, had these buildings ever existed, will probably never be found. To the north and east of the villa the plough scrapes bedrock yearly; a little farther to the east and immediately to the south, then curving up to the northwest, modern farm roads cut through the periphery of the site.

Not until fairly recent times were tarred and bedded farm roads laid down throughout the *tenuta*. These roads and other farm-related construction have undoubtedly taken their toll on the ancient remains. Immediately to the southwest of Site 11, across from the southern road restricting the site, there was a small hay barn, open in its upper part for ventilation. The roof of the barn had already burned when we arrived at the site in 1976, and its interior was soon used as a compost heap. By 1981 all that was left of the building had been demolished. Some 50 meters to the east, in an angle of the southern and eastern roads referred to above, stands an electrical relay tower, a proud testimony to our technological age.

[24] A fine discussion and analysis of the engineering techniques appear in Ward-Perkins, "The Via Gabina," app. 3, 122–126.

SITE 10

When we began the excavation of Site 10 in 1978 we had no idea that the task would prove so formidable.[25] Since 1981 we have been working only at this site. Although the Late Antique *horreum* or barn was the first building discovered, for this paper I will begin with the adjacent villa of the Early Empire and its possible predecessor.

The Republican Villa

An abundance of sherds dated to the second and first centuries B.C., especially from the area at the southern end of the *horreum* and farther south beyond its walls, assures us of the presence of a villa in the Late Republic. Finding evidence for its plan and its construction materials is the problem.

Wherever we cleared to bedrock in this southern area, we discovered a network of shallow channels appropriate for foundations. Some of these channels had embedded fragments of hard, reddish tufa. Since the bedrock tufa of the site is soft and gray in color, we think the red tufa intrusions may be all that remains of *opus quadratum* foundations, the blocks later pried up to be used in subsequent building operations.[26] So far the channels do not give us any coherent plan for a building, and it may be that several related buildings are represented.

The Augustan Villa

We are far from finishing the excavation of the enormous villa constructed here in the Augustan period. We have, however, most of its plan (Fig. 18) and know that much of its area was assigned to agricultural or industrial functions.

The villa had, from the start, a peristyle form. Although its northern and southern outer walls follow somewhat different alignments, thus creating an irregular plan, pottery finds suggest they are contemporary in construction.[27] The skewed position of the

---

[25] The first published mention of Site 10 is Cotton, "Una villa" (above, no. 10); see also Widrig, "Two Sites," 129–132 and fig. 13. Widrig, *NS* (forthcoming), discusses at some length the Late Antique *horreum*, or barn, and its immediate area. Here complete plans and possible reconstructions of the elevation of the *horreum* are presented. *Horreum* is used in its singular form because of the unique character of the building and to distinguish it from the type of building that usually comes to mind with the plural form *horrea*.

For the Augustan villa at Site 10 see Widrig, *NS* (forthcoming); *AJA*, 85 (April 1981), 224; and *AJA*, 87 (April 1983), 269; the most recent discussion is P. Oliver-Smith, *AJA*, 89 (April 1985), 344. These last papers read at the general meetings of the Archaeological Institute of America all treat the possible economic role of the villa. In addition consult Oliver-Smith and Widrig, "Nine Centuries" (above, n. 11).

[26] See Widrig, *NS* (forthcoming). The reuse of blocks from the dismantlement of walls is consistent with the procedures at Site 11.

[27] As a result of the 1985 season of excavation the probable original plan of the Augustan villa has been carefully reviewed. The northern and southern outer walls of the villa as they appear in Fig. 18, indeed contemporary, may have been initially terrace walls of different alignments. It now seems that both the northern and southern walls of the villa in its Augustan phase were set closer and parallel to the peristyle. The same method of moving walls outward to increase the size of the villa appears to have been adopted for the eastern perimeter wall and for the creation of the U-shaped portico on the west.

peristyle helps mask the discrepancy of the outer walls. We can only guess that preexisting terraces or the natural terrain made the awkward alignments necessary. Two seasons ago we thought we had identified the atrium, but last season we found the space to be another bathing room.[28] As a result we are still in doubt about the orientation of the villa or which of its facades served as the principal entrance into the interior. This is true for the Augustan as well as later phases. Nevertheless, from the beginning the agricultural facilities seem to have been located on the south. The walled garden on the west was always a feature of the total plan since it incorporates into its terraced layout the extension of both the northern and southern perimeter walls of the villa.[29]

We are certain of at least two phases of major rebuilding and reworking of the villa's internal plan and organization. The first of these seems to be in the reign of Domitian and the second in the Hadrianic Age. Probably between A.D. 81 and 96 a bath suite was created from the rooms in the northwest section of the villa, and this suite was then rebuilt and extended eastward in the third decade of the second century. The eastward expansion of the bath suite could have destroyed a standard atrium leading into the peristyle from the north (this would account for the area's persistent resemblance to an atrium). A latrine that juts out from the northern facade is an amenity constructed in this last phase.

The villa had an eastern wing which, as yet, we are unable to assign to any particular phase. For the moment it would appear to be an addition to the original rectangular form of the villa, but we need to dig further for confirmation. The function of the wing could be either farm-related or residential. Unfortunately in this area of the site all floors have been lost to the plough, so the determination of an exact use for the wing may never be possible. However, the wing does form, along with the central block of the villa, a large courtyard area to the north. If not a service courtyard, this space could prove to be an enclosed garden, even a kitchen garden.

The formal garden of the villa was certainly the walled area on the west. A U-shaped portico (Fig. 19) of Doric columns comprised the western facade of the villa and overlooked several terraces descending the western slope. An outbuilding or portico to the south not only defined the garden on that side but would have effectively hidden any of the industrial or storage buildings beyond. On the other hand, the far western wall of the garden would have been kept low to permit a view out over the fields and surrounding countryside. What a beautiful panorama this would have been! Both Frascati and the city of Rome can be seen even today from this vantage point. We will never

---

[28] Widrig, *AJA*, 87 (April 1983), 269. In 1984 traces of the impluvium were discovered in lower layers and its small cistern and overflow channel excavated. We had identified the space of the atrium correctly (see below), although we had not dug sufficiently to obtain the evidence. Unfortunately the original orientation of the villa as determined by its main entrance may continue to elude us because, if our postulated Augustan plan is right, the atrium occupies almost a corner position (the northwest corner) in the overall plan. It may even be that the main entrance was on the south and that one moved through the peristyle before coming upon the atrium.

[29] As stated in n. 27, the U-shaped portico is probably not contemporary with the walls that define the terrace on the north and south.

know how the western garden was planted. This is the place where the Late Antique *horreum* or barn was built (see below). In fact, it was probably the existence of the terraces that determined both the location and orientation of the later building.

The residential rooms of the villa were handsomely, even lavishly, decorated. Mosaic floors, some plain with borders and others quite complex in their black and white geometric patterns, are found throughout, and quantities of colored-marble veneer fragments attest to extensive wall revetments. It may be that a few of the smaller rooms were fully revetted. Marble pilaster capitals (Fig. 20), elaborate molding fragments in both stucco and marble, and *campana* reliefs give us more information about the decorations; so, too, do the fragments of painted wall plaster (Figs. 21, 22). Some of the vaults of the bathing rooms were covered in colored glass mosaic depicting floral tendrils.

The entire southern section of the villa was always devoted to agricultural activities. What we believe to be treading and collecting basins, all with runoff channels (Figs. 23, 24), have been uncovered next to an emplacement for a small screw-type press. We wonder if these facilities did not serve for wine making, perhaps even on a commercial scale. Several phases in the life of the villa can be accounted for since a concrete floor was laid over a destroyed basin similar to those that replaced it at the new floor level. Unusual, however, are the interconnecting bedrock-cut passageways that run under these facilities (Fig. 25). For now, we can only speculate that they helped in the collection of must and its transfer in jars to a fermentation area.[30]

Should there be wine making at Site 10, it was not the only agricultural or industrial activitiy carried on here. Attached to the southeastern corner of the villa is a round structure we believe to be a silo.[31] On the south outside the villa are two separate build-

---

[30] Our digging in 1985, much to our surprise, quickly uncovered an *opus spicatum* emplacement for a mechanical press in the northeastern quadrant of the villa. Liquid from the press would have flowed into a small concrete-lined and stepped tank to the west. In a later phase this tank was replaced by a sunken dolium closer to the press itself. To the north of the press an extensive area of concrete covers the bedrock. The plough has removed the surface of the concrete, so positive evidence of tanks or basins is lost except for a drain to the outside and changes in the method of laying the concrete. If this area constituted tanks and basins, their floors would have been at a level considerably above the floor of the press room, a condition that would allow a flow of liquid in the same direction or directions as that from the press. Immediately to the south of the press room all physical remains of structure mysteriously disappear. Unfortunately we did not have time to dig here to bedrock. Our guess is that further excavation in 1986 will produce a small yard or room with cavities for dolia, the dolia themselves long since pulled out and salvaged from their bedrock-cut positions. The eastern corridor of the peristyle contains at least two (when completely cleared, probably many more) such bedrock-cut cavities for dolia.

It is too soon to say whether our large mechanical press would have been for wine or oil, although we are inclined to believe wine. However, we can say with somewhat more certainty that the whole installation represents a later phase in the life of the villa since it partially surrounds what was either a tablinum or a principal triclinium of the initial residential section. The conversion of the eastern corridor of the peristyle for storage dolia also supports a late date.

Another future task will be to search for any possible linkage of this area of the villa with the cuniculus system found to the south. We do know that the system is multiphased and does continue northward from those passages we have already cleared of their debris.

[31] The 1984 season of excavation concentrated on the area southeast of the peristyle. Here we found three enigmatic small basins which drain into the cuniculus system. The space that contains two of these

ings, one to the east still unexcavated and one to the west dug in 1980 (Fig. 18). A large part of the western building (it appears to have been a long rectangle in plan) has been lost to the plough and to the erosion of the slope, but it had a concrete floor and a small doorway on the east. Most likely these outbuildings were for produce or equipment.

It is difficult to reconstruct what the villa at Site 10 would have looked like during its more than two hundred years of occupation. So far only one space on the plan is appropriate for a staircase leading to an upper story. Its location could indicate an upper floor above either the garden range of rooms or the work facilities, perhaps both. We may be deceived by what seems to be a tightly circumscribed overall plan, and perhaps we should visualize fairly autonomous units grouped around the peristyle. Depending upon the needs of the resident family and the household staff, these units might have been single or double storied.

Coins as well as pottery tell us the villa was abandoned and decaying by the fourth decade of the third century, a date close to that which marks the end of occupation for the villa at Site 11. Perhaps the same local disturbances (the construction of the aqueduct?) affected both villa sites. However, unlike the villa-factory at Site 11, the villa at Site 10 was later razed to provide materials for the construction of the *horreum*. The evidence is clear on this point.[32]

The Augustan villa at Site 10 was occupied for somewhat more than two hundred years. Judging from the topography, the field divisions of today, and the proximity of other Imperial Age villa sites, we estimate the landholding of this villa was, at most, 10 hectares (ca. 25 acres). This suggests the villa was supported more from its role as processor than from its surplus of crops. Again we have a situation where cooperative organization for processing might be applied to advantage. Admittedly, a vineyard of eight or so hectares would supply ample grapes for commercial production of wine. But not all the land held by the owner of this villa can be assigned to vines. Some grain crops and perhaps grazing animals should be figured in as well.[33]

---

basins is paved in concrete-covered *opus spicatum* and, like the basins, has a drain into a branch of the same underground system. In fact, this space, although fairly large, could itself be a tank or basin. The only parallels we can establish for this configuration are some of the fulleries at Ostia. Might we have here facilities for the washing and dyeing of raw wool? Even, perhaps, the making of wool cloth? See Oliver-Smith, *AJA*, 89 (April 1985), 344. In 1985, as we explored farther to the north, no continuation of these facilities was discovered. They may, however, continue eastward into the large east wing of the villa. In this wing one small basin has already been identified. We also wonder if the two rooms to the south that once had floors raised over a rudimentary hypocaust are possibly drying rooms. At one time we thought the hypocausts might instead be ventilating space for grain storage above. At any rate, our "silo" must now be considered within a new context. Rather than grain storage, it might better serve for winter fodder to feed flocks of sheep.

[32] Particularly in the area west of the peristyle, we came upon the remaining courses of walls only below still existing floor surfaces from late phases. In fact, some concrete walls seemed to have been sheared by intentionally pushing them over. Where walls had been composed of red tufa blocks, as we found to be the case in the north near the atrium, revetments and upright plaster remain in situ, sometimes to a height of 10 or 12 cms, while the blocks they once covered are gone. A good example is the marble revetment of the tablinum or triclinium, a room excavated in 1985.

[33] See above, n. 31.

This villa, too, was a country retreat on the outskirts of Rome. There is no doubt that its owner was fairly rich. How much time he would have spent on the estate is impossible to say. I think this would depend upon the personal preferences of each generation of owners. The enhancements to the bathing facilities in the time of Domitian and again in the Hadrianic Age indicate interest in the estate was not lost over the years.

The Horreum or Granary

Sometime in the late fourth or early fifth century A.D. an enormous building, 79 meters in length and 19 meters across, was constructed over the terraces of the western garden of the former Augustan villa (Figs. 26, 27). It is easily identified by its masonry: *opus vittatum* above massive concrete rubble foundations. The rooms to the north formed a unit consisting of a corridor with flanking rooms preceding a large cross-axis chamber. One approached this unit by way of steps and a porch with a monumental doorway (Fig. 28). The enclosed space running southward from here was divided by parallel foundations which carried piers, thus creating a long central area with aislelike passages on either side. No cross walls partitioned the aisle spaces and apparently only the central area was paved.

The farthest chamber of the northern unit had a concrete vault and concrete floor over a ventilated space, in part cut out from the bedrock. This sealed chamber was certainly for grain storage, and probably the two other rooms of the unit served the same function. The divided space to the south is more difficult to interpret. It is really a barn attached to the storage unit, but it lacks sufficient definition to know if it sheltered livestock or was also for the storage of agricultural produce. We have been unable to find the kind of flushing drains one would expect were the area for livestock.

In past publications we have offered several alternatives for reconstructing the elevation of the *horreum*.[34] I am now convinced that the building was roofed throughout and that it looked much like many barns in the region today (see Fig. 27). This is a type heretofore unknown from the Late Antique or medieval periods. The type also raises another issue: were there residential quarters above the northern storage unit? The incorporation of a dwelling into the basic form would correspond to present practice. If our arguments hold, we have a *horreum* that is also a *villa rustica*. The thickness of its outer walls and their solid character would have given to this new type of *villa rustica* something of the sense of a fortress. Since the building seems to have been occupied until the ninth century,[35] perhaps well into the century, need for a defensible and contained form is not so far-fetched.

---

[34] First in Widrig, "Two Sites," 130. Here it is suggested that only the central area to the south of the storage unit was roofed. Exterior walls are too thick (at least .70 m) not to share with the piers in the support of a roof; drainage would have been necessary had the aisle spaces been unroofed, and no drains have been found. A more standard courtyard (one resembling a peristyle courtyard) is offered as one of two alternatives in Widrig, *NS* (forthcoming). The first of these alternatives is now thought unlikely because then the tile-paved central area, open to the sky, would have required a drain system. Again none was found.

[35] Pottery does not help in determining the end of occupation. So far I have not mentioned that the

The *horreum* of Site 10 represents a watershed in economic terms for the region. Not only does it show that grain became the main crop (as might be expected with the elimination of Rome's overseas sources in the troubled Late Antique world), but that the land was organized and held according to a new system. The *horreum* is too large not to be regarded as a facility for more than 10 hectares of fields. In fact, the consolidation of the former small parcels in the region may be a result of the shift to large-scale grain production. We now must determine what authority might have initiated such changes and what authority would have remained in control. I am not asking who were the workers and who were the owners.[36] I am postulating, instead, that the church might supersede the state as the authority over lands previously confiscated or at least redistributed.

In 1976, when we began our project, we were unaware how rich the villas along the ancient Via Gabina would prove to be in their economic and social information. Transformations in land use and economic organization are paramount in understanding the succession of architectural forms and cultural artifacts from this region bordering Rome. We still have a long way to go before we have exhausted the full potential of our sites, but each year brings us closer to achieving, even exceeding, our original goals.[37]

---

northern end of the *horreum* is surrounded by burials. These were pushed up against and aligned with its walls. Carbon 14 gives a range from the 3rd to the 13th century (plus or minus 150 years) for those skeletons already excavated. See app. 2 by Marshall Becker, in Widrig, *NS* (forthcoming). The upper range of carbon dating, aside from possible contamination, might be questioned on the basis of the medieval history of the region. Surely the designations for today's *tenuta*, the Tor Bella Monaca and Tor Angela, are medieval in origin and represent a system of landholding and organization different from that of the Late Antique period. It does not seem probable that our *horreum* would survive any large-scale reorganization, especially since its physical condition must have deteriorated over the centuries. However contradictory the evidence of Carbon 14, the 9th century appears to us the most likely time for the abandonment of the building.

[36] *Pace* Carandini (above, n. 3). It seems reasonable that only the state could exercise sufficient authority for the consolidation of land on this scale. Once a new system evolves or is imposed, what entity or person holds title is of lesser consequence than defining the ultimate authority for maintaining that system.

[37] A worthwhile catalogue has recently been published which begins to assemble the archaeological materials necessary for a consideration of economic and social issues in the area of Rome: *Misurare la terra: Centuriazione e coloni nel mondo romano. Citta, agricoltura, commercio: Materiali da Roma e dal suburbio*, Modena, 1985. This catalogue was issued for the exhibition of the same name organized by the Soprintendenza Archeologia di Roma in collaboration with the Sezione di Topografia Antica del Dipartimento di Scienze Storiche, Archeologiche e Antropologiche dell'Antichità, Università degli Studi di Roma and presented at the Museo Nazionale, Rome, in April–June 1985. We are pleased to note that plans from early publications of the villa at Site 11 are here reproduced, 96 and 97.

A good summary of the "state of affairs" for determining the role of the suburban villas of Rome, with a particularly useful bibliography, is found in L. Quilici, "La villa nel suburbio romano: Problemi di studio e di inquadramento storico-topografico," *Archeologia classica*, 31 (1979), 309–317. This article is the result of a colloquium, "The Roman Villas in Italy: Current Research," held at the American Academy in Rome in December 1979.